Please remember that this is a library book,
and that it belongs only temporarily to each
person who uses it. Be considerate. Do
not write in this, or any, library book.

CREATIVITY AND LIBERAL LEARNING

Problems and Possibilities in American Education

edited by
David G. Tuerck
Suffolk University

 Ablex Publishing Corporation
Norwood, New Jersey 07648

Library of Congress Cataloging-in-Publication Data

Creativity and liberal learning.

   Papers of two conferences organized by the College of
Liberal Arts and Sciences of Suffolk University in 1984
and 1985.
   Bibliography: p.
   Includes index.
   1. Education, Humanistic—United States–Congresses.
2. Creative thinking (Education)—Congresses. I. Tuerck,
David G. II. Suffolk University. College of Liberal
Arts and Sciences.
LC1011.C76 1987   370.11′2   87-11404
ISBN 0-89391-415-0

Ablex Publishing Corporation
355 Chestnut Street
Norwood, New Jersey 07648

Contents

Acknowledgments

David G. Tuerck

Credit for the publication of this volume is owed to many persons, some—but not all—of whom are represented in the pages that follow. I would first like to thank Michael R. Ronayne, Dean of the Suffolk University College of Liberal Arts and Sciences, who provided steady support and encouragement.

David L. Robbins, chairman of the college's fiftieth anniversary committee, assisted with the organization of the creativity conferences while simultaneously coordinating those conferences with other fiftieth anniversary events. I would like to offer my thanks to him and to his committee.

Daniel H. Perlman, President of the University, provided the support of his office and participated actively in the conferences. His then Executive Assistant, Diane T. Rudnick, provided crucially timed encouragement in our efforts to bring the conference proceedings into print.

Ellen Foley of the Office of Institutional Advancement and Jeffrey Robillard of the Department of Economics deserve special mention for their assistance with the conferences. My secretary, Jenny Stanzel, assisted with the conferences and produced a large portion of the manuscript. The College of Liberal Arts and Sciences and the Lowell Institute provided financial support, which, on behalf of the fiftieth anniversary committee and the contributors to this volume, I would like gratefully to acknowledge.

Among those who assisted in our search for a publisher, I would like to thank, in particular, Lillian Feder, Henry Giroux, Joseph M. McCarthy, and Zenon Pylyshyn. I would also like to thank Barbara Bernstein, Karen Kronman and Carol Davidson of Ablex for their advice and patience.

Several members of the Suffolk faculty and administrative staff generously agreed to chair the conference panels. They are Bette Mandl, Joseph M. McCarthy, David L. Robbins, Michael R. Ronayne, Diane T. Rudnick, Joseph Strain, and Malcolm Wetherbee. They deserve the thanks of their panelists and audiences for keeping the panels lively and on schedule.

Finally, we would like to acknowledge permissions to quote from the following materials:

Ballard, D. H. & Brown, C. M. *Computer vision.* Figure 1.1 (c), (d), p. 3. Reprinted with permission of Prentice-Hall, Inc. Copyright 1982.

Brecht, B. *Selected poems.* Reprinted with permission of Harcourt Brace Jovanovich, Inc. Copyright 1947 by Bertolt Brecht and H. R. Hays; renewed 1975 by Stefan S. Brecht and H. R. Hays.

Freud, S. *The interpretation of dreams.* In A. A. Brill (Ed. and Trans.), *The basic writings of Sigmund Freud.* New York: Modern Library. Reprinted with permission of Gioia B. Bernheim and Edmund R. Brill.

Hawkes, T. *Metaphor.* Reprinted with permission of Methuen & Co.

Hofstadter, D. R. *Metamagical themas: Questing for the essence of mind and pattern.* Reprinted with permission of Basic Books, Inc. Copyright 1985 by Basic Books, Inc.

Pryor, K. Behavior modification: The porpoise caper. Reprinted with permission of *Psychology Today Magazine.* Copyright 1986 (APA).

Pylyshyn, Z. *Computation and cognition: Toward a foundation for cognitive science.* Figure 1, p. 68. Reprinted with permission of MIT Press.

Rogers, C. R. Toward a theory of creativity. In H. H. Anderson (Ed.), *Creativity and its cultivation.* New York: Harper Bros. Reprinted with permission of the author and publisher from *Etc. A Review of General Semantics,* Summer 1954, *11* (4), 249–260.

Contributors

John C. Berg is Professor of Government at Suffolk University, where he is a leader in experiential education. He received his Ph.D. at Harvard University and has published in the professional literature on seniority reform in Congress.

Gloria M. Boone is Associate Professor of Communications and Speech at Suffolk University, where she has participated in the debate and rhetorical communication program. She received her Ph.D. at Ohio University, is coauthor of *Rhetoric, Argument and Communication*, and has engaged in consulting for business and government.

Mark H. Curtis is President Emeritus, Association of American Colleges. He received his Ph.D. at Yale University and has been a Guggenheim Fellow and a Folger Shakespeare Library Fellow. He is an authority on undergraduate curriculum and adminstrative issues and is the author of many books and articles, including *Oxford and Cambridge in Transition*.

Daniel C. Dennett is Professor of Philosophy and Director, Center for Cognitive Studies at Tufts University. He received his D.Phil. at Oxford, has been the recipient of numerous fellowships and guest lectureships, and is a member of the editorial board of *Cognitive Science*. He has published widely in the fields of cognitive science and artificial intelligence and includes, among his publications, *Brainstorms: Philosophical Essays on Mind and Psychology* and *The Mind's I: Fantasies and Reflections on Self and Soul* (with Douglas Hofstadter).

Rebecca McBride DiLiddo is Assistant Professor of Biology at Suffolk University, where she has been coordinator of the biotechnology program and coordinator of the Eastern New England Biology Conference. She received her Ph.D. at Ohio State University and has published on the subject of plant physiology in the professional literature.

Leslie Epstein is Professor of English and Director of the Graduate Program in Creative Writing at Boston University. He received his D.F.A. at Yale Drama School and has been a Rhodes Scholar, recipient of a Guggenheim Fellowship, and a Fulbright Teaching Fellow. He has published five books of fiction in addition to many articles and book reviews.

Paul Ezust is Professor and Chairman, Department of Mathematics and Computer Science at Suffolk University. He received his Ph.D. at Tufts University.

Lillian Feder is Distinguished Professor of English and Comparative Literature at Queens College and at the Graduate School, City University of New York, where she has served as Executive Officer of the Doctoral Program in English. She received her Ph.D. at the University of Minnesota, has been the recipient of many honors and awards, and has written widely on classical and comparative literature. Her books include *Madness in Literature* and *Ancient Myth in Modern Poetry*.

Henry A. Giroux is Associate Professor, Department of Educational Leadership at Miami University, Ohio. He is an authority in the areas of curriculum theory, cultural studies, and the new sociology of education. He received his D.A. from Carnegie-Mellon University and includes among his many publications *Ideology, Culture and the Process of Schooling* and *Education under Siege* (with Stanley Aronowitz).

Stuart Goldkind is Member, Artificial Intelligence Group at Mitre Corporation. He received his Ph.D. from the University of Rochester and has served on the faculty of Washington University in St. Louis and as a Research Associate in the Computer Science Department at the University of Rochester. He has taught and published in the fields of computer science, philosophy, and artificial intelligence.

Ronda Goodale is Program Advisor, Support Services, Boston Public Schools. She received her Ph.D. at Boston College and has published and spoken widely on special education and on problems of minority students and disadvantaged children. She was a principal planner in the establishment of the first international high school program, which opened in September 1983 at Copley High School in Boston.

Kenneth S. Greenberg is Professor of History at Suffolk University, where he serves as coordinator of the program in Integrated Studies. He received his Ph.D. at the University of Wisconsin and has spoken and published widely on the history of the South. His publications include *Masters and Statesmen: The Political Culture of American Slavery*.

John C. Holley is Associate Professor of Sociology at Suffolk University, where he is a leader in the application of computer methods to the social sciences. He received his Ph.D. at the University of Edinburgh and has published widely on the subject of technology and society and on the effects of industrialization on women. His publications include *Romantic Capitalism in 19th Century S.E. Scotland*.

Laura Hourtienne is Associate Professor of Humanities and Modern Languages at Suffolk University, where she teaches art and German. She received her Ph.D. at Bryn Mawr College and is the recipient of many fellowships, awards, and prizes. She has shown her art in galleries and at exhibitions in Massachusetts, Michigan, and New York.

Ann D. Hughes is Assistant Professor of English at Suffolk University, where she has served as faculty advisor to *Venture* magazine. She received her M.A. at the University of Kansas and has published and spoken on biblical literature.

Kevin M. Lyons is Director, Learning Resources for Student Athletes at Boston College. At the time of the symposium he was Assistant Professor of Education and Director, Learning Resource Center at Suffolk University. He received his Ed.D. at Boston University and has directed numerous workshops in competency testing and learning style diagnosis.

Joseph M. McCarthy is Professor of Education and directs graduate programs in educational administration at Suffolk University. He received his Ph.D. at Boston College and has published and lectured widely on medieval history as well as on educational theory and practice. He has served on numerous editorial, advisory, and accreditation committees and has authored more than seventy books, articles, and scholarly reviews, among them *Humanistic Emphases in the Educational Thought of Vincent of Beauvais* and *Training School Administrators*.

Maria Teresa Miliora is Professor of Chemistry at Suffolk University, where she has chaired the Department of Chemistry. She received her Ph.D. at Tufts University. She recently completed a Master of Social Work program in preparation for work in psychotherapy. Her contribution to this volume is based on her experience in psychosynthesis, a nontraditional psychological system.

Zenon W. Pylyshyn is Professor of Psychology and of Computer Science and Director, Centre for Cognitive Science at the University of Western Ontario. He received his Ph.D. at the University of Saskatchewan and has published many scientific books and articles on cognition and artificial intelligence, including *Cognition and Computation: Toward a Foundation for Cognitive Science*. He serves on the editorial boards of several scientific journals and is advisor to several granting agencies in the sciences and humanities. He currently holds a Killam Research Fellowship as well as a Senior Fellowship from the Canadian Institute for Advanced Research. He is also Director of the Program in Artificial Intelligence and Robotics of the Canadian Institute for Advanced Research.

Gerald Richman is Associate Professor of English at Suffolk University. He received his Ph.D. at Yale University, has participated in a National Endowment of the Humanities Summer Institute on medieval civilization, and has published in the professional literature on the subject of old English.

David L. Robbins is Professor of History at Suffolk University, whose history he has chronicled in a number of pamphlets documenting the evolution of the University since its founding. He received his Ph.D. at

Yale University, is active in several Boston area historical societies, and has written on French history in the professional literature.

Michael R. Ronayne is Dean of the College of Liberal Arts and Sciences and former Chairman of the Department of Chemistry at Suffolk University. He is a member of the Town of Winchester School Committee, on which he has served as Chairman. He has served on a number of reaccredication visiting teams for the New England Association of Schools and Colleges and has authored numerous scientific and educational articles. He received his Ph.D. at the University of Notre Dame and has published widely on the subject of gamma-irradiated chemical systems.

Kevin Ryan is Professor of Education at Boston University. He received his Ph.D. at Stanford University, has been a Whitehead Fellow at Harvard University, and has published over fifty articles, reports, and reviews. He is contributing editor of the *Encyclopedia of Educational Research*. His books include *Those Who Can, Teach* and *Moral Education: It Comes with the Territory*.

Sarah Smith is Director of Documentation, Bachman Information Systems, Inc. At the time of the colloquium she was Director of Documentation, LMI (LISP Machine, Inc.). She received her Ph.D. at Harvard University, has taught in the Departments of English at Tufts and Northeastern Universities, and has published widely on eighteenth-century literature and history and on the theory and use of film.

Alexandra Todd is Associate Professor of Sociology at Suffolk University. She received her Ph.D. at the University of California, San Diego and has spoken and written on women's issues in doctor-patient relationships. She is coeditor of *The Social Organization of Doctor-Patient Communication* and of *The Structure of Discourse and Institutional Authority: Law, Medicine, Education*.

David G. Tuerck is Professor and Chairman, Department of Economics at Suffolk University. He received his Ph.D. at the University of Virginia, has directed a project on the economics of advertising at the American Enterprise Institute, and has been a director in the economic consulting practice of Coopers & Lybrand. He has published books and articles on the economics of education and of advertising, on international trade policy, and on supply-side economics.

Robert C. Webb is Professor of Psychology at Suffolk University, where he has served as Chairman of the Department of Psychology. He received his Ph.D. at Tufts University and has taught and lectured in the field of experimental psychology.

Introduction: Creativity and Cognition

David G. Tuerck

Late in 1983, the College of Liberal Arts and Sciences of Suffolk University decided to conduct a series of panels on the subject of creativity as part of its approaching fiftieth-anniversary celebration. The panels would be organized into two conferences bearing the title, *Creativity and the Implementation of Change: Liberal Learning in the Practical World.* This volume presents the papers and proceedings of these conferences.

The choice of creativity as the subject of these conferences grew out of a conviction on the part of the college that a fresh examination of the creative process and of the role of liberal learning in understanding and enhancing that process represented both a fitting act of celebration and a promising intellectual endeavor. The decision to conduct two conferences was owed partly to the fact that the anniversary celebration would span the entire 1984–1985 academic year and partly to a feeling that the events to be celebrated called for two different panel formats. The first conference would mark the meeting of the first college classes in the fall of 1934, and the second would mark the signing of the college charter on February 21, 1935. The setting for the first would be more intimate and less formal than that for the second, the hope being that by varying formats in this way, the college would achieve a suitable blend of depth and informality.

The words *symposium* and *colloquium,* though close in meaning, seemed to offer a useful distinction. Webster's *New Collegiate Dictionary* defines a symposium as "a social gathering at which there is free interchange of ideas" and a colloquium as "a usually academic meeting at which one or more specialists deliver addresses on a topic or on related topics and then answer questions relating thereto."

The college conducted its first conference as a faculty symposium on Tuesday afternoons, over the period from October 16 to November 13, 1984. It conducted its second conference as a colloquium, featuring addresses before a widely recruited audience by "specialists" from outside the university, on February 20 to 21, 1985. Although the symposium gave more time to discussion than did the colloquium, both conferences included the presentation of prepared papers and comments. This volume contains these papers and comments.

1

In a *Prospectus* distributed in advance of the conferences, the college offered two hypotheses for consideration by prospective contributors: (1) that *the*, or at least *a*, principal mission of a college of liberal arts and sciences is to enhance the creative skills of its students in a way that furthers their ability to bring about useful change in a practical world and (2) that a college of liberal arts and sciences should turn to cognitive science, and particularly, within that domain, to artificial intelligence, for clues as to how it might go about performing that mission more effectively. The *Prospectus* cited a "curriculum in design" proposed by Herbert A. Simon in *The Sciences of the Artificial* (1981) and *Gödel, Escher, Bach: An Eternal Golden Braid* (1979) by Douglas R. Hofstadter as particularly rich in clues of this kind.

SOME OBSERVATIONS ON COGNITIVE SCIENCE

Cognitive science describes thinking, in the words of speaker Zenon Pylyshyn (this volume), as a "representation governed process." Insofar as computers are capable of exhibiting intelligence, they, like humans and other highly developed creatures, "can only be understood if we assume that aspects of their internal states are representations—that they are physical instantiations or tokens of symbols that stand for something." Cognitive scientists disagree over the sense in which, and over the degree to which, thinking is reducible to computation. Where they agree is on the importance of representations for explaining the behavior of cognizers, human and artificial.

The importance of representations for explaining this behavior follows from a fundamental distinction that separates cognizers from other entities. This is the fact that, whereas one could offer a purely material explanation for the behavior of the latter, one could not offer a purely material explanation for that of the former. Cognizers have, in their brains, physical characteristics that symbolize someone's intentions for them to do certain things (just *whose* intentions—the cognizer's or someone else's—is a sticky issue, with which Drs. Pylyshyn and Goldkind grapple in their remarks in this volume). In order to explain the behavior of such entities, it is necessary, therefore, to know the intentions that their physical characteristics instantiate. It is necessary to know the meaning behind their actions. The idea that computers exhibit, or might conceivably exhibit, intelligence rests on the argument that it would be impossible to explain their behavior without recourse to a representational interpretation of their physical characteristics.

A Computational View of Cognition

One possible implication of this line of reasoning is that computers can exhibit genuine intelligence, at least in principle. If people conduct essentially the same kind of symbol processing when they think as computers do when they compute, then, considering the pace at which computers have grown in power and versatility, the prospects for artificial intelligence are good. Dr. Pylyshyn, Herbert Simon, and other cognitive scientists appear to accept this view. Simon (1982) has put it as follows:

> Like a modern digital computer's, Man's equipment for thinking is basically serial in organization. That is to say, one step in thought follows another, and solving a problem requires the execution of a large number of steps in sequence. The speed of his elementary processes, especially arithmetic processes, is much slower, of course, than those of a computer, but there is much reason to think that the basic repertoire of processes in the two systems is quite similar. Man and computer can both recognize symbols (patterns), store symbols, copy symbols, compare symbols for identity, and output symbols. These processes seem to be the fundamental components of thinking as they are of computation. (p. 430)

Simon predicted, in a 1957 article, that in ten years computers would be winning world chess championships, discovering and proving important mathematical theorems, writing music "accepted by critics as possessing considerable aesthetic value," embodying "most theories in psychology," and, in general, performing many tasks previously performed by men. Simon admits that he and his coauthor (Simon & Newell, 1982) have had to dodge a lot of brickbats as a result of these predictions. Perhaps, as he says, the reason lies not only in their overoptimism but also in worries they caused about technological unemployment and about the diminished uniqueness of man (pp. 266, 386–387).

In *The Sciences of the Artificial* (1981), Simon considers some implications of computer technology for higher education. Dividing sciences between the natural and the artificial, he characterizes the artificial sciences as falling properly within the domain of the professional schools. It is the business of the professional schools to design artifacts and thus to teach and to organize their curricula around the science of designing artifacts. Unhappily, the professional schools have been surrendering in recent years to a misguided desire to turn their curricula away from the artificial and toward the natural sciences. The cookbook nature of much professional school curricula may, at one time, have explained the feelings of insecurity that underlay this desire. But, if justified before, the expanding arsenal of problem-solving methods made available by advances in management science and in computer science make these feelings obsolete and wrongheaded today. The now-available inventory of computer simulation models provides a rich empirical base for the development of a curriculum in design, an outline of which he offers as a guide to the revitalization of professional education.

The conferences' *Prospectus* proposed a marriage of Simon's curriculum in design to the liberal arts and sciences. Although this might appear as role reversal, much of Simon's own logic argues for placing his curriculum there rather than in the professional schools. Simon points out how the emergence of computer science has created a common language and, perforce, an opportunity with which persons from fields as diverse as music and engineering "can begin to perceive the common creative activity in which they are both engaged, can begin to share their experiences of the creative, professional design process." The communication thus made possible across disciplines has given rise to a "new intellectual free trade" in our "thought processes, our processes of judging, deciding, choosing, and creating." "If I have made my case," Simon writes, "then we can conclude that, in large part, the proper study of mankind is the science of design, not only as the professional component of a technical education but as a core discipline for every liberally educated person" (Simon, 1981, pp. 158–159).

Several of the contributors to this volume address themselves directly or indirectly to Simon's argument. Although the bulk of opinion appears to be negative, there is much that sees a bright future for artificial intelligence and, to that degree at least, for curricular changes of the kind that Simon proposes.

A Noncomputational View of Cognition

In *Gödel, Escher, Bach: An Eternal Golden Braid* (1979) and in some follow-up articles, Douglas Hofstadter rejects the computational view of thinking in favor of an alternative view that stresses the role of analogy and imagery. Hofstadter sees a distinction between computation and thinking, the latter being the kind of brain activity that machines must capture in order to claim intelligence.

Computation takes place at a low (which is to say, hardware or neural) level of brain activity. At this level, symbols are "empty" and "passive" in character, governed by some set of formal rules or program. Symbol processing of the kind that occurs in computation does not characterize true thinking (or, therefore, creativity), although it does still characterize, for the most part, what computers, including supposedly intelligent computers, do (Hofstadter, 1979, p. 570; 1983, pp. 274–279, 285).

Thinking, in Hofstadter's model (1979, 1983), takes place at a high level of brain activity, where symbols mix with each other and emerge unpredictably from their computational substrate to group themselves into meaningful, neurological " 'clouds.' " The clouds thus formed are "active symbols" that "flow and act on their own," incorporating "within their own structures the wherewithal to trigger and cause actions" (1979, p. 570; 1983, p. 278).

Cognizers form a new symbol or concept by creating around it what Hofstadter calls an *"implicosphere"* or *"implicit conterfactual sphere."* This is a cloudlike set of variations on the core theme of the concept that, when properly connected, give meaning ("representation") to the concept in the mind of the cognizer. The very existence of a concept depends on the cognizer's ability to connect in a meaningful way the variations that make up the implicosphere of its core theme:

> The gist of my notion is that having creativity is an automatic consequence of having the representation of *concepts* in a mind. It is not something you add on afterward. It is built into the way concepts are.... If you have succeeded in making an accurate model of *concepts,* you have thereby also succeeded in making a model of the creative process, and even of con-sciousness. (1985b pp. 238, 245–247, 1985a, pp. 528)

The process of creating a concept is one of letting the imagination conjure up (perhaps nondeliberately but always nonaccidentally) coun-terfactual or subjunctive ideas that at once resemble and reify its core theme. "We select from our fantasy a world which is close, in some internal mental sense, to the real world. We compare what is real with what we perceive as *almost* real. In so doing, what we gain is some intan-gible kind of perspective on reality" (Hofstadter, 1979, p. 643). An ac-curate model of the creative process, therefore, is not one in which the cognizer changes the real world but one in which it uses the imagination as needed to produce concepthood:

> When we daydream or imagine situations, when we dream or plan, we are *not* manipulating the concrete physical world, nor are we sensing it. In imagining fictional or hypothetical or even totally impossible situations, we are still making use of, and contributing to, the meaningfulness of our symbolic neural machinery (Hofstadter, 1983, p. 282).

In order to create new concepts, cognizers must be able not only to build up the implicosphere that surrounds a concept but also to spot the regularities in their thinking processes that identify the implico-sphere by which those processes are bound. A true cognizer can look down upon itself, spot regularities in the way it thinks about things, and, in doing so, escape these regularities for new ways of thinking about things. Hofstadter (1985a) uses the term "jootsing" to describe the process of thus creatively "jumping out of the system" to create new concepts (p. 541).

A cognizer might devise some method of spotting regularities in its thought processes that would, in turn, exhibit regularities of the kind from which it might wish eventually to escape. It would, in this fashion, attempt to create certain "metarules" for finding the rules that govern the original thought processes. But the possibility of creating metarules implies that of creating metametarules, and so forth, up to some set of metameta . . . metarules. This possibility, in turn, creates that of an infinite regress, one in which the cognizer would trap itself in an everwidening hierarchy of rules whose very effect would be to subject thought, at all levels below the very highest, to computational regularity of the kind that suppresses creativity (Hofstadter, 1979, pp. 687–688; 1985a, p. 544).

In fact, the ability to "joots" saves the cognizer from this trap. By jumping out of the system (or metasystem or metametasystem . . .), the cognizer sees the infinite regress unfolding and collapses the whole hierarchy into one "tangled hierarchy" of rules. The result is a kind of self-modifying game in which thought processes produce strange loops that take a given thought out in one direction only to bring it back to where it began. The fugues of Bach and the paintings of Escher illustrate this phenomenon.

The mind, in Hofstadter's model (1979), is forever "jootsing" from one tangled hierarchy of thought to another, more tangled hierarchy, even reaching up, perhaps, to encompass the "inviolate" level at the top (which, if accomplished, would necessitate the creation of another inviolate level, and so forth) (p. 688). Is it possible, after all, then, to develop a formal system of rules that would encompass this process in its entirety? The answer, thanks to Gödel's proof, is no. Gödel's proof says that in every such system of rules, certain propositions are true but unprovable. A proposition of this kind is one that asserts its own unprovability. Because of Gödel's proof, there is no system of formal rules by which a brain, mechanical or nonmechanical, could anticipate every jump out of the system with which a cognizer might create new concepts.

> This endless jootsing is a process whose totality (so says Gödel) cannot be formalized, either in a computer or in any finite brain or set of brains. Thus one need not fear that the mechanization of creativity, if ever it comes about, will mark the end of art. Quite the contrary: It is a day to

look forward to, for on that day our eyes will open—as will those of computers, to be sure—onto whole new worlds of beauty. (Hofstadter, 1985a,
p. 541)

Gödel's proof not only protects art from formalization (if not from
mechanization) but also makes the search for truth, at least in part, an
art. Tangled hierarchies are everywhere, in science as well as art. The
fact that we *know* this—that we can *see* them in the genetic code as well
as in the fugues of Bach—proves that we cannot rely on logic for knowing the truth: "My feeling is that the process by which we decide what
is valid or what is true is an art; and that is relies as deeply on a sense
of beauty and simplicity as it does on rock-solid principles of logic or
reasoning or anything else which can be objectively formalized" (Hofstadter, 1979, p. 695).

While thus dismissing the possibility of formalizing the creative process, Hofstadter (1985a) also dismisses the idea that creativity somehow
transcends ordinary thinking. "Creativity is part of the very fabric of all
human thought, rather than some esoteric, rare, exceptional, and fluky
by-product of the ability to think, which every so often surfaces in places
spread far and wide" (p. 527). He thus rejects as "mystical" the theory
offered by Arthur Koestler and considered in this volume, whereby it is
the "bisociation" or fusing of two old concepts that gives birth to new
concepts. Koestler's theory errs, according to Hofstadter (1985b), by ignoring the internal characteristics of the constituent elements whose
bonding gives rise to the creation of new concepts (p. 250). Furthermore, it is a mistake to believe

> that Einstein and other geniuses are "cut from a different cloth" from
> ordinary mortals, or at least that certain cognitive acts done by them in-
> volve principles that transcend the everyday ones.... If you look at the
> history of science, for instance, you will see that every idea is built upon
> a thousand related ideas. (p. 249)

THE SUFFOLK CONFERENCES ON CREATIVITY

As mentioned, the conferences' *Prospectus* cited the writings of Simon
and Hofstadter, among others, as literature worth considering for its
bearing on the subject of creativity. Nevertheless, the college deliberately avoided limiting the conferences to papers that would take a cognitive science approach or any other approach in particular to the study
of the creative process. Rather, it attempted only to invite papers that
would contribute at least indirectly to our understanding of that process

and that would, in the aggregate, represent a suitable balance between the major academic disciplines into which the college is organized—the humanities, the natural sciences, and the social sciences. This stemmed not only from a wish to offer invited speakers the greatest possible latitude in approaching their topics but also out of a feeling that there is much in the cognitive science approach itself that argues for offering such latitude.

The result, as my contribution to the Final Remarks section in this volume points out, is a set of papers and comments that divide themselves roughly into four categories:

1. those that attempt to reveal the cognitive foundations of the creative process;
2. those that offer practical suggestions for the teaching of creative skills within the framework of the existing educational system;
3. those that support the idea of teaching creative skills but find the existing educational system flawed in some way that, without correction, poses a barrier to such teaching; and
4. those that question the desirability of attempting to teach creativity as part of the liberal arts curriculum.

Throughout the papers, there is a tension between a "computational" or "rational" view of the creative process, on the one hand, and a "noncomputational" view of that process, on the other. Predictably, as the foregoing observations would suggest, papers that offer a computational view appear generally to argue for a "design" or "problem-solving" approach to education. Papers that offer a noncomputational view emphasize, instead, what might be called the imaginative, introspective, aesthetic, or humanistic domain of creative thought and the importance of that domain to problems of educational reform. If these papers produce any one view concerning the creative process, it is to show that the tension between these alternative views is real and perhaps inherent to that very process.

The Symposium
This section of the proceedings consists of remarks made in an informal setting by Suffolk faculty to an audience consisting mainly of Suffolk faculty and students. The printed version that follows contains complete versions of the prepared papers and comments. Some of this material contains allusions to the Suffolk College of Liberal Arts and Sciences curriculum, in particular to a one-year course in integrated studies and to a one-year course in finite mathematics that the college requires of freshmen. The course in integrated studies stresses, as its name suggests,

an integrated approach to the study of the major academic disciplines and exposes freshmen to a variety of writings representative of those disciplines. Finite mathematics has the purpose of providing its students with what the college has determined to be a minimum amount of mathematical literacy.

In Panel 1, Robert Webb and Kenneth Greenberg offer contrasting views of the creative process. For Dr. Webb, that process is amenable to scientific scrutiny at the level of the individual. His approach is to examine the literature on psychology for ways of identifying the characteristics of creative people, of the processes by which people engage in creative thought, and of the nature of the products that they create. He is able, by virtue of this examination, to suggest a number of ways to enhance people's creative skills.

For Dr. Greenberg, by contrast, the group is the appropriate level for analyzing creativity. Rejecting, much as does Hofstadter, the idea that creativity is the province of only a few great geniuses, he draws parallels between the lives of Copernicus and of P.T. Barnum to illustrate the importance of social context for understanding the creative process. The idea of a creative process stripped of this context is illegitimate, as is that of attempting to teach creativity as a functional skill.

Dr. Webb and several other contributors to this volume take up the question of how the consequences of success or failure affect people's ability to create. Although Webb and most others appear to favor a nonthreatening environment, Webb's paper argues also for a high energy level and strong ego. (But, see also Maria Miliora's paper, this volume, on the importance, at the "primary stage" of creativity, of *abandoning* "egoic defenses.") On the prospects for artificial intelligence, Webb makes an observation in the spirit of Hofstadter: "Since creativity essentially involves the manipulation of patterns into new arrangements, pattern recognition is almost where one has to start."

In his comments on their papers, David Robbins sees agreement between Drs. Webb, Greenberg, and himself on the notion that there is a creative process and that certain techniques, particularly bisociation, are useful in fostering that process. Dr. Robbins, however, rejects Greenberg's view of creativity as removing any reliable basis for assessing creative worth or for holding the individual responsible for the moral consequences of his creations.

In Panel 2, Gloria Boone and Gerald Richman draw on their professional and classroom experience to identify methods of enhancing creativity in speech and in writing. Dr. Boone traces the evolution, from ancient to modern times, of "topoi" and metaphor. Topoi are "places of arguments" or "commonplaces" from which one can generate ideas for a speech. A distinction traceable to Aristotle divides rhetoric between the logical and the figurative, with topoi and metaphor serving, respectively, as the principal vehicle for each. Dr. Boone proposes a system of "metaphorical topoi" that would overcome the stultifying effects on creativity of this division, illustrating her proposals with examples of interdisciplinary topics drawn from the liberal arts and sciences.

Dr. Richman describes a method called "idea combining" that he employs in his English composition courses. Idea combining consists of taking "ideas that have never been combined before to create new ideas distinct from the originals." Richman cites examples of institutions, products, academic disciplines, and scientific principles whose creation may be seen as having resulted from idea combining. Drawing on his experience in the classroom, he describes the results of idea combining as it has been performed by students in selected writing assignments. In a hypothetical assignment, he draws on *Wuthering Heights* and *Frankenstein* to illustrate diagrammatically what might be called the "implicosphere" around the concept of a main character talking through a narrator. "Idea combining," he argues, helps turn "pencil and a blank piece of paper" into "powerful creative tools."

Ann Hughes cites "the great iconoclast of the 'sixties, Abby Hoffman," to provide still another example of topoi. She offers some additional insights to both papers by considering, with an example, the consequences of applying Boone's proposed method of metaphorical topoi to Richman's method of idea combining.

The papers by John Holley and Rebecca DiLiddo provide lessons from the history of science for enhancing our understanding of the creative process. Dr. Holley's paper encapsulates, perhaps more than any other contribution to this volume, the core issues around which it is organized. In his review of the life of Charles Babbage, Holley exposes the tension that exists between what we characterize above as the computational and the noncomputational views of cognition.

In Babbage, we have both the "Father of the Computer" and the "Father of Scientific Management." Babbage, as Holley explains, observed in one of his writings how the French had successfully used the principle of the division of labor to construct a table of logarithms. (The person retained to construct the tables had spied a copy of Adam Smith's *Wealth of Nations* in a bookstore and, on reading the section on the division of labor, realized that he could, by using this principle, shorten greatly the time it would take to complete the project.) Babbage, seeing the applicability of the same principle to the idea of mechanizing the production of mathematical tables, set out on what was to be his unfulfilled quest to build machines that, in design, anticipated the modern computer. Tragically, by Holley's account, Babbage became lost in the details of his project and thereby failed to live up to his own principles of management science. The moral is that the very principles of management science, of which the computer is so much the embodiment, are antithetical to the development of creative products like the computer.

In her paper, Dr. DiLiddo describes instances in which a scientist, equipped with a large knowledge base, was able to turn some entirely surprising result into a great discovery. In her model of creativity, the fact gathering with which a scientist builds a knowledge base is not aimless wandering but "an essential part of the process which creates the fuzzy outline [implicosphere?] that insight brings into clear focus." She sees the liberal arts and sciences curriculum as well suited to the task of fostering creativity, owing to its commitment to the principle of imbuing students with analytical skills and with a wide knowledge base.

In his comments on the papers by Holley and DiLiddo, Paul Ezust turns the discussion back on the teaching profession, which he finds populated with "a class of pseudo-professionals" who smother our children in a "cloud of psycho-babble that has been substituted for knowledge and competence." Ezust calls for a restructuring of teacher training paradigms that would shift priorities away from "methods" and towards "academic" subjects.

In Panel 4, Maria Miliora and Kevin Lyons examine the cognitive foundations of creativity: Dr. Miliora as a practioner of psychosynthesis and Dr. Lyons as a teacher of learning skills. In her paper, Dr. Miliora directs her attention to the intuitive or "primary stage" of the creative process, where ideas and images emerge prior to their becoming finished products in the rational or secondary stage. The primary stage requires the capacity to "disidentify" from the secondary stage—to suspend rational thought in favor of what Miliora calls "the creative attitude," one characterized by "trust, curiosity, and the capacity to take risks." She outlines some techniques from the field of psychosynthesis for expanding the creative attitude.

Kevin Lyons, in a paper that anticipates a number of points raised by Mark Curtis and Henry Giroux in the colloquium, identifies and condemns a drift to vocationalism and competency testing in secondary and postsecondary education. The desertion by students of the liberal arts and sciences for the business schools has paralleled this trend, causing the liberal arts and sciences to lose ground in the competition for resources. The result has been a decline in the very skills—the ability to think critically and conceptually and the ability to communicate effectively in speech and writing—that are needed in order to perform creatively in a business environment. Facing head-on the pressures to produce marketable graduates under which the liberal arts now operate,

Lyons recommends a model of cognitive objectives for revitalizing the liberal arts curriculum. The propagation of this model, he believes, would encourage "a congruity of student and teacher goals" and provide "evidence of the revelance of liberal learning to the world of work."

Laura Hourtienne applauds Dr. Lyons' condemnation of everincreasing vocationalism in education but dissents from what she sees as his placing the liberal arts in the service of practical, material values. Indeed, she sees a world dominated by such values as deeply inhospitable to Dr. Miliora's suggestions for promoting a creative attitude. In her comments she anticipates at least two ideas that would surface again in the colloquium sessions: (1) that material values stultify creativity and (2) that a sharp division exists between cognizing of the kind that can be called creative and of the kind that can be called practical (that is, "rational" or "computational").

In his paper, Joseph McCarthy reviews the literature on teaching creativity and offers his assessment of the prospects for successfully integrating the methods produced by that literature into the curriculum of the liberal arts and sciences. Dr. McCarthy shares Dr. Webb's feeling that creativity remains a "slippery beast." Despite "excellent reason to think that creative behaviors are teachable," the verdict, based on the hitherto dominant mode of testing (that is, experimental psychology) is " 'not proven.' " In place of this method, McCarthy recommends an anthropological approach that would evaluate observed teacher characteristics and teacher–student interactions for clues to the effective teaching of creative behavior. The paper contains a bibliography and suggestions for identifying additional sources.

In his paper, John Berg reviews the curriculum of the Suffolk College of Liberal Arts and Sciences and observes that, for good reason, it contains no requirement in creativity. Berg adopts a squarely noncomputational stance, rejecting any idea of a marriage between the liberal arts and Simon's curriculum in design. The problem-solving approach typified by management-school curricula and methods fails as a paradigm, not only for liberal education but also, it would appear, as a form of management education. Indeed, the openmindedness and broad knowledge base characteristic of a liberal arts graduate might be seen as fostering problem *creation* or problem *rejection*, as well as problem *solving*. He offers several examples of political issues whose resolution succeeded or failed in part as a result of the knowledge base and openmindedness of the parties who were engaged in the process of resolving them.

In her comments, Alexandra Todd offers the opinion, based on her reading of Dr. Berg's paper, that Dr. McCarthy makes an excessively pessimistic assessment of the prospects for teaching creativity. Berg's own reservations notwithstanding, his conceptualization of the liberal arts mission represents an aspect of creativity that the liberal arts *do* successfully teach.

The Colloquium

Whereas the symposium speakers address themselves in several instances to specific methods of teaching creativity and to the problems of implementing such methods within the framework of the liberal arts and sciences, the colloquium speakers generally take a broader view. The colloquium speakers tend to think about creativity from the perspective of a broadly defined field of knowledge or endeavor: technology, schooling, literature. A keynote address by Mark H. Curtis of the Association of American Colleges turns the discussion back to the liberal arts and sciences, but the panel sessions themselves tend to focus inwardly on the professional or scholarly orientations of their participants, producing in the process a number of points of controversy.

In Panel 1, Zenon Pylyshyn offers what is characterized above as a computational interpretation of cognitive science. Technology has provided an important "imagination prosthetic" in the form of the notion "of a *symbolic* or *computational* process." The idea that human cognition is just such a process leads to the identification of a new "natural kind" of species, one in which human and machine cognizers are close cousins. Owing to their plasticity and capacity for modularization, computers are becoming an adept and powerful member of this species, offering to perform more effectively tasks now performed by humans and, at the same time, creating new opportunities for the division of human labor.

In her comments on Dr. Pylyshyn's paper, Maria Miliora questions the notion, first, that computers are capable of exhibiting humanlike plasticity and, second, "that humans are like computers in all aspects of their respective cognitive processes." While welcoming the technological advances that artificial intelligence appears to promise, she cautions against any polarization of cognitive paradigms that would favor rational over creative kinds of thinking.

Daniel Dennett comments first on Dr. Miliora's comment on Dr. Pylyshyn. Dr. Miliora errs, in his opinion, by drawing a false boundary between the creative, on the one hand, and the rational, on the other. He cites recent progress in artificial intelligence as evidence of the inseparability of creative from rational processes. Dr. Dennett also disputes an example with which Pylyshyn illustrates the boundary between representational and nonrepresentational systems. For Dennett, the important issue is not so much the boundary between these systems but rather the capacity of one kind of representational system—namely, the computer—for informing us about the way our own minds work.

Stuart Goldkind raises the question of whose representations a computer represents. Where do the representations come from—the computer or somewhere else? "The exact explication of the functional role a representation must play in order to qualify as a belief (or a representation for an entity) is," in his view, "one of the greatest challenges faced by cognitive scientists."

In his reply, Dr. Pylyshyn agrees with Dr. Goldkind about the difficulty of ascertaining the cause of representations. Although this difficulty does not hinder cognitive scientists in their "day-to-day work," it does raise the philosophical question whether machine cognition is "strongly equivalent to human cognition." Dr. Dennett correctly, in Pylyshyn's view, admonishes Dr. Miliora and others not to underestimate the importance of rationality in human cognition. While accepting Miliora's claim that important kinds of thinking (e.g., learning and moods) go on outside the rational domain, he argues that some kinds of thinking once believed to go on outside that domain (for example, "subitizing") are, in fact, a form of computation. Although his "natural kind" of cognition is thus not all-inclusive, it does encompass many kinds of thinking that are not transparently computational in nature.

In his keynote speech, delivered over lunch on the first day of the colloquium, Mark Curtis reviews some of the principal findings of the then just-published report of the Association of American Colleges on baccalaureate education. The report, entitled *Integrity in the College Curriculum*, responds to a perceived "disarray in undergraduate education" that has roots in "the collapse of any coherent educational philosophy." Contributing to this collapse is both a trend toward vocationalism in college curricula and failure by college faculty to attend seriously to their teaching responsibilities. Dr. Curtis describes a proposed " 'minimum required program of study' " that would work across the curriculum to develop skills in logical analysis, computation, literacy, scientific reasoning, appreciation of the arts, and other areas deemed essential to the development of fulfilled and socially responsible human beings. It is to the development of such skills rather than any "tinkering with the curriculum" that we must turn if we are to revitalize the liberal arts and sciences or, for that matter, undergraduate education.

In Panel 3, Henry Giroux identifies a "growing crisis in public education" that threatens "not merely the ability of students to be creative, but the very capacity for conceptual thought itself." The cause of this crisis is the increasing deskilling of teachers, who, denied any opportunity to grow and act as intellectuals or as educational leaders, have been reduced to a role of serving and propagating the prevailing corporate, technocratic ethic. The consequence is the disenfranchisement, not only of the teachers themselves, but also of a substantial component of their student constituency.

Dr. Giroux proposes as a solution that teachers assume the role of "resisting intellectuals" who would undertake "the task of making the pedagogical more political and the political more pedagogical." In assuming this role, they would place the school at the center of the political process, wherein it would "become part of a fundamental social project to help students develop a deep and abiding faith in the struggle to overcome injustices and to further humanize themselves." As resisting intellectuals, teachers would work "to create the ideological and material conditions in both schools and the larger society that give students the opportunity to become agents of civic courage." Students bring to school their own "cultural capital," whose affirmation can help to establish the conditions necessary for the implementation of change.

Kevin Ryan finds much to applaud in Dr. Giroux's paper but finds counterproductive any effort to produce a class of teacher intellectuals. While decrying the overemphasis on "technication," he faults Giroux for overvaluing the idea of an "oppositional" approach to teacher training. He warns, in this context, against producing students who automatically oppose "those in power without understanding the need for power in human affairs."

In his comments, Michael Ronayne makes some observations based on his service on a local school committee. One difficulty is the trend toward placing a greater and greater burden on the schools to provide elements of child care that are not related to any educational mission. A second difficulty arises from teacher certification procedures that overemphasize methods courses at the expense of academic achievement and intellectual capacity.

Ronda Goodale finds Dr. Giroux's paper "exciting and timely" but notes the practical problems that cause school administrators to impose the strictures Giroux condemns. It is often the teachers themselves who demand methods courses. Tightly controlled curricula in reading are in large part mandated by the need to assure minimum competency on the part of the individual student.

In his reply, Dr. Giroux elaborates on the idea that teachers should be intellectuals, explaining that he intends, in suggesting this role, "to begin to use a language that allows us to rethink the very nature of the work that teachers do, the social functions they perform, and the conditions under which they work." Technical competency is important, but it is necessary, in applying a particular teaching method, to recognize the ideological content that it embodies. What teachers must recognize is the capacity of even commonsense methods and remarks to disconfirm cultural capital and thus inhibit learning.

In her paper, Professor Feder considers the ways in which the study of literature is involved in the processes by which human beings create a concept of the self. She regards the experience and concept of the self as continual creations of the individual mind, involving multiple processes, chiefly internalization, integration, and expression. The study of literature, especially the limits and potentialities of the fictive self, unites the individual writer and reader with literary, cultural, and social history.

Not only the fictive self but the whole created world of a literary work—its setting, plot, atmosphere, and narrative and thematic structure—become part of what D. W. Winnicott has called the " 'intermediate area of *experiencing* to which inner reality and external life both contribute' but which is different from both." Using examples from ancient and modern literature, Professor Feder demonstrates that significant works of imaginative literature create an aesthetic structure of the "intermediate area of experience." By so doing, they incorporate and challenge a society's prevailing assumptions and provide an alternative view of reality. Feelings and ideas stimulated by such an alternative view and directed by the aesthetic structure of a literary work demand new forms of cognitive assimilation and linquistic expression. The creative connections between language, thought, and feeling are thus reawakened.

Leslie Epstein interprets Dr. Feder's argument as aiming to address the areas of the psyche that are "accessible to conscious manipulation and control." This has the "great strength" of helping us experience reality "with our wits sharpened, our very capacity for thought and judgement invigorated." He describes the passage from *Don Quixote* in which the Don spares Sancho Panza from the lash as illustrating the power of literature to exert this effect.

In his comments, Gerald Richman describes Professor Feder's argument as "an interesting and sophisticated version of an old idea . . . that literature is didactic." Although he finds this argument "appealing," Dr. Richman expresses doubts that the study of literature can contribute to the development of the self. Charging a lack of evidence to support Dr. Feder's argument, he cites the Nazis' reading of Goethe as evidence of the failure of literature to contribute in any constructive way to this development.

In her comments, Sarah Smith predicts the birth of a new form of creativity made possible by advances in computer technology. This new form will be the modular, nonlinear narrative. Through narrative of this kind the reader will have the ability to interchange and interact with modules (i.e., episodes), thus losing a sense of closure but gaining a new and more effective way of simulating real-world choices.

In her reply, Professor Feder disagrees with Dr. Richman's comment that hers is an "old idea." His comment, she says, confuses what *is* an old idea—that literature provides moral judgments—with her own argument—that the study of literature induces a psychological process of self-creation. The fact that the study of literature has not prevented *some* persons from taking on evil personalities is correct but too complex to enter usefully here as evidence for or against her argument. On the prospects for nonlinear narrative, Dr. Feder observes that such narrative predates the computer. Though welcoming the creative possibilities offered by computer technology, she says, in concluding, that "it must never replace the feel of a book, the turning of a page, the owning of a book, just the whole experience of being alone and yet communally involved as you sit and read."

The final panel of the colloquium was organized as a roundtable discussion in which I served as moderator. Here, we reproduce as Final Remarks the statements with which the speakers and I began this panel. I direct my own contribution to these remarks mainly at Dr. Giroux. My argument has to do with his politicization of knowledge and with my support for Kevin Lyons' position that the liberal arts must address the task of preparing students to participate creatively in the business world.

In his reply, Dr. Giroux warns about the threat to critical pedagogy that is posed by narrow considerations of economic efficiency and argues for turning our attention to the needs of democracy and of social empowerment. Dr. Feder points out how literature questions society—not by politicizing knowledge, but by revealing how the characters and personae of a literary work simultaneously internalize and question the assumptions of their time. Dr. Pylyshyn offers his judgment that it is one of the consequences of science and technology, as it is of great literature, to question the assumptions of our time, pointing out how artificial intelligence has brought about the latest in a series of great challenges to man's view of himself.

CONCLUSION

It is neither surprising nor discouraging that the papers and comments contained here have not resolved the major issues posed above and in the conferences' *Prospectus*. In important respects, the issues posed by modern cognitive science appear to mirror those raised here. The tension exhibited here between alternative conceptions of the creative process and of the proper mission of the liberal arts and sciences parrallels the computational and noncomputational modes of thought that are contrasted above. Perhaps the existence of this tension indicates that both modes of thought are present in the creative process, sometimes opposing and sometimes reinforcing one another. Perhaps, therefore, it is the process of bringing together diverse and divergent views, such as this volume contains, that advances our understanding of the creative process and of the role of that process in educational reform.

REFERENCES

Hofstadter, D. R. (1979). *Gödel, Escher, Bach: An eternal golden braid.* New York: Basic Books.

Hofstadter, D. R. (1983). Artificial intelligence: Subcognition as computation. In F. Machlup & U. Mansfield (Eds.), *The study of information: Interdisciplinary messages.* New York: Wiley.

Hofstadter, D. R. (1985a). On the seeming paradox of mechanizing creativity. In D. R. Hofstadter (Ed.), *Metamagical themas.* New York: Basic Books.

Hofstadter, D. R. (1985b). Variations on a theme as the crux of creativity. In D. R. Hofstadter (Ed.), *Metamagical themas.* New York: Basic Books.

Simon, H. A. (1981). *The sciences of the artificial* (2d ed. pp. 129–156). Cambridge: MA: MIT Press.

Simon, H. A. (1982). From substantive to procedural rationality. In H. A. Simon (Ed.), *Models of bounded rationality, II.* Cambridge, MA: MIT Press.

Simon, H. A., & Newell, A. (1982). Heuristic problem solving: the next advance in operations research. In H. A. Simon (Ed.), *Models of bounded rationality, I.* Cambridge, MA: MIT Press.

WAYS OF THINKING ABOUT CREATIVITY

Creativity: The Need For Definition

Robert C. Webb

The word creative is an adjective, and we use it freely in conjunction with any number of nouns, as in creative cooking, creative accounting, creative management, and so forth. We seem to understand what is meant by these terms, though there is a mild air of anticipation that accompanies their use, so that we are often motivated to find out just what they mean "this time." We feel cheated if it turns out to be the same old thing we already knew. Our initial interest in such cases probably results from a built-in fascination with the novel. The psychology of perception has clearly documented that the novel stimulus attracts attention, a principle well understood by those in the marketing and advertising trades. In other words, because creative things are novel, if nothing else, we exhibit at least mild curiosity when we see a book entitled "creative this" or "creative that" (which, of course, is why such titles are chosen in the first place), and we seem to have a pretty good notion of what to expect.

It is when the word moves from its adjectival status to assume the role of noun that a number of difficulties arise. Creativity is the noun, of course, and I was surprised to find that it is a newcomer to our linguistic scene. I do not know when it quietly moved to its dominant position as a noun, but *Webster's Fifth Collegiate Dictionary* (1947) does not even list it. The 1980 edition does list it, however, and says there are

19

two meanings: (1) the quality of being creative and (2) the ability to create. Notice, right in the first definition, that a subtle change has oc-curred from our earlier usage. We are no longer speaking of being cre-ative "something"; we are now simply creative. The implication is clearly that one can, in fact, be creative, with no reference to what it is one is doing. That is, creativity is the same thing regardless of task or person. The second definition picks up the same implication when it refers to an ability to create as though there is such an ability that applies across the board to all endeavors. Unfortunately, however, psychologists have been engaged in the pursuit of such an ability for a number of years now, and have concluded that no such general creative ability exists. D.N. Perkins (1981) makes the point particularly well:

> Sometimes I feel we ought to do away with the word *creativity*. What need is there for a word that removes us one step further from the key meaning of a creative result? To see what an odd and unnecessary idea creativity is, consider this. Just as we speak of creative people, we speak of athletic people. So suppose we coin a word to mean whatever athletic people have that makes them athletic—say *athleticity*. Now we can talk about how much athleticity people have, and maybe even try to measure athleticity in re-lation to IQ, sex, and race. All this sounds scientific because athleticity sounds like a single fixed stuff we could measure. But perhaps people are athletic for many different reasons and in many different ways, even rea-sons and ways which change with time. We could just as well talk about how athletic a person is, instead of how much athleticity a person has, and the first way of talking doesn't make all those misleading suggestions. (p. 245)

Our semantic extensions seem to have led us into a corner of mis-understanding. But sometimes it is even worse than Perkins says—for instance, when we lose sight of the term's relative nature and speak as though creativity is something either present or not, like blue eyes. Because one can be more or less creative, then creativity (and I am afraid the word is here to stay) must be something one can have more or less of. For example, suppose someone comes across plans for a birdhouse in a popular magazine and decides to build it. He follows the plans and produces a birdhouse. This certainly is creative: A bird-house exists where there was not one before. But we would have to say that a person who designed his own birdhouse is more creative because he created the design as well. Even more creative would be the person whose design was unusual in some way. In other words, anyone can show creativity, but some show more of it than others. So it can be placed on a scale from low to high, but what else do we know about it? Because the dictionary is no help, we must turn to those who have used the term, and here I shall confine myself to psychologists.

When you begin to examine how the term creativity has been used by psychologists you see that about the only part on which they agree is the necessity that novelty be present in the process. Now, novelty means new, but because mere mortals cannot create from nothing, that is, literally new, what we really mean is a new arrangement of old materials or ideas. But novelty alone is not enough; because if novelty is our only requirement, we are led to problems such as this: Would the productions of a monkey which is hitting typewriter keys at random qualify as creative? We tend to think not, but why not? It certainly is different from any collection of letters seen before. It is novel alright, but is it creative? Most would say no—some quality is clearly missing. Simple random activity is not what we mean by creativity; so it seems that simple novelty is not enough.

An approach based on utility is favored by some psychologists, for example, Bruner (1961). According to this view, creativity is that which leads to products which are novel and useful. This would be a definition that those engaged in industry would favor. They would consider as creative one who could come up with new products or new ways of producing them. We cannot argue with their use of the term; such people are clearly creative. But if we are looking for a general concept of creativity, we find the requirement that the production be useful a bit confining. For instance, what about a work of art? It would seem that to say a painting on the wall is useful stretches the notion of useful a little. But there is a more important problem even than this. The picture on the wall may be useful, but what about the one in the attic? Suppose no one likes the artist's works and they gather unsold in the attic? Are they useful hidden away up there? Or, what if the artist becomes discovered 50 years later and is recognized as having been years ahead of his time—what then? Has he suddenly become creative years after his death? The need for usefulness clearly applies only in some cases of creativity. In addition it carries the implication that someone must judge whether it is useful or not, and judges may not always agree.

Nor do our problems end there. Suppose that a useful product occurs totally by chance as someone is pursuing something else. Can he be considered creative? The element of intent must be dealt with. The question of serendipity is not the issue here. Often researchers find something they were not looking for but their creativity is in their recognition of its importance. Rather, here we are talking about that admittedly unusual case where a person creates a useful something and someone else recognizes its value. That is, the creator did not intend to create. Is the creator creative in this case?

Consider one more twist, if you will. What if someone designs a product only to find out that it has already been done, perhaps by many others? Should not the designer still be considered creative? But clearly there is no useful product. In other words, what may be quite creative, given the individual, still may not produce a useful product. It would seem we must consider the intent and the resources of the individual who is attempting to create when judging his creativity.

If useful is not quite the right word, nonetheless there is agreement that some distinction from randomness is necessary. Ryan (1984) sums it up:

> Newell and Simon called it appropriate originality; Wallach and Kogan, unique, effective formulation; Barron, uncommon adaptation; and most recently Amabile, appropriate novelty. Each of these definitions has been chorused by numerous others, highlighting the two central qualities of creative endeavor—its departure from conventionality and its skillful, organized character. (p. 533)

Note that Ryan wisely used the term *creative endeavor*, not creativity, but the people he cites are not so circumspect. They are clearly talking about creativity, but by now it should be understood that we are dealing with a slippery beast.

I want to leave the direct discussion of definition at this point, becoming indirect by turning to an overview of the ways in which psychologists have pursued the topic. It is certainly not my intention to provide a review of the research as such; the topic is much too vast and others far better qualified have already done an admirable job with it. Rather, what I would like to do is to provide a flavor of how psychologists have proceeded in order to show that the question of definition is not just an academic one. How you cast your definition to a large extent determines what you find. Some of the apparent discrepancies will dissolve when it becomes clear that they are not really talking about the same thing. Finally, definition becomes particularly important if one is going to implement a program to produce more of it.

We turn, then, to the considerable literature in the psychological field of creativity. Barron in his review (Barron and Harrington 1981) noted that, whereas in 1956 there were about 400 references in the *Psychological Abstracts* on the topic of creative imagination, by "1965, the comprehensive bibliography of the Greater Education Foundation ... contained 4,176 references" (p. 440). He goes on to say that the current production has leveled off at about "250 new dissertations, articles, or books every year since 1970" (p. 440).

When one peruses a bit of this literature, one notices that there are three main concerns in the field of creativity: product, person, and process. Psychologists have been concerned with all three aspects, particularly over the last 35 years, but their findings have not always fit together as nicely as one might hope.

We will consider product first. I am, of course, using the term *product* here not in the narrow sense of physical objects only, but in a wider sense that also includes ideas. In psychology the creative product has chiefly been used as a means of identifying the creative producer, and what has emerged is a clear understanding that I must know what you want to produce before I can find you creative people to do it. Although this may seen obvious in some cases, that is, you look for creative scientists among scientists, not among artists, in other cases we seem to forget the principle. For example, we set out to make students simply more creative, assuming that the same approach will work no matter where they are headed. We seek a single creativity innoculation. But, whereas all creatives share some common characteristics, their creativity is always partially structured by its raw materials. The products of the scientist and the artist are totally different because their goals are different. The scientist is trying to explain logically, whereas the artist is trying to express emotionally. Although they both must work within some rules and, to be creative must discard some, how they do this is bound to be quite different.

An approach to creativity which starts with product has recently appeared. Amabile (1983) has found that products can be reliably rated as to their inherent creativity, even sorting it out from technical goodness or aesthetic appeal. She takes this information not so much to find out about the people themselves as to find out about the social climate that has produced their creativity. She focuses mostly on motivational aspects of the social climate and finds that "the intrinsically motivated state is detrimental" (p. 91).

Amabile finds that tying rewards or other kinds of evaluation to creativity has deleterious effects. Ryan (1984) concludes, "Creativity, like intrinsic motivation, is most likely to emerge when we *allow* it, rather than attempt to prompt or produce it" (p. 533). This is probably why the president of a small computer company recently said on national television that 90% of what his creative innovators produce is unusable. Clearly he feels that the pressure to make them more efficient would lose him that precious 10%. The climate he provides for his innovators to work in would probably be described as relaxed and permissive, rather than demanding and competitive. Now a company which adopts a new idea and goes into production with it by those very actions is certainly rewarding the idea. But there is no negative evaluation of ideas that are not adopted, and that is the point Amabile has empirically found to be necessary.

The rewarding of desired behaviors is a well-established way to behavior change. Its relationship to creativity burst upon the scene in a remarkable way more than 15 years ago:

> In 1965 the trainers of Sea Life Park, Makapuu Oceanic Center, Hawaii decided to demonstrate to audiences the first step in shaping the behavior of their performing porpoises. At each demonstration a completely new behavior had to be reinforced because once an action has been rewarded, it can no longer be used to demonstrate the *first step* in shaping. Within a few days all the normal causal actions of the porpoise had been used up and unusual spontaneous stunts emerged. The porpoise had apparently learned that the trainer wanted new acts, not repetitions. The trainers unexpectedly encouraged an animal to demonstrate creative behavior.
>
> To see if this kind of training could make another animal creative, a formal experiment was set up using another porpoise which was considered a docile, timid animal with little initiative. Thirty-two training sessions each lasting five to twenty minutes with half-hour rest periods between them were conducted with only new responses being awarded. At first, responses that were reinforced were performed repeatedly; as many as one hundred and ninety two times in twenty-three minutes.
>
> In session thirty-one, the porpoise repeated a new reinforced act fourteen times and in session thirty-two, another new one only ten times. The porpoise had produced a new behavior in each of six out of seven consecutive sessions and, by this time, its aerial acrobatics had become so complex that they exceeded the ability of the observers to describe them. The experiment had to be concluded.
>
> After the experiment was over, the trainers found a tendency toward increased activity and original response in other situations by the porpoises in this study. In one instance, a porpoise jumped from the water, skidded across six feet of wet pavement and tapped the trainer on the ankle with its snout—a bizarre act for an aquatic animal. (Pryor, 1969, p. 46)

The behavior of these animals is certainly novel, intended, and appropriate, so that we would conclude it is creative. This series of studies expanded the concept of reinforcement to include creativity. What is needed, however, to bring this demonstration in line with Amabile's findings is an understanding of the complexity of reinforcement in humans. Humans are cognitively complex enough that they are going to feel not only reward when one action is reinforced, but also disappointment or even anger that another action at the same time was not reinforced. This is the thin ice on which Amabile cautions us to tread lightly.

Although psychologists have often started from product, the bulk of their concern has quite naturally been on person. In this approach they have tried to isolate the characteristics that people have which make them creative. It asks, who has it, where did it come from, and can it be taught to others? Any attempt to answer these questions will illustrate at once that the problem of definition is no longer simply an intellectual exercise.

J. P. Guilford (1967) was one of the first to meet this problem head-on by using the tried and true psychological research technique of operational definition. The method involves defining a quality or state in terms of the operation used to produce it. It is used extensively in psychology because there is no other alternative. For example, hunger, which can only be inferred to exist and certainly cannot be measured directly, is defined as that state produced in animals by depriving them of food for so many hours. We can then equate animals at least to a first approximation on the variable hunger. Although operational definitions are admittedly incomplete, they do allow progress toward understanding.

Guilford's approach was to devise a test of creativity which seemed to have some face validity in that it attempted to measure associative fluency. It required one to produce a variety of responses in a short period of time. For example, one of the items asked for as many uses of a brick as you could think of. The test later became known in psychology circles as the uses-of-a-brick-test and served as a model for many variants. One's score is derived not only from the number of responses, but also from the amount of variety contained in them.

Note that the creative person here is defined as one who scores high on the test, and that there is no reference to product at all. You might in fact identify creative persons who never produced anything. It would be assumed, of course, that they were potentially creative. Guilford was interested in many mental abilities besides creativity and identified up to 120 of them; but tests which evolved from his creativity test have shown that they are consistently measuring some unique quality.

Another way to study creative people is to ask others to identify them. A company president, for instance, might be asked to identify the most creative person in his or her company, the person they found to be indispensable for new ideas. We can then make a group of such people and see what characteristics they have that others lack. Note that in this method we are again working from product backward, but our concern here is with the persons themselves, not the characteristics of their environment. The type of product is left unspecified but will of course be reflected in whom we select to identify our creatives. If no controls were applied one might have scientists, inventors, and artists all mixed in

together. Now that would not matter if there were a common characteristic that all creatives share, but it would obscure things if such were not
the case.

We should note before going on to the findings that both approaches,
giving a test or identifying a group, are looking for people who have a
lot of whatever this is. The idea is to isolate the beast by finding the
strongest or most obvious examples of it. Here again, without care, we
could easily conclude that creativity is something only these best examples have and lose sight of its relative nature.

Perhaps the most obvious question to ask about these groups of identified creatives is whether they are extra intelligent. Thus, their most
extensively researched personality variable has probably been their intelligence. Caution is advised here since the concept of intelligence itself
has been changing in recent years, but it does seem fairly clear nonetheless that highly creative people also tend to be of high intelligence
(Barron & Harrington, 1981, p. 445). The reverse is not the case, however. That is, highly intelligent people will not necessarily be creative.
In other words, high intelligence is necessary, but not sufficient for high
creativity.

The reason for this connection seems fairly clear. Creativity involves
the manipulation of materials into new relationships, whether the materials be nuts and bolts or ideas. Intelligence provides the materials—
the more intelligent, the more materials—but it does not necessarily
mean that the materials will be rearranged at all. The same logic applies
to the principle that long years of learning a discipline precede creative
advances there. Knowledge, like intelligence, is necessary but not sufficient.

Personality variables other than intelligence have also been extensively explored. In a nutshell:

> In general, a fairly stable set of core characteristics (e.g., high valuation of
> esthetic qualities in experience, broad interests, attraction to complexity,
> high energy, independence of judgement, autonomy, intuition, self-con-
> fidence, ability to resolve autonomies or to accomodate apparently op-
> posite or conflicting traits in one's self-concept, and finally, a firm sense
> of self as "creative") continued to emerge as correlates of creative achieve-
> ment and activity in many domains. (Barron & Harrington, 1981, p. 453).

Most of the information that Barron has reviewed above is based on
empirical studies, but a second source of information is available in the
reports of clinicians. It is reassuring that their picture is essentially the
same as the empiricists. Eric Fromm (1959), for example, gives five char-

acteristics of personality necessary for creativity; the capacity to be puzzled, the ability to concentrate, a sense of self as the true originator of
many acts, the ability to accept conflict, and the willingness to let go of
certainties and illusions. He goes on to remark that these are conditions
not just for the gifted, but ones that everybody can attain. "Education
for creativity is nothing short of education for living" (p. 54).

Carl Rogers (1959) echoes the importance of concepts of self, and, in
anticipation of the findings of Amabile, relates them to a climate in
which external evaluation is absent:

> When we cease to form judgements of the other individual from our own
> locus of evaluation, we are fostering creativity. For the individual to find
> himself in an atmosphere where he is not being evaluted, not being mea-
> sured by some external standard, is enormously freeing. Evaluation is al-
> ways a threat, always creates a need for defensiveness, always means that
> some portion of experience must be denied to awareness. If this product
> is evaluated as good by external standards, then I must not admit my own
> dislike of it. If what I am doing is bad by external standards, then I must
> not be aware of the fact that it seems to be me, to be part of myself. But
> if judgements based on external standards are not being made then I can
> be more open to my experience, can recognize my own likings and dislik-
> ings, the nature of the materials and of my reaction to them, more sharply
> and more sensitively. I can begin to recognize the locus of evaluation
> within myself. Hence I am moving toward creativity.
>
>   To allay some possible doubts and fears in the reader, it should be
> pointed out that to cease evaluating another is not to cease having reac-
> tions. It may, as a matter of fact, free one to react. I don't like your idea
> (or painting, or invention, or writing), is not an evaluation, but a reaction.
> It is subtly but sharply different from a judgement which says, What you
> are doing is bad (or good), and this quality is assigned to you form some
> external source. The first statement permits the individual to maintain his
> own locus of evaluation. . . . The second statement, whether it praises or
> condemns, tends to put the person at the mercy of outside forces. He is
> being told that he cannot simply ask himself whether this product is a
> valid expression of himself; he must be concerned with what others think.
> He is being led away from creativity. (p. 79)

The tie between creativity and such basic elements of personality as
ego strength and self-image suggests that not everyone can become creative without a major effort of therapeutic self-improvement. For many,
nothing less than a restructuring of their personality is what is involved.
A quick course on thinking techniques will not be of much help for one
who is deeply involved in ego defense. To experiment with the new may
often result in criticism, ridicule, and even rejection. Only strong egos

need apply. Still, our reference here is to high creativity, and, just as we can all grow from therapy, so we can all become somewhat more crea-tive.

Perkins (1981), after reviewing the extensive literature, expresses a final note of caution on the personality of creatives when he warns that "whatever trends emerge, exceptions are exceptionally easy to find" (p. 269).

Before leaving this whirlwind tour of psychological research on cre-ativity oriented toward person, one other factor might be mentioned that has come under increasing analysis, particularly in the last decade. I refer to the repeated finding that men and women are not necessarily creative in the same ways. When creativity is defined in terms of a test score, clearly the content of the test is crucial to the findings. It appears that at least some of these tests may be biased, not only against women but against other groups as well. Likewise, a company which hires no women in its research and design department will not be likely to iden-tify women who are creative. (See Barron & Harrington, 1981, pp. 456–458 for a summary of this extensive literature.)

Psychologists have been concerned with creativity not only as person, but also as process, and we turn to that now. The question here is whether there is a particular mode of thinking that leads to creative conclusions. Researchers have proceeded here also by devising tests of various kinds, but the approach is slightly different than that outlined above. Here, a test is used to model some sort of thought process. Then, to see whether that process is involved in creativity, one validates it against a group of creatives. High scores by high creatives, in other words, means that they are particularly efficient in thinking in this way. A few examples will serve to illustrate the approach.

Mednick (1962) formulated a theory of remote associates in which he hypothesized that the associative patterns among words and ideas dif-fered between creatives and noncreatives.

As expressed by Mendelsohn (1976) "Mednick proposes that persons of low creativity have a small number of strong, stereotyped, associative responses to a given stimulus, while remote responses to the stimulus have very low associative response strengths. This is designated a steep hierarchy of associative response strengths. In contrast, the hierarchy of highly creative persons is described as relatively flat, the response strengths of primary and remote associates being more nearly equal. They should consequently emit a larger variety of associates as well as more unusual associates, i.e., show greater associational fluency" (p. 341).

Martindale (1981) summarizes how Mednick tested his theory by de-vising a Remote Associates Test in which the subject is confronted with 30 sets of three items. For each set, the task is to find a fourth word that is related to all three of the stimulus words. The trick is that the fourth word is associatetively rather than logically related to the stimulus word. Here is an example of the sorts of items that the test contains:

Railroad	Girl	Class	_____
Surprise	Line	Birthday	_____

(The answers are working and party.) People who are creative (as defined by their having produced work that is creative) do in fact score higher on this test than do uncreative people. (p. 376)

Support is thus marshalled for a theory of creativity which says the ability to think with a flat gradient of remote associates is essential for creativity.

Mendelsohn (1976) formulated a theory that differences in attentional capacity play a major role in forming one's associations and thus in one's potential for creativity. Creative people are hypothesized to have less-focused attentions than uncreatives. Martindale (1981) reports a study by Dykes and McGhie of the performance of creative and uncreative subjects on shadowing tasks." This "shadowing" involves trying to repeat back a message as it proceeds. Thus, the "shadowed" ear is getting the message one is trying to repeat back, whereas the "unshadowed" is getting a different message one is trying to ignore. Martindale does not report how the subjects were determined to be creative or uncreative, but the study is an interesting one:

In one part of the experiment, the words coming to the shadowed ear consisted of a meaningful prose passage. Random words were presented to the unshadowed ear. After the experiment, a recognition-memory test was given for words presented in both the shadowed and the unshadowed channels. Creative subjects recalled more of the words from the unshadowed channel than did the uncreative subjects.... As compared to less creative people, creative subjects switched (that is, mistakenly repeated the word from the channel they were supposed to disregard) more often when highly associated word pairs were presented. Both of these results—better memory for the unshadowed message and more intrusions from the unshadowed channel—support the contention that creative people have less focused attention. (p. 372)

Note that both the studies reported here use verbal materials. It is possible that creativity is being confounded with verbal fluency, as Mendelsohn (1976, p. 360) found, because high creatives would also likely be highly intelligent. It seems clear that an underlying assumption of studies of this type is that creatives in general will show some special ability with words. Perhaps it is because our education is so completely verbal that we tend to regard all thinking as verbally based.

Many studies have been done of this type in the areas of verbal learning, problem solving, span and focus of attention, and cognitive fluency. Note that this approach cannot avoid the problems of definition, because confirmation of a process as essential to creativity occurs by reference to a group of known creatives whose selection assumed a definition. The crucial question tends to remain whether the selected group represents all creatives, that is, creativity in general, or whether it reflects some narrower group.

In the late nineteenth century, evidence began to accumulate that damage to the left side of the brain affected language whereas right-side damage did not. However, only in the last 25 years has the corresponding right-side function been known. In general, visual imagery is affected by right-side damage, but the brain's function is not simple. Gardner (1982), drawing on his work over many years with brain-injured patients, has recently described a more comprehensive role of the right hemisphere. He writes that some patients with right-hemisphere damage, particularly in the frontal lobes, when hearing a story read to them,

> have difficulty accepting the story on its own terms. To borrow from Coleridge, they are unable to adopt a 'willing suspension of disbelief'. They argue with points that should be accepted, even as they accept the bizarre elements that we sometimes put in just to see whether they have any sense of what is appropriate. The patients fail to respect the boundaries of the story, to accept its premises, but cross those boundaries at will to suit their own purposes.
>
> • • •
>
> a related conclusion is that they lack the ability to set up a 'scaffolding' for a story. They are unable to figure out the underlying architecture or composition of a story—the nature of and relationship between the various parts and characters. Instead, each part stands alone, a single brick unrelated to any other—or to the entire edifice. (pp. 314–315)

Ornstein (1977) has characterized the difference between the hemispheres as related to mode of processing. The left side is characterized as a sequential processor and thus is suited to verbal material in which the sense of a sound must be determined by comparing it to other sounds immediately preceding or following. The right side, rather, is a simultaneous processor and is more suited to visual input in which the whole scene is perceived at once, not in successive pieces.

An interesting contribution on this topic has come from an unlikely

source, Japan's Nobel Prize-winning physicist, Yukawa. In writing about
the role of intuition in science, Yukawa (1973) refers to a psychological
experiment in pattern recognition, involving a triangle stimulus:

> ... the same psychologists tell us about the result of an experiment which
> is even more striking and interesting. They tried to follow the line of
> vision of a normal adult. The motion of his line of vision is very much
> simplified compared to that of the formerly blind man recently operated
> upon. The restored line of vision of the latter totters along one side of
> the triangle and when it comes to the corner, the motion is ended. In this
> simplified way he can recognize the triangle. How is it possible at all? The
> information which the man obtains by moving his line of vision is twofold.
> One is the sharp and clear perception of a small part of an object to which
> the line of vision is directed. This one may call quantitative or digital
> information. The other is the more obscure but wide-angled perception
> of the larger part of an object surrounding the small part on which the
> vision is focused. This may be called qualitative or analogue information.
> These two kinds of information work together so as to abridge the process
> of pattern recognition to a great extent. (p. 117)

To say that his description fits the left and right hemispheric brain
functions well is probably too simple. However, the parallel with Gardner's findings is remarkable.

Pattern recognition is, of course, one of the concerns of researchers
in the field of artificial intelligence. The computer has given a boost to
the psychology of cognition ever since it first appeared after World War
II. Up until that time, thinking had been considered by most to be a
magical realm completely beyond the reach of science. Behaviorism had
all but ruled it out as not measureable. When the computer appeared,
it provided a physical model for thinking and the magic began to disappear. At that time the controversial issue was whether computers could
think. Simon reportedly said, "Tell me what you mean by thinking and
I will build a computer to do it." The position is well taken, for thinking
defies easy definition. The question is no longer a volatile one, but it
seems to have been replaced by other questions even more difficult to
answer. Do computers feel and can computers be creative? Just as in the
question of thinking, the key is definition. With feeling we have almost
no way of knowing that even other humans feel, except they tell us so;
but in the case of creativity we have a product. On the other hand, we
have seen how hard it is to specify what makes a product acceptable.
This is why we still have to fall back on terms like *appropriate*.

Pattern recognition involves the distillation of a constant feature out
of endless variations. How does the human mind recognize even the
letter *A* upside down in a strange handwriting, not to mention the face

of a friend across the street? Because creativity essentially involves the manipulation of patterns into new arrangements, pattern recognition is almost where one has to start. In addition to the pieces, the rules for combination must also be verbalized and this is proving even more difficult.

The human being follows many rules he or she cannot verbalize. Brown (1973) showed some years ago that children have internalized all the rules of grammar before they enter the first grade. We know this from errors in their speech, among other ways. For example, when a child says, "That's mines," she is using a word that she has probably never heard, but has constructed from the rule that with possessives you add an "s." Only, in this case, it happens to be an exception to the rule and incorrect. The exceptions will be learned later. The point is, we are often not aware of this side of ourselves, and we find it very hard to verbalize why 'mines' sounds wrong to us as adults. We say, we just know.

It is interesting that Yukawa's main concern was with intuition, feeling that it is essential for theoretical advances, because that topic has seen a renaissance since the hemispheric duality became known. If one defines intuition as "knowing, without being able to verbalize how one knows," it would seem to describe right-side knowing, which is separated from the left-side verbalizer. Perhaps some of the magic of intuition will also begin to disappear. The role of the unconscious in creative production has long been acknowledged, but it may turn out that some of this function should more properly be considered nonverbal thinking, rather than unconscious. However, lest we make the mistake of trying to make creativity a right-side function and locate it in a particular part of the brain, Gardner (1982) leaves us with a word of warning: "To produce something well organized, let alone something fresh and original, it may be necessary to have an essentially intact nervous system. . . . One needs to have all, or at least most, regions of the brain performing at top form" (p. 334).

The process of creative thought has also been considered a result of divergent thinking. Without reviewing the considerable body of literature on divergent thinking (see Guilford, 1967), suffice it to say that it appears that convergent thinking is also needed and the creative person may be one who can shift between these two modes as needed. Kris (1952) proposed a theory of creativity based on the Freudian notions of primary and secondary process thinking, hypothesizing that the creative person is able to shift between these levels. Martindale (1981, p. 387) sees parallels in both Mednick's and Mendelsohn's proposed cognitive mechanisms and the ability to shift when required. The brain's ability to shift modes is doubtless one of the problems which makes harder the task of the modelers of artificial intelligence trying to design a computer worthy of the label "creative."

Another approach to creativity as process can be seen in the work of Perkins (1981). He has interviewed creative people from different fields of endeavor, especially poets. His particular interest has been in how they describe their process of creating rather than in what personal characteristics they have. Surprisingly, their process appears to be quite ordinary and not magical at all.

Study of creativity as process has seen applications from the early brainstorming techniques to the more elaborate "synectics" promoted by Gordon (1961). These approaches have involved methods to increase the production of ideas and to apply various types of analogies for the juxtaposition of unusual ideas. Koestler (1964) proposes a similar process he calls "bisociation," which seems to consist of placing together in the unconscious, frames of reference which don't normally occur together. He feels that the unconscious then works creatively because the interaction process is allowed to proceed with fewer constraints than in the conscious level.

Probably these approaches do help improve some sorts of creativity. Koestler is, of course, referring mostly to writers, and the other techniques are related mostly to problem solving. It is doubtful, however, how much they can do to produce high creativity where it does not already exist.

Psychologists have used many approaches to the study of the elusive creativity. What it is remains questionable. However, while we wait for synthesis, what application can be made (of what we have learned) to creativity in the college classroom? It would appear most important that a decision be made to clarify the objectives: Is the goal to raise the creativity level of average people or to foster the creativity of a few individuals at a high level? The approaches are different, though they are not, of course, mutually exclusive. The evidence certainly suggests that if one wants highly creative individuals, one must start with highly intelligent people, well integrated psychologically, educate them well in a discipline, and provide a supportive environment in which they may develop.

On the other hand, to raise the level of creativity in the average person would appear to be a bit easier task. Climate of support would seem to be the key, with some exposure to techniques of creative thinking as a probable help. For some, opportunities to improve their level of psychological functioning would appear to be necessary. Beyond that, however, it would seem that we must also define the type of creative endeavor we wish to see, because creativity comes in many forms.

REFERENCES

Amabile, T.M. (1983). *The social psychology of creativity.* New York: Springer-Verlag.

Barron, F., & Harrington, D.M. (1981). Creativity, intelligence and personality. *Annual Review of Psychology, 32,* 439–476.

Brown, R. (1973). *A first language.* Cambridge, MA: Harvard University Press.

Bruner, J. (1961). *The process of education.* Cambridge, MA: Harvard University Press.

Fromm, E. (1959). The creative attitude. In H.H. Anderson (Ed.), *Creativity and its cultivation.* New York: Harper Bros.

Gardner, H. (1982). *Art, mind, and brain.* New York: Basic Books.

Gordon, J.J. (1961). *Synectics.* New York: Harper and Row.

Guilford, J.P., (1967). *The nature of human intelligence.* New York: McGraw Hill.

Koestler, A. (1964). *The act of creation.* New York: Macmillan.

Kris, E. (1952). *Psychoanalytic exploration in art.* New York: International Universities Press.

Martindale, C. (1981). *Cognition and consciousness.* Homewood, IL: Dorsey.

Mednick, S.A. (1962). The associative basis of the creative process. *Psychological Review, 69,* 220–32.

Mendelsohn, G.A. (1976). Associative and attentional processes in creative performance. *Journal of Personality, 44,* 341–69.

Ornstein, R.E. (1977). *The psychology of consciousness* (2d ed.) New York: Harcourt Brace Jovanovich.

Perkins, D.N. (1981). *The mind's best work.* Cambridge, MA: Harvard University Press.

Pryor, K. (1969). Behavior modification: The porpoise caper. *Psychology Today, 3,* 46.

Rogers, C.R. (1959). Toward a theory of creativity. In H.H. Anderson (Ed.), *Creativity and its cultivation.* New York: Harper Bros.

Ryan, R.M. (1984). An appropriate, original look at appropriate originality. *Contemporary Psychology, 29,* 533.

Yukawa, H. (1973). *Creativity and intuition.* Tokyo: Kodansha International.

SYMPOSIUM

PANEL 1

Creativity: From Asexual to Sexual Production

Kenneth S. Greenberg

I would like you to conjure up the image of a creative genius. What do you see? If you are like most people I asked to perform this feat of imagination you have probably visualized a middle-aged or elderly man, disheveled in appearance, with a kind of wild look about the eyes. You have probably imagined him sitting alone in his study working furiously over some piece of creative work. Perhaps you have seen Einstein or someone very much like him.

This popular image of the creative genius is actually little more than a simplified vision of creativity which has achieved a remarkable level of acceptance for centuries in the history of Western thought. The central message embodied in this image is that creativity is an activity performed by men acting in isolation. The purpose of this paper is to demonstrate that such an image of creativity is inadequate and incomplete in several significant ways. A more complete image of creativity must recognize that individuals do not perform their creative work divorced from the world in which they live. Creativity is a social production and must be understood in the context of particular peoples living in time and space.

The traditional image of the creative genius has deep roots within Western culture. Not that there haven't been great disagreements about the nature of creative people, processes, and products. But, with few exceptions, disagreements about creativity have left the traditional image remarkably untouched. In fact, these debates have often served to reinforce this image. The issue has hardly ever been seen as whether or not creativity is performed by men sitting alone. What always seemed to be at stake was exactly how they came to emit their creative product. Put in its most basic terms, the problem of creativity has been conceived of as the problem of how individual men could produce something new.

The debate has almost always been about the exact nature of this asexual production. The central question has always been, "How do men give birth?" The central issue posed by the problem of creativity has always been a sexual issue, although almost no one has explicitly understood it this way before.

The question of how something new comes into existence,—of how men give birth—has traditionally been answered in two main ways: Either the something which is new is thought of as something old which has been transformed through a natural process, or it is something which is created out of the void from nothing (at least from outside the natural universe). The first answer, that new things arise from natural processes and transformations, can be seen earliest in the writings of Aristotle: "... It is impossible," he wrote, "that anything should be produced if there were nothing existing before" (Ross, 1983, p. 793). Hence, all new things are old things transformed. It is at the heart of many psychological explanations of creativity; it is imbedded in theories of the physical universe which assume the conservation of matter and energy; and it is assumed by advocates of computer-generated artificial intelligence (see Hofstadter, 1979).

The second answer, that new things emerge from outside the natural world, can be seen in Plato's idea that "lovely poems are not of man or human workmanship, but are devine and from the gods, and that the poets are nothing but interpreters of the gods, each one possessed by the divinity to whom he is in bondage" (Plato, 1961, p. 221). It is also the answer given in the Bible which describes the creation of nature from nothingness: In the beginning, we are told, "... the earth was without form, and void." It is the explanation offered by many creative thinkers when they are questioned about their work. Mozart, for example, described the sudden flow of his ideas by noting that "*Whence* and *how* they come, I know not; nor can I force them." Samuel Taylor Coleridge apparently composed "Kubla Khan" while under the influence of opium "without any sensation or consciousness of effort." The poet Amy Lowell believed that "(t)he words seem to be pronounced in my head, but with nobody speaking them." Perhaps Friedrich Nietzsche best characterized this experience of creativity: "The notion of revelation describes the condition quite simply; by which I mean that something profoundly convulsive and disturbing suddenly becomes visible and audible with incredible definiteness and exactness. One hears—one does not seek; one takes—one does not give; a thought flashes out like lightening, inevitably and without hesitation—I have never had any choice about it."[1]

---

[1] Quotations found in Ghiselin (1952, pp. 34, 84, 111, 193, 209–210).

Despite these clear differences of opinion, what is noteworthy about such visions of creativity is that they all view the creative process as the production of objects occurring through individuals isolated from their social and cultural world. In this sense, they all evoke images of asexual production, of creativity through male masturbation. It has always been the same story: Athena emerging in full armor from the head of Zeus; God creating light through words spoken from His mouth; creative ideas emerging from the unconscious portions of individual human minds; students isolated in their classrooms, training themselves to solve problems; Nietzche, sitting alone, possessed by a force he does not understand, spewing forth a creative product; and artificial intelligence experts designing computers to perform strange loops and recursions within the confines of a small box in order to achieve creative release.

Such an image of creativity (and all that it implies) should be drastically modified. Perhaps we should not abandon it entirely but, as it presently stands, it unnecessarily narrows our understanding of human creativity. Moreover, it contains within it certain moral and political judgments with which we ought to disagree once they are made explicit. First of all, this is an image which presents creativity as a completely male activity. What, after all, do we have in this vision: people acting alone furiously generating creative products. It is not simply that this standard image of creativity almost always involves men, but rather that they are engaged in a distinctly masculine activity. The product is an object which is produced asexually and comes from within. There is no place for women or other people in this vision of the creative genius. This is an image of the male on a lonely, heroic quest. If we imagine women engaged in this activity it is only because they have become traditional male heroes. Secondly, this traditional image of creativity is hierarchical at its core. These men are exceptional and stand alone above the crowd. They are to be worshipped with a kind of awe. They have access to a truth hidden from ordinary people. This image of creative genius is both inaccurate and degrading to us all. Finally, as a corollary to this second point, the traditional image too narrowly defines creative achievements. It severely restricts our vision of human potential. Once we imagine that creativity is the province of men working alone we no longer regard group productions as creative human achievements. Wasn't the American Revolution a creative product? Isn't the city of Paris a product of human creativity? Moreover, the standard image makes us forget that those men lived in a culture with other people. Didn't they live in rooms built by others, read books by others, have friends and families, or speak a language? Didn't they eat? Who grew the food? Perhaps Bertolt Brecht (1947) stated the issue most clearly in poetic form. His subject was not creative men at their desks, but rather creative men of action. The point, however, is the same. These men of action, at least as Brecht indicates we have often imagined them, are in the same isolation as the men at their desks. Let us listen to him raise some questions about this view of the world:

Who built the seven towers of Thebes?
The books are filled with names of kings.
Was it kings who hauled the craggy blocks of stone? ...
In the evening when the chinese wall was finished
Where did the masons go? ...

Young Alexander plundered India.
He alone?
Caesar beat the Gauls. Was there not even a cook in his army?
Philip of Spain wept as his fleet
Was sunk and destroyed. Were there no other tears?
Frederick the Great triumphed in the Seven
Years War. Who
Triumphed with him? ...

Every ten years a great man,
Who paid the piper?

So may particulars.
So many questions.

I would like to replace the image of male creative geniuses sitting alone in their rooms with a new image. I would like to view the world as a place in which people and their productions are linked together by webs of association. It is a world where people exist as individuals but also one in which they are rooted in the culture and society of a partic-ular time and place. It is a world where created productions need not be objects such as inventions or theories or words spoken or written, but can also be transformations in consciousness or the destruction of oppressive conditions. I do not intend this as a utopian vision but as a way of describing real human societies. Creativity in such a world should not be conceived as simply the product of individuals but rather of individuals acting with and within groups. I would like to imagine the walls of those isolating genius-chambers crumbling. I would like to imag-ine the end of asexual creativity and the emergence of a kind of sexual creative production. In such a world, creative products are not spurted out by individuals but they are nurtured by groups into existence. They grow in social wombs.[2]

Now you may wonder about the validity of simply wishing an old image away. "Where is the proof?" you say. "You can't change the past just by imagining it a different way."

Of course, there is no "proof" for the validity of either set of images in any simple empirical sense. This is not a question like "What is the birth date of Abraham Lincoln?" What we have here in the clash of these images is a clash of world views and worlds. We can find data and arguments to support either image. I am suggesting that we choose the image with more appealing moral and political consequences. I am suggesting that we choose the image which more closely conforms to our experience of how the world really works. I am suggesting that we choose the image which seems more complete.

I believe that a refurbished image will greatly enrich our understanding of human creativity. In fact, without such a new image of creativity we have no hope of ever answering one of the fundamental questions which must precede all creativity investigation: How can we distinguish creative human activity from other kinds of human activity? Precisely how a transformed image of creativity as a social production can help us answer such a fundamental question is worth considering in some detail. First, we need some illustrative material. Let me begin by sketching the achievements of two rather different people in order to provide some raw material for analysis. Let me describe the accomplishments of P. T. Barnum and Copernicus.

P. T. Barnum, one of the great practitioners of what he and other nineteenth-century Americans liked to call "humbug," began his career as a clerk in a Connecticut store. After floundering around for a number of years in a variety of clerking and sales positions, after trying to make money by inventing numerous shady lottery schemes, Barnum finally began to make it big in 1835. It was then that he initiated his great career as a discoverer, purchaser, and advertiser of what can rather judiciously be termed "entertainments." He bought Joice Heth, a slave who was reported by her owner to be 161 years old *and* to have been George Washington's nurse. Lesser men might have been more cautious. Lesser men might have asked for greater evidences of proof of her age. Lesser men might have wondered whether it was wise to invest in someone who was partially paralyzed, totally blind and toothless—and clearly

[2] The kind of contrast in imagery which I am suggesting here is rooted in the distinction between male and female views of the world suggested by Gilligan (1982). I do not intend to argue that a female should replace a male view of the world, but only that a full account of human creativity must somehow embody truths contained in both visions.

quite near death. Barnum, however, plunked down a thousand dollars to buy Joice Heth, rented a giant saloon hall in New York, wrote a biographical pamphlet, splattered the city with thousands of handbills and poster portraits, and then announced that "she was the most aston-ishing and interesting curiosity in the world"; that she was "the first person to put clothes on George Washington"; and that she was "the most ancient curiosity Americans were ever likely to encounter." (Har-ris, 1973, p. 2). After making a small fortune in New York he took her on tour through New England. When Boston audiences failed to attend in the proper numbers, he wrote an anonymous letter to a local paper denouncing Joice Heth as a fraud: She was "a curiously constructed automaton, made up of whalebone, india rubber, and numberless springs, ingeniously put together, and made to move at the slightest touch. . . ." Such a fraud, of course, would even have been more aston-ishing than the real thing. Even staid Bostonians flocked to see her.

And all this, of course, was only the beginning. He soon signed "Sig-nor Antonio," a juggler; changed his name to what seemed a more for-eign-sounding "Signor Vivalla," and arranged for several fake contests with competitors. With the money from such "entertainments," Barnum then established his famous American museum in New York. That must have been a sight. On any given day or night an American of the mid-nineteenth century could come to see magicians, tattooed men, albino women, a model of Niagara Falls with running water, a fortune teller, a one-armed Civil War veteran who could guess your weight, giants, dwarves, wax figures of Napoleon and Christ, Ned the smart seal, a large ball of hair found in the stomach of a sow, petrified pork, Turkish shoes, as well as a portion of the throne of Louis XVIII. And to top it all off, on the uppermost floor of the museum was Barnum's famous happy family of monkeys, dogs, rats, cats, pigeons, owls, porcupines, guinea pigs, cocks, and hounds all living in absolute peace in a single enclosure (Harris, 1973, p. 41, 165).

Of course, Barnum's greatest achievement undoubtedly rests in the discovery and marketing of Tom Thumb. Barnum first met the perfectly proportioned midget Charles S. Stratton (as he was then called) when he was 5 years old, 2 feet tall and weighing only 15 pounds. Then Bar-num went to work. He changed Stratton's name to Tom Thumb, dou-bled his age (who, after all, would be interested in paying to see a small 5 year old child—they are all rather small), changed his place of birth from Connecticut to England, taught him how to sing and dance, had him engage in mock battles with giants, made him sometimes wear a specially designed Yankee Doodle suit, and had him dress up in tights in imitation of such figures as Cupid or Hercules. And Barnum flooded the nation with the usual biographies, handbills, posters, and lithographs. Finally, with enthusiasm reaching a fever pitch in America, Barnum took him on tour to Europe. This was Tom Thumb's finest hour. Due to Barnum's remarkable publicity, thousands came to the dock to send him off. Despite Tom Thumb's apparent British birth, Barnum somehow portrayed him as an American democratic representative sent to deflate the aristocratic pretensions of the old world. Once in England, Barnum took up residence in an elegant mansion where neighboring nobles called to pay their respects and meet the curiosity. Barnum and Thumb were the talk of the town. Not even the queen could resist. She called them in for a special audience. They were greeted in Paris in a similar fashion. The old-world aristocracy seemed to love Tom Thumb's remarkable ability to caricature and mock it. And the masses followed the aristocratic lead. Barnum had an uncanny sense for fitting his discovery into the old European tradition of court jester or royal dwarf (Harris, 1973, pp. 93–104).

One could go on and on with this discussion of Barnum's career. One could describe the triumphs on the tour of one of the great singers of the nineteenth-century—the "Swedish Nightingale" Jenny Lind. One could describe his famous New Jersey buffalo hunt; or his remarkable exhibition of a mermaid (probably a monkey skillfully sewn onto a fish). But the general type of Barnum's achievements are already quite well illustrated. Now let us turn to Copernicus.

Copernicus's great achievement rests in the conception of the universe described in his *De Revolutionibus*, published in 1543. In order to appreciate the significance of this conception it is necessary first to understand the generally accepted vision of the heavens and earth on the eve of Copernicus's radical break with tradition. Since the time of Aristotle, Western astronomers (and many others) had adhered to a set of ideas best described as the tradition of the "two-sphere" universe. These ideas, of course, had been greatly modified during their nearly two thousand years of domination, but they still retained the central features outlined by Aristotle. First was the assumption that the universe was finite. Second was the idea that no empty space existed within the universe. Even the apparently empty space of the heavens was filled with a colorless, tasteless, odorless substance known as "ether." Third was the belief that the heavens (the moon, stars, sun, and planets) were fundamentally different from the earth. In fact, this is the reason for designating this theory the "two-sphere" universe: heavens and earth were separate and distinct spheres. The difference manifested itself in several ways. The heavens were made of a perfect substance, the ether, not found on the earth (and the area immediately surrounding the earth). The heavenly bodies were concentrations of this ether which never changed or mixed with anything else. These bodies were embedded in unseen rings of the ether (heavenly spheres as they were called) which slowly rotated around the earth in perfect and unchanging circular motion. The earth, on the other hand, did not rotate and was at the center of this universe. But it consisted of four elements (earth, air, fire, and water) mixed together in different ways and in constant transformation. Fourth was the idea that all physical motion of the heavenly spheres could be traced to a "first mover" (or God, as the Christians conceived it) pushing the sphere of the stars furthest from the earth, which (because they were embedded in a universe with no empty space) also pushed the spheres within which the sun, moon, and planets were embedded, which in turn stirred up and mixed the four earthly elements.[3]

All this may seem rather strange to modern sensibilities. It is always hard to understand a dead world view. But in order to appreciate the Copernican achievement, it is important to recognize just how powerful this way of looking at the universe seemed to people for two thousand years. It conformed to most observations available to ordinary people (and experts of the times). Just as they do to unaided observers today, the heavens did seem to be unchanging points of light which contrasted dramatically with a constantly shifting earth. The notion of empty space did seem to be absurd to people living on the earth. In common experience, objects always did seem to move because they were in direct physical contact with other objects. Why not extend this notion to the heavenly sphere? The earth did seem to be stationary at the center of the universe. All heavenly bodies did appear to rotate around it in perfect circles. If mathematical predictions of this motion did not work perfectly, the theory of circular motion could be slightly modified to include the idea of circles rotating within circles (or epicycles, as they were called). Even if the mathematics never quite worked perfectly, it came very close.

Not only did this vision of the heavens conform to common sense and observation, but by the time of Copernicus's writing, it had been fully absorbed by two other powerful traditions: Christianity and astrology. The "two-sphere" universe fit into a view of Christianity which placed humans at the literal center of a great heavenly drama. God, existing outside the physical universe, was the first mover pushing the outer sphere of the heavens. He could look down on humans from above. Hell was below, at the very center of the earth. Humans lived with their feet near hell and their heads near the heavens in this universe structured in a literally hierarchical fashion. They could be tempted in either direction. Moreover, the central assumption of the rather different tra-

---

[3] The clearest and most complete discussion of the "two-sphere" universe can be found in Kuhn (1957).

dition of astrology was that movement in the heavens affected events on the earth. Notice how nicely this fit with the idea of a stationary earth at the center of the universe with rotating heavens pushing against the elements of the earthly sphere. Both Christianity and astrology had proved quite compatible with the idea of the "two-sphere" universe.

The Copernican achievement of 1543 rests in his suggestion that the earth was not the center of the universe. He believed that the sun was the center and that the earth rotated around it. This was his only modification of the "two-sphere" universe. His new idea of earthly motion was in tension with virtually every aspect of the older view of the universe, but his own work focused only on a mathematical description of the movement of the earth and the centrality of the sun.

With this discussion of Copernicus and Barnum behind us, let us now turn to the central matter at hand. How can the conception of creativity as rooted in culture and group help us identify genuinely creative human activity? How can we distinguish the substantial from the inconsequential? How can we distinguish the merely clever from the really creative? How do we know when something is genuinely new? In other words, is it possible to differentiate P. T. Barnum from Copernicus?

The importance of such a question cannot be overestimated. It is a question which is prior to almost all other questions one can ask about creativity. How can we discuss the nature of creative processes and products without having some way of determining exactly how they are to be valued? The traditional image of creativity, of men sitting alone spewing out creative products, is of little help in answering this kind of question. If we study Copernicus and Barnum as if they were in social isolation, we would very likely discover that they were remarkably similar. It is very likely that the physical structure of their brains did not significantly differ in a way which could account for their dissimilar achievements. On the psychological level, they both probably had "aha" reactions and engaged in what one psychologist calls "bisociation" (the mixing together of two frames of reference).[4] Moreover, we cannot differentiate between Copernicus and Barnum by suggesting that Copernicus somehow got closer to some kind of great truth. Certainly by today's standards he had it all wrong. The sun is not at the center of the universe. Perhaps some believe that the universe is finite today, but for reasons quite different from those of Copernicus. Certainly Barnum did not discover any new and great truth, but one would be hard pressed to show that Copernicus did either. Moreover, it would be virtually im-

---

[4] For a discussion of "aha" see Taylor & Getzels (1975, pp. 224–248). For a discussion of bisociation see Koestler (1964). I do not mean to suggest that these works are without merit. My point is that they cannot be used to answer the question of value.

possible to show that Copernicus started a kind of chain of inevitable reasoning which led to the present conception of the universe. The connections are too remote.

There are, of course, many different ways of making judgments of value, but I believe that, in the case of creativity, context provides a very useful starting point. Let us consider a few aspects of the webs of association which connected Barnum and Copernicus to their worlds. Barnum, I suggest, should be regarded as a rather typical American who was simply a bit more skillful at doing what most Americans of the nineteenth and twentieth centuries loved to do: He made money. He was an extremely skillful and clever entrepreneur. Born in Connecticut in 1810, he grew up in a world of commerce and sharp business practices. As Barnum described his early business career, "the slightest inattention on the part of the storekeeper, and he is fooled on weight and measure; the least heedlessness on the part of the farmer and he is swindled" (Harris, 1973, p. 11).

Barnum grew up in the world of the shrewd and became the shrewdest of them all. Moreover, Barnum was born into Jacksonian America, an age of irreverence of established traditions and customs. The people of such an age loved the hoax. Even as we do today, they loved to be fooled and then to discover how the trick was accomplished. This seems to go along with the American desire to learn about the workings of complicated machinery. Barnum's hoaxs appealed to American sensibilities in the same way that robots appeal to us today. We like to see it perform and to learn how the trick was done. We are now and have long been a society that loves the "how to" book. As Barnum's ticket seller once so ably put it, "I believe if he [Barnum] should swindle a man out of twenty dollars, the man would give a quarter to hear him tell about it" (Harris, 1973, p. 77). In other words, Barnum was an extremely clever American, doing what extremely clever Americans have been doing for two hundred years—following along in a tradition which began long before he was born and continued long after he died.[5]

Copernicus in historical perspective, however, can be seen as one of the early innovators associated with a major change in Western culture. Consider the way in which we can connect Copernicus to the transformations of his age. His movement of the earth out of the center of the universe also moved man out of the center. What would happen to the hierarchical universe of heaven above and hell below? What would happen to the hierarchies in human society—hierarchies which were rooted in, and parallelled the order of, the heavens? In many ways, Coperni-

[5] The best discussion of the context of Barnum's work can be found in Harris (1973, especially pp. 207–231).

cus's challenge was a challenge to the very order of a Catholic and aristocratic world, threatening the order similarly attacked by the various
Protestant movements and peasant rebellions of his time. He did not
burn down the old churches and castles but he was certainly a part of
the movement which tempted others to do so. In some ways, he exhibited (at least covertly if not overtly) the same irreverence to authority as
Barnum and yet he preceded him by a considerable span of years.

The point of this rather too-brief discussion of context is simply to
argue that it can provide a basis for differentiating between Barnum
and Copernicus. Although Copernicus certainly had antecedents, he was
one of the early innovators of a tradition which established a new world
order.[6] He was a part of something genuinely new in the largest social
and cultural context. Barnum, on the other hand, was a part of an established world which he did not fundamentally challenge. Perhaps we
should award him the designation of a different order of creativity; he
was clever in the sense that American entrepreneurs are clever. This
seems different from the creativity of Copernicus.

Even if critics disagree with such an analysis and judgment, even if I
have misrepresented Copernicus or Barnum, even if I did not understand their context properly, my point still stands: The place to begin
judgments of value about creativity is through a consideration of context.[7]

This discussion brings me to a second major insight derived from the
rooting of creativity in culture: There are no such things as creative
people, processes or products.[8] At least there are no such things independent of social and cultural context. The same person, process, or
product may or may not be regarded as creative depending on the circumstances of the surrounding world. This is so obvious that it amazes
me that it is often forgotten in creativity investigation. Suppose Copernicus suddenly appeared in one of my classes. Suppose he wrote *De
Revolutionibus* as a final paper. I might at some level be impressed. But
I would probably fail him. I might regard him as an *idiot savant* but
certainly not as a creative genius. Perhaps a modern Barnum could sign

[6] Antecedents to Copernicus might be found in changes in the medieval analysis of
falling stones, a Renaissance revival of the ancient mystical notion of the sun as God, or
the Atlantic voyages which opened the terrestrial horizons of man. See Kuhn, 1957, pp.
100–133.

[7] Please note that I am well aware that this analysis raises another question. What
exactly is the appropriate context for making these judgments? My feeling is that there is
no set or simple answer to such a question. Our ways of organizing the world into contexts
constantly shift with changes in our experience and thought. Hence, we should expect
that our visions of what is creative will shift as well.

[8] For a denial of the notion of creative process from a different perspective, see Dutton
& Krausz (1981, pp. 47–73)

such a person up and put him on display. Similarly, suppose that Barnum had brought Tom Thumb to Europe one hundred, or even fifty, years earlier. Suppose Tom Thumb had thumbed his nose at the British aristocracy in 1776. In fact, many Tom Thumbs and Barnums did exactly that and the British did not pay them for it, or rather they paid them in a different way. Such earlier Thumbs and Barnums might legitimately be regarded as creative. Clearly, the search for creative people, processes, and products outside of culture seems to miss the whole point of creativity investigation.

A third insight to be derived from this brief discussion of Barnum and Copernicus involves the need to praise the group along with the individual. This is true at several different levels. Although Copernicus certainly was skillful as an astronomer, his skills considered alone should not inspire awe. He was no more technically proficient than many other scientists of his time. Moreover, given the then-current state of discourse about the heavens, his ideas were a good deal more absurd. A critical contemporary might well have wondered—"If the earth moves why don't we feel it?"—"If we are not at the center of the universe then where is heaven and hell?" Copernicus could not answer these questions. He was, quite legitimately, regarded as an oddball in his time. Every age has many such oddballs. It was only others—Galileo, Kepler, and Newton— who years later built onto Copernicus's original idea and created the Copernican revolution. Copernicus himself had little inkling of what he had wrought. But Copernicus's dependence on a larger social world (and, incidentally, the dependence of Galileo, Kepler, and Newton) was even deeper. The reconceptualization of the place of humans in the universe could not possibly have been constructed by a bunch of scientists working in isolation. They were as much consequence as cause of such a large change. We must look elsewhere for the other agents involved in the process: to European explorers of the new world, to a newly emerging bourgeois culture, to the Protestant Reformation, and to new patterns of trade. It was all this, and probably a great deal more which helped make Copernicus creative in ways he could not possibly have understood. We need not stand in awe of him. The Copernican revolution was only marginally connected to Copernicus as a person. Perhaps we should find a new name for it.

There are lessons in this analysis which might prove very useful in our attempt to understand the relationship between creativity and the modern American University. First of all, it would seem a remarkably fruitless endeavor for a university to try to develop a vision of a timeless creative process which could be taught to its students. As I have already argued, such a process does not exist. We could teach our students to be clever—in the sense that P.T. Barnum was clever. That, after all, is what schools of management, law schools, and even large parts of liberal arts and sciences colleges are really up to. We could teach our students to solve certain problems, to put together unusual frames of reference, or to write new words on blank pages, but we could not teach them to be creative in the sense that Copernicus was creative. Moreover, it is well to keep in mind that because we are embedded in the passing moment of history it is virtually impossible to distinguish with any certainty a contemporary Barnum from a contemporary Copernicus. Even Freud thought that his friend Fliess, the man who believed that all neurosis was rooted in the nose, was a great creative genius. We would need to look far into the future in order to begin to get it all in perspective. Let us have a little humility.

In fact, there is much about the modern American university which makes it a natural enemy of creativity. If creativity involves the production of something genuinely new, then it always threatens the existing order. Just as the learning establishment of the sixteenth century found Copernicus to be a threat, we should expect the same reaction from contemporary universities when they are confronted with a modern Copernicus. It happens all the time. We can all think of examples from our various academic fields.

If a university cannot teach a creative process, then what exactly can it do to promote creativity? First of all, it can continue to develop the clever. We all love P. T. Barnum and none of us would mind very much if our students were sometimes like him. And every once in a while a Barnum might become a Copernicus. Secondly, we need to make ourselves vitally aware of context—vitally aware of our connection to society, to culture, and to history. This is the way to begin to give ourselves the ability to distinguish the clever from the creative. We all need to be made aware of a wide variety of contexts, because contexts are the way we determine value. Even if we will never be able to distinguish the creative from the clever with a high degree of certainty, the attempt to do so does cast some light on the subject. A student in a science course needs to see his or her work in the context of other scientists working in the same field. But such students also need to be made aware of the connections of their work to other sciences, and to the scientific tradition at large. At an even higher level our students should understand that what they do in their science classes is intimately connected to what they do in their history, literature, or philosophy classes. (This is one of the functions of the course in integrated studies at Suffolk University). They need to see those connections. At a higher level still we need to understand the larger world in which we are embedded. How does our social structure, our economic relations, our habits of dress, our sexual tastes—and a hundred other factors—relate to our intellectual and material productions. Only when we begin to understand all this can we begin to distinguish that which is genuinely new. Only when we remove ourselves from our isolated desks, only when we begin to see ourselves in the womb of our history, society, and culture can we hope to understand creativity.

Finally, even while trying to teach ourselves and our students about context, we should remain aware that we are unlikely to get it right. The future contains contexts which will remain hidden from us until we experience them. Hence, our humility should encourage us to tolerate wide and wild diversity in the university. The contemporary creative person, at the beginning of a world which is genuinely new, will always appear to be an oddball. Most often, these strange minds in our world deserve to be forgotten. But we must never forget that sometimes— rarely, but sometimes, nonetheless—they become part of a new world. We need to remember not to burn, exile, or hospitalize them.

REFERENCES

Brecht, B. (1947). *Selected poems* (H.R. Hays, Trans.). New York: Harcourt, Brace, Jovanovich.

Dutton, D. & Krausz, M. (Eds.). (1981). *The Concept of creativity in science and art.* The Hague: Martinus Nijhoff Publishers.

Ghiselin, B. (Ed.). (1952). *The creative process: A symposium.* Berkeley: University of California Press.

Gilligan, C. (1982). *In a different voice: Psychological theory and women's development.* Cambridge, MA: Harvard University Press.

Harris, N. (1973). *Hambug: The art of P.T. Barnum.* Chicago: University of Chicago Press.

Hofstadter, D.R. (1979). *Gödel, Escher, Bach: An Eternal Golden Braid.* New York: Basic Books.

The Holy bible: Old and new testaments in the King James version. (1970). Nashville: Thomas Nelson, Inc.

Koestler, A. (1964). *The act of creation.* New York: Macmillan.

Kuhn, T.S. (1957). *The Copernican revolution: Planetary astronomy in the development of western thought.* Cambridge, MA: Harvard University Press.

Plato. (1961). *The collected dialogues* (L. Cooper, Trans.). New York: Pantheon Books.

Ross, W.D. (Trans.). (1983). *The Oxford translation of Aristotle,* (Vol. 8). Oxford: Oxford University Press.

Taylor, I.A. & Getzels, J.W. (Eds.). (1975). *Perspectives in creativity.* Chicago: Aldine Publishing Co.

SYMPOSIUM

PANEL 1

Comments

David L. Robbins

I begin, as I believe this symposium does, from the belief that creative thinking—the kind of innovative evaluation that can produce change for the better—is the most practical and marketable skill produced in students by an extended exposure to the disciplines of the liberal arts and sciences, and that this immensely important skill is taught better in a college which specializes in liberal learning than in any other component of the American university structure.

Having stated that premise, let me fall back momentarily on the guidance of Francis Bacon, Copernicus's fellow "natural philosopher." The simplest, most rudimentary kinds of generalizations, Bacon observed, differ too little from bare empirical experience to be very useful, whereas the most complex and abstract generalizations are too far removed from empirical experience to be very useful; it is, rather, middle-level, intermediate generalizations—those that connect the empirical with the abstract—that have the "solidity" and practical applicability to affect the affairs and fortunes of humanity (Bacon, 1960, p. 98).

Those whose intellects concentrate on formulating low-level generalizations, Bacon (1960, p. 93) characterizes as "ants," who "only collect and use"; the formulators of abstract, high-level generalizations, he terms "spiders," who "make cobwebs out of their own substance." But those who concentrate on discovering middle-level generalizations, Bacon labels "bees," whose "middle course" of mediation between the highly abstract and the highly concrete represents "the true business of philosophy," the most significant concern of intellectual endeavor.

Following Bacon, let me try for a few moments to play the "bee" among the "ants" and "spiders"—and thus attempt to synthesize from the material presented in Dr. Webb's and Dr. Greenberg's papers several middle-level generalizations with practical application to two principal middle-level questions regarding the teaching of "creativity" in a college of liberal arts and sciences: 1) What practical, marketable creative habits of thought (if any) can be developed by studying the liberal arts and sciences? and 2) What are we doing or can we additionally do to inculcate these creative habits of thought in our students?

Let me start by addressing the practical implications of Dr. Greenberg's attempt (this volume) to distinguish between "creativity" and "cleverness." "Creativity," he says, is "substantial"; "cleverness," "inconsequential." Any attempt to "develop a vision of a timeless creative process" would, according to Greenberg, of necessity be "fruitless." Yet he also acknowledges that teaching students to be "clever"is what the college of liberal arts and sciences is "really up to," and that "every once in a while a Barnum [a "merely clever" individual] might become a Copernicus [a "truly creative" person]." Thus, teaching "clever" habits of thought to our students may not be as "fruitless" an endeavor as Dr. Greenberg led us initially to believe.

But what are "clever" (and potentially "creative") habits of thought? Dr. Greenberg and Dr. Webb (this volume) both invoke Arthur Koestler's suggestion that "bisociation"—the mixing or juxtaposition (by placing them together in the unconscious, where the interaction process is allowed to proceed with less constraints than at the conscious level) of unusual ideas or frames of reference that don't normally occur together—leads to the manipulation of patterns or materials into new arrangements or relationships (the definition that both Webb and Greenberg seem to agree upon for "creative thinking"—Dr. Webb's protestations about the difficulty of coming to such a common understanding notwithstanding). Koestler, Webb, Greenberg, and I, at least, seem to be, therefore, in agreement that (1) such an entity as "creativity" does exist, with synthesis as the essence of "creative" thinking, and that (2) exposure of students to a broad cross-section of materials and approaches from various disciplines, with gentle encouragement (such as is provided in the freshman integrated studies course) to interrelate them, can (and does) help to develop in those students a flexibility and agility of mind which transcends the boundaries of individual disciplines, an awareness and a sensitivity which, tolerant of different analytic frameworks and languages, can readily modulate between different perspectives, knowing that each may embody a portion of the truth and that parallax between different viewpoints may provide a truth all its own—that is, "clever" habits of thought that, in certain circumstances, can become "creative." In short, we agree that, although we cannot aim to produce a Copernicus, if we inculcate (as we should) in our graduates—most of whom are "average" people who will nevertheless be rendered more "marketable" as a result—the "clever," flexible habits of thought that Dr. Greenberg associates with a Barnum, we will, rarely but predictably, produce the "creative" skills of a Copernicus.

One critical question grows out of this conclusion: How can we prevent most of those whom we train in "clever," flexible habits of thought from employing the practical skills that liberal education has taught them in the kind of shameless exploitation, imposture, and self-promotion that were characteristic of P. T. Barnum, and are characteristic of Dr. Greenberg's "Barnum" stereotype. In addressing this issue, let me begin by stating clearly my disagreement both with Dr. Greenberg's belief that "creativity" can most usefully be viewed as a social product and with his view that the only way to "liberate" us from the old stereotype of the "creator" is to dissolve the notion of the individual creator in the notion of society as creative agent. Creativity is an individual product with social implications, not a social product. To view creativity, or the creator, any other way is epistemologically inadequate; the sociology of knowledge can neither account for "revealed" (intuited) creative insights—which "revelations" can and frequently have come to people very different from Dr. Greenberg's excessively narrow "creator" (or "Copernicus") stereotype—nor provide any reliable basis for assessing the truth value of, and resolving the conflicting claims of, different kinds of "creative insights," whether they are regarded as social products or as a species of revelation/conclusion deriving from a realm of ideas (Christian, Kantian, or Platonic) outside/beyond/above materialistic society. Greenberg's paradigm of creation/creativity as a social product may offer, as he indicates, certain analytic advantages; but, as with all things, his paradigm has the defects of its virtues—and those defects, along with the resulting disadvantages to the paradigm's use, are too significant to permit its substitution for the "individual creator" paradigm.

In addition, to assign the function of creativity to the society and not to the individual is to abolish the individual moral/ethical responsibility of the "creator" for her/his creation on which must depend any effort to maximize the number of "clever" potential Barnums (and hence of potential "creative" Copernicuses) while minimizing the number of these potential Barnums who actually turn their "cleverness" to exploitation, humbug, and deceit. If we accept Dr. Webb's judgment, creativity flourishes only in a "relaxed and permissive" atmosphere in which there is no negative evaluation extrinsic to (outside of) the creator of the ideas produced by the creative process. If the "creative" atmosphere is not to be poisoned by extrinsic evaluation, but if responsible limits are to be produced concerning which "clever" ideas (all of which ideas might have been acceptable to Barnum, or would be to a "Barnum") will be acceptable, and which unacceptable, to their "creator," then such limitation will have to be intrinsic, to come from within the "clever" potential Barnum/Copernicus—from her/his conscience or sense of ethical responsibility. Just as the tragic should be infused with a sense of "high seriousness" that sets it apart from the "merely unfortunate," so creativity—or at least the creator—needs to be characterized by "high seriousness" to be set apart from the "merely clever." It has long been a central mission of liberal education to expose the student to subjects and situations that not only encourage flexibility ("cleverness") of mind but that also raise questions which encourage the development of a personal hierarchy of ethical values, a strong sense of responsibility to fellow human beings based on that hierarchy, and a "high seriousness" about the adventure of living. Thus, if the highly marketable "creative" skills are to be effectively taught by the study of the liberal arts and sciences, practical limitations on the application of these skills can originate only in the individual ethical aspect of liberal learning. In understanding and encouraging these complementary (and central) endeavors of liberal education, the "individual responsibility" paradigm, rather than the "social responsibility" paradigm, is indispensable.

It is difficult to frame middle-level operational generalizations about the immensely important practical question of how to encourage (and yet keep responsible) creative habits of thought; but it is absolutely necessary to try. For, as George Santayana has observed:

> When there is real profundity,—when the living core of things is most firmly grasped,—there will accordingly be a felt inadequacy of expression, and an appeal to the observer to piece out our imperfections with his thoughts. But this should come only after the resources of a patient and well-learned art have been exhausted; else what is felt as depth is really confusion and incompetence. The simplest thing becomes unutterable, if we have forgotten how to speak. And a habitual indulgence in the inarticulate is a sure sign of the philosopher who has not learned to think, the poet who has not learned to write, the painter who has not learned to paint. (Santayana, 1896/1955, p. 82)

and, I would add, the teacher who has not learned to teach.

REFERENCES

Bacon, F. (1960). F.H. Anderson (Ed.), *The new organon and related writings* (Book I, Aphorisms CIV & XCV). Indianapolis, IN: Bobbs-Merrill.

Santayana, G. (1955). *The sense of beauty.* New York: Dover. (Original work published 1896)

METHODS OF TEACHING CREATIVITY

Topoi and Figures of Speech: The Place of Creativity in Rhetorical Studies

Gloria M. Boone

In Greco-Roman education, "teaching was generally focused on invention, that part of rhetoric which deals with the discovery of arguments appropriate to the theme under discussion" (Clark, 1966, p. 211). Invention has been the dominant concern of rhetoricians over the centuries. The concept of invention has evolved from the classical rational art of discovering arguments to a modern process of creating reality. Invention is the creative process of forming ideas and meanings for communication. In 1972, Karl R. Wallace observed that "inventing is at the heart of all communication behavior" (p. 395).

Invention is the creative process at the heart of a liberal education. First, invention of ideas or of meanings involves the discovery of existing options and the creation of new choices. A speaker chooses the meanings of the messages, chooses a strategy of persuasion, and chooses how to adapt to the audience. This act of creative choice is the essence of a liberal education: "The liberal arts have the primary responsibility for preparing human beings to make the informed choices which arise from technology and art" (Dance, 1980, p. 329). Second, invention is a process that forms the relationships among speaker, message, audience, and situation. For example, the speaker initially forms the relationship with the audience by choosing the tone of his message. The speaker may address the audience as peers, superiors, or subordinates. Understanding these relationships in the communication process is "in a very real sense to understand the essence of our humanity" (Smith, 1960, p. 344). Third, the creation of a piece of rhetoric allows the speaker to draw upon his prior liberal education and past experiences. A speaker needs a well-rounded education to find the materials for arguments and to appreciate the creative possibilities of a given rhetorical situation. A story will illustrate the point:

> After Daniel Webster gave his famous "Reply to Hayne," a friend asked him how long he stayed up preparing his speech. When Webster informed him that he went to bed at the usual time, his friend expressed amazement that Webster had spent no time in the preparation of his famous reply. Webster immediately corrected him by saying, "I spent all my life in preparation for that speech!" (Walter, 1954, p. 161)

A speaker needs a broad, humanistic education "both for the direct knowledge that these studies give him and for their value as stimulators of imagination and thought" (p. 161). As Otis M. Walter has noted, "No one who would be a creative speaker dare neglect the insights to be obtained from the reading of literature, the study of history, and an understanding of man's biological relationships" (p. 161). Overall, rhetorical invention is an important part of a liberal education because it reveals the choices open to the speaker and the relationships among speaker, appeals, audience, and situation; and it uses and expands the speaker's creative skills.

Rhetorical invention, like the liberal arts, is evolving and changing. Liberal arts are changing to adapt to the different needs and perceptions of society. Invention is changing both theoretically and pedagogically. Let's explore the placement of creativity or invention in rhetorical studies by examining the changing concepts of topoi and metaphor. First, the terms topoi and metaphor will be defined. Second, the interaction of topoi and metaphor in the development of rhetoric will be analyzed. Third, a modern system of metaphorical topoi will be proposed to enhance rhetorical invention in theory and practice.

Definitions of Topoi and Metaphor
Creativity in rhetorical studies has traditionally been divided into two separate aspects: invention and stylistics. Invention was viewed as the creation of arguments and was often associated with logic, dialectic, or philosophy. The main focus of invention was logical discovery. These logical discoveries were based on topoi which were seen as places of arguments. Topoi consisted of terms such as: more or less, past fact,

future fact, possible or impossible, and so on. From these common-places, a speaker could generate ideas for a speech. For example, if the speaker's topic was taxation, he could talk about whether more or less taxation was needed, past examples of tax changes, the future conse-quences of taxes, and possible reforms to the tax system. The other separate aspect of creativity in rhetoric was stylistics. Stylistics focused on figurative language that changes other standard meanings of a term to another meaning. Figurative language uses the substitution of words, the juxaposition of words, or the transference of implied meaning. Fig-urative language was most often associated with the art of poetry. Sty-listics usually featured the metaphor.

> The various forms of "transference" are called figures of speech . . . that is, "turning" of language away from literal meanings toward figurative meanings. Metaphor is generally considered to manifest the basic pattern of transference involved and so can be thought of as the fundamental figure of speech. The other figures tend to be versions of metaphor's prototype. (Hawkes, 1972, p. 2)

Metaphor can be as simple as "time is money" or as complex as:

> All of them hope that the storm will pass before their turn comes to be devoured. But I fear—I fear strongly—that storm will not pass. It will rage and it will roar, even more loudly, even more wildly. (Churchill, 1940, p. 141)

Michael Leff (1983) summarizes the traditional division of invention from style in rhetorical studies: "In short, whether we are dealing with the rhetorical divisions of antiquity or the divided rhetorics of contem-porary theory, we still regularly encounter a wall of separation between topic and trope" (p. 215).

Evolution of Topoi and Metaphor as Creative Elements in Rhetoric
This separation between topoi and metaphor begins with Aristotle (1960) and is solidified in the writings of the later Roman rhetoricians.

Aristotle's definition of rhetoric reveals the emphasis that he places on the importance of invention. "So let Rhetoric be defined as the fac-ulty of discovering in the particular case what are the available means of persuasion" (p. 7). Aristotle emphasizes the discovery or creation of arguments and thus places invention at the forefront of rhetoric. Aristo-tle sees rhetorical invention as a *rational art:* "Rhetoric is the counterpart of Dialectic . . . for this act consists of proofs [persuasions] alone—all else is but accessory" (p. 1). Aristotle notes that rhetorical proofs are accomplished by the enthymeme, which he describes as a "rhetorical syllogism," "a kind of demonstration" with seldom as many links as in "a normal chain of deduction. Thus if one of the premises is a matter of common knowledge, the speaker need not mention it, since the hearer will himself supply the link" (pp. 5, 10, 12).[1]

In order to create the enthymeme, Aristotle suggests that the speaker use topoi.

> Let me say, then, that the proper subjects of dialectical and rhetorical syllogisms are those with which the so-called Topoi [commonplaces, lines of argument] are concerned; and by these I mean arguments that are applicable in common to the study of justice and physics, to the study of politics—to a large number of inquiries of diverse sorts. (p. 15)

Aristotle divides the topoi into two categories: the universal and the particular or special topoi. Four universals—possible and impossible, past fact, future fact, and more or less—can be used to invent ideas when speaking on any subject (p. 16).[2] A list of particular topics would include drawing arguments from:

1.   the opposites,
2.   inflections of words,
3.   correlative terms,
4.   degree,
5.   time,
6.   definition,
7.   ambiguous terms,
8.   division,
9.   induction,
10. existing,
11. decision,
12. the parts to the whole,
13. simple consequences,
14. contrasts,
15. inward thoughts,
16. proportional results,
17. identical antecedents,
18. altered choices,
19. attributed motives,
20. incentives and deterrents,

[1] For a discussion of the enthymeme, see Conley (1984) and Bitzer (1959).

[2] In the *Topics,* Aristotle (1941) also distinguishes between universal and specific topics. See Sections 9.9, 1.10, 14, and 3.5.

21.   incredible occurrences,
22.   conflicting of act,
23.   meeting slander,
24.   cause to effect,
25.   course of action,
26.   actions compared,
27.   previous mistake, and
28.   the meaning of names (pp. 159–171).

The topoi or places of arguments are analytic guides where arguments can be found. Leff (1983) has noted the logical nature of the topoi as "a source for discovering a middle element in argument . . . the universal topic . . . suggest principles of inference capable of generating warrants" (p. 220).

Aristotle's use of the term topoi seems to shift occasionally from meaning the discovery of a logical inference to meaning common arguments to be used for a particular type of discourse. For example, Aristotle (1960) suggests that in deliberative speeches, the themes tend to be (1) ways and means, (2) war and peace, (3) national defense, (4) imports and exports, and (5) legislation (p. 21). Thomas M. Conley (1984), in an excellent article, observes:

> Enthymemes, therefore, are informed inferences. In Bitzer's familiar scenario, the rhetor argues A, so C, with the audience filling in the missing B to understand how the connection between A and C could be asserted. In inventing a rhetorical argument, a speaker will try to choose as the suppressed premise . . . viz., a commonplace notion possessed by everybody; for only in that way could the audience make the inferential leap demanded of it. (p. 170)

For example, a speaker may leave out of a speech a definition that an audience will supply on its own.

Aristotle spends a great deal of time on the *rational discovery of arguments* but he does not fully consider the metaphorical nature of creativity. In *The Rhetoric*, Aristotle strictly divides topoi/invention from metaphor/style. In Chapter III on Style, Aristotle (1960) states: "It is the metaphor above all else that gives clearness, charm, and distinction to the style" (p. 187). Metaphors should be "appropriate" and "derived from something beautiful" (pp. 187, 189). Metaphors should not be overused or artificial. Aristotle uses metaphors to separate poetry and rhetoric. Poetry uses more metaphors than does rhetoric. It is in the Poetics that Aristotle defines and classifies the metaphor: "Metaphor consists in giving the thing a name that belongs to something else; the transference being either from genus to species, or from species to genus, or from species to species, or on grounds of analogy" (McKeon, 1971, p. 1476). For Aristotle (1960), the metaphor is creative only in a stylistic sense. Metaphors can add an "air of novelty" or "liveliness" and are "in the highest degree instructive and pleasing" because they "set an event before their (the audience's) eyes" (pp. 108, 207, 210). This separation of topoi and metaphor reveals:

> ... two fundamental ideas about language and its relationship to the "real" world; first, that language and reality, words and the objective world to which they refer, are quite separate entities; and second, that the *manner* in which something is said does not significantly condition or alter *what* is said. (Hawkes, 1972, p. 9)

Cicero extends Aristotle's ideas on topoi and metaphor. The Roman rhetoricians divided rhetoric into five classical canons: invention, disposition (organization), elocution (style), memory, and pronunciation (delivery). Cicero defined commonplaces as "seats (sedes) or sources of argument ... he used places as fundamental devices in invention and in memory" (McKeon, 1973, pp. 199–200). When discussing memory, Cicero (Watson, 1970) states: "Certain places must be fixed upon, and that of the things which they desire to keep in memory, symbols must be conceived in the mind, and ranged, as it were, in those places" (p. 187). In Cicero's system, memory and invention become intertwined. A speaker draws upon his memory of topics to create arguments for a particular situation. In the *Topics,* Cicero (1976) reforms the topoi of Aristotle.

> Inherent in the nature of the subject are arguments derived from the whole, from its parts, from its meanings, and from the things which are in some way closely connected with the subject which is being investigated. . . . Arguments are also drawn from circumstances closely connected with the subject which is under inquiry. But this class has many subdivisions, for we call some arguments "conjugate," others we derive from genus, species, similarity, difference, contraries, adjuncts, antecedents, consequences, contradictions, cause, effect, and comparison with events of greater, less or equal importance. (pp. 387, 391)

A speaker would go through this checklist of commonplaces so that no arguments remain to be explored (p. 387).

Cicero (1976) adds a dynamic nature to invention when he develops the concept of stasis, or "where the defense takes its stand."

> There are four ways of dealing with conjecture or inference: the question is asked, first whether anything exists or is true; second, what its origin is;

third, what cause produced it; fourth, what changes can be made in anything. (pp. 445, 455)

This place is where the clash of opposing arguments should occur. Another feature added by Cicero was the educational uses of topoi. Students were taught how to discover arguments based on topoi and how
to select the best arguments to adapt to a given situation. Although
Cicero adds to the concept of topoi, he just extends Aristotle's notion
of metaphor as an ornament of language.

Quintilian adds to the classical understanding of invention and metaphor without completely departing from the path established by Cicero. Quintilian emphasized the idea that topics should be *created* by the
speaker. He urged students not to be satisfied with the textbook list of
topics but to try to discover new topics. In Book V of *The Institutio
Oratoria*, Quintilian

> ... emphasized the asking of questions concerning the subject at hand ...
> persons and things. To draw their arguments from persons, the students
> were urged to study such things as birth, nationality, sex, age, and country.
> The topoi concerning "things" focused around questions about why or
> where or when or how or by what means the action is performed. . . . The
> student, for example, inquires. . . . "What could have caused this particular
> effect?" (Dick, 1964, p. 317)

He also separated the concept of topics from that of commonplaces.
During this time period, commonplaces were phrases or sayings that
speakers memorized for "immediate use, with a view to employing them
when occasion arose as a species or ornament to be inserted into their
extempore speeches" (Dick, 1964, p. 317, quoting Quintilian II, iv, p.
27). He discouraged the use of these commonplaces because they were
often superfluous. Quintilian (1888) does see these memorized commonplaces as figures of speech, but he does *not* see them as creative. As
for the metaphor, he divides figurative language into two parts, tropes
and figures. A metaphor was a trope or the "artistic alteration of a word
or phrase from its proper meaning to another. . . . [T]he changes involved
concern not merely individual words, but also our thoughts and the
structure of our sentences" (Book VIII, v-35, vi-39). Tropes also included
synecdoche, allegory, and hyperbole. A figure was a form of speech
differing from the common mode of expression and included forms
such as interrogation, personification, and irony. Quintilian gives greater
importance to tropes and figures than does Aristotle or Cicero, but he
does not realize their creative potential for unifying topic and trope.

One of the last significant works during the classical period is *The*

Rhetorica ad Herennium. It suggests that the metaphor be used for: vividness, brevity, magnifying, minifying, and embellishing (Caplan, 1954, Book IV). The enthymeme is often viewed as "unashamedly stylistic" (Conley, 1984, p. 179). However, the creative connection between invention and metaphor is not completed in this work.

The Rhetorica ad Herennium, which subdivided 45 Figures of Diction, was a very influential work during the Middle Ages because it was falsely attributed to Cicero. Aristotle's and most of Cicero's works were unknown during the Middle Ages. In the Middle Ages, the five canons of rhetoric were divided up into three disciplines of the trivium in the liberal arts: "logic (or dialectic): the art of reasoning, defining, investigating, and discovering truth; grammar: the art of syntax, meter, figures of speech, and the study of poetry; and rhetoric: the art of expression, style and organization" (Golden & Corbett, 1968, p. 98). Creativity in speeches declined due to the lack of political freedom, the disintegration of civil governments and the all-pervasive influence of the Church. For rhetoric, the topics were used to remember past knowledge or religious revelation, but not to discover new ideas.

> In a phrase, *invention becomes revelation.* Christianity posited not a socially constructed but a divinely created world. Medieval and Renaissance scholars thus began to treat conceptualization primarily as a matter of assessing previously learned material in a formulary manner. Meanings were not viewed as created in the categorization process but as learned ... The topical system of analysis began to be thought of as an information storage, rather than as an information generating, system. (Harper, 1979, p. 111)

In one aspect, the Middle Ages added to the concept of metaphor. The primary focus of rhetoric on preaching led to the development of methods to interpret the bible. Because many statements in the bible are metaphorical, the rhetorician learned to discover the different levels of meaning. Near the end of the Middle Ages, Dante summarized the four levels of biblical meaning.

> These are, first, a *literal* meaning (the 'story' ...) and then three higher levels of meaning, the *allegorical* (the symbolic meanings appropriate to this world), the *anagogical* (those appropriate to the spiritual world), and the *tropological* (those appropriate to a personal or moral level). (Hawkes, 1972, p. 17)

The rhetorician was concerned not with the creation or discovery of personal ideas, but with the interpretation of God's revelations or signs.

Proof was extrinsic, based on prior authority, and not intrinsic, based on personal experience or observation. The nature of creativity could not be fully developed in the Middle Ages due to the categorization of the inventional process.

The Renaissance brought some changes in the concept of invention and metaphor. Peter Ramus in the sixteenth century divided rhetoric and dialectic into distinct divisions. For Ramus, rhetoric was the art of speaking well and dealt with style (tropes and figures) and delivery (voice and gesture). Dialectic was the art of disputing well and included invention, organization and memory. Metaphors or other tropes would be ornaments added *after* the logical arguments had been created. Furthermore, metaphors used to embellish discourse should not detract from the logical relationships developed in the arguments. This Ramist concept influenced both rhetoricians and poets in the seventeenth century when they composed

> ... metaphor from "public" elements with "established" ranges of relationships. In general, [their] metaphors are self-consciously "artificial" rather than sensuously vivid, designed to please on grounds of formal excellence rather than by means of any "likeness to the staff of life." (Hawkes, 1972, p. 19)

The division of Ramus had extended influence:

> This trend was given additional impetus by Francis Bacon's subordination of rhetoric to inductive logic, by the Cartesian and Port Royalist subordination of rhetoric to formal deductive logic, and by the Elocutionist's reduction of rhetoric to the techniques of oral delivery. (Kneupper & Anderson, 1980, p. 318)

Thus, creativity in the Ramist tradition consisted of the formal topics from dialectic. Rhetoric lacked the creativity of ideas and consisted only of orderly metaphors and delivery.

Another development during the Renaissance followed somewhat different lines. The English stylistic rhetorician concentrated on figures of speech. Henry Peacham expanded the concept of metaphor by analyzing its psychological effects. More importantly, Peacham "... developed an elaborate system of the 'places' of metaphor which, in historical retrospect, tends to cloud the traditional distinction between invention and style" (Osborn, 1967, p. 125). He lists 16 places used for "teaching where apt translations may be found," such as "from living creatures without reason, to man, partaker of reason ... from man to the brute creatures ... from the four elements" (Osborn, 1967, pp. 125–126). Unfortunately, because of the lack of consideration of invention itself, Peacham could not follow through with the development of creativity in discourse. Furthermore, due to the influence of the Ramist system, Peacham's contribution was not extended by other theorists or educators during this time period.

A dispute arose in the seventeenth century among a variety of epistemologists who challenged the use of topoi in creativity. Francis Bacon challenged the classical dependence on syllogisms and deduction. He instead proposed an experimental method based on induction. He dismissed the role of the topics in the discovery of new ideas. For him, the commonplaces were an element of remembrance. He even suggested the use of commonplace notebooks to enhance the memory. Bacon's early notions of faculty psychology—understanding, reason, imagination, memory, appetite—allowed him to say, "[T]he duty of office of Rhetoric is to apply Reason to Imagination for the better moving of the will" (Dick, 1955, p. 309). The later epistemologists—Decartes, Locke, and Hume—attack rhetoric and the system of topics. For example, Locke (1970) attacks the existing nature of rhetoric when he states:

> If we would speak of things as they are, we must allow that all the art of rhetoric, besides order and clearness; all the artificial and figurative application of words eloquence hath invented, are for nothing else but to insinuate wrong ideas, move the passions, and thereby mislead the judgments. (III, x, p. 34)

The downgrading of rhetoric was based in part on the attack of the syllogism. Syllogisms were faulted because they could be based on vague and insufficient facts; they do not produce new knowledge; and they do not lead to the truth. David L. Vancil (1979) summarized the disputes of the seventeenth century epistomologists to a system of topoi:

1. The process of proving is essentially the same as coming to know ... the new logic subordinated the process of advocacy and justification ... and held that (scientific) inquiry is the primary concern of logic.
2. ... All of our mental operations are performed naturally.... Thus it was categorically denied that topical systems performed the functions of finding materials of argument, or recollecting materials.
3. (Since) the syllogism itself is portrayed as, at best, unnecessary, than *a fortiori* any system which merely aids one in finding the materials for syllogisms is also unnecessary.
4. ... That topical systems are unsound epistemologically because they are based upon rational procedures rather than cognitive processes. (pp. 32–35)

It was up to the "Father of Modern Social Science," the Italian rhetorician Giambattisba Vico, to first respond to the attacks on rhetoric and the topical system in the early eighteenth century. In his work, *On the Study Methods of Our Time*, Vico (1965) disputes the first argument.

> In our day . . . philosophical criticism alone is honored. The art of 'topics' from being given first place in the curriculum, is utterly disregarded. . . . This is harmful, since the invention of arguments is by nature prior to the judgment of their validity, so that, in teaching, that invention should be given priority. (pp. 14–15)

For the second argument, Vico believed that students need to be trained by the topics so they can be more perceptive. Experiments conducted recently by Nelson, Infante and others (see Nelson, 1970, pp. 121–126; Infante, 1971, pp. 125–128) support Vico's idea that topoi are effective in helping people remember and generate more ideas than they would without topoi. Vico's answer to the third and fourth arguments is summarized as follows:

Rhetoric, contrary to what Descartes believes, is rooted in a probability-based reality.

1. By using topical philosophy, it has the power to create knowledge.
2. Rhetorical invention precedes demonstration; and rhetorical discovery precedes truth.
3. Rhetoric creates data and hypotheses.
4. Only through rhetoric can we communicate our ideas and impressions to others (Golden, 1968, p. 14).

Vico believed that "minds are formed by the character of language, not language by the minds of those who speak it" (Hawkes, 1972, p. 38). His works, which discussed the metaphors and myths of different cultures, seemed to indicate that:

> Metaphor, in short, is not fanciful "embroidery" of the facts. It is a way of experiencing the facts. It is a way of thinking and of living; an imaginative projection of the truth. As such, it is at the heart of the "mode." (p. 39)

Vico defends the creative nature of rhetoric by expanding the notion of topical invention from argument creation to a form of perception of the world.

During the early modern period, the concept of invention changed because of the influence of the epistemologists.

> By eliminating the role of discovery from invention, Campbell, Blair, and Whately altered the starting point to be used in speech preparation. Speakers can assume that since arguments and proofs are present from the outset, their principle challenge is to learn how to manage rather than invent or discover ideas. (Golden & Corbett, 1968, p. 14)

Discovery was natural and could not be taught by rhetorical topics. Although the concept of topics declined, the concept of metaphor was expanded during this period. For example, Campbell defined the ends of rhetoric as "to enlighten to move the passions, or to influence the will" (p. 145). The concept of imagination stressed the association of ideas, imagery, and comparison. Here metaphor, analogy, simile and other comparisons were arguments and ornaments (pp. 206–208). Lord Kames (1845) summed up the idea when he said, "Metaphor is an act of the imagination, figuring one thing to be another" (p. 370).

All of these diverse previous works set the stage for the twentieth century views on topoi and metaphor. In 1936, I.A. Richards shaped a modern concept of metaphor:

> The traditional theory ... made metaphor seem to be a verbal matter, a shifting and displacement of words, whereas fundamentally it is a borrowing between and intercourse of *thoughts,* a transaction between contexts. Thought is metaphorical, and proceeds by comparison, and the metaphors of language derive therefrom. (p. 94)

Richards uses the term metaphor for the "whole double unit" that is created by the "tenor— ... the underlying idea or principle subject the vehicle or figure means" (pp. 96–97). If someone says, "He is a teddy bear," the tenor would be "he" and the vehicle would be "teddy bear." It is in the interaction of these terms that a new thought is created. As Richards notes, "the copresence of the vehicle and tenor results in a meaning (to be clearly distinguished from the tenor) which is not attainable without this interaction" (p. 100). This interaction changes the concept of reality:

> So metaphor is hardly an amusing embellishment or diversion, an "escape" from the harsh realities of life or of language. It is made out of, *and it makes,* those realities.... Given this, the chief use of metaphor ... is to *extend* language and, since language is reality, to expand reality. By the juxaposition of elements those interactions bring about a new dimension

for them both, metaphor can reasonably be said to create *new* reality. (Hawkes, 1972, pp. 61, 63)

Although Richards presents a new concept of metaphor, he does not discuss the topics.

Kenneth Burke (1950) only mentions the commonplaces directly when he states that the "commonplaces" are a "quick survey of opinion . . . things that people generally consider persuasive" (pp. 56–57). The commonplaces, like the figures of speech, help to create identification which is the cornerstone of rhetoric. For Burke's views on invention seem to follow a pattern found among other recent theorists: "Modern theorists tend to reject the medieval doctrine of topics and commonplaces. Instead, they focused on 'principles of human nature' as guides to artistic conceptualization" (Harper, 1979, p. 275). Burke (1954) directly discussed metaphor more often than the topics. He recognized the metaphors have heuristic functions: "Classifications are heuristic by reason of the fact that, through the process of abstraction and analogy, they dictate new groupings, hence new discoveries" (p. 103). The significance of this extends to all fields of knowledge when he asks, "Indeed, as the documents of science pile up, are we not coming to see that whole works of scientific research, even entire *schools*, are hardly more than the patient repetition, in all its ramifications, of a fertile metaphor" (p. 95). Examples are taken from different eras of history: man as son of God, man as animal, man as machine, etc. According to Burke, these metaphors have a profound impact on the way we argue.

> When a writer gives us a sequence of logical propositions framed to show why he got to his conclusions, he is almost reversing the actual processes of his thought. He presents data which supposedly lead to a conclusion— whereas the conclusion had led to the selection and arrangement of the data . . . of metaphor in science, we should say that the "data" evolved by those who would prove that men are machines . . . are observations moulded by the informing point of view. (pp. 98–99)

This concept is similar to the ideas expressed by Thomas Kuhn (1976) in *The Structure of Scientific Revolutions*. What "differentiated, the various schools" was not a "failure of method—they were all scientific" but their "incommensurable ways of seeing the world" (p. 4). The paradigm shifts change what relationships will be examined, what questions will be asked, and what language will be used.

In *Counter-Statement* (1931), Burke showed that "form in literature is an arousing and fulfillment of desires. A work has form in so far as one part of it leads a reader to anticipate another part, to be gratified by the sequence" (p. 124). For Burke, the syllogistic-progression is a form just as a metaphor is a form. Both, if "correct," allow the audience to anticipate something further, such as a conclusion or a new idea. Thus, "form is the appeal" (p. 138).

Another prominent contemporary theorist who has expanded the concept of creativity in rhetoric is Chaim Perelman. In his 1969 book, *The New Rhetoric: A Treatise on Argumentation*, written with L. Olbrechts-Tyteca, topics are redefined as loci. They note the differences between Aristotle's topics and their concept of loci.

> First of all, we do not wish to bind our viewpoint to any particular meta-physical system. Secondly, we shall only apply the term *loci* to premises of a general nature that can serve as the bases for values and hierarchies . . . each *locus* can be confronted by one that is contrary to it: thus to the classical locus of the superiority of the lasting, one may oppose the ro-mantic *locus* of the superiority of that which is precarious and fleeting. It is accordingly possible to characterize societies not only by the particular values they prize most but by the intensity with which they adhere to one or the other of a pair of antithetical loci. (pp. 84–85)

The specific loci dealt with by Perelman included: "loci of quantity, quality, order, the existing, essence and the person" (p. 85). Rhetoric is looked at as a process of connecting links and dissociations—presented to the audience (even to the self). Some examples of philosophical pairs created by this process of dissociation are: appearance/reality, body/soul, means/end, individual/group. In a more recent book, *The Realm of Rhetoric* (1982), Perelman states: "A figure is argumentative if its use, leading to a change in perspective, seems normal in relation to the new situa-tion" (p. 38).

Toward a Modern Inventional System of Metaphorical Topoi

The concept of topoi has evolved substantially. Topoi have been thought of as lines of arguments, places of discovery, points of memory, common themes, places of clashing arguments, and as warrants in syllogistic rea-soning. Topoi have traditionally been placed under the general heading of invention. Usually with this placement has come several attached ideas:

1. Topoi can be discovered.
2. Topoi can help the speaker create messages.
3. Topoi can be both universal and specific to a given context.
4. Topoi are analytic guides.

5. Topoi can help the speaker produce *reasonable* ideas to justify arguments to some audience.
6. Topoi demonstrate some *relationship* among ideas.
7. Topoi can help speakers to remember ideas.

The major inadequacy in present theory is that topoi are often viewed as a "sequential . . . temporal or logical progression." (Leff, 1983, p. 216. It should be noted that this is not Leff's viewpoint.) This narrows the potential range of topoi's heuristic value. It also seems to conflict with the growing evidence on human conceptual behavior. William Nelson, in his 1969 article, "Topoi: Evidence of Human Conceptual Behavior," summarizes the conclusions of decades of research on human conception by many authors:

—A kind of categorizing behavior (contiguity transfer) is intrinsic within man.
—Categorizing behavior is a necessary antecedent to language propensity.
—Categorizing is of significant utilitarian value in virtually all forms of human behavior. (p. 2)

Nelson suggests that meaning, cognitive activity, and rhetorical arguments cluster according to categories. The categorizing behavior is not always sequential but is always associational. Mednick (1976) points out the relationship of associations and creativity: "The greater the number of associations that an individual has to the requisite elements of a problem, the greater the probability of his reaching a creative solution" (p. 232). J.P. Guilford (1962) believes that factors involved in creativity include associational fluency, adaptive flexibility, spontaneous flexibility and redefinition. These factors led Guilford to propose convergent and divergent production of ideas (pp. 156–168). Using somewhat different terminology, Edward deBono (1970) makes a distinction between lateral and vertical thinking in creativity. Vertical thinking is selective, sequential, analytical, and, therefore, has to be correct at every step, uses the negative to block off certain pathways, concentrates and excludes what is irrelevant, uses fixed classifications, and focuses on problem solving or critical judgment. Lateral thinking is generative, provocative, makes jumps to new points, does not have to be correct at every step, welcomes chance intrusions, has open classifications, focuses on changing patterns, and gains new ideas without being judgmental (pp. 7–14, 39–59). What needs to be recognized is that rhetorical invention should not be straitjacketed into dealing only with justifying arguments to an audience. Before justification must come the generation of ideas and discovery:

Some people are unhappy about lateral thinking because they feel that it threatens the validity of vertical thinking. This is not so at all. The two processes are complementary not antagonistic. Lateral thinking is useful for generating ideas and approaches and vertical thinking is useful for developing them. Lateral thinking enhances the effectiveness of vertical thinking by offering it more to select from. (p. 50)

Modern rhetorical invention and topoi need to consider both lateral and vertical thinking.

Another inadequacy is in the use of topoi in educational settings. Unfortunately, topoi in any form—classical or modern—are rarely given the treatment they merit in public-speaking courses or in textbooks on public speaking. Michael Leff (1978) points out that there has been a lack of scholarship on speech composition as it relates to educational use (p. 90). Kneupper and Anderson (1980) found that

... in current pedagogy, the most important of the classical rhetorical canons, invention, is seriously neglected. A survey of textbooks in public speaking will show that there is seldom any significant or extended treatment of invention. What most contemporary textbooks present is a fairly detailed discussion of the extrinsic sources of content.[3] (pp. 320–321)

In public-speaking courses, students need to learn the process of creating intrinsic arguments. How to come up with ideas, how to think about a topic needs more attention. Ruth Anne Clark and Jesse G. Delia, in 1979, suggested that topoi could be used to examine and develop rhetorical competency (pp. 187–206). The topoi system can provide us with an understanding "of the *message choices* made by the potential persuader" (Walter, 1954, p. 160). In the article, they advise that topoi systems should be used more often in theorizing, research and teaching. Clark and Delia (1979) state that there are at least four steps involved in message strategy and development. These steps are: (1) identify communication objectives; (2) identify obstacles to communication objectives; (3) discover lines of argument; and (4) examine ways of casting arguments. This four-step process can be used by teachers when using topoi for training and development. Otis M. Walter, as early as 1954, expressed the need for the teaching of creativity in public speaking. He suggested the use of a four-step process: the preparation process, a plateau period, the moment of insight, and the process of verification (p. 160).

Despite this overall neglect, let's briefly examine the few topoi sys-

[3] Two exceptions to this problem were noted by Kneupper and Anderson (1980), Wilson & Arnold (1974), and Walter (1976). Some other books mention brain-storming but few other intrinsic inventional techniques are usually mentioned.

tems currently used in speech education. Wilson and Arnold (1974) offer one topoi system based on classical rhetoric:

ATTRIBUTES

1. *Existence* or nonexistence of things.
2. *Degree* or quantity of things, forces, etc.
3. *Spatial* attributes, including adjacency.
4. Attributes of *time.*
5. *Motion* or activity.
6. *Form,* either physical or abstract.
7. *Substance:* physical, abstract, or psychophysical.
8. *Capacity* to change, including predictability.
9. *Potency:* power or energy, including capacity to further or hinder anything.
10. *Desirability* in terms of rewards or punishments.
11. *Feasibility:* workability or practicability.

RELATIONSHIPS

1. *Causality:* the relation of causes to effects, effects to causes, effects to effects, adequacy of causes, etc.
2. *Correlation:* co-existence or co-ordination of things, forces, etc.
3. *Genus-species* relationships.
4. *Similarity* or *dissimilarity.*
5. *Possibility* or *impossibility.*

Karl Wallace (1972) presents a topoi system that focuses more on values, value hierarchies, affective states, and character traits of the speaker along with some of the more traditional terms like classification, fact, causation, disagreement, and the possible (pp. 393–394).

Debate and forensic coaches have been far ahead of most of their colleagues in the use of topoi as an education technique. Four modern conceptions have received the most notice in forensics. The topoi of policy argument or stock issues (need, inherency, policy, practicality, advantages, counterplan, etc.) are often used in debate (McCroskey, 1982, pp. 154–155). Ralph Towne develops a system of nine topoi that deal with public policy (justice, waste, confusion, security, morality, efficiency, strength, prestige, and destruction) (p. 156). B.G. Blackburn suggests a typology of anxiety-arousing arguments (such as loss of security, loss of democracy, death, loss of a loved one, professional loss, social disapproval, financial hardship, loss of status, failure, lack of meaningful relationships, mental anxiety, etc.) (McCroskey, 1982,pp. 156–157). Wayne Minnick presents a topoi of American values (theoretical values,

economic values, aesthetic values, social values, political values, and religious values) (McCroskey, 1982, pp. 158–160). There are several problems with the aforementioned classical and modern topoi systems. First,
they are often viewed as proving logical arguments and fail to adequately consider the discovery process. They tend to emphasize vertical
thinking to the exclusion of lateral thinking. Second, some of the systems are not expandable. They do not challenge the student to add to
the list of topoi. Third, the categories are hard to remember. The problem with most of the topoi systems discussed is that a student would
have to memorize a rigid classification system that does not easily correspond to their lives. For example, Aristotle's topoi of correlative terms,
division, and crisscrossed consequences do not come right to mind when
looking for ideas for a speech.

The fundamental problem with the classical and modern topoi systems is that it fails to link the two major creative processes in communication—topoi and metaphor. This is probably due to the traditional
division of invention and style, the relative neglect of topoi by modern
theorists, and the relative late development of the idea that metaphors
are creative forms of appeal.

What is needed is a system of metaphorical topoi. By joining the
metaphor with the concept of topoi, we could take advantage of the
metaphor's creative nature: "Truly creative and non-mythic thought,
whether in the arts, the sciences, religion, or metaphysics must be invariably and irreducibly metaphorical" (Berggren, 1962–1963, p. 472).
The following metaphorical topoi system is offered:

Arts
Biology
Business
Chemistry
Communications
Economics
Education
English
Film
Foreign Affairs
History
Law
Military
Philosophy
Politics
Psychology

Religion
Science
Sociology
Sports
Television

This flexible and expandable list follows the already existing academic categories or majors. Students using this list would simply take their speech topics and generate ideas by asking a series of questions:

—How does this relate to the arts?
—How does this relate to biology?
—How does this relate to business? and so on.

These questions produce association between the speech topic and the topoi. The topic for an entire speech assignment could even be generated by using such a set of topoi. For example, if the student was asked to give a persuasive speech about some problem in society, the student could go through such a list and ask: Are there any problems in the arts? Problems in business? And so on.

In a creative writing course, if the student was asked to write a creative paper about trees, then the writer could try to associate trees metaphorically with those topoi not usually associated with trees. For example, by this process of forced association, the student might generate an entire paper on the role of trees in religion (i.e., the tree in the Garden of Eden, the Cross of Christ). This would take the concept of "tree" out of its normal role in agriculture or biology and see the tree from a different metaphorical framework.

This list is easily expanded. Students could add any other major (math, agriculture, journalism, engineering, medicine, fashion design, etc.) or any subdivision of a major with which they are familiar. Someone knowledgeable about biology might discover topics under the subdivision of anatomy, bioethics, botany, ecology, genetics, microbiology, or zoology.

Such a set of topoi would allow the student to explore both the familiar and the novel in the development of ideas. Students would be encouraged to develop intrinsic ideas first and then look for extrinsic examples from books and articles. Both vertical and lateral thinking could be encouraged. The "logical appeals" of an existing field could be used or the student could be asked to break the typical associations of one field by inserting the ideas of another field. So the concepts from the arts could be applied to sports to reveal arguments. A television sports reporter uses metaphors such as "the drama of athletics," "a climatic game matching two antagonists" and "this was a beautiful display of boxing" to keep the audience interested and tuned in to a particular channel.

This topoi system meets the needs of students at various levels in college. A beginning student might generate ideas from only the area of his or her major interest. But as the speaker gains confidence and knowledge, other more creative and challenging approaches might be tried. A more experienced speaker may use the topoi to develop extended metaphors across fields.

A metaphorical system of topoi based on academic areas is easy for the students to remember. From the first day of their college career, they are asked: What is your major? Such an approach more easily corresponds to the categories in education and careers experienced by people today. It can be used for a variety of rhetorical presentations: an impromptu speech, a prepared speech, an essay, or even an extended term paper.

Most importantly, this approach links two theoretical systems and unites the theory of metaphor with educational practice. This system of topoi relates to what we know about metaphors:

—Most of our fundamental concepts are organized in terms of one or more spatialization metaphors.
—Spatialization metaphors are rooted on physical and cultural experience; they are not randomly assigned. A metaphor can serve as a vehicle for understanding a concept only by virtue of its experimental basis.
—So-called purely intellectual concepts, e.g., the concepts in a scientific theory, are often—perhaps always—based on metaphors that have a physical and/or cultural basis. (Lakoff & Johnson, 1980, p. 17)

Metaphorical topoi would fulfill a criteria established by Richard McKeon in his 1973 article, "Creativity and the Commonplace," because it would "allow for 'creative interplay of philosophies . . . their facts, their data, their methods, their universes' " (p. 207).

It would apply various results from brain research and creativity to the field of communication. It would develop vertical and lateral thinking and hemispheric interaction by encouraging both analytic and imaging abilities (Leaffer, 1981, p. 242).

A metaphoric topoi system would allow metaphor finally to take its place in rhetorical invention. It would allow for the enhancement of creativity in rhetoric by having the student interrelate different fields of study in a metaphorical way. Finally, it would provide a philosophy of communication on both the theoretical and practical levels. As Lakoff and Johnson (1980) state,

Metaphor is thus imaginative rationality. Since the categories of our every-day thought are largely metaphorical and our everyday reasoning involves metaphorical entailments and inferences, ordinary rationality is therefore imaginative by its very nature. . . . Metaphor is one of our most important tools for trying to comprehend partially what cannot be comprehended totally: our feeling, aesthetic experiences, moral practices, and spiritual awareness. (p. 193)

So placement of metaphor and topoi does not have to remain divided as in the traditional approach. Metaphor and topoi can be cojoined in rhetorical invention to enhance the creative process.

REFERENCES

Aristotle. (1941). Topics. In R. McKeon (Ed.), *The basic works of Aristotle* (pp. 188–206). New York: Random House.

Aristotle. (1960). *The rhetoric* (L. Cooper, Trans.). Englewood Cliffs, Prentice-Hall.

Berggren, D. (1962-1963). The use and abuse of metaphor. *Review of Metaphysics 16,* p. 472.

Bitzer, L.F. (1959). Aristotle's enthymeme revisited. *Quarterly Journal of Speech 45,* 399–408.

Burke, K. (1931). *Counter-statement.* Berkeley, CA: University of California Press.

Burke, K. (1950). *A rhetoric of motives.* New York: Prentice-Hall.

Burke, K. (1954). *Permanence and change: An anatomy of purpose.* Indianapolis, IN: Bobbs-Merrill.

Caplan, H. (Trans.). (1954). *The Rhetorica ad herennium.* Cambridge, MA: Leob Classical Library.

Churchill, W. (1940). Unpublished speech.

Cicero (1976). *Topics* (H.M. Hubbell, Trans.). Cambridge, MA: Harvard University Press.

Clark, D.L. (1966). *Rhetoric in Greco-Roman education.* New York: Columbia University Press.

Clark, R.A. & Delia, J.G. (1979). Topoi and rhetorical competence. *The Quarterly Journal of Speech, 65,* 187–206.

Conley, T.M. (1984). The enthymeme in perspective. *Quarterly Journal of Speech, 70,* 168–187

Dance, F.E.X. (1980). Speech communication as a liberal arts discipline. *Communication Education, 29,* 329–343.

de Bono, E. (1970). *Lateral thinking: Creativity step by step,* New York: Harper Colophon Books.

Dick, H.C. (Ed.). (1955). *Selected writings of Francis Bacon.* New York: The Modern Library.

Dick, R.C. (1964). Topoi: An approach to inventing arguments. *The Speech Teacher, 13,* 313–319.

Golden, J.L., & Corbett, E.P., (Eds.). (1968). *The rhetoric of Blair, Campbell, and Whately.* New York: Holt, Rinehart and Winston.

Golden J.L. (1968). *The rhetoric of western thought* (3d ed.). Dubuque, IA: Kendall/Hunt.

Guilford, J.P. (1962). Creativity: Its measurement and development. In *A source book for creative thinking*. New York: Charles Scribner's & Sons.

Harper, N. (1979). *Human communication theory: The history of a paradigm*. Rochelle Park, NJ: Hayden.

Hawkes, T. (1972). *Metaphor*. London: Methuen.

Infante, D.A. (1971). The influence of a topical system on the discovery of arguments. *Speech Monographs, 38*, 125–128.

Kames, Lord (1849). In A. Mills (Ed.), *Elements of criticism*. New York: Huntington & Savage.

Kneupper, C.W., & Anderson F.D. (1980). Uniting wisdom and eloquence: The need for rhetorical invention. *Quarterly Journal of Speech, 66*, 313–326.

Kuhn, T.S. (1976). *The structure of scientific revolutions* (2d ed.). Chicago: University of Chicago Press.

Lakoff, G., & Johnson, M. (1980). *Metaphors we live by*. Chicago, IL: The University of Chicago Press.

Leaffer, T. (1981). Left brain—right brain: Domination or cooperation. *Journal of Creative Behavior, 15*, 238–245.

Leff, M.C. (1978). In search of Ariadne's thread: A review of the recent literature on rhetorical theory. *Central States Speech Journal, 29*, 73–91.

Leff, M.C. (1983). Topical invention and metaphoric interaction. *The Southern Speech Communication Journal, 48*, 214–254.

Locke, J. (1970). *An essay concerning human understanding*. London: D. Browne.

McCroskey, J.C. (1982). *An introduction to rhetorical communication* (4th ed.). Englewood Cliffs, NJ: Prentice-Hall.

McKeon, R. (Ed.). (1941). *The basic works of Aristotle*. New York: Random House.

McKeon, R. (1973). Creativity and the commonplace. *Philosophy and Rhetoric, 6*, 199–200.

Mednick, S.A. (1976). The associative basis of the creative process. In A. Rothenberg & C. Hausman (Eds.), *The creativity question*. Durham, NC: Duke University Press.

Nelson, W.F. (1969). Topoi: Evidence of human conceptual behavior. *Philosophy and Rhetoric, 2*, 1–11.

Nelson, W.F. (1970). Topoi: Functional in human recall. *Speech Monographs, 37*, 121–126.

Osborn, M.M. (1967). *Western Speech, 31*, 125 (Quoting from H. Peacham, *The garden of eloquence*, 1577).

Parnes, S.J. & Harding, H.F. (1962). *A source book for creative thinking*. New York: Charles Scribner's Sons.

Perelman, C. (1982). *The realm of rhetoric*. Notre Dame, IN: University of Notre Dame Press.

Perelman, C., & Olbrechts-Tyteca, L. (1969). *The new rhetoric: A treatise on argumentation*. Notre Dame, IN: University of Notre Dame Press.

Quintilian (1888). In J.S. Watson (Trans.), London: G. Bell and Sons. *Institutes of oratory*.

Richards, I.A. (1936). *The philosophy of rhetoric*. London: Oxford University Press.

Smith, H.L. (1960). Linguistics: A modern view of language. In L. Bryson (Ed.), *An outline of man's knowledge of the modern world*. Garden City, NY: Doubleday.

Vancil, D.L. (1979). Historical barriers to a modern system of topoi. *Western Journal of Speech Communication, 43*, 32–35.

Vico, G. (1965). *On the study methods of our time.* (E. Gianturco, Trans.). Indianapolis, IN: Bobbs-Merrill.

Wallace, K.R. (1972). Topoi and the problems of invention. *Quarterly Journal of Speech, 58,* 387–395

Walter, O.M. (1954). Creativity: A neglected factor in public speaking. *The Speech Teacher, 3,* 159–168.

Walter, O.M. (1976). *Speaking intelligently: Communication for problem solving.* New York: Macmillan.

Watson, J.S. (Trans.). (1970). *Cicero on oratory and orators.* Carbondale, IL: Southern Illinois University Press.

Wilson, J.F. & Arnold, C.C. (1974). *Public speaking as a liberal art* (3d ed.). Boston: Allyn and Bacon.

SYMPOSIUM

PANEL 2

Idea Combining

Gerald Richman

"As long as students take exams, there will be prayer in the public schools" has been a frequent quip since the Supreme Court banned school prayer. Equally true, as long as students write papers, there will be creativity. For, if necessity is the mother of invention, the necessity to fill blank pages (or screens or whatever the writing surface of the future will be) will inevitably lead to invention (discovery, creation) of ideas to fill up the blankness. Writing itself is thus a stimulus for creativity, a tool for thinking and discovery rather than just a means of communicating what already has been discovered.

But how can we as writers—for the most part not geniuses—create ideas like Newton, Freud, Einstein? Is genius a prerequisite for creativity? Do the minds of geniuses create ideas in ways alien to the minds of ordinary people? My first college writing instructor, Charles Kay Smith (1974), made a deep impression on me by arguing that all of us can create new ideas the way geniuses do: by combining ideas that have never been combined before to create new ideas distinct from the originals. (Smith calls the process "cross-structuring" rather than combining.) Thus, in 1891, in Springfield, Massachusetts, James Naismith combined a basket with a ball to create basketball. The combination of a container for peaches and a round, bounceable object led to something startlingly different from the original ideas—the Boston Celtics.

Of course, the Boston Celtics did not appear immediately after Naismith's invention of the game of basketball. Instead, a whole series of idea combinings (some of which turned out to be dead ends) had to occur before the establishment of the National Basketball Association (NBA). The first professional teams barnstormed around the country

I would like to thank Ann Hughes and David Tuerck for their valuable suggestions.

playing matches against local teams. The game of basketball was thus combined with the barnstorming techniques of challenge boxing matches. What could make money for boxing could also make money for basketball. Later, leagues were formed on the model of professional baseball and hockey. This culminated, after WW II, in the founding of the Basketball Association of America (later combined with the National Basketball League to form the NBA). Under the guidance of Walter Brown, founder of the Celtics, the Basketball Association of America was formed by the owners of hockey arenas to fill Boston Garden and similar buildings when the home hockey team was playing in other cities. Empty arenas cost money and professional basketball was seen as the answer to this problem. The team structure of professional hockey, the need to fill empty arenas, and the game of basketball were thus combined. In 1954, a further instance of idea combining saved the league from being abandoned by fans bored with the stalling techniques that led to 22–20 scores. The 24-second clock, requiring a team to shoot the ball at least every 24 seconds, saved the league and led to the Larry Birds and Robert Parishes of today. The idea of a clock to control playing time was borrowed from other sports, most likely, football (Mokray, 1983).

Many combinations of ideas can be easily recognized because they have been encapsulated in language as compounds, whether written as one word or not. Consider the compound idea, *law school*. Both ideas had existed separately for a long time before they were first combined in 1784 with the foundation of the Litchfield Law School. Against the strong objections of traditionalists, who argued that law, in the English system taught through apprenticeship, couldn't be taught in a school, with formal classroom instruction, set curricula, and exams, law schools became established as the main method of training lawyers in the years after the founding of Harvard Law School in 1817 (Harno, 1953). Similar charges have failed to stop other instances of idea combining, such as medical school, business school, driver education, and sex education. Today, we can even speak of parent education, formal instruction in the art of parenting. In the future, this conference may be recognized as a contributor to a new compound idea, one that would seem impossible to those who believe that creativity can't be taught: creativity education.

Idea combining, of course, is not limited to education. Many of the most successful instances of idea combining in the twentieth century have combined the automobile with other technological innovations. In 1913, Henry Ford combined the assembly line, which he had observed in the meatpacking industry, with the automobile to mass produce a new product, the Model-T. By the 1920's, automobiles and radios, which had developed separately in the preceding decades, were combined. Similarly, the Packard Motor Car Company combined air conditioning and the automobile in 1939. Today, perhaps stirred by the divestiture of AT&T, several companies are actively promoting the combination of automobiles and telephones, hoping that car phones will become as common as car radios, or at least car stereos. Sometime in the near future, we may see the combination of the automobile and the home computer, as auto computers specialize in audio games and computer versions of Trivial Pursuit.

As the almost unlimited combinability of the automobile demonstrates, there can be a contagiousness to idea combining. Once one combination proves to be useful and profitable, other combinations naturally spring up. Professional baseball's success led to professional football, professional hockey, professional basketball, and all the other professional sports of the 1980s. Similarly, the success of the New York baseball team named the Mets led to other New York sports names ending in -ets: Jets, Nets, Sets (Word Team Tennis), and Bets (Off Track Betting). McDonald's is another example of an idea that has proved contagious in combinations. Fast-food techniques have spread from hamburgers to tacos, chili, subs, Chinese food, and beyond food to dental and medical care. Although the automobile is the undisputed combinability champ of the first three-quarters of the twentieth century, the computer is likely to be the champ of the rest of the century and perhaps far into the twenty-first century as well. The massive institutional computers of the early days have given birth to the compact home and office computers of today. We already have portable computers and, in the future, we may have beach computers (for summer use), school computers (for the classroom), combat computers (for the battlefield), and football computers (for the sidelines). The possibilities are limitless and the success of early combinations will inevitably lead to further combinations.

Similar contagiousness can occur in the intellectual realm. After WW II, when French existentialism became the vogue, this philosophy was combined with literature to produce existential literature and with psychology to produce existential psychology. Another vogue from France, structuralism, spread from linguistics to anthropology, philosphy, and literary criticism. Likewise, we can speak of Marxist economics or psychology or sociology or art. As these examples show, one instance of idea combining can lead to many others.

Idea combining has been particularly fruitful in the natural and social sciences. New hybrids like astrophysics, biochemistry, and geophysics have joined the traditional disciplines of astronomy, biology, chemistry, geology, and physics. Anthropology, linguistics, psychology, and sociology have combined to create anthropological linguistics, psycholinguistics, social anthropology, social psychology and sociolinguistics. Psychoanalysis has combined with history to form psychohistory. Combining ideas from one discipline with ideas from another has created insights and approaches that would not have been generated otherwise. In the future, we can look forward to the creation of new disciplines by idea combining, perhaps, compulinguistics (the linguistics of computers), compuphysics (the physics of computers), psychochemistry (the chemistry of psychology), and even linguaphysics (the physics of language).

So far we have seen idea combining produce new institutions, new products, and new disciplines. But idea combining can also create new ideas to help us understand the world and our position in it. Idea combining can combine ideas from within economics to explain inflation or ideas from within literary criticism to explain *Ulysses*. Idea combining can also cross disciplinary lines, combining ideas, say, from literary criticism and economics to explain inflation. Let's look at a few examples.

Idea combining led Charles Darwin to discover "the principle of natural selection, one worthy to rank with Newton's discovery of the principle of gravitation, as providing at one bound a natural explanation for an enormous number of unrelated, puzzling and hitherto unexplained facts of nature" (Huxley, 1939/1959, p. 90). Darwin arrived at this principle by combining his observations of the fossil record and animal and plant life with the economic theories of Thomas Malthus. As Darwin wrote in his *Autobiography* (1887).

> In October, 1838, that is, fifteen months after I had begun my systematic enquiry, I happened to read for amusement Malthus on *Population,* and being well prepared to appreciate the struggle in existence which everywhere goes on from long-continued observation of the habits of animals and plants, it at once struck me that under these circumstances favourable variations would tend to be preserved, and unfavourable ones to be destroyed. The result of this would be the formation of new species. Here, then, I had at last got a theory by which to work. (quoted in Huxley, 1939/ 1959, p. 90)

Malthus had written about the economics of human population, not animals and plants. Roughly, he had argued that an inevitably limited food supply means that only the most efficient survive. Darwin applied this idea to animals and plants, for which it is more valid than for humans, because animals and plants lack the means to increase the food supply artificially. Darwin succinctly formulated his new principle in Chapter 3 of *The Origin of the Species* (1859):

> A struggle for existence inevitably follows from the high rate at which all organic beings tend to increase. Every being, which during its natural lifetime produces several eggs or seeds, must suffer destruction . . . , otherwise, on the principle of geometrical increases, its numbers would quickly become so inordinately great that no country could support the product. Hence, as more individuals are produced than can possibly survive, there must in every case be a struggle for existence, either one individual with another of the same species, or with individuals of distinct species, or with the physical conditions of life. It is the doctrine of Malthus applied with manifold force to the whole animal and vegetable kingdoms; for in this case there can be no artificial increase of food, and no prudential restraint from marriage. (quoted in Huxley, 1939/1959, pp. 92–93)

Without the ideas of Malthus, Darwin might not have been able to formulate his theories.

No less controversial than Darwin's theory of evolution was Sigmund Freud's combination of his clinical observations of psychoneurotics and Sophocles' *Oedipus Rex*. Freud explained this combination of ideas in *The Interpretation of Dreams* (1900/1938).

> It is far more probable—and this is confirmed by incidental observations of normal children—that in their amorous or hostile attitude toward their parents, psychoneurotics do no more than to reveal to us, by magnification, something that occurs less markedly and intensively in the minds of the majority of children. Antiquity has furnished us with legendary matter which corroborates this belief, and the profound and universal validity of the old legends is explicable only by an equally universal validity of the above-mentioned hypothesis of infantile psychology.
>
> I am referring to the legend of King Oedipus and the *Oedipus Rex* of Sophocles. (p. 307)

Indeed, Freud acknowledged that Sophocles has already stated the theory through the mouth of Jocasta, Oedipus's wife-mother:

> For many a man hath seen himself in dreams
> His Mother's mate, but he who gives no heed
> To suchlike matters bears the easier life. (p. 309)

It is possible that without knowledge of *Oedipus Rex*, Freud would not have been able to make a coherent theory out of his observations. As

Darwin combined ideas from economics and the observation of nature, so Freud combined ideas from literature and psychiatry.

But idea combining is not limited to the Darwins and the Freuds of the world. Last spring, while studying Shakespeare's tragedy *Othello*, my students were asked to combine two ideas, culled from different critics, about seemingly unconnected aspects of the play: the soldiering profession and romantic love. The first critic, Wolfgang Clemen (1951), points out that for Iago, the villain who convinces his superior officer, Othello, that Desdemona, Othello's wife, has committed adultery, being a soldier is merely a job. In act 1, scene 1, lines 28–31, Iago regrets the loss of the higher pay to be gained by an appointment as Othello's lieutenant; and in act 1, scene 2, line 1, he speaks of soldiering as a "trade." In contrast, being a soldier is a grand and fully satisfying career and vocation for Othello. Othello speaks of "hair-breadth 'scapes" (1, 3, 136), "plumed troop," "big war / That make ambition virtue," and "the neighing steed and the shrill trump, / The spirit-stirring drum, the ear-piercing fife, / The royal banner and all quality, / Pride, pomp, and circumstance of glorious war" (3, 3, 346–351). The contrast could not be stronger (pp. 126–127). The second critic, Leo Kirschbaum (1944), observes that

> Paradoxically, Othello loves Desdemona so much that it is questionable whether in human terms he loves her at all. He loves not Desdemona but his image of her. . . . To Othello, his wife is not a woman but the matrix of his universe: "My life upon her faith" (1, 3, 294), "Excellent wretch! Perdition catch my soul / But I do love thee! And when I love thee not, / Chaos is come again" (3, 3, 91–93, and "If she be false, O, then heaven mocks itself!" (3, 3, 282). (292–293)

The assignment was to combine these two ideas into a single unified and coherent paragraph, creating new ideas as necessary to provide the missing connection between the original ideas. A sample response to the assignment follows.

Othello throws himself so wholeheartedly into whatever he takes up that he loses touch with reality. Thus, as Clemen (1951) notes, unlike Iago, who views being a soldier as simply a job to be paid for and earn a living (see act 1, scene 1, line 30–33, and scene 2, line 1), Othello sees war as something grand and fully satisfying (see act 1, scene 3, lines 158–59, and act 3, scene 3, lines 405–10) (pp. 126–127). This view totally eliminates the boredom, monotony, and cruelty of war, for Othello loves not war itself but his image of it. Othello exhibits a similar fantasy about Desdemona. As Leo Kirschbaum points out, "Othello loves Desdemona so much that it is questionable whether in human terms he loves her at all. He loves not Desdemona but his image of her" (pp. 292–293). In support of his position, Kirschbaum (pp. 292–293) shows that Othello trusts the image of Desdemona so much he bets his "life" on her (1, 3, 294), believes that his love for her is the only force in the universe preventing a collapse into "chaos" (3, 3, 91, 93), and almost equates her with God Himself (3, 3, 282). In the same way, though neither Clemen or Kirschbaum makes the extension, Othello throws himself into killing Desdemona, which act he wishes to see as "a sacrifice" (5, 2, 68), not a murder. In all three cases, what controls Othello is not the reality of war, of Desdemona, of his taking of Desdemona's life but the picture in his vivid and sometimes skewed imagination. Othello's murder of Desdemona, then, is in part in character—he's used to acting as if the fantasy in his mind is reality.

In the sample, a new idea is created by combining two already existing ideas. Here, a general idea is abstracted out of the combination of two particular ideas: There is a trait in Othello that leads him to glamorize what infatuates him. (Note that the paragraph applies Kirschbaum's phrase about love, "He loves not Desdemona but his image of her," to war, "Othello loves not war itself but his image of it.") The general idea in turn generates a third example to be added to war and Desdemona, as Othello is said to glamorize his murder of Desdemona into "a sacrifice." The conclusion following from this argument is that Othello acts as he does in all three instances because he mistakes the fantasy in his own mind for reality. By combining two already existing ideas, the writer creates a new general concept, a new example, and a new conclusion. Without preexisting ideas and the injunction to combine them, however, the new ideas would not have been generated.

The two ideas combined in this example come from the same discipline, literary criticism and, in fact, from the even narrower subset of literary criticism of *Othello*. But idea combining is not limited to ideas about the same topic or within the same discipline. Indeed, combining ideas from different disciplines may create new and unexpected ideas more stimulating than those created by idea combining within a discipline.

A few years ago, a student in a course on medieval literature was taking an introductory psychology course at the same time. To write a paper on two of the greatest poems of the Middle Ages, Dante's *Divine Comedy* and William Langland's *Piers Plowman*, he combined two ideas from the psychology course with an idea from medieval theology.

While studying the psychology of learning, he was struck by two ideas in particular:

1. *Vicarious classical conditioning* occurs when one learns from the ex-

perience of others. "One experiment ... showed that people could be conditioned to give an emotional response to a light, merely by watching another person get an electric shock each time the light came on. Even though subjects never directly received a shock, they developed a conditioned emotional response to seeing the light come on" (Coon, 1983, p. 178).

2. *Modeling* occurs when one learns from observation. "By observing a model (someone who serves as an example) a person may ... learn to carry out or avoid previously learned responses, depending on what happens to the model for doing the same thing" (pp. 205–206). The student combined these ideas with the medieval idea of *imitatio Christi* (imitation of Christ), succinctly defined by the opening of Thomas à Kempis's (1426/1957) *Imitation of Christ*:

> *He that follows Me shall not walk in darkness*, says the Lord [John 8:12].
>   These are the words of Christ, by which we are urged to imitate His life and virtues, if we wish to be truly enlightened and freed from all blindness of heart. (p. 17)

The student argued that Christ is not the central character of *The Divine Comedy* or *Piers Plowman*, because a perfect being would not make an effective model for the vicarious conditioning of imperfect human beings. Instead of imitating perfection, readers would give up in despair because of the impossibility of the task. For this reason, the main characters of the two poems, Dante and Long Will, respectively, are imperfect human beings who try to imitate Christ but constantly fail to do so by making wrong decisions that readers are led to concur with and, so, in theological terms, to sin along with the characters. Dante and Long Will, who are punished for their failures, provide readers with models of what to avoid and follow (because neither gives up the quest), thus leading to vicarious classical conditioning in the direction of *imitatio Christi*.

Without the ideas from psychology and medieval theology, the student would never have created this interpretation of the two poems. Yet the interpretation is a new idea that is not an obvious development of the original ideas. Modern psychology, grounded in experiments with dogs and rats, and medieval poems, grounded in exegesis of the New Testament, would seem to have nothing to say to each other. But, as this example shows, idea combining can bridge even the gap between science and theology and lead to the creation of new and illuminating ideas. (See Katz, Greenberg, & Warrick, 1977, for interesting examples of idea combining between science fiction and psychology.)

Invention, the creation of new ideas out of old ideas, is only part of creativity. Good new ideas need to be developed and bad ones, improved or abandoned. Thus, whereas a folding bicycle, capable of being ridden for miles before being folded into a light-weight case for easy carrying and safe storage, may be practical, a folding automobile is not. Sure, a folding automobile could solve the parking problem in crowded cities and eliminate auto theft as motorists wheel their cars from street to office or home. But the folded automobile would be too heavy for easy carrying and storage, and such an automobile would not be strong enough to withstand the impact of a crash. In this case, the marketplace would reward the good product and ignore the bad one. Similarly, saunas and tennis clubs make a good combination, but a company would have a difficult time marketing saunas designed for Hondas.

While the marketplace tests products, and a laboratory tests scientific hypotheses, the challenge of the blank page tests ideas. In writing it is not enough merely to assert new ideas. Writers must convince skeptical readers of their validity and value. This forces writers to check their ideas thoroughly, often leading either to the rejection of ideas that had seemed promising or to the improvement of the original idea. Thus, an inventor seeking to capitalize on the combinability of the automobile by proposing to produce saunas for autos may discover the drawbacks of the project while drafting a prospectus for potential investors. He or she then might modify the proposal to design the saunas for specially built limousines or luxury campers to meet the objection that operators of automobiles couldn't enjoy the sauna and drive at the same time.

Of course, the discipline imposed by writing for skeptical readers is no more infallible than the discipline imposed by the marketplace or by science. Bad ideas can avoid detection and elimination, and half-good ideas (though better than no ideas at all) may not be modified and improved. But idea combining in writing, though not perfect, is an inexpensive and convenient tool to promote creativity. The result may be a new invention or a new advertising campaign. The important point is that idea combining can be taught in schools to force students to integrate seemingly unconnected parts of the curriculum and to train them to be creative in performing real-world activities like inventing and marketing. Idea combining does not require expensive equipment or retraining in radically new skills but rather, builds on skills already taught in our schools. In a time when money is tight (is money ever not tight?), it is more practical to turn to new ways of using old resources than to invest in new technology.

Teachers can use idea combining as early as elementary school to foster creativity. Students could be asked, say, to combine what they have learned about arithmetic with what they have learned about sentences. They could be asked to combine what they know about the 1s, 10s, and 100s columns in the decimal system with what they know about the parts of a sentence, subject, verb, and sentence completer. Combining these ideas could lead students to the general idea that order has meaning. Thus, as 378 differs from 873, so does "Brutus killed Caesar" differ from "Caesar killed Brutus." In numbers, the right-hand column indicates 1s, the next column, 10s, and the third column, 100s, whereas in English sentences, stripped to basic patterns, the right-hand word is the sentence completer, the next word, the verb, and the third word, the subject. Given "Caesar killed Brutus," we know that Caesar did the action to Brutus, as given 378, we know that 300 is greater than 70 is greater than 8. Similar assignments would accustom students to seek to create new ideas by combining ideas within and across disciplinary boundaries. Such assignments in idea combining will teach students that the subjects they study at different hours or on different days have much in common and will teach them to look for similarities beneath obvious differences. When we call mathematics a language, we are combining ideas, as this exercise shows, that deserve to be combined.

In my teaching, I certainly haven't exhausted all the possibilities of idea combining, but I have used it to develop long and short writing assignments. I begin the semester with several assignments like the *Othello* assignment we looked at earlier. For these assignments, about one paragraph in length, I supply the ideas to be combined. Sometimes, I simply give students two ideas to begin with, but at other times I give them four or five different ideas (often in the form of quotations) and ask them to choose two to combine. I choose the initial ideas because they add to the students' understanding of the subject. Through these short assignments, students get the hang of idea combining. They discover that idea combining does not mean explaining one idea in the first half of the paragraph and a second idea in the last half but rather, requires the ideas to be blended together.

Once students understand how idea combining works, I give longer writing assignments with the same directions but with the ideas to be combined left up to the students. In a linguistics course, for instance, I might ask students to combine an idea from class discussion of phonology (sound systems) with an idea from the discussion of names. Let's say a student picked out the two following ideas:

1. The sounds *p* and *b* are made in the mouth in exactly the same way, by stopping and then releasing the flow of air out of the mouth by bringing the upper and lower lips together. They are called bilabial (two-lips) stops. The only difference is that *b* is voiced (vocal chords vibrate) and *p* is voiceless (vocal chords don't vibrate).

2. Entertainers often change their names to advance their careers. Marion Morrison became John Wayne, Frances Gumm became Judy Garland, and William S. Pratt became Boris Karloff. Faced with such seemingly different ideas, the student will have to create like mad to combine them into an organized and coherent argument. I'll just sketch a possible solution to this problem.

Both ideas stress important distinctions between the sound *p* and *b* and the old and new names (if the distinction were not important, why change names?). Language is a signaling system based on a limited number of distinctions. Thus, the large difference between *bit* and *tap* is based on a small number of narrow distinctions such as the voicing that differentiates *p* and *b*. These signaling devices that operate on the level of sound also operate on the level of individual words. As *p* differs from *b*, so Marion differs from John. The important distinction here is that Marion is usually a girl's name in our culture. An actor who wanted to be taken seriously as a he-man cowboy simply would not go far with a girl's name. So John Wayne was born. Both of the original ideas, then, illustrate a more general idea: Language works by signaling differences. By combining these two ideas in this way (only one of many possibilities), the student will create a new general idea about language and will realize that there is a connection between physical phenomena (sounds) and mental phenomena (meanings and associations).

If the assignment is part of the preparation for writing a research paper, I ask students to read several sources and combine an idea from one source with an idea from another, giving proper credit for the borrowings. For these assignments, students must find the initial ideas as well as combine them.

Other assignments require students to combine ideas taken from different readings. For instance, I might ask students to combine an idea about Mary Shelley's classic monster story, *Frankenstein*, with an idea about Lord Byron's dramatic poem, *Manfred*, in order to provide an organized and coherent analysis of some aspect of Emily Brontë's *Wuthering Heights*. Sometimes I stipulate the ideas to be combined, but at other times I leave the assignment as general as the preceding sentence.

If I were to stipulate ideas for this assignment, I might ask students to combine the following ideas:

1. The structure of *Frankenstein* is a series of boxes within boxes. The story is told to us by means of letters written by Robert Walton to his sister. These letters report what Victor Frankenstein told Walton, part of which is a report of what Frankenstein's creature told Frankenstein. This can be schematized as follows:

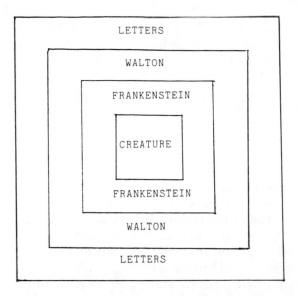

(This scheme does not take into account the complication of Walton's one meeting with the creature.)

a. In Lord Byron's, *Manfred*, we are left ignorant of the exact relationship between Manfred and his sister, though incest is suggested. These two ideas could be combined in a number of ways to form an analysis of *Wuthering Heights*.

One possible combination would go like this. We can never know what another person is feeling or thinking unless we are told in a believable and sincere manner (as in *Frankenstein*), but sometimes the power and impact of ideas and feelings can be made more powerful through suggestion than through explicit statement (as in *Manfred*). *Wuthering Heights* has a box-within-a-box structure similar to *Frankenstein*:

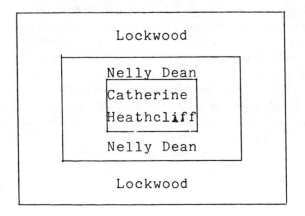

Lockwood, the narator, tells us what Nelly Dean told him about Catherine and Heathcliff. But Catherine and Heathcliff, the main characters, never get a chance to speak for themselves at length as does the creature in *Frankenstein*. Consequently, their relationship remains suggestive rather than explicit and therefore all the more powerful, like that between Manfred and his sister. To make a good paper, these ideas would have to be fleshed out with details and further interpretation. Without the two original ideas, dealing with *Frankenstein* and *Manfred* and the injunction to combine them, this new idea about *Wuthering Heights* may never have been developed.

In Integrated Studies, my assignments require students to combine ideas from sources as diverse as *Oedipus Rex* and the Gospel of Luke, *Gilgamesh*, and Nietzsche. For instance, I might ask students to apply Nietzsche's famous distinction between Apollonianism (roughly, rationality) and Dionysianism, (roughly, passion) to the characterization of three women in the ancient Sumerian epic, *Gilgamesh*: Ninsun (mother of Gilgamesh), Ishtar (goddess and would-be lover of Gilgamesh), and Siduri (another would-be lover of Gilgamesh). Nietzsche developed his distinction on the basis of Greek culture and probably gave no thought to *Gilgamesh*, if he were aware of it at all. Yet the distinction between Apollonianism and Dionysianism can provide insight into the presentation of women in the poem, insight perhaps not possible without the combination of ideas. These assignments will, I intend, force students to be creative without leading them by the nose to preconceived conclusions. The assignments are designed to strike sparks, not to require students to guess ideas I have already developed—I want to learn something new, too. Similar assignments using idea combining can be used to produce creative sparks in any course.

Idea combining does not always lead students to create new and convincing ideas, or to see the connections between widely different readings and fields, but it frequently leads them in the right direction. Idea combining in writing can help all of us create interesting and significant ideas without the expense of fancy and bulky equipment. A pencil and a blank piece of paper are powerful creative tools that are readily available and always at hand.

To be successful, idea combining requires writing, in the first place, to record the ideas to be combined and the results created; but more importantly, to combine the ideas and test the validity of the new idea. The challenge of the blank page or its equivalent provides the motivation to find and combine already existing ideas to create new ideas to fill the blankness. But the challenge of explaining and proving to skeptical readers the validity and value of these newly created ideas forces us to evaluate our creations, separating what is valuable from what is not. Though, in theory, both the combining and testing of complex ideas could take place in the mind, most of us need to work out our ideas in the laboratory of writing—creating hypotheses, testing them, and revising them. Idea combining in writing is a tool that can foster creativity throughout life—in school, in work, and in our private lives.

REFERENCES

Clemen, W. (1951). *The Development of Shakespeare's imagery.* London: Methuen.

Coon, D. (1983). *Introduction to psychology: exploration and application* (3d ed.). St. Paul, MN: West.

Freud, S. (1938). *The interpretation of dreams.* In A. A. Brill (Ed. and Trans.), *The basic writings of Sigmund Freud.* New York: Modern Library. (Original work published 1900)

Harno, A. J. (1953). *Legal education in the United States.* San Francisco: Bancroft-Whitney.

Huxley, J. (1959). *The living thoughts of Darwin.* Greenwich, CT: Fawcett. (Original work published 1939)

Katz, H. A., Greenberg, M.A., & Warrick, P.S. (Eds.). (1977). *Introductory psychology through science fiction* (2d ed.). Chicago: Rand McNally.

Kempis, T. à (1957). *Of the Imitation of Christ.* (Abbot J. McCann, Trans) New York: New Americans Library-Mentor. (Original work published 1426)

Kirschbaum, L. (1944). The Modern Othello. *English Library History, 2,* 282–296.

M[okray], W. G. (1983). Basketball. *Encyclopedia Britannica: Macropaedia* (Vol. 2), 750–757.

Shakespeare, W. (1908). Othello. In S. Lee (Ed.), *The complete works of William Shakespeare.* Vol. XVI. New York: Harper & Brothers.

Smith, C. K. (1974). *Styles and structures: Alternative approaches to college writing* New York: Norton.

SYMPOSIUM

PANEL 2

Comments

Ann D. Hughes

The idea combining that Professor Richman discussed—and explains very clearly—is similar to the bisociation—the mixing together of two frames of reference—that Professor Greenberg spoke of in his paper. So, in a less direct way, is Professor Boone's subject.

Professor Boone has given us the history of two separate rhetorical concepts: first, topoi, essentially a list of things to consider that would be applicable to just about any subject of a speech or essay. The iconoclast of the sixties, Abby Hoffman, didn't use the word "topoi," but he found them useful in getting through college. He said once that he managed to pass essay exams, even when he knew nothing about the subject, by beginning his answer with: "Let us examine this question three ways, politically, economically, and socially." That's an example of topoi, though in his case obviously misused in order to put something over on the tired professor reading his exam.

The second aspect of rhetoric of which Professor Boone traces the history is figures of speech, used to ornament the topoi, or more importantly to argue them persuasively. She suggests that though these two have traditionally been considered separate elements of rhetoric, they can in a sense be combined. The topoi can serve—not as figures of speech in themselves—but to encourage thinking in figurative ways, which is to say, in creative ways. The word "metaphor" comes from the Greek root meaning "to carry over, to transfer." And one of the functions of metaphor is to provide us with displacement of perspective, so we approach something obliquely, rather than merely head on.

To test Professor Boone's theory, I decided to apply her proposed method to Professor Richman's concept of idea combining, as she would have a student do. How can one think in a new, creative way about

Professor Richman's subject, as a result of using Professor Boone's method and by looking at the list of topoi she suggested for students—the list of academic categories in the college catalogue? Alphabetically, in the old catalogue, the first department listed is biology.

Biology—fertile ideas—eggs. (I had one for breakfast, so I must admit that my mental experiment was "contaminated" by the outside factor.) An egg and a new idea both carry the "germ" of something; each is merely a potential. Both the idea and the embryo in the egg need time to develop fully before being exposed to the harshness of the outside world. Metaphorically speaking, Professor Richman, then, is asking students to take two ideas, like two fertile eggs, brood over them to let them mature sufficiently, and see what hatches out. As the next step, the student would cross-breed the results and get a vigorous, new off-spring with a separate life of its own; not a hybrid, but a new species.

So Professor Boone's method was productive of a new way of looking at Professor Richman's subject. (I hasten to add that I did not run through the entire list of academic departments and try to apply each in the same fashion.) But the process of going through such a list, though it might be a little mechanical, *can* produce something—undoubtedly something much more illuminating than my rather trifling analogy between eggs and ideas.

As teachers, we need anything along these lines that will help us over-come a real handicap that is built into the structure of academic life. The structure within which we work obviously influences us. And the very structure of the college schedule, unfortunately, discourages students from thinking across academic disciplines, discourages them from seeing the relationships that do exist among these disciplines. Instead, the schedule of students' days inclines them to think of their academic subjects as coming in separate, discrete lumps that are spooned out in 50-minute portions—some of them pretty undigestible.

Finite math at 9:00 A.M. on Monday, Wednesday, and Friday seems to have nothing to do with American history at 10:00, and neither appears to have any connection with psychology at 11:00. That problem is built into the system. One purpose of Integrated Studies is to help overcome this way of seeing—or of failing to see. Another way we, as teachers, can help alleviate this problem is to make the kind of creative assignments Professor Richman recommends.

For those of us in the classroom, on either side of the lectern, inter-disciplinary approaches can also be productive of this kind of cross-fertilization. Though it is not idea combining in the sense that Professor Richman defines the term, a teacher of *Othello,* to use his exemplar, might have his or her students read a brief classical myth, the tale of Pygmalion. Pygmalion, you will remember, was an idealist of sorts who sculpts a statue of a beautiful woman and promptly falls in love with his creation. Ask students to put Ovid's myth side by side with Shakespeare's play and look at them until the parallel emerges. The student might even go on to ask what would have happened to Galatea, the statue who comes alive, if she *really* came alive—if she became an independent person with ideas or values separate from those of Pygmalion, and hence no longer a reflection of him. Would Pygmalion have smashed the statue the way Othello destroys Desdemona because she has become both more than, and less than, the lovely image that he created to satisfy his own needs?

The comparatively new academic area of women's studies often draws on one discipline to illuminate another. On that same subject, *Othello*, Professor Gayle Green in an article in *The Journal of Women's Studies in Literature* argues—very convincingly—that the tragedy of Desdemona's murder is the direct result of the socially imposed conceptions of manhood and womanhood that constrain both Othello and Desdemona.

As an English teacher, I might make a more conventional writing assignment on *Othello*, for example, asking the students to analyze the several dramatic functions served in the play by the seemingly minor character of Roderigo. My assignment would not be productive of creative thinking to the extent that an idea-combining assignment would be. On the other hand, given specific instructions, all students could do something with such an assignment. It has been my experience that "creative" assignments offer a fine chance to the highly intelligent and imaginative student, but that the less capable student is merely bewildered and helpless when faced with such an assignment. Since bewilderment and helplessness are not responses we want to elicit from our students, perhaps a reasonable solution is to offer them a choice of writing assignments.

LESSONS FROM THE HISTORY OF SCIENCE

Creative Genius and Control over Innovation: Reflections on the Life and Work of the "Father of the Computer," Charles Babbage

John C. Holley

Two related current developments have spurred interest in individual creativity and the social arrangements which might encourage it. The first is the growth of the high technology industry of computers and microchips here in Massachusetts, and the second is the increasing need to train people to work in computing industries. Does the creation of new technology require inventive and original thinking, and do our schools and universities train young people for such work? These are the questions which provide a current challenge to politicians, developers of computer industries, and educators who aim to expand high technology here in Massachusetts. With these questions in mind, it is revealing to look at the education and social circumstances of the man known as the "Father of the Computer," Charles Babbage, as he struggled to create a new technology in the nineteenth century. Babbage was a man who possessed creative genius in plenty. He produced a bewildering variety of discoveries and inventions in a wide range of fields, and from a social scientist's point of view, the greatest of these was his analysis of the conditions under which scientific invention itself could flourish. Yet, despite his genius, it is one of the great ironies of this man's life that, in identifying the laws under which creativity could take place, Babbage failed to apply them to his own work. Babbage's computers were never built, and his life was filled with bitterness and anger as a result. What can we learn from Babbage's successes and failures about the progress of creativity? The inexorable conclusion is that individual genius alone is not enough, that success depends upon support from the institutions around, and that the hostility of surrounding institutions dooms even the most creative individual to failure.

In the first section of this paper, I describe Babbage's original contribution to understanding how institutions relate to the creation of new ideas. His understanding of the complex structure of human organization, needed in order to bring a scientific project to completion, makes him a founder of scientific management and of operations research. Babbage's failures to apply these principles in his own life are summarized in the second section. His hostile relations with the institutions of organized science and government frustrated the completion of his advanced technology because a highly original product calls for new industrial techniques and capital to support it which are beyond individual capacity to supply. The third and final section considers the consequences of organizational forms for the creative use of computers today. Which of Babbage's brainchildren will be more important, his calculating machines, the computers, or his organization of managerial control? The answer to this question will tell us the direction in which our latest round of technology is heading.

BABBAGE'S RULES FOR SCIENTIFIC RESEARCH

Charles Babbage's finest written work was published in 1833 under the title, "On the Economy of Machinery and Manufactures" (Babbage, 1963). In it, he described many aspects of the use of machinery resulting from his many years supervising the construction of his calculating engine (machine), the "Difference Engine." But his most original and insightful contribution was his explanation of the advantages of industrial production's central technique, the division of labor. The decision to divide up the necessary tasks into related groups and have the simplest jobs done together by untrained workers, while the difficult tasks were reserved for the highly trained few was the essential goal of industrial management and provided the basis for the economic profitability of the division of labor. The "Babbage Principle" has rightly been recognized in recent years as the central organizing rule of Taylorist "scientific management" (Braverman, 1974), and as such has been used in every major modern industry. Babbage identified the source of the economic benefits of being selective in the kind of workers employed, which continues to be so important in societies divided by great differences in training and in the pay levels different kinds of workers command. The principle was to use as much cheap labor as possible on the many unskilled tasks and as little expensive labor as needed on the few skilled tasks.

This logic in the division of labor has been applied most obviously to the manufacturing of such physical objects as cars on an assembly line. But Babbage was quite clear that the same principle was most suitable for organizing mental work, too, and he supplied an extended example in his account of how the French produced their logarithmic tables. Chapter 20, (Babbage, 1963) "On the Mental Division of Labor" makes it absolutely clear that there were great economic and managerial advantages to dividing up the mental work involved in any great scientific research project. The scale of the project was huge. Just one of the tasks included the calculation for a table of logarithms of all the logarithms of the numbers from 1 to 10,000, each calculated to 19 decimals. The tasks were allocated according to a strict division of labor by rank of skill: there were 5 or 6 of the finest mathematicians to set up the method of calculations to be used; there were 7 or 8 skilled calculators to put the results together; and there were 60 to 80 minimally skilled workers who knew only addition and subtraction to do all the repetitive work.

With this arrangement, there were numerous advantages coming from the scientific management of this project. Firstly, there was control over the project as a whole from the top: The organizers knew the current state of the work, and how much remained to be done at any given time. Secondly, they could control and estimate the cost of the project with some accuracy. Expensive labor was limited to a few individuals, and the bulk of the work was done cheaply. Finally, not the smallest advantage was that the work was done highly accurately. It was found that the unskilled mathematicians who knew only the two rules of addition and subtraction were actually more accurate in their calculations than were people who were more skilled and knew more mathematical rules. A paradoxical conclusion, therefore, is that the best quality mental work can be done by those who know least. The explanation of this riddle is that the intelligence lies in the organization of the project as a whole. The thinking was done at the top and the lower workers in the hierarchy did best if they remained uncreative and instead worked simply and reliably.

A further conclusion must be drawn from this example because it has immense consequences for the creative role of individuals. The vast majority of the employees of the French logarithm project not only did not require great skill but moreover were not expected by their employer to become more creative individuals. The routine workers were expected to be reliable and bound by their fixed set of work rules. They would, in fact, have been breaking the rules if they had deviated from their narrow set of instructions; they would have disrupted the project's organization if they had tried to invent new ways of doing their jobs; and they would no doubt have been punished with dismissal if they had been so creative as to do something different at work. Under the rules of management for the division of labor, it is therefore clear that creativity by the wrong kind of people—those low down in the organization— is subversive of good order, is a dereliction of duty, and probably falls under the definition of crime.

If this example of Babbage's is thought for a moment to be unusual, the literature shows that it is typical of the organization of modern scientific research. A look at the way scientific research is done today suggests that the day of the individual inventor has gone. Although it is clear that both the total sum spent on research and development (R&D) and its share of America's gross national product (GNP) have increased, this money does not go to support the creativity of individual geniuses. Bell (1973) claims that R&D accounted for 9% of GNP, whereas a narrower definition puts the figure at 6% (Kumar, 1978, p. 224). But the typical research project is not for basic research, that is, research not for an applied goal but as an end in itself, which is only about 10% of all research and development. The typical scientific research is likely to be for a military contractor (of which we have so many here in Massachusetts), because over 60% of all R&D goes to meet the "external challenge" (Kumar, 1978, p. 229). And the way in which research on military contracts is carried out is strictly hierarchical, according to the Babbage principle of the division of labor.

Gorz (1976) has shown that scientific research has become institutionalized. Discoveries are expected to come from large organizations set up to produce new products, not from individuals or small teams working out of garage workshops. Even though the Wright brothers invented the airplane out of their home workshop, space inventions should come only from the biggest corporations or government agencies. The same applies to the development of the next generation of microchips: These can be developed only with major funding in a laboratory; they won't surprise us by coming off somebody's basement workbench. The difference is what makes "high technology" so high: it is out of the reach of the ordinary inventor. The typical worker in the new scientific corporation is the technician, someone with a specific skill in operating one kind of machine, and doing but a fragment of the whole project in a routine way, repeating it many times. Is this not exactly one of the third class of logarithm calculators?

How Babbage came to understand that this was a necesary result of scientific research, and how he dealt with this in his own life are described in the next section.

BABBAGE'S LIFETIME OF CREATIVE GENIUS

Charles Babbage's life began in opposition to formal organization and continued that way. As a boy, he had very little formal schooling. Although his father was a wealthy provincial banker, Charles was a sickly child and went to a variety of private schools, liking none of them. But his one passion was algebra, at which he was entirely self-taught. This hobby he developed by his own reading until there were few who could teach him anything. Having exhausted the materials in the English language, he began translating mathematical work from the French, which in the early nineteenth century was advanced far beyond that of the English. Indeed, English education was so backward and decayed that when Babbage went to Cambridge University in 1811, "he thus found himself far in advance of his tutor's mathematical attainments" (*Dictionary of National Biography*, 1885.). This naturally frustrated him, and he had contempt for the academic institution which set itself up to teach people when its teachers were, in fact, ignorant. This kind of self-assurance, which came from being an autodidact, made him highly critical of institutions which did not meet his high standards and which he saw as holding back, rather than fostering, the creative genius of the best.

Because there was no adequate textbook or teacher, Babbage and some of his fellow students, Herschel, Peacock, and Woodhouse, literally sat down to write the book themselves. What they did was use the new notation to modernize algebra, and the text they created, with its problems and examples, became a standard for years (Becher, 1980). Babbage went on to make a number of important contributions to mathematics and became Lucasian Professor of Mathematics at Cambridge University, although he was never inclined to do any teaching. Had he done no more, he would have been an interesting mathematician. But Babbage had two things in his favor which were to take him on to greater things. Firstly, he had a restlessly inquisitive mind which constantly took him on to new topics and more challenging problems. Secondly, he had the kind of private income which permitted him to live as a gentleman scientist, employed by no one, working in his house in London at whatever project took his fancy.

After some work with the properties of electromagnetism, a social problem attracted his attention which he quickly saw could benefit from the application of mathematics. The problem was one of establishing accurate life-expectancy tables. This might not seem like a pressing social problem but, in early nineteenth-century Britain, it was not simply a dry actuarial problem of mortality rates. The breakup of traditional means of support for old age and for descendents was accelerating with the advance of industrialization and the modern economy. The rich could no longer rely solely on the value of the argicultural land they owned and had to diversify into modern occupations of financial and business management. When a man was actively engaged in business or employed for the services he rendered, death cut off that supply of income; that could be disastrous for a man's family if he left business debts. At the time, the law did not permit incorporation with limited liability, so a man's personal assets were at risk in any business venture, while, in addition, the debt law was such that men were still thrown into prison for the nonpayment of debts. The public sought an answer to the financial disaster of sudden death in a money-making society.

The answer people sought was life insurance, and insurance societies sprang up rapidly. The big problem of the time, though, was to find sound financial principles upon which life insurance companies could be run. And it was here that Babbage came in. First, he applied himself to calculating the necessary life tables, an important demographic and statistical achievement in itself. Babbage's tables were copied and used throughout Britain and Europe wherever insurance and friendly societies formed. Then he went on to master the economics of running an insurance company and wrote a book on the subject in 1826 entitled "A Comparative View of the Various Institutions for the Assurance of Lives" (Babbage, 1967). In estimating the comparative benefits of spending a certain sum of money on a life insurance policy or alternatively investing it in a savings bank, Babbage produced lots of tables with many cells, increasing step by step with each year or different assumption. It was from this concern with printing large tables accurately that Babbage derived his next project: it was to be fateful, for it occurred to him that such printing could be done by machine, hence his concern with calculating machines.

Babbage went beyond the calculating engines which had been known since Pascal by adding the mathematical idea that a whole series of numbers in any given table could be created by the repeated addition to fundamental numbers of a common "difference" or element. Hence, Babbage called his machine the Difference Engine, "engine" at that time meaning any kind of machine. He read a paper on this idea before the Astronomical Society (which he helped found in 1820) and was encouraged to continue. But the history of this machine was not to be a happy one, for it was beset with difficulties, some of which were of Babbage's own making. A look at the problems of this calculating machine is instructive, for it shows how much more than individual creative genius is needed in order to bring a new piece of scientific technology into being.

Few people doubted that Babbage's first calculating machine could have been built and made workable; he was too good a mathematician and engineer for any doubts about that. The real doubts existed about how long the whole project would take and how much it would all cost. Babbage had himself to blame in that he kept wanting to make changes to his design. It was obvious to him that they were improvements, but for the progress of the work it would have been better to stick to one early design even if better ones were discovered later. But this was not the most serious problem at all. The root problem of the Difference Engine was money.

Babbage sank a considerable part of his personal fortune into making this first machine, but he saw that even his £6,000 was not going to be enough. He sought funding from the government and eventually got some support, but the agreement was so badly made that money was late in arriving and hard to control on either side. In a word, the project had money-management problems. Babbage frequently had to pay the workmen out of his own pocket because the government money arrived late. The government was slow, corrupt, and not geared up to fund research and development. Babbage met the indifference of government officials and the hostility and jibes of politicians. Understandably, his opinion of government declined to equal the low level in which he held other institutions, like the universities. Interestingly, Babbage stood for parliament twice in the London borough of Finsbury as a Liberal, but came out bottom of the poll on both occasions. He was not a man who could tolerate fools. He thought that simply to state the truth was enough to convince every person of it, while his espousal of various novel ideas and causes made him look very eccentric. It is not surprising that politics was one area in which Babbage failed.

Another area that went creditably well was the construction on all the new machinery and tools for making the new calculating engine. This took far longer than Babbage had anticipated, but his ingenious mind produced many new engineering tools for the cutting of the toothed gears and all the other operations in building a complex mechanical device. In such a computing machine, each number was represented in the circles of geared wheels, which turned as the calculations progressed. Babbage had the workshop for constructing all this built next to his London house and spent many hours on the workbenches, doing not only all the detailed engineering drawings, but also designing and building new tools for making the machine. He even devised a new notation for use in engineering to describe all the possible movements of a piece of machinery. In this area we can see his detailed attention to the process of production, in particular the substitution of mechanical for hand labor, which concepts were so important in his book *On the Economy of Machinery and Manufactures* (1963).

What was good from the point of view of harnessing Babbage's creative ideas was not so good from the point of view of rapid progress. Like another Victorian engineer, I.K. Brunel, Babbage was not good at delegating. Actually, he proposed the idea that the government provide a supervising engineer to run the whole project. Babbage had plenty of other things to get on with and did not want to waste 20 years of his life supervising a scheme beyond which his lively mind had long since progressed. But, typically, the government did not follow his suggestion or put the finances on a sound footing. When the money flow ceased one day, the subcontractor ran off with all the tools (as he was apparently legally entitled to do) and the project came to a complete stop. Despite Babbage's many letters and meetings with various administrations, incredibly, the government left him without an answer for 8 years as to whether or not he would get any more funding.

When an answer finally came, it was in the negative. Although the government was ready to forget all the debts and give Babbage title to the machine, there was to be no more money. Hence, the Difference Engine was dead. The machine was never completed and the fragment that was built went to rest in the museum at South Kensington. An ironic footnote is that a Swedish father-and-son team, the Scheutzs, read a description of Babbage's machine and built a simpler version with some help from the Academy of Sweden and the Diet of Sweden. Their machine was put into use, and Babbage was generous in praising the Scheutzs when they won the gold medal at the Great Exposition of Paris in 1855. The final irony was that the British government, which had treated Babbage so badly, ended up buying a version of the Scheutz machine in 1864 in order to calculate its tables (Dubbey, 1978, p. 192), when Babbage had worked out the principles some 40 years earlier.

Some conclusions on the failure of the Difference Engine to be completed are firstly, that new technology requires more resources than even an independently wealthy man can bring to it, and secondly, that the economics of its production require scientific management or an open funding policy. On the first point, the so-called spin off from a new technology project is, in fact, a retooling of industry; the bigger the project, the bigger the new industrial production techniques it calls into being. The Difference Engine required great advances in mechanical engineering, and engineers in the nineteenth century would agree that Babbage's scheme had more than repaid its cost in the engineering improvements it brought. But the point was that the government had not agreed to finance the retooling of the engineering industry; it just wanted to build one machine. This leads to the second point, the need to control costs. The logical way to reduce costs was to impose a division of labor on the project, as Babbage well knew in theory because he had written the book on the subject. But he failed to apply the mental division of labor to himself. We may well ask, Why not? The answer lies, as everyone knows, in the quality of work life which results. When someone is so dedicated to a project that it becomes his life's work, it has emotional and intellectual satisfactions for him. In a word, it is the spiritual side of human work which is lost under the Babbage-style division of labor; and although he recommended it to others, Babbage wanted none of it imposed on himself.

What were the alternatives to the chaos of Babbage's first calculating engine-building project and the soulless rigor of his managerial division of labor? Babbage's own answer was to abandon all outside help, to ignore the government and the learned societies, and to do his next project entirely by himself. His great aim was to build a far superior calculating machine, one with greater flexibility and power than the Difference Engine—in fact, the machine which was to earn him later the title, "the Father of the Computer." This new machine would be able to do almost all calculations, indeed to be programmable, and we must give him credit for all the aspects of later computers which he anticipated. But his chosen method of producing this machine was weak, given the resources needed (as we have seen). To attempt to go it alone was heroic, but Quixotic, too. His mother encouraged him to devote himself to the new project, even if it meant living on nothing but bread and cheese (Dubbey, 1978, p. 195). Although he spent nearly 40 years on it, he could not complete the new machine, even though he had solved all the major problems and completed engineering drawings of all the main mechanisms. One man's resources in time and labor were too little to create what was a minor industry of its own, and the new machine was never built, either.

Lest we think that Babbage's whole life and work were a failure, we should pause to note the great achievements which distinguished Charles Babbage from just any failed and eccentric inventor. Babbage's reputation has risen only in the last generation since modern electronic computers have become important. In recent years there has been a rush to write the history of computers and, as this has happened, the magnitude of Babbage's achievement has grown in the public perception. At the end of his life he was known only as an eccentric whose machine would never be built. Babbage never lost faith in the idea that computers would someday be built—if not by him, then perhaps 50 years later. Most scoffed at him, however, and remember him only for his vituperative attacks on those people and institutions which had thwarted him, and for his obsession with the irritating noise made by organ grinders, the street musicians of his day. But today there is an institute named after him, the Charles Babbage Institute for the History of Information Processing at the University of Minnesota, and his reputation continues to rise along with the number of publications about him.

Babbage's fame rests on the achievements of his second machine, the "Analytical Engine," and it is best to get an appreciation of this from someone who understands both Babbage's mathematics and modern computers. Such a review comes from John Dubbey, a professor of mathematics and computer science, who gave the following review recently. The Analytical Engine anticipated the modern computer in six ways, according to Dubbey (1978):

1. Babbage identified the five basic units of a computer:
    a. the "store" containing the data, instructions and intermediate calculations.
    b. the "mill" or core in which basic arithmetical operations are performed.
    c. the "control" of the whole operation, in Babbage's case this was done by means of a Jaquard loom system.
    d. the "input" by means of punched cards.
    e. the "output" which automatically prints results.

    Babbage also anticipated the following:
2. The registering apparatus by means of which instructions could be repeated many times as desired, i.e., looping.
3. The capability of the Analytical Engine to make decisions in the course of a calculation, and reverse the sequence of cards to continue the operation at any desired place in the program.
4. The logically contrived program to analyze any calculation into basic steps that the engine could perform in sequence.
5. The realization that the engine was capable of performing any analytical calculation.
6. An estimate of the amount of storage space required. (p. 217)

Nor are these all, for they are only the main achievements. Given that Babbage had put so much in place, many things followed from it. For example, he wanted to save his cards (making the first program library), and his collaborator, Ada Augusta Byron, Countess Lovelace, wrote the world's first computer program for Babbage's engine. The list will probably lengthen as we find out more about Charles Babbage's remarkable mind.

THE LESSONS OF BABBAGE'S LIFE AND WORK FOR TODAY

Now that Babbage's brainchild, the computer, has come into widespread use, what can we say about the process of creativity which goes into the making and use of computers today? And what can Babbage's life and work tell us about such creative use in our own time? When we look behind all the boosterism of the latest "high technology" industry, some remarkable and old-fashioned patterns emerge. How is the new technology of computers used? and, how are new computer programs and systems created? A number of important studies of these subjects have been conducted by Philip Kraft and Steven Dubnoff and show that the newness of the industry has not exempted it from the organizational rules which govern older enterprises. When we look at how people work in the computer industry in the Boston area, we find that there is an increasingly strict division of labor being applied in which all the various tasks of computer systems are being separated out and graded according to pay. Kraft and Dubnoff show, by looking behind titles like "systems analyst" and "systems programmer" at the job tasks actually done, that there is more and more of a distinction being drawn between those who buy hardware and who supervise others and those who actually write computer code and document programs. Increasingly, the latter are lower paid, whereas the former are becoming higher paid (Kraft and Dubnoff, 1984).

If all this sounds familiar, it should, because it was described by Babbage in 1835 as a feature of the division of labor in big industry. The people working in such industries find themselves subject to a narrowing definition of their tasks, which they must complete as technicians with only a limited repertoire of solutions. The pay levels reflect this differentiation of tasks. While the code writers actually do the software programming, they are amongst the lowest paid in their industry, according to Kraft and Dubnoff. The highest paid are those with managerial tasks like supervising others and buying hardware. The kinds of people who typically fill these roles reveal the endurance of social stereotypes: the low-paid programmers are frequently young women, whereas the high-paid managers are typically middle-aged men. The result is a gender gap in computer programming which regenerates sexual stratification in this new industry (Dubnoff and Kraft, 1984).

Of course, computers have brought some changes to organizations, chiefly of a temporary, dislocating kind. Some managers have resisted

computerization of their departments, fearing the retraining and dislocation involved. But, increasingly, it is being seen as a time for the
redefinition of the managerial processes and an opportunity for the
recentralization of information in the hands of senior managers. This
reassertion of hierarchical control promises to accentuate the overskill-
ing of a few in control at the top and to routinize and deskill the work
of the many, just as Babbage asserted it would. Probably, the best opportunities for creative originality remain in small software companies
where there are low capital barriers to entry and the small scale of the
enterprises means that the Babbagian division of labor has not been
taken very far. We can conclude, therefore, that in modern times it is
not Babbage's computer which is more important but his managerial
division of labor. Even in his own industry of computing, the principle
of hierarchical control over the new has asserted itself and, as a result,
Babbage should be known rather as the Father of Scientific Management than as the Father of the Computer.

Are there alternatives to the control of computer work by a few? Are
there opportunities for the innovative and creative use of computing
technology? I believe that the answer is in the affirmative, and there is
evidence of this around us. The people who are making the most imaginative use of computers today are those freelance computer owners
who have become devoted to their machines and spend many hours of
their own time in unpaid pursuit of new knowledge. Many of these
people are young, although they do not need to be in order to be computer devotees. They have linked the small personal computer, the microcomputer, to the telephone to add the power of telecommunications
to their own. In this way, with relatively little initial cost, they can communicate with other micro users via bulletin boards and hence build up
networks of peers with whom information can be shared on any subject,
from football through electronics to recipes. Such people's style is non-
hierarchical and mixes work with pleasure. It is often done at home,
which adds to the blurring of the distinction between work and leisure.
And, what is more, their techniques are unstandardized, self-indulgent,
and expressive of their character rather than strictly instrumental. A
study of their programming style indicates that private programmers
write very long, undocumented programs that are unique and personal.
Wilkes concludes that they are more like an art form than a businesslike
science (Wilkes, 1984). And, with these shared resources and improvised
programs, small-scale users can communicate with large mainframe
computers and gain all the scope of memory and analytical power they
desire.

Not everyone is enthusiastic about the creativity of these self-taught
programmers. When they share access codes, which permits them to dial

up and log on to computers, they may be unwelcome guests; and when they deliberately try to break into communications networks where they are not wanted, they are called "hackers" facing the threat of legal action. Are they really breaking the law when they take what is an open and communal resource? Is this the direction in which we want the law to be rewritten so as to deny the public access to computer systems? These are many-sided issues, and our answer to them must depend upon whether we value more the creativity which yields access to information or the hierarchy which seeks to centralize and limit access to electronically transmitted knowledge. The issue is not an easy one, because it seems, at first sight, easy to distinguish the professional from the hacker. But are they really so far apart? The question is whether we are ready to accept some costs associated with this freedom as the price of creativity. Included in such costs are the conflicts between those who like the sociologist Robert Merton (1959), would define innovation as crime, and those who see today's deviance as tomorrow's truth and progress.

CONCLUSIONS ON CREATIVITY

What conclusions can we draw from Charles Babbage's life and work about the conditions under which creative genius can flourish? From Babbage's own education we might infer that some skepticism about formal education was warranted, but this is not the main lesson, in my view. The overwhelming evidence shows that a creative individual mind is not enough, and that it must be supported and encouraged by sympathetic institutions which are willing to provide their resources in assistance. Babbage floundered and then suffered isolation because he was supported neither by governments nor by professional societies like the Royal Society in England. One of the most important inhibitors of creativity is the hierarchical principle of organizing large research projects, which Babbage identified as being so economical and efficient and yet so deadly to a person's creative genius that he shunned it himself. Our need is to find alternatives to this kind of scientific management, which divides labor, and encourage organizational forms which support individual creativity.

Babbage's life suggests the following requirements for a practical scheme to encourage creative thinking when it occurs: Firstly, we should avoid the Babbagian division of labor and, instead, encourage a diversity of tasks and a pay structure which avoids excessive difference between team members. Secondly, organizations which want to develop creativity should not set definite and narrow goals. They should, on the contrary, expect the unexpected, the innovative, and the original. Thirdly, they should not count costs and estimate benefits in terms of a fixed set of goals and results. They should be prepared to spend money according to their means and admit that many of the benefits are un-measurable in terms of specifiable goals. They should frankly accept that the payoff comes in spin-off inventions and external benefits to the people involved. Finally, our new creative organizations must not be overworried about change and dislocation; on the contrary, they should be tolerant and forbearing. Creativity needs space in which to grow and should not be shut in by those who would rush to stigmatize innovation as deviance. Too often, creative genius has been called eccentric, dan-gerous, and illegal, and Charles Babbage in his time was called all of these. Our aim must be to judge creative people by their potential for improving our lives, not by their challenges to our traditional ways.

REFERENCES

Babbage, C. (1967). *A comparative view of the various institutions for the assurance of lives.* New York: Augustus Kelley Reprints. (Original work published 1826)

Babbage, C. (1963). *On the economy of machinery and manufactures* (4th ed. enlarged). New York: Augustus Kelley Reprints. (Original work published 1835)

Becher, H. W. (1980). Woodhouse, Babbage, Peacock and modern algebra. *Historica Mathematica, 7* (4), 389–400.

Bell, D. (1973). *The coming of post industrial society: A venture in social forecasting.* New York: Basic Books.

Braverman, H. (1974). *Labor and monopoly capital: The degradation of work in the twentieth century.* New York: Monthly Review.

Bromley, A. G. (1982). Charles Babbage's analytical engine, 1838. *Annals of the History of Computing, 4* (3), 196–217.

Bromley, A. G. (1983). Inside the world's first computer: Charles Babbage. *New Scientist, 99* (1375), 781–784.

Dictionary of national biography (1885). Babbage, Charles (1792–1871).

Dubbey, J. M. (1978). *The mathematical work of Charles Babbage.* Cambridge: Cambridge University Press.

Dubnoff, S., & Kraft, P. (1984). *Gender stratification in computer programming.* Paper presented to the annual meeting of the Eastern Sociological Association, Boston.

Gorz, A. (1976). On the class character of science and scientists. In H. Rose & S. Rose (Eds.), *The political economy of science.* London: Macmillan.

Kraft, P. (1977). *Programmers and managers: The routinization of computer programming in the United States.* New York and Heidelberg: Springer–Verlag.

Kraft, P. & Dubnoff, S. (1984). *The division of labor, fragmentation and hierarchy in computer software work.* Paper presented to the annual meeting of the Eastern Sociological Association, Boston.

Kumar, K. (1978). *Prophecy and progress: The sociology of industrial and post industrial society.* Harmondsworth, England: Penguin.

Laver, M. (1983). A century of catching up with Babbage. *New Scientist, 99* (1375), 778–780.

Merton, R. K. (1959). Social structure and anomie. In R. Bendix & S. M. Lipset (Eds.), *Class, status and power*. Englewood Cliffs: Prentice-Hall.

Roth, N. A. (1983). Charles Babbage Institute preserves info processing's rich history. *Data Management, 21* (4), 44–45.

Wilkes, J. M. (1984). *The Hacker challenge: Artistry, addiction or subversion?* Paper presented to the annual meeting of the Eastern Sociological Association, Boston.

SYMPOSIUM

PANEL 3

Scientific Discovery: A Model for Creativity

Rebecca McBride DiLiddo

Albert Szent-Giorgi once said, "Discovery consists of seeing what every-one else has seen and thinking what no one else has thought" (Johnson, 1983, p. 16). These words have been used to define both the process we call science and the quality we call creativity. Creativity, the motivating force behind works of art, has not traditionally been seen to be so close an ally of the works of scientists. Discovery in science is seen by many as the end result of a systematic search directed by the scientific method. The scientific method is the stepwise process of hypothesis formation and testing that leads to the proof or refutation of the original hypothesis. Observers of the process behind scientific discoveries see this visible process which overshadows the motivating force that first sparked the search. The scientific method is a blueprint that plans what is to be done but tells us nothing about the ideas that produced the plan. It is the framework within which discovery can occur but shows us nothing about the moment when that framework becomes a three-dimensional form in the mind of the creator. This is the moment when something which has never been known before becomes known. This is the moment when the quality of creativity is displayed. This is the creative event.

This moment is described by Laura Levine as she remembers the creative event that resulted in her realization of the relationship of the molecules of actin and myosin in muscle tissue. "[I]t's like one of those moments in analysis when you see ... the truth of something that you have been staring at unseeingly for years." (Gornick, 1983, p. 60).

An idea is born in a creative event and is validated by the application of the scientific method. Without creativity, scientific research would be merely a laboratory exercise performed to verify what is already known to be true. That a creative event is backed by a period of plodding, mechanistic, tedious work should not be surprising. Art and music also require long periods of concentrated technical work after the moment of inspiration, which initiated the work, has long passed. K.C. Cole (1983) has written that "it would be a sloppy artist who worked without tight creative control and no scientist ever got very far by sticking to the scientific method" (p.63). Both the arts and the sciences have a creative and a mechanistic component. Each generates ideas in a moment of creativity that receive validation through an extended period of labor.

The nature of the creative event in science is best understood through an examination of scientists who have experienced such a moment. Through this examination we will see that Richard Fenyman (Fenyman, 1975) was right when he said, "A new idea is extremely difficult to think of. It takes fantastic imagination" (p. 129).

Charles Darwin was an unlikely candidate to start a scientific revolution. He spent his youth and young manhood as a typical English aristocrat. He entered the university at the insistence of his father to earn a degree in medicine. He spent nearly as much time in the taverns and the fields as he did in the classroom. Finding medicine distasteful, he settled on a career in theology. It was a respectable field and as pastor of a small country parish he would have time for his other interests of hunting and the collection of beetles. But his mentor, John Henslow, was to disrupt these plans with an offer for Darwin to be a naturalist on a British sailing expedition to South America. This voyage launched Darwin into a search to answer questions about the very nature of living organisms and their origins (Stone, 1980).

The answers to these questions would cause man to change irreversibly his view of nature and himself. Darwin spent 5 years on the journey collecting specimens, studying geological formations, and absorbing experiences. On his return to England, as he worked over his specimens and remembered all he had seen and experienced, a question kept gnawing at him. How could one explain the variety of new organisms he had encountered as well as the absences of familiar species such as rabbits. The South American interior was a perfect habitat for rabbits, but there were none there. Instead, there was a rabbitlike animal that performed as a rabbit in the habitat and even looked like a rabbit (Wallace & Sanders, 1981). The endemic species of tortises and finches on the Galapagos Islands also were a puzzle. Each species was exactly matched morphologically to the food sources and habitat of its island of origin.

As Darwin pondered these observations, an idea to explain them began to form that linked the form of the organism to the demands of its native environment. Others had proposed such a linkage before but had lacked either the solid evidence to support the ideas or a mechanism by which the theory could work. Darwin had the evidence. He had volumes of data on anatomy, embryology, breeding experiments, and geology. What he lacked was a mechanism. One afternoon, as he lay recovering from a recurring illness, he picked up a copy of Thomas Malthus's work, *A Theory of Populations* (Johnson, 1983). Applying Malthus's ideas to his data on animals and plants, Darwin saw a way by which some features of a species could be maintained within a population and others could be eliminated. He saw that, over time, this process could generate forms distinct from the forms of previous populations. The theory of natural selection upon which his theory of evolution was based was born in this moment. Johanson writes that Darwin speaks of insight as a sort of instinct unsupported by reasons (Johanson and Eddy, 1982). This modesty does not acknowledge the prodigious work upon which his ideas were based or his own gift for synthesis. Darwin's genius lay in his ability to draw together hundreds of isolated facts into a coherent explanation. His "instinct" was a tremendous synthetic energy we call creativity. He had the ability spoken of by Samuel Butler (Keyes, 1951) to "draw sufficient conclusions from insufficient premises" (p. 222).

A similar moment of insight is described by Melvin Calvin in an interview with Frank Salisbury (Salisbury & Ross, 1985) as Calvin recalls the moment when he understood the process of carbon dioxide fixation in photosynthesis.

> I can remember being at home reading a JACS article on sugars. I realized how a carbon dioxide could add to a keto-sugar. . . . It was this recognition which allowed me to draw the whole thing out. It was done almost at once, because the pieces had been accumulating over several years. (pp. 214–215)

The light bulb had flashed again and another new idea was born.

In both cases, the moment of creativity was powered by the slow accumulation of a large base of knowledge over a long period of time. What appears to be an instantaneous flash is a discharge of creative energy that has been building for some time. The fusion of the pieces into a complete idea requires a spark—that moment of insight. We see the fact-gathering process as an aimless wandering and give the full credit to the instantaneous flash that saved the lost soul from the abyss of ignorance. The seemingly aimless wandering is really an essential part of the process which creates the fuzzy outline that insight brings into clear focus.

Another strong force in generating creative events is the observation of the unexpected. When a scientist performs an experiment, there is usually an expected result. Often this result is not obtained. The unpredictable nature of science has been a constant source of bewilderment for beginning students and frustration for seasoned scientists. Unexpected results challenge the belief in the predictability of the natural world and the immutability of scientific laws. The fact is that predictability is, itself, a nebulous concept. Exactness of predictability is only as precise as the ability to reproduce the conditions under which the observation was first made. This unpredictability of science leaves the door open to the unexpected.

Wilhelm Roentgen was performing experiments on electrons using a cathode ray tube. When an experiment was in progress, he noticed that fluorescent materials, some distance from the tube, glowed. Photographic film near the tube was exposed during experiments. These effects were not expected. To Roentgen, they implied that some previously unobserved force was liberated from the electron activity in the cathode ray tube. Further research identified X-rays and harnessed them for use (DeRopp, 1972). The behavior of the fluorescent materials and the film could have been overlooked or dismissed as unimportant. A trained observer was able to see the events for their true significance. The realization of the importance of the unexpected event requires the special abilities of a creative mind. A mind that sees not two and two, but four.

Albert Michelson and Edward Morley set out to measure the speed of the earth as it moves through space. At the time, light was thought to move as a wave through a substance called the ether that filled all of the "vacuum" of space. They based their experimental design on the premise that, when the speed of light measured from a point moving into the ether is compared to the speed of light measured from a point moving away from the ether, an absolute speed of the earth's motion could be calculated. But even though their instrument was able to detect differences in the speed of light as small as 0.0000001%, the speed of light remained constant regardless of the relationship of the site of measurement to the "ether." This constancy was unexpected and called for an explanation (Swenson, 1972). Lorentz and Fitzgerald, well-known physicists of the time, tried to reconcile these startling results with the physical "reality" of the ether. They explained that the speeds of light only appeared to be the same. They explained that this illusion was caused because the apparatus and ether were bent by the earth's gravitational field just enough to offset any actual changes in speed which occurred. He could provide no reasonable explanation for why the bending should be so synchronized, however (Wertheimer, 1981). The true meaning of the lack of a detectable change in the speed of light under these circumstances was used by another—Albert Einstein. He said that such a constancy of the speed of light meant that there was no ether and that velocity becomes a ratio of distance travelled to time. Space and time became independent quantities and all motion became relative (Hewitt, 1971).

There is argument about the true influence of Michelson and Morley's experiment on the development of Einstein's theory of relativity. There is no argument, however, that he used their results to support his contentions that the speed of light is a constant. This idea formed a cornerstone in Einstein's renovation of physical theory that set the foundations of modern physical laws (Wertheimer, 1981). He was able to observe the unexpected and to see its true significance, even though it meant embracing a new reality.

There always exists the possibility that the unexpected event was the result of a mistake and, therefore, without significance. The importance of the unexpected as a motivator of creativity does not lie in the validity of the event. Even an error can lead to discovery when observed by a creative mind.

A drug maker mixed up a batch of synthetic heroin. Being greedy, he took some shortcuts to increase his profit margin. With his heroin, he also got a large amount of MPTP (1,2,5,6-tetrahydropyridine). His customers turned up in the emergency room with symptoms of advanced Parkinson's disease. Their symptoms were puzzling because they had no history of the degenerative process of the disease. Ballard and Langston, the doctors investigating the case, sensed that this was more than a usual drug poisoning. A coworker remembered a report of a similar incident some years before in an obscure psychology journal (Lewin, 1981).

The study of diseases of unknown origin, such as Parkinson's, is made difficult because scientists have no reliable method by which to induce the disease in lab animals. All research requires human subjects which puts severe ethical restrictions on the types of data that are obtainable. The discovery that MPTP induces the symptoms of Parkinson's disease made possible the use of animals in the search for the organic cause and eventually a cure. The first team had been looking for a cure, not a cause. To them, the poisonings were interesting but of no importance in reaching their goal.

The first event had not impressed the researchers observing it. The second event found more fertile ground. A decade of research time had been lost because the unexpected had failed to alert the minds of researchers that something significant was happening. It has been said that a mind which can not be surprised will never make a great discovery. In this case, it was true.

The importance of the unexpected as a motivating force in creativity lies in its ability to startle. After the initial jolt, the mind must decide whether the unexpected observation was a fluke, a mistake, or a valid occurrence justifying closer scrutiny. The observer must first be able to recognize that the unexpected event is important. Because experimental results are unpredictable, this is not always an easy task. An unexpected event is not always of itself enough to trigger interest. It is in the evaluation process that follows where the creative mind can succeed where others fail. The creative mind steps beyond the obvious into the imaginative interpretation. This imaginative approach grows out of a trust in one's own work even in the face of surrounding dissent. T.S. Painter reported in 1921 that the human-cell nucleus had 48 chromosomes. The report was given with such conviction that the count stood unchallenged until 1955. Two Swedish workers demonstrated that the true number was 46 chromosomes. After their announcement, others stepped forward to say that they, too, had counted 46 but had felt that they had made errors in their counts (Kottler, 1974). Their minds were not jolted to discovery, but stunned to silence. The perception that the true number was 48 overpowered their trust in their own work and shielded their minds from the startling power of the unexpected.

This is not unusual. The powerful force of the unexpected often acts in opposition to the numbing force of dogma. The dogma of science serves as a reservoir of all the accepted explanations of natural phenomena. A scientist depends upon this base of established facts to predict and interpret experimental results. This base of stability is constantly assulted by the unexpected. A scientist must embrace a body of knowledge whose validity can change at any moment.

A mind which is open to seemingly outrageous ideas is open to the creative experience. A mind that works in closed patterns seeing all events as results of known forces will not be known for its inventiveness.

The interpretation of observations to produce new knowledge requires one to be able to see beyond the obvious and the predictable. It is this vision which can fire creativity. Those who have this vision discover new ideas; those who do not are doomed to repeat the ideas of others. A scientist works with a dependence on dogma but must not allow the dogma to block the creative forces of the unexpected and vision.

One morning, Donald Johanson (Johanson & Edey, 1982) surveyed the piles of work in his tent. He heard their urgent call, but listened instead to a quiet voice which told him today he was going to find something big. He and Tom Gray set out across the Afar plains to search for hominid fossils. As noon approached, the oppressive heat drove them back toward camp. But the feeling of imminent discovery drew Johanson over one more hill. As he descended the rise, he looked down.

There it was—a jaw; then a femur; then many more. Together they comprised the most complete hominid fossil found to that date, and the
most amazing.

The fossil, later named Lucy, shook the foundations of paleontological dogma and rewrote the fossil history of mankind. Dogma had said
that it was man's bigger brain that led to tool use which, in turn, freed
the hands for walking upright. Dogma had also said that the line from
man to the ancestoral primate was a straight evolutionary sequence with
no branches or dead ends. A study of the Lucy fossil and accompanying
data led Johanson and his coworkers to another interpretation of the
evolution of humans. Lucy had a skull with features that represented an
intermediate stage in the evolution from primates to humans. Although
her features and geological age indicated that she was primitive, she
had the advanced behavioral trait of upright gait. The order of the evolution of human traits was reversed with upright walking coming first,
followed by tool usage, and then increased brain size. The family tree
of man became one of many branches, not a straight twig. The careful
study of the new information gave the Johanson group the courage to
face the dogma and the vision to see beyond it to a new view of reality.

The Leakeys—Louis, Mary, and their son, Richard—have added
greatly to our knowledge of the fossil record of human evolution. Louis
Leakey developed definite ideas about the record, including such concepts as the "dogma." Upon his death, these ideas were inherited by
Mary and Richard. They held to these ideas even in the face of supporting evidence which was contradictory and questionable to many
other paleontologists. Dedication to personal preconceptions clouded
their vision and kept them from the consideration of the validity of new
approaches. Both the Johanson and Leakey groups had access to the
same information. Johanson's group derived courage and vision from
the data to leap beyond the dogma into a new chapter in the fossil
history of humans. The Leakeys remained locked into the dogma, continuing to interpret new finds with old ideas. They were held back from
creative insights by the dike of dogma (Johanson, 1982).

The Johanson group was also helped by another force that can support creative thought. This is the force generated by the clashing of
minds of differing backgrounds and views. Within the Johanson group
were scientists with widely different ideas about the fossils and their
interpretation. These minds thrashed around in the evidence, challenging one another until a final hypothesis emerged that fit all the data.
The Leakeys were of one mind. They received no stimulation from the
conflict of opposing views. Without new approaches, the recent finds
were analyzed with ideas focused with foggy spectacles.

This stimulus provided by the conflict of minds is a vital force in creativity. Watson and Crick worked together to decipher the structure of the DNA molecule. Some feel that neither may have been able to accomplish the feat on his own. (Wallace & Sanders, 1981) It was the creative energy produced by the interplay of two minds that forged the pattern upon which the structure of DNA was based. Rosalind Franklin, working in another laboratory in England, provided, without her knowledge, through Maurice Wilkins, the X-ray crystallographs upon which Watson and Crick based their theory of DNA structure. Her notes provided them with two vital pieces of information. Her data confirmed that the sugars and phosphates formed the outer surface of the molecule and that the molecule was an *a*-helix. She died of cancer without ever realizing how helpful she had been. Rosalind was isolated from Watson, Crick, and Wilkins by her femaleness. She was shielded from the creative sparks those minds could have provided (Sayre, 1975). Donald Johanson (1982) writes, "She needed that last push—another mind. She never got it" (p. 293).

The discovery of the structure of DNA shows us that the energy generated by more than one brilliant mind can fall short of precipitating the creative event when cut off from the stimulus provided by the interplay of ideas from others.

The forces that motivate a mind to creativity are varied. But it is not enough for a creative event to occur. In order for a creative event to impact scientific thought and add to our knowledge base the genius of the idea must be recognized. Sometimes it takes as much imagination to recognize a creative event as it does to generate one.

Creativity in science faces the same challenges for acceptance as creative works in other fields. Creative works challenge our concept of reality by expanding it and rewriting the rules by which we judge the value of a new work. T.S. Eliot (1964, p. 5) explains it this way:

> When a new work of art is created ... something happens ... simultaneously to all works of art which have preceded it. The existing order is complete before the new work arrives; for order to persist ... the whole existing order must be ... altered. (First Essay)

Before a new theory is verbalized, the world of science is ordered. Afterward, the scientific world must readjust to the rules of the new order. This resistance to new ideas makes recognition of creativity dependent on timing. The creative event must occur at the right time. The work of many scientists goes unrecognized at the moment of the creative event, but must wait for a time when minds are more receptive to new ideas.

Gregor Mendel announced his work on pea genetics in the late 1860s. His paper presentation met with no response. There was no outcry, no applause—just silence (Ritchie & Carolla, 1983). Barbara McClintock presented her theory of jumping genes to the 1941 and 1943 Cold Spring Harbor Symposia. There was silence—born of awe at the magnitude of the work and of ignorance due to a lack of ability of others to understand what she was saying (Keller, 1981). In 1961, Peter Mitchell proposed a theory of energy production in the cell that required the cooperative efforts of many molecules organized into a system enclosed within an organelle. His theory was so unorthodox that it was considered little better than fantasy by most established scientists (Wallace & Sanders, 1981).

Each of these scientists has since been vindicated. For Mendel and Barbara McClintock, the recognition took over 40 years. For Mitchell, it took about 15 years. McClintock and Mitchell have since both received Nobel prizes for their work. These scientists were all three victims of the expectations that we all have for creative works. We expect that creative works are produced by those who are designated as talented and are developed according to established rules. All three of these scientists were not recognized as legitimate workers. Mendel was a monk who crossed peas as a hobby. He was not a professional scientist or associated with a prominent laboratory. In the 1940's, Barbara McClintock's gender was sufficient to keep her outside the ranks of the established order. Peter Mitchell was kept outside the world of recognized workers by his propensity for developing ideas in his mind instead of in the lab. Such practices made him suspect in the eyes of more serious workers (Wallace & Sanders, 1981). Creative works that do not conform to established rules and techniques for the production of new works are often slow to be accepted. Those who feel that a painting should be constructed using the established techniques of proportion, perspective, and light of the old masters will find modern art hard to accept. Scientists construct new works using accepted ideas. Theories that use ideas not yet imagined or unconventional approaches are often slow to be assimilated into the dogma.

Our ability to comprehend new ideas lies in our repertoire of assimilated facts and preconceptions of reality. Creative minds are able to see realities not yet experienced by others and thus invisible to the less inventive mind. It was an established "fact" that an individual was a blend of characters inherited from both of its parents. The physical attributes of offspring were a mixture of traits midway between the forms of the parents. To think of traits as being inherited as independent units, some of which could cancel the effects of others, was not feasible. Mendel's ideas were so outside the perception of reality of his listeners that his ideas made little impression. For similar reasons, the ideas of Mitchell and McClintock were also dismissed as mere fantasy.

Science depends upon previous knowledge to generate new ideas. These ideas accumulate as new knowledge as they provide answers to previously asked questions. As each question is answered, a new question is generated. A creative mind answers questions that have yet to be asked. When the unsolicited answer appears, it goes unrecognized as a great leap forward because its companion question is missing. A creative mind skips over layers of the question-answer hierarchy to find answers by a different process—the creative event. When a creative mind encounters an experience, it allows the experience to lead it to a conclusion irrespective of all prior experiences.

When Michelson and Morely showed that the ether did not exist, Einstein saw that if this were true then the speed of light is a constant and motion becomes a relative quantity. Einstein used this new knowledge as a support for a whole new view of the universe. These were conclusions totally outside the experience of physicists at the time. Less creative minds rejected the results that did not fit into their perceptions about the basic nature of the universe. Physicists at the time of Einstein could not conceive of a universe without the bonding powers of ether. They struggled to explain the absence of the ether using incorrect assumptions about its existence. A creative mind can see things as they must be, not just as they are. This ability allowed Einstein to step outside the constraints of accepted physical theory into a new vision of reality. This same ability allowed Mendel, McClintock, and Mitchell to see explanations for phenomena not yet even imagined by others. There would be years of questions and answers that would have to accumulate before the world would have the necessary tools with which to properly judge their works.

The forces that work for creativity act to produce creative events and to assure the recognition of the genius of those events by others. Any program to increase creative abilities must address both the creative event itself and its recognition. In order to participate in the creative event, one must see creative acts as possible occurrences. We must understand that (1) creativity is not a gift and (2) that it is not the result of luck. Creative ideas can come to anyone who is prepared to receive them. Few creative people started out as recognized talents. There are prodigies, but they are the exceptions.

The assumption that creativity is a gift leads to the attitude that nothing can be done to stimulate creativity. This attitude can suppress talent that could be released if given the proper training and environment in which to fluorish. The climate for creativity must also provide courage to believe in one's own ideas even if they are unconventional and outside the accepted dogma. We have seen that those who cling to old approaches will often come to the old conclusions. In order to have the courage to experiment, one has to understand that there have been experimental thinkers who have gone before.

A creative event is not the result of an accident or good fortune. Most examples of the role that luck plays in the creative process are really illustrations of how the unexpected triggers a creative event. The event has often been observed by others before and dismissed as a freak occurrence. The observer who discerns the true importance of the event is not lucky, but creative. This realization gives one courage to be innovative and outrageous.

Creativity is not a gift and it is not available to only the lucky. Each person has a potential to be creative, just as each has the potential to learn. The extent of the ability to think in creative ways can be increased by educational programs that open the mind to the forces for creativity. A liberal arts education is one such educational experience. It is the challenge of the liberal arts education to encourage both the production of creative ideas and the ability to recognize the contributions of others. A liberal arts education is well-suited to the task because it prepares the mind to be open to the forces which promote creativity. It includes a broad knowledge base, quantitative skills, practice in skeptical thinking, and application of knowledge to real situations.

A liberal arts education is based on a foundation which exposes a student to all areas of study. No field so relies on the multidisciplined approach as does science. Drawing boundaries between scientific disciplines is not easy because few areas of study in science exist independently. Each area blends into its adjacent field, making pure areas of study hard to maintain. For example, biology and geology would seem to be quite distinct fields. Rocks have few of the attributes of living organisms. A complete geological record requires proper dating of the rocks as well as correct identification of the fossils which they contain. Dating requires the knowledge and tools of the geologist whereas the identification of fossils involves knowledge traditionally held by biologists. Both must work together to gain from the rocks the full message which they hold. A lack of appreciation for the importance of both types of data can lead to serious errors in the search for valuable mineral and fossil fuels or in the interpretation of a fossil.

The importance of broad knowledge to creative thought was best illustrated by Darwin's work. Darwin was not just a zoologist, or a botanist, or a geologist, or a breeder; he was all of these and more than the sum of all of them. Lack of expertise in any one of these fields would have left a void in the knowledge base that fueled his insight into the problem of the generation of variability in organisms. When he read Malthus, he used another area of knowledge—economics—to provide a new perspective. This new field of study provided a view that triggered the creative event leading to the development of the theory of evolution.

Workers in artificial intelligence recognize the dependence of creative solutions on a wide knowledge base. The computer being programmed for creative thought requires a large pool of facts to provide for cross-checking and evaluation of a problem. The information necessary to solve a problem may come from areas of knowledge that are not closely related to the question itself. Florence Nightingale has been immortalized for her career as a nurse to the British troops. In fact, she might be better known for her application of statistics to medicine. It was her imaginative use of statistics that proved to the British military that more soldiers were dying from disease than from battle wounds (Cohen, 1984). A less creative mind would have missed the opportunity to bring together such disparate fields to provide an answer to the problem of massive numbers of soldiers dying on the battlefield.

This dependence of a scientist on a multifaceted background was addressed by Louis Leakey who was asked how one could prepare for a career in paleontology. He replied,

> There is no single course of study which could fit a person for what I am doing. I did a tripos in modern languages, then a tripos in archeology and anthropology, and thereafter a post-graduate course in meterology. (quoted in Johanson & Edey, 1982, p. 7)

What he has described is a liberal arts education which is composed of coursework from the humanities, social, and natural sciences. Such a diverse background provides the foundation upon which observation and experience can work to generate creativity. But diverse knowledge is not sufficient, in all cases, to produce creative answers to questions.

A knowledge base is important, but analytical tools are the keys to unlocking the secrets of the unexpected and to freeing one's mind of the trap of dogma.

After the initial jolt given by the observation of the unexpected, one must determine the status of the observation. Without the ability to discern the important from the mere anomolous, the force for creativity generated by the unexpected will be dissipated. Analytical tools that can test an event's validity and confirm its veracity are essential to the critical judgment that opens the mind to receive the forces for creativity. The quantiative component of a liberal arts education provides such analytical tools. Mathematics, the sciences, statistics, and computer science comprise this vital component. Each provides training in the collection, analysis, and the interpretation of data. The laboratory part of the science component of the curriculum provides an essential element in training to the student. Laboratories provide firsthand experience in handling encounters with the unexpected and testing the validity of preconceived ideas.

Analytical tools aid creativity by allowing for the critical evaluation of incoming information. Without analytical expertise, the true nature of an event may be overlooked and the force for creativity can be lost. Scientific research is littered with the skeletons of such ill-tested truths.

The discovery of the "missing link" was announced in 1912 with the unveiling of the Piltdown man skull. The fossil stirred controversy because of its odd mix of characters. If the fossil were a link between primates and man, it should have had features that were between those of apes and humans. Instead, it had a fully human cranium and teeth and an ape-like jaw. Its discoverers defended the fossil, but a little careful analysis could have revealed the fossil for the sloppy forgery that it was (Millar, 1974). Any amateur paleontologist could have easily spotted the hoax. Even seasoned scientists were fooled because they took the anomalous features of the skull as proof of its validity, not as affronts to its authenticity. Careful analysis could have established the true nature of the features and determined whether the features supported or refuted the claims made for the skull. Theories that are founded on shaky, unverified data can dissolve into fantasy, not spring into inspired wisdom. Creativity can be defeated when one substitutes wishful thinking for the harsh glare of analysis.

The quantitative aspects of a liberal arts education are not the sterile mechanistic anatagonists of creativity, but are tools in the process of the verification of significance vital to sorting the important from the meaningless. Analysis is not the enemy of creativity, but its facilitator, by opening the mind to be acted upon by the forces of the unexpected.

Quantitative tools also provide protection from the trap of dogma that hampers creativity. Even a scientist who is open to novel ideas needs solid information with which to overthrow the accepted interpretation and replace it with a new approach. Tim White felt that the whole picture of human evolution was incorrect but, to convince Donald Johanson to overthrow the accepted dogma and turn the paleontological world upside down, he needed facts, not feelings. It is facts that lead the mind from the obvious to the ingenious. Solid facts focus doubts into new ideas. Analysis becomes a framework upon which new ideas can be hung. The Michelson-Morely experiment became the framework upon which Einstein could hang his impression that the speed of light is a constant. Creativity brings together the fantasy of feelings with the proof of analysis to convince oneself and others of the truth of a new reality.

Knowledge and analytical skills are facilitators of creativity, but the force which powers the search for new ideas lies in a skeptical approach to knowledge.

Skepticism, testing of the established view of the natural world, frees the mind from dependence upon dogma and leaves it open to the forces for creative thought. A mind released from the black and white of certainty into the greyness of maybe is on its way to discovery.

Chambers (1969) has shown that creative scientists have the ability to think autonomously and in original thought patterns. This originality will not find a welcome in a mind dedicated to the conservation of dogma. A liberal arts education stimulates creativity by facilitating the development of a skeptical attitude. Such an education exposes a student to the many perspectives of a variety of disciplines and can develop an appreciation for the chameleonlike nature of our perceptions of reality. One can begin to understand how an observation can be influenced as much by the approach of the observer as by the causative factors of the events themselves. Skepticism opens the mind to be ready for new explanations of old observations as well as for the unexpected. Mansfield and Busse (1981) refer to many studies that show that a skeptical approach to observation and knowledge is an essential component of a creative mind. The encouragement of skeptical thinking gives minds courage to think in new ways and and to express controversial opinions. A skeptical attitude is especially important in a discipline like science in which the foundation principles are constantly being updated. Karl Popper (1965) spoke to this changeability when he wrote, "Science does not rest upon rockbottom ... Its theories rise, as it were, above a swamp. The piles are driven from above ... We simply stop when we are satisfied that they are firm enough for the time being" (p. 111).

The continued process of skepticalization is further encouraged when history is included in the curriculum. History is a chronicle of the process by which humankind has changed its perception of reality. Through the study of this chronicle, a student understands that change is the result of the natural process by which we discover knowledge. A scientist with an understanding of history will not see change as an assault on truth, but a goal after which to search.

The scientific mind needs the company of other creative minds to perfect its questioning process and to gain increased intellectual courage. Zuckerman (1977) in her study of Nobel laureates found that more than one-half of all American Nobel recipients had studied under Nobel prize winners. Austin (1978) interviewed many famous scientists who prized their one-on-one relationship with an established scientist during their graduate careers.

An undergraduate liberal arts institution can be lacking in this highly charged atmosphere, which is usually created by the presence of state-of-the-art research. Most focus their energies on the academic side of intellectual pursuits. This approach to education allows a student to get the important knowledge base, quantitative skills, and skepticism essential to creativity. However, without a period in which to put these into practice under the direction of a skilled observer and experimenter, an essential piece in the armor of intellectual courage will be missing. Laboratory components of courses provide a taste of this process but more is needed if one is going to do truly great work in science. Addition of a research program on top of a solid teaching effort may not be possible due to constraints of space, budget, and faculty time—or even desirable. Necessary research experience can be provided through a well-designed internship program. It is an exciting addition to a liberal arts curriculum. Internship programs are often viewed with scorn or even as a threat to a liberal arts education. These feelings stem from a view of internships that sees them as a compromise to assure the employability of the liberal arts student upon graduation. Internships need not be a compromise for which we must apologize but can be an exciting intellectual exercise that encourages analysis of data and demands original conclusions based upon the research done during the internship. One gains through this that essential extra confidence one needs to soar to new insights on one's own. The opportunity to do research allows the mind of the student to be opened up fully to the forces for creativity. Just as a test flight allows one to experience the true feeling of flight, so an internship allows one to experience the feel of the creative process.

An internship paired with the knowledge base of the liberal arts gives confidence.

Confidence in one's own observations gives one the courage to think independently, to express opinions, and to stand up against the pressure of dogma. Without this type of belief in oneself, none of the scientists cited in this paper as creative thinkers would be remembered for their contributions to our knowledge of the universe. Creative ideas do not spring from the minds of the timid. A creative mind has to have the courage to take risks and the talent to back up that originality with hard work. Chambers (1969) found that the creative not only take intellectual risks, but have a deep need to be original thinkers. Their courage to take risks comes from strong feelings of autonomy and independence instilled by parents during early childhood. These scientists had special parental support, but a program such as described in a liberal arts education could be an adequate substitute.

The forces which power creativity are varied. We have seen how broad knowledge, the unexpected, analysis, skepticism, and vision all work to allow the prepared mind to see the new idea in the common observation.

The liberal arts education is a unique approach to the development of the scientific mind. It attempts to maximize the potential for creativity by the exposure of the mind to all the forces which power creative events. A liberal arts education forces a student into all areas of knowledge, including those which seem at the moment to be useless. A liberal arts curriculum realizes that no knowledge is ever useless, only perhaps little used. It also recognizes that one can not preknow what one will need to know and so guards against potential ignorance with a potpourri of knowledge.

A liberal arts education also realizes that a creative event is fueled by more than knowledge alone. The importance of analytical training is not forgotten. Those who seek to diminish the analytical portion of the liberal arts curriculum contribute to the perpetuation of lackluster ideas based on innuendo and sloppy thinking.

It is upon these two pillars—broad knowledge and analysis—that the ediface of the creative mind is built. Through knowledge and analysis is forged a skeptical, courageous mind open at all times to the unexpected and prepared to see beyond the obvious.

A liberal arts education treats the mind as an integrated circuit composed of individual elements, but functioning as a single unit. No one element is more important than the other and all are required to produce the desired result. All are required to produce a mind that sees the potential for discovery in every event, can value the genius of others, and will be a force for changing the knowledge of humankind.

REFERENCES

Austin, J. (1978). *Chase, chance, and creativity.* New York: Columbia University Press.

Chambers, J. (1969). Beginnings of a multidimensional theory of creativity. *Psychological Reports, 25,* 779–799.

Cohen, B.I. (1984). Florence Nightingale. *Scientific American, 290* (3), 128–137.

Cole, K.C. (1983). The scientific aesthetic. *Discover, 4e* (3), 54–63.

DeRopp, R.S. (1972). *The new prometheans.* New York: Dell.

Eliot, T.S. (1964). Tradition and the individual talent". In T.S. Eliot (Ed.), *Selected essays* (new ed.) New York: Harcourt, Brace and World.

Fenyman, R. (1975). Seeking new laws. In R.J. Tukodi (Ed.), *A taste of science.* Lancaster, PA: Technomic.

Gornick, V. (1983). *Women in science: Portraits from a world in transition.* New York: Simon and Schuster.

Hewitt, P. (1971). *Conceptual physics: A new introduction to your environment.* San Francisco, CA: Little, Brown.

Johanson, D., & Edey, M. (1982). *Lucy: The beginnings of humankind.* New York: Warner Books.

Johnson, L. (1983). *Biology*. Dubuque, IA: W.C. Brown.

Keller, E.F. (1981). McClintock's Maize. *Science, 81* (12), 55–68.

Keynes, G. and Hill, B. (1951.). *Samuel Butler's notebooks*. New York: E.P. Dutton.

Kottler, M. (1974). From 48 to 46: Cytological technique, preconceptions, and the counting of human chromosomes. *Bulletin of Historical Medecine, 48,* 465.

Lewin, R. (1981). Trail of ironies to Parkinson's disease. *Science, 224, 48,* 465. 1083–1085.

Mansfield, R., & Busse, J. (1981). *The psychology of creativity and discovery*. Chicago, IL: Nelson Hall.

Millar, R. (1974). *The Piltdown men*. New York: Ballantine.

Popper, K. (1965). *The logic of scientific discovery*. New York: Harper & Row.

Ritchie, D., & Carolla, R. (1983). *Biology*. Reading, MA: Addison-Wesley.

Salisbury, F., & Ross, C. (1985). *Plant physiology*. Belmont, CA: Wadsworth.

Sayre, A. (1975). *Rosalind Franklin and DNA*. New York: Norton.

Stone, I. (1980). *The origin*. Garden City, NY: Doubleday.

Swenson, L.S. (1972). *The ethereal aether*. Austin, TX: University of Texas Press.

Wallace, R.A., & Sanders, G.P. (1981). *Biology: The science of life*. Glenview, IL: Scott, Foresman.

Wertheimer, M. (1981). Einstein: The thinking that led to the theory of relativity. In R. Tweny, M. Doherty, & C. Mynatt (Eds.), *On scientific thinking*. New York: Columbia University Press.

Zuckerman, H. (1977). *Scientific elite: Nobel laureates in the United States*. New York: New York Free Press.

SYMPOSIUM

PANEL 3

Comments

Paul Ezust

John Holley and Rebecca DiLiddo have raised very important points about the nurturing of creative individuals. DiLiddo has discussed the importance of providing these hungry minds with diverse, liberal educations which will tend to "maximize the potential for creativity by exposing the mind to all the forces which power creative events." Holley has called for a restructuring of the priorities and the expectations of organizations so as to foster creativity by anticipating the inevitable disruption of the status quo and by maintaining sufficient flexibility to move in new directions and reap the fruits of the creative process.

I find myself in very close agreement with the proposals stated in both papers. I would like to comment, however, on a much earlier stage of the process.

As a teacher of mathematics, I have become increasingly alarmed over the past two decades by the growing number of people whom I have met who possess a very debilitating disorder which has been given the rather forbidding name, "math anxiety." Typically, this condition manifests itself by rendering otherwise intelligent individuals incapable of dealing with even the simplest mathematical concepts. This condition generally proves to be equally incapacitating with scientific concepts.

Unfortunate individuals who have contracted this disease are unlikely to be able to make creative use of unexpected results the way that a Roentgen or an Einstein might or to have sufficient courage to "believe in their own ideas even if they are unconventional and outside the accepted dogma" (DiLiddo, this volume).

I puzzled over this phenomenon for a long time before I arrived at a model which seems to fit all of the data that I have gathered over the years. My theory, in explaining why vast numbers of intelligent citizens

125

have this intellectually crippling disease, also implies an appalling decimation of the population of potential creative scientists and mathematicians. Consider the following imaginary scenario:

> We are in a second-grade classroom. It is math time and a bright little girl has just asked her teacher a question that occurred to her as she was working. The question concerns some experiments that the little girl was doing with numbers. She has already worked out the answer and is looking for validation from her teacher. The teacher, who has taken several courses dealing with the social and psychological development of children, is very sensitive to the emotional needs of her pupils but is "math phobic" herself, doesn't understand the question, and gives a mathematically invalid answer. The little girl, who takes pride in being cooperative and obedient and who respects and admires the teacher, accepts the teacher's answer and superimposes it upon the mathematical system that she has been constructing in her questing mind.

In this scenario, a bright child has learned two disastrous things. First, by "learning" an invalid mathematical concept, the child has introduced an explicit contradiction into her mind. The inconsistency of the invalid concept with correct concepts can give rise to an infinite stream of nonsensical mathematical ideas. Second, and more important, the child learned that it is not safe to trust her own intellect—because it leads to "wrong" answers. What can the child do if she cannot trust her own powers of reasoning?

The solution of choice for bright, achievement-oriented children, like our hypothetical little girl, is to memorize. There we have the crux of math anxiety: It is not possible to memorize enough to feel secure and comfortable because mathematics is infinite!

Is the scenario far fetched? Can such things happen in real classrooms? Why didn't I picture the teacher as a cruel, overbearing ogre?

Unfortunately, if anything, the scenario is understated. In two different elementary schools in Cambridge, my own children have described (and I have personally verified) classroom horror stories which surpass the mild scenario described above. It is an unfortunate fact of life that elementary education in America has traditionally been a "safe" way for math-phobic people to get college degrees and enter a profession.

Suffolk's own elementary education program is typical. Prior to the establishment (2 years ago) of a universal math requirement for all undergraduate students, there was absolutely no mathematics requirement for students who enrolled in the elementary education programs. Students in that program were, however, required to take a course given by the education department, entitled "Methods of Teaching Elementary Mathematics."

At present, students in elementary education programs at Suffolk must satisfy a six-credit math option requirement and a six-credit science option requirement. The mathematics course sequence of choice tends to be the course that we call "Finite Mathematics." This course sequence consists of a selection of elementary topics that prepare students in management or liberal arts major programs to take other required quantitative courses (e.g., statistics, economics, physical science, etc.). Finite Math is a general-purpose "service" course. It does not attempt to provide students with the basic understanding of crucial mathematical concepts that they would need in order to teach young children. The most popular course sequence for satisfying the science requirement is an elementary survey course called "Physical Science." Thus, students in elementary education programs can graduate and become certified to teach all subjects in grades K thru 6 with only the most superficial understanding of mathematics and science—in an era when these subjects are more crucial than ever for the intellectual development of all children. We require "methods" courses of several types, however: methods for teaching subjects about which the teacher will probably know essentially nothing!

I do not wish to leave the impression that Suffolk is unique or even unusual in structuring its elementary education curriculum. Our education department is simply satisfying guidelines set down by the Massachusetts State Board of Education. When the guidelines for secondary education certification were changed, the education department worked closely with the science and mathematics departments and developed excellent programs to prepare students for careers as high school math and science teachers.

My little story emphasized the teaching of invalid methods and concepts. Such occurrences have great destructive potential, indeed. I am equally concerned, however, with a concomitant problem which, being more subtle and more pervasive, has far more devastating capabilities.

When a teacher with a sixth grade (or lower!) level of understanding of mathematics attempts to teach mathematical ideas to a class of bright young children, even if he or she explains these ideas "correctly" (having internalized a lesson plan obtained from a teachers' guide), many additional messages are transmitted to the class. The teacher's own insecurity and anxiety (and, hence, loathing of the subject) are very difficult to hide. Because what is being taught is so very close to the ragged edge of the teacher's own understanding of the subject (which was probably obtained by rote), the presentations will tend to be inflexible and dogmatic. In many ways, the teacher will convey his or her own attitudes

and learning methods to the class. The essential mathematical foundations which teach children to reason and to approach problems with
analysis instead of fear will not be built. Perhaps we have found the real
reason why so many pathetic individuals are clamoring for school prayer:
No viable alternatives for problem solving are being taught in the
schools!

Over the years, we have been populating our public schools with
hundreds of thousands of teachers who are not competent to introduce
our children to the basic ideas of mathematics and science. These individuals, well versed in child development and crowd control, are causing widespread damage and depriving this nation of powerful, creative
thinkers. The most common product of their teaching is a growing population of compulsive memorizers who have suffered irreparable intellectual damage and whose creative possibilities have been drastically
curtailed.

Mathematics and science are areas in which students who are com-
petently taught can and should learn not only basic skills and basic
knowledge, but also basic intellectual pride. It is this intellectual pride
that empowers an individual to think "autonomously and in original
thought patterns" (DiLiddo, this volume). The child that has been de-
prived of competent basic training in these areas during the crucial
formative years has been intellectually mutilated. The amount of energy
that is required in later life to compensate for this tragic omission is
often prohibitive. The population of children that is most likely to be
damaged in this way is precisely the group that contains the potential
Rosalind Franklins and Barbara McClintocks.

DiLiddo's call for a liberal arts education "to develop the responsive
mind needed by a scientist" seems like a cry in the wilderness when
heard in the context of the appalling state of our primary education
system. By the time that our potential scientists reach college, it is often
too late to help them. Many have already given up on learning and are
simply trying to survive their courses and get their degrees. The curiosity and love of learning that characterizes all healthy children has
been smothered in the cloud of psycho-babble that has been substituted
for knowledge and competence. One wonders how many little Charles
Babbages in our modern urban elementary schools have managed to
hold onto their self-assurance and healthy "contempt for the academic
institution which set itself up to teach people when its teachers were in
fact ignorant" (Holley, this volume).

I do have a modest proposal. Our children are our most precious
resource. For decades, we have been entrusting their education to a class
of pseudo-professionals who have become entrenched in our public education system. I am not so naive as to suppose that such a well-estab-

lished population can be easily modified. I do believe, however, that it is possible to exert pressure on the state certification agencies and force them to raise their standards.

Universities could generate a substantial amount of pressure by eliminating the undergraduate education degree. There is an indisputable need for teachers of young children to study and understand the psychology and sociology of children and to be thoroughly trained in the special methodologies that have been developed for teaching various subjects to children. But the study of this important material should take place after an aspiring teacher has earned a *legitimate* bachelor's degree in an *academic* subject area. When that has happened, I believe that an individual who then goes on to take the appropriate "methods" and child development courses, should be certified to teach in grades K thru 6—but only in those areas in which he or she can demonstrate a reasonable level of competence.

For teachers who are already in the system, I propose that an orderly process of competence inventory be started. Ultimately, these teachers should be recertified to teach those subjects in which they can demonstrate competence. Recent educational research (Hawk, Coble, & Swanson, 1985) suggests that the results of such a certification program will be positive and dramatic.

This would be a substantial departure from our present, virtually standardless system. Furthermore, it would be extremely expensive to implement such a system because qualified individuals would be relatively rare at first and are likely to be sought after by other employers. But our children are worth the expense and the risk. Presently, elementary education attracts our weakest students. Elementary school teachers command little professional respect and relatively low salaries. Elevated standards such as those suggested above would gradually transform the teaching profession into one which would deserve respect and which would, therefore, be attractive to competent individuals who could stimulate and motivate bright, creative young people and help them to develop into the powerful creative individuals that we so desperately need to deal with the awesome problems that face our planet.

REFERENCES

Hawk, P.P., Coble, C.R., & Swanson, M. (1985). Certification: It does matter. *Journal of Teacher Education, 36* (3), 13–15.

SYMPOSIUM

PANEL 4

DEVELOPING SKILLS FOR CREATIVE THOUGHT

The Creative Attitude

Maria Teresa Miliora

INTRODUCTION

I know of no more elegant expression of joy, trust and spontaneity—qualities that epitomize the creative attitude, than these words written by Joseph Zinker (1977):

> Creativity is a celebration of one's grandeur, one's sense of making anything possible. Creativity is a celebration of life—my celebration of life. It is a bold statement: I am here! I love life! I love me! I can be anything! I can do anything! Creativity is not only an expression of the full range of each person's experience and sense of uniqueness, but [it is] also a social act—a sharing with one's fellow human beings this celebration, this assertion in living a full life. [Creativity] is the breaking of boundaries,

Integrated throughout this paper is experimental material that I obtained by interviewing the artists, writers, educators, and psychotherapists listed here during the preparation of the manuscript. I express my deep gratitude to them for sharing their personal experience of the creative process with generosity and trust and for the truly creative moments that each encounter represented: Blair Gelbond, Mariel Kinsey, Ellen Milan, Ramsay Raymond, Priscilla Sanville, Steven Schatz, Gary Whited, and Thomas Yeomans.

I also extend special thanks to Thomas Yeomans, Holly Beardsley, Ramsay Raymond, and Alex Kronstadt for their helpful suggestions.

the affirmation of life beyond life—life moving beyond itself. Out of its own sense of integrity, life asks us to affirm our own intrinsic nature, our essences as human beings. Creativity is an act of bravery. It states: I am willing to risk ridicule and failure so that I may experience this day with newness and freshness. The person who dares to create, to break boundaries, not only partakes of a miracle, but also comes to realize that in his process of being he is a miracle. (pp.3–4)

The ideas, beliefs, and values which I express in this paper represent an integrated personal perspective, one derived from my training in both the physical and social sciences, my experience in these fields as an educator and a psychotherapist, and my personal explorations within the consciousness disciplines. The essential aspect of the creative process is change, the change from one form into another, that is, transformation. Ideas are transformed into words, dreams into creation solutions, feelings into actions. The processes of education and psychotherapy have much in common. Both attend to growth, to the evocation of human potential from within, to transformation. Thus, creativity is the essential underpinning of both. A creative attitude, one that allows that something new can emerge and encourages unfoldment, irrespective of discipline or field of practice, is the instrumental condition that facilitates the awakening and flowering of human potential.

The focus of this paper is twofold: first, the primary stage of the creative process, the stage from which emerge ideas and images, some of which materialize into form; and secondly, the creative attitude which I hold as fundamental to the realization of the creative potential to which each of us has access. The intuition and the imagination, two functions whose development and utilization I consider crucial to the creative process, and the role of dreams and disidentification are also considered.

I am not addressing what might be called the secondary or elaboration stage of the creative process, the one which results in completion of artistic and scientific endeavors or socially useful products. There is a tendency, I believe, to think of creativity or the creative individual as a relatively rare phenomenon. This derives from viewing the products, the forms into which some creative insights materialize, rather than examining the creative process at its essential level within ourselves. If we consider creativity the province of a select few "others," if we don't experience ourselves as creative, as capable of change, if our attitude is one of discounting our creative potential, then we miss the insights we can access. I believe that the primary stage of the creative process is available to all in varying degrees and that creativity can be manifested in all facets of everyday life. Because I also believe that our capacity to access creative energy can be expanded, I have chosen to focus on this stage of insight.

The broad theoretical perspective which this paper reflects is drawn from the literature within humanistic and transpersonal psychology. "The term 'transpersonal' means, literally, beyond the personal or beyond the personality" (Vaughan, 1982, p. 39). Transpersonal psychology is considered the fourth major force of Western psychology and emerged because of perceived limits in the first three: psychoanalysis, behaviorism, and humanistic psychology. Thus, it may be viewed as representing the growing edge of psychology and, as such, it is outside the mainstream of traditional Western models. The traditional models, represented in particular by the psychoanalytic and behavioristic schools tend to emphasize the personality, psychopathology, and adaptation. The humanistic movement and, to a more extensive degree, transpersonal psychology, are concerned with expanding human potential and optimal psychological health and well-being. "Transpersonal psychology recognizes the potential for experiencing a broad range of states of consciousness in some of which identity may expand beyond the usual limits of the ego and the personality" (Walsh, 1980, p. 16). It does not seek to replace the earlier models but rather to include them within an enlarged context of what constitutes human nature and the full range of human experience.

One particular transpersonal psychological system to which I make reference is that termed *psychosynthesis*. As a model of human growth, psychosynthesis provides both a theoretical framework that is useful for conceptualizing the creative process and a set of techniques for developing greater awareness of the process. Extending from its original psychoanalytic base, this model of the human psyche includes a realm of the unconscious called the "higher" unconscious or "superconscious," from which it is posited that we receive the so-called "higher intuitions and inspirations—artistic, philosophical or scientific . . ." The superconscious is considered the realm of the ethical, esthetic, heroic, and humanitarian drives. These inspirations and drives flow as energy into the personality and are experienced as intuitive insights, feelings, thoughts, images, and impulses to action (Assagioli, 1976, pp. 17–18). Psychosynthesis affirms the value of developing all of the functions of the psyche, including the imagination and intuition, both of which are intimately involved in the primary stage of the creative process. For many of us, these functions are little used and appreciated as ways of apprehending reality. Psychosynthesis contains specific active techniques to encourage contact with the superconscious and to encourage development of these functions.

PRIMARY STAGE OF THE CREATIVE PROCESS

The core of the primary stage of the creative process is inspiration, illumination. Words such as intuitive insight and flash are often used to describe the experience. Individual perception of the insights can occur at different levels of experience and at more than one. For some, dreams may be a primary source, for others the waking imagination or intuition may be the principal access vehicle. Some experience it through a felt body sense, an actual inner movement which signals change. The people I interviewed described their experience of the process in ways which underscore the uniqueness of creative experience:

> I begin to feel tension which is an intensity and I come into relationship to something that doesn't exist yet. That's how it begins.

> If I'm being creative through dance, it comes out of my body.

> I experience a lot of creative energy in relationship to others ... a lot of metaphors and images come in my mind. Each metaphor is intuitive, it comes up suddenly as a picture.

> Imagery gives me a satisfied feeling in my body, gives me the idea to communicate, this is what comes through.

> When I have accessed dreams, I have traveled back in my mind to the void, to darkness, to nothing, and then suddenly, coming over the line, suddenly something is created. Out of nothing something new is created. I felt I had a stream of the creative mind.

> It depends on the amount of resonance between me and the word, image, color, moment of experience. It's mostly in my body, though it's not a physical sensation. It's an energetic sensation of aliveness and response that tells me that that's it. It's intuitive, imaginal and it could be ideational, an idea that I try to clothe in form. I could call it an abstraction. I use images to serve an abstraction.

> Dreams are major sources of information for me. I use them in my painting.

> A lot of the times that I have felt truly creative, like something new has come out of me, it has come out of relationship with something outside myself, whether it's a person or a tree. Out of the exchange, I am open to letting things come in. It involves listening, to a person or a tree.

> In writing I try to get the essence of the matter and a lot of that is intuitive.

In one sense the primary stage is no big deal. We all experience fleeting inspirational moments, perhaps a simple insight while walking in the woods or a sudden awareness of a solution to a problem with which we had been struggling. These creative moments seem to come out of nowhere and most are disregarded. No big deal, indeed. We tend to pay more attention to the creative products of others. But the forms into which some creative insights do materialize occur because some people are more open to and aware of them and more willing to carry through their inspirations to completion. The "no big deal" primary stage is obviously an essential step in all creative effort.

I believe that creative energy is available to all as a potential energy source, that access to this insight stage is inherent in our humanness, that it is as basic to the life process as breathing and that, like breathing, it is largely unconscious but one to which we can bring greater consciousness.

From one point of view the primary stage involves what has been described as "regression in the service of the ego" (Heath, 1983, p. 187). This alludes to the capacity to temporarily abandon one's normal egoic defenses and self-control in order to explore alternative and primitive ways of knowing, for example, expressive body movements, fantasies, intuitions. When we do so we can connect with what Maslow calls "aspects of the unconscious and preconscious (or poetic, metaphoric, mystic, primitive, archaic, childlike)" (1976, p. 66). This regression within ego control can be suspended at will by the mature and integrated person who then recovers his previous level of organization, according to Heath (1983, p. 187).

Writing within the psychosynthesis perspective, James Vargiu presented a model of the creative process that shows how it "emerges out of the close and purposeful interplay among our main personality functions—mind, feelings and imagination—so as to tap the energies that make up our superconscious or transpersonal processes" (1977, p. 18). Consistent with French mathematician Henri Poincaré's depiction, Vargiu gave a general description of the creative process as including some or all of the following stages: preparation, frustration, incubation, illumination, and elaboration.

During the preparation stage we may consciously and purposefully be seeking a solution to a problem, manipulating ideas, trying to find one that fits, one that feels right. At this stage we are, in effect, supplying material and collecting data at the intellectual level. Sometimes we come to what seems like a dead end, we can't find a solution, we feel blocked, perhaps confused and frustrated and we put the problem aside, that is, out of our consciousness. During the next or so-called incubation stage we let go of consciously manipulating our mental constructs but unconscious processes continue to operate. Then, sometime later, seemingly by chance, the solution becomes apparent at the third illumination, or what I refer to as the primary, stage. Perception of the insight at this stage may be through the intuitive function, the imagination, dreams, or the senses. Vargiu (1977) described this stage as arising from the influence of an energy field which "pervades the elements and images within our mind," combining them into a meaningful pattern (p. 21). According to Vargiu, the creative field has reached such a peak of intensity at this stage that it acts "simultaneously on all mental elements, arranging them in well-defined shapes which correspond to its own harmonious patterns." He attributed the suddenness of illumination to what he described as an "avalanche effect" (p. 24). The flashlike, unexpected, or sudden nature of the insight is different from the stepwise process that occurs when we use the rational intellect for problem solving.

The intensity described by Vargiu that may occur prior to the illumination appears to be consonant with the experience of some of the people I interviewed:

> There's a tension and a restlessness. I feel really bothered about something, a lot of confusion. If I stay with the agitation and try to listen, then a phrase will just pop in and then everything (referring to a poem) comes out of that phrase.

> It requires a tremendous pressure to build up before I find the way out and it is uncomfortable.

> The discomfort is important, something doesn't feel right. It means I have to push my boundaries.

Recognition of the insight is usually followed by a positive emotional reaction with qualities such as joy, a sense of harmony and beauty accompanied by the certain conviction of the correctness of the solution. During the final elaboration, or what I have termed the secondary, stage of the process, intellectual activity, application of learned skills, and disciplined attention are utilized to complete the task.

CREATIVE ATTITUDE

From what I have observed of my own creative process and learned from others I have come to believe that the qualities intrinsic to a creative attitude are trust, curiosity, and the capacity to take risks, to be spontaneous in the moment. Trust can be conceptualized as receptivity to what emerges, to change, to the unknown, without needing to manipulate, concretize, and analyze. Trust also implies a nonjudgmental, accepting attitude toward oneself at all levels of experience—feelings, thoughts, sensations, images—and a willingness to let go of control when appropriate. One person described his attitude as including the "willingness to take a leap into the unknown, listening to the impulse of truth, to what is attempting to be expressed through me." I think of curiosity as a playfulness, a childlike innocence that manifests as wanting to explore that which isn't known, to go toward the new. It implies having a dynamic and open view of life, courage and a willingness to learn, to change and to grow. The capacity to take risks, to be spontaneous requires trust in oneself and the environment, some freedom from attachment to a self-image, from self-doubt and concern of how others will judge us. The person who can be spontaneous in the moment experiences being oneself as joyous. One person cited "openness" as an important element of the creative attitude and added:

> ... having an open mind, open to different models of reality, it's the attitude of learning, learning from life, being receptive to life—that's creative.

Another cited "curiosity, honesty in the sense of depth, inventiveness in the sense of playfulness, and trust." One person exemplified the creative attitude in describing the role of imagery in artistic creations:

> No, I don't use imagery. Part of the process is discovering the image. I'm just going to find it. It's going to happen. If I saw it ahead of time I probably wouldn't do it because the excitement of doing something is not knowing how it's going to turn out. To have pre-packaged answers is fooling yourself. You never have the thrill of being alive. Being alive involves decision-making through a process.

These qualities of attitude have some correlation with studies of the attributes of creative persons in the psychological literature. These have included findings that creative persons are "less repressed and defensive, more intuitive and open to admitting turbulent inner conflicts, more curious, ... and more maturely autonomous and so less dependent upon views that others have of them" (Heath, 1983, pp. 187–188).

Abraham Maslow (1976) described what for him was the essential quality for creativeness of any kind as the "ability to become 'lost in the present.'" He observed "that the creative person, in the inspirational phase of the creative furor, loses his past and his future and lives only in the moment. He is all there, totally immersed, fascinated and absorbed in the present, in the current situation, in the here-now, with the matter-in-hand" (p. 59). He noted that creativeness had something to do with the "ability to become timeless, selfless," and that it was a "diluted" version of the mystical experience described as a loss or "transcendence of self" and "fusion with the reality being observed" (pp. 59–60). One person expressed it in this way: "Creativity has to do with being, with the way it unfolds. A creative space opens in me when I get a whiff of the being of things." Another commented on making "creative decisions" when deeply into the present moment:

> When I am fully present, there I am able to process a situation and respond to it freshly, just with the variables that are present rather than according to an old pattern in my mind. Then I am just being appropriate to the situation.

Maslow's description of this absorption in the present can be applied to a variety of ordinary life experiences and appreciated when viewed from the perspective of the familiar. In working on a problem we can speak of putting other matters aside and concentrating our attention on it, studying it from the inside, in a sense, becoming one with it. In interactional situations, this would translate as approaching another without inhibitions and expectations, forgetting oneself, really listening to another, truly empathizing. If one is absorbed in the process of listening to music or reading poetry, then one can be said to have lost oneself to the experience of hearing and letting that experience evoke feelings, sensations, images. If we are totally present to our experience during these moments, then we have lost our past and our future, that is, we have put aside our concerns in thinking about the past and planning for the future and, in effect we have let go of controlling, striving, manipulating and we are one with the reality of the moment. One person expressed this precise experience:

> When I hear music evoke a creative response in me, I always feel my body open up in the middle, a sense of expansion and coming into the present moment in a way where I'm stepping back from time and I don't feel compelled by everyday concerns.

The qualities of trust, curiosity, and spontaneity are essential elements of presence, for absorption in the experience of the moment. They are needed for our conscious cooperation with what may be happening beyond our conscious control and for attending to insights we may be open to receive. We can see how these apply to the model of the creative process previously described. As noted by Vargiu (1977), there needs to be a movement from the preparation to the incubation stage before illumination. During this process, one needs to let go of the conscious mental activity of the preparation stage and allow unconscious processes to work. One needs to be receptive, quietly curious and alert toward that which may emerge and indeed to trust that something will emerge. One person commented on the importance of "honoring the blocks encountered during this stage, of not panicking, of trusting that it will come" and the importance of being able to get away from it when stuck. Another spoke of "paying attention and simply staying in the presence of a core thing ... eventually something just pops out." At the illumination stage, there is an alignment with the creative field which may be experienced as a sense of synchronicity with something originating from "outside" (Vargiu, 1977, p. 21). One person described the experience in these words:

> It comes from a place of being. This is a potent place, a place where you're connected up with everything. There's tremendous power and energy in that place. To create art I tap into that. There's some kind of synchronicity going on and it permeates all if you're moving in the real flow.

The recognition of the insight derives from a fusion or absorption with the particular perceptual process—intuition, senses, feelings, imagination—through which we derive the recognition, the knowing. At the moment of insight we are not identified with, for example, thoughts, concerns, and judgments about the past or the future, but rather, we are "lost in the present," in the experience of the insight.

How we respond to the insight largely determines our attitude toward our creative potential. Here again, trust in the form of a nonjudgmental attitude, curiosity to, for example, further explore the information received and courage to take risks come into play. My emphasis on the need for trust and receptivity in the creative process does not imply that we should indiscriminately take action on the basis of our insights without the utilization of the rational intellect. Often it is important to apply care in interpreting the insights, to see if the inspirations are genuine and if they should be followed in the elaboration stage. Assagioli (1974) commented on the need for balance between stifling creative inspiration by an overly critical attitude on the one hand and acting hastily and without careful scrutiny to all psychic influences that we access on the other (pp. 156–157).

INTUITION

Intuition is considered by some to be the highest form of human cognition (Deikman, 1983, p. 48). It is defined in *Webster*'s as follows: "immediate apprehension or cognition; the power or faculty of attaining to direct knowledge without rational thought and inference; quick and ready insight." In contrast to cognition via thinking, cognition via intuition has the following characteristics: immediate and direct knowing of the totality of a situation; experiential and synthetic or holistic. It does not operate from the part to the whole as the analytical mind does (Assagioli, 1974, p. 218). Ferrucci (1982) described it as the way "one jumps directly to understanding rather than slowly walking to it with the aid of reasoning" (p. 221). One person said of the intuitive experience: "The best poems were those that came whole." Some consider the intuition one of the least recognized and appreciated and one of the undeveloped and devalued functions (Assagioli, 1974, p. 217). For those that choose to pay attention to it, the awareness of intuition can be developed as a valuable faculty in the creative process.

Some attribute scientific breakthroughs to the intuitive faculty. Deikman (1983) commented on the place of intuition for the scientist as follows: "Although the scientific method is taught as if data plus logic equal discovery, those who have actually studied how discoveries are made come to different conclusions." He quoted Eugene Wigner, a Nobel prize-winning physicist:

> The discovery of the laws of nature requires first and foremost intuition, conceiving of picture and a great many subconscious processes. The use and also the confirmation of these laws is another matter . . . logic comes after intuition. (p. 280)

Michael Polanyi, a physical chemist and philosopher, researched the process used by scientists to arrive at their breakthroughs. He is quoted by Deikman as follows:

> And we know that the scientist produces problems, has hunches, and, elated by these anticipations, pursues the quest that should fulfill these anticipations. This quest is guided throughout by feelings of a deepening coherence and these feelings have a fair chance of proving right. We may recognize here the power of a dynamic intuition. The mechanism of this power can be illuminated by an analogy. Physics speaks of potential energy that is released when a weight slides down a slope. Our search for deeper coherence is guided by a potentiality. We feel the slope toward deeper insight as we feel the direction in which a heavy weight is pulled along a steep incline. It is this dynamic intuition which guides the pursuit of discovery. (pp. 280–281)

The model of creativity that Wigner and Polanyi described, one in which intuition plays the preeminent role, correlates with the primary stage of the creative process previously described. During the incubation stage, it was noted that conscious mental activity was put aside but unconscious processes continued to operate. At the illumination stage, the insight is perceived via intuition at one of the levels of awareness.

Wigner's and Polanyi's words—"intuition," "picture," "subconscious processes," "feelings of a deepening coherence," "dynamic intuition," "potentiality"—are consonant with Vargiu's depiction. It is at the elaboration stage, *after* the insight or primary stage, that intellectual activity is preeminent, as Wigner noted.

According to Vaughan (1979), intuitive experience can be perceived at four distinct levels of awareness although awareness of any single experience may be registered at more than one level. These levels are (1) the physical, where intuitions are perceived as bodily sensations; (2) the emotional, where intuition comes into awareness through feelings; (3) the mental, where awareness of intuitions is through images (p. 66). The fourth level is the spiritual or mystical. "At this level intuition is 'pure'," that is, it does not depend on sensory, emotional or mental cues (p. 77). Vaughan makes the point that the intuitive insights of the artist may be perceived more on the emotional level and that of the scientist more on the mental, where it is "often associated with problem solving, mathematics, and scientific inquiry" (p. 73). In both cases, the creative inspiration of the scientist and the artist, the important role of intuition in the creative process seems clear. Indeed, it appears that intuition provides the link between scientific and artistic creativity.

Although intuitions at all levels of awareness are usually experienced as arising spontaneously, seemingly outside of our conscious control, there is much that can be done to awaken intuition and expand awareness of it. Within psychosynthesis theory, its development is consonant with the goal of attaining a fuller expression of human potentiality.

The first step in awakening the intuition is having a clear intention to do so, thus acknowledging the value of this function. The development of intuition is accomplished primarily by quieting the other functions. Calming the mind, body, and emotions facilitates our attending to this mode of awareness. Thus, silence and relaxation are needed to help establish a receptive mode, one that allows the intuition to emerge. It is important to suspend critical judgment and to develop a trusting, noncontroling attitude. A variety of exercises and techniques can be used to awaken and develop the intuition. These include meditation, body-mind disciplines, the visualization and disidentification exercises within psychosynthesis and exercises whose intention is the evocation of particular qualities, such as serenity and patience used to enhance the attitude of quiet waiting. This attitude is particularly important during the incubation stage of the creative process.

Although awakening and developing the intuition is considered essential to the creative process, as previously noted, the role of the rational intellect, particularly with regard to discrimination and interpretation of intuitive insights, should not be ignored. A harmonious coordination between the intuition and intellect can be attained gradually, each function playing its appropriate role in the creative process. As the intuition is the faculty capable of the immediate grasp of a situation, the intellect is used to check the validity of the intuition and to include the insight into one's accepted body of knowledge. With increasing development and use of the intuition comes progressively greater trust of it as a reliable source of knowing.

IMAGINATION

Developmentally, cognition via imagination precedes conceptual thinking and this primary mode of cognition continues to operate throughout our lives in the form of dreams, spontaneous imagery, and that which is deliberately induced. Imagery is not limited to visual images, but extends to all levels of sensory perception—auditory, tactile, olfactory, gustatory, and kinesthetic (Assagioli, 1976, p. 144, 157). The process of attending to images connects consciousness with unconscious processes; it is a way of becoming conscious of what is unconscious. Thus, through imagery we can bring conscious insight into the experience of the unconscious. Because the imagination is a vehicle for intuitive insight, developing the imagination is useful for expanding intuition and awareness of creative insights.

Within psychosynthesis, images are conceived of as channels, transformers, lenses of the energy of the unconscious. Psychosynthesis affirms the value of the imagination and encourages development of this function through exercises and techniques that use both guided and spontaneous imagery.

Assagioli (1976) considered the imagination to be a synthetic function because it "can operate at several levels concurrently: those of sensation, feeling, thinking and intuition" (p. 143). The image is perceived by the senses, there may be feelings associated with it, an intuitive insight may result, and the intellect may interpret it. According to Vargiu (1977), "the interaction between the mental elements and the emotional field constitutes the very essence of the imagination." He considered the imagination to be the "bridge" between our minds and our feelings (p. 28). The capacity of images to unite physical, mental, and emotional levels of experience accounts for its potential usefulness to effect healing, growth, and learning. Imagery can be used to discharge and transform emotional energy and conversely, to evoke desirable emotional states such as joy and tranquility. It can be used to effect physiological states such as relaxation, to decrease pain, and to control physiological processes. The condition of physical, mental, and emotional relaxation which can be promoted through visualization allows for the awakening of intuition and thus greater awareness of intuitive insights. Learning may be enhanced by using visualization to transform the emotional and mental states that block receptivity to new ideas and images and symbols can be used for creative problem solving (Vaughan, 1979, p. 87). As expressed by Vargiu (1977), discordant emotional energy released through imagery can transmute discordant mental patterns. A "stable harmonic relationship can then develop between emotional and creative fields," that is, feelings, mind, and creative field are in alignment (p. 30). Thus, greater clarity, receptivity, and creative insights are possible.

As with awakening the intuition, developing or expanding the awareness of images requires an intention to do so and a receptive, trusting, and accepting attitude. One needs to let go of conscious control, to allow images to emerge and to observe them without judgment, that is, without expectation of what should happen and without judging what does happen. Without this attitude, which I describe as creative, the imagination is resisted. Resistances can take the form of self-doubt and judgment. The conscious, rational mind may criticize the imagination as silly, illogical. We may conclude that we are making up what is happening and that therefore it is worthless, that what is in the unconscious has no significance (Watkins, 1977). A receptive, trusting attitude would simply allow images to be as they are, registering what is in the moment. If we allow, indeed focus, our attention on images, the experience will become progressively stronger. The more we use imagery the easier it becomes to do so and increasingly we learn to trust the process.

In the early phase of working with imagery, it is not important to interpret the inner experience using the rational intellect. With experience in this realm, interpretation can be done more easily and more meaningfully. Indeed, increasingly we develop our capacity to use our will to shift back and forth from imagery, including its affective components, to a more rational, analytic framework from which we can observe, interpret, and integrate these experiences.

Psychosynthesis includes techniques for evoking sensory perception, to train the use of the will, and to encourage symbol indentification. Visualization exercises include guided imagery to both the "lower" unconscious, the realm of our personal history, and the "superconscious." These exercises encourage use of and train the creative imagination.

DREAMS

Dreams are said to be a "vast storehouse of unconscious wisdom" and the consciousness of dreams, "a form of intuitive, nonrational, experiential knowing" (Vaughan, 1979, p. 143). Dreams communicate both unconscious material related to one's personal problems and inspirations and intuitive insights. As the mode least controlled by the rational, conscious mind during its operation, dreams allow for the emergence of creative insights most clearly. Dreams "often contain the seeds of future possibilities and reflect what is unfolding from within us in our lives." Thus, information of a precognitive nature and creative problem solving may be accessed through dreams (p. 137). One person described the value of dreams in this way:

> Just to dream is a creative act. To be aware of my dreaming connects me with the source of being creative and that in itself has value, whether I do anything with it or not. Sometimes elements of higher consciousness will come in and present visions, solutions, what I need to do. I get a lot of creative information through dreams.

Another described the role dreams played in the process of writing poetry:

> Dreams often gave me the images to start with. Some poems came directly from dreams because they would touch deeply into feelings. The dreams' images drew me, fascinated me.

Within the field of organic chemistry, Kekule evolved the cyclic structure of benzene in a dream and it is said that Poincaré used dreams to solve mathematical problems (Vaughan, 1979, p. 145).

According to Vaughan, research has indicated that everyone dreams every night, but it appears that many of us do not remember the contents of dreams. There are several ways that have been suggested to increase our recall capacity and thus tap this mode of creative potential. These include formulating a clear intention to do so, recording all recollections including fragments of dreams immediately upon waking, and keeping a dream journal.

DISIDENTIFICATION

Throughout this paper I have alluded to particular qualities of attitude—allowing, receptive, nonjudgmental, noncontroling, trusting—that are important in enhancing awareness of the primary stage of the creative process. The awakening and development of the intuitive faculty, however intuitive awareness is individually perceived, requires this trusting, receptive attitude. If we are overidentified with the controling, conscious, rational mind, we may miss other forms of reality, particularly that which occurs within ourselves. Thus, I believe the capacity to disidentify from those personality aspects that obstruct our full-functioning creativeness and inhibit self-expression and spontaneity to be instrumental to the development of greater consciousness of the creative process.

The processes of disidentification and its obverse, identification, can be conceptualized as letting go and attachment, respectively. Attachment or exclusive identification with particular personality elements, roles, attitudes, beliefs, or mental-emotional patterns limits our perception of who we are, our sense of identity. To disidentify from a limiting attachment means to step back from it and to observe it with a nonjudgmental attitude. If we can observe, be aware of, a particular mental pattern, we are at least partially disidentified from it and thereby freed from its dominating influence. On the other hand, when we are strongly identified with a particular personality aspect, our consciousness of other aspects is necessarily limited (Assagioli, 1976, pp. 22–23). If we are exclusively identified with the rational, analytical mind, we are not aware of other functions—sensations, feelings, intuition, imagination. Therefore, our perception of what is happening at these other levels is obstructed. Thus, in so far as the creative process is concerned, I believe it is essential to develop the capacity to observe our psychic processes and to direct at will our energy and attention to those functions that may need expansion.

Techniques aimed at expanding awareness and the capacity to develop an observer function, visualization exercises, all forms of meditation and mind-body disciplines, exercises involving expressive body movements, spontaneous drawing and writing all contribute to increasing the capacity for disidentification and thereby to expanding self-awareness (Assagioli, 1976, pp. 116–123).

CONCLUSION AND SUMMARY

The creative attitude requires a lessening of our defenses and inhibitions, controls we place on self-exploration and expression. In essence, it amounts to having a positive, trusting attitude about ourselves, the world, and the unknown. By trusting we allow change to emerge. The creative attitude requires a holistic view of reality, awareness of all levels of experience—physical, emotional, and mental, and a balance of inner and outer directedness.

The creative process may be conceptualized as involving all or some of the following stages: preparation, frustration, incubation, illumination, and elaboration. The first three may viewed as preliminary to the primary or illumination stage. It is here that insights are perceived. I believe all of us have access to a creative energy source, energy available in potential, and that our capacity to access this source of creative insights increases with greater self-awareness. One person I interviewed expressed it particularly well:

So maybe the creative process is tapping into what is truly happening from someplace deep inside of you and finding a way to express that.

It is through the intuitive function that we realize creative inspirations and insights, but we may experience the realization at any level—sensory, emotional, imaginal. Thus, if we develop greater awareness of these levels, we develop greater sensitivity and receptivity to creative insights.

Because it seeks to develop balance and coordination among all of the human functions, psychosynthesis is a valuable resource for developing greater intuitive awareness. Conceptually and methodologically, psychosynthesis provides a basis for the linkage of imagination, intuition, and creativity and a framework within which their enhancement can be facilitated. Viewed from this perspective, the ideas expressed in this paper can be applied to many fields, and within the educational process, across a wide range of disciplines.

REFERENCES

Assagioli, R. (1976). *Psychosynthesis: A manual of principles and techniques.* New York: Penguin.

Assagioli, R. (1974). *The act of will.* New York: Penguin.

Deikman, A. (1983). Sufism and the mental health sciences. In R. Walsh & D. Shapiro (Eds.), *Beyond health and normality: Explorations of exceptional psychological well-being* (pp. 273–292). New York: Van Nostrand Reinhold.

Ferrucci, P. (1982). *What we may be.* Los Angeles, CA: Tarcher.

Heath, D. (1983). The maturing person. In R. Walsh & D. Shapiro (Eds.), *Beyond health and normality: Explorations of exceptional psychological well-being* (pp. 152–205). New York: Van Nostrand Reinhold.

Maslow, A. (1976). *The farther reaches of human nature.* New York: Penguin.

Vargiu, J. (1977). Creativity. *Synthesis, 3–4,* pp. 17–53.

Vaughan, F. (1979). *Awakening intuition.* Garden City, NY: Anchor Press/Doubleday.

Vaughan, F. (1982). The Transpersonal perspective: A personal overview. *Journal of Transpersonal Psychology, 14* (1), pp. 37–45.

Walsh, R. & Vaughan, F. (Eds.). (1980). *Beyond ego.* Los Angeles, CA: Tarcher.

Watkins, M. (1977). *Waking dreams.* New York: Harper & Row.

Zinker, J. (1977). *Creative process in gestalt therapy.* New York: Random House.

Creativity and Competence: Challenges for the Liberal Arts College

Kevin M. Lyons

It is difficult to imagine that any school would set among its purposes that of producing Einsteins, Mozarts, Darwins, or Newtons as a primary mission of its daily experiences for students. It is equally difficult to imagine any school that does not explicitly or implicitly include among its purposes that of encouraging and rewarding creativity among its students. Conventional wisdom suggests that creative thought is not defined by its products, but rather, defines its products. That is, it is desirable to think in certain manners even if much of this thinking produces little that is recognized as unique, novel, and having far-reaching effects on mankind. Process as well as product is regarded as creative in this dualistic definition of creativity. Creativity of a novel or unique nature is recognized for what it is and creativity as a process of living and thinking (occasionally producing the recognized novel product) underlies this culture's concern for passing on the cultural heritage and modes of thinking to succeeding generations. Creativity can be viewed as a very narrow or as a very broad concept. Definitions of either nature are valuable in certain contexts. The cognitive researcher seeks to narrowly define creativity in a scientific manner, looking for evidence of observable or definable behaviors that will explain the nature of the creative process. The social scientist may view creativity more broadly, perhaps seeking to explain cultural trends and innovations.

Pearlman (1983) posited that

> Creativity taken by itself is an ambiguous and vague concept. It has several meanings in most particular contexts. Furthermore, when trying to reflect on creativity in general, it can be interpreted as having one or all of these

meanings. This ambiguity is the source of the richness and vibrance in describing something or someone as creative. The ambiguity provides the flexibility which allows the application of the term "creative" in a wide variety of contexts. (p. 294)

The concept of creativity has little meaning outside of its cultural context. Clifford (1964) commented that underlying all approaches to creativity is a characteristically American preoccupation with novelty. One conception of creativity is product oriented while others are clearly process oriented. Indeed, some argue that creativity is defined by the emotional experience of the creator (Bronowski, 1958; White, 1959, 1960). Golann (1963) and Dellas and Gaier (1970), and others developed complex models of creativity which focused on creative products, intelligence as a factor in creativity, personality traits of the creative, environmental factors affecting creativity, and the nature of creative process.

Creativity must be redefined in order to speak intelligently about different problems. The creative artist, sculptor, or poet may fit one or more conceptions of creativity. The labor negotiator, aerospace engineer, or floor polisher can also be creative although each approaches problems quite differently than does the artist. A third conception of creativity, which will be a working definition here, is even more broadly construed, for it encompasses creativity of the first two conceptions and also captures thinking and behaviors associated with what has been called problem solving of a critical and reflective nature or, more traditionally and philosophically speaking, the "liberated" thinking skills needed to pursue the good and just life. Although some will object to this definition as being too ambiguous or amorphous, it is a suitable definition for this paper, for the problem under consideration concerns the purposes of education and current trends in curriculum evolution.

It is an interesting definition of creativity to which formal education subscribes; it is seldom forwarded in operational terms or specifics of content to be taught but is universally held to be important. Most everyone has a concept of what creative teaching is, but the explicit teaching of creativity conjures up an exotic notion for most of us. This essay describes how foundations for creativity have been approached by American education, particularly at the postsecondary level. It is argued that the value of these historically sporadic endeavors is presently threatened by a growing attitude of vocationalism that will, if left unchecked, allow creativity to disappear from the agenda of liberal arts and professional schools. The result of this trend will be a generation of college graduates less prepared than any previous one for work in its future. This essay will focus on the relationship of schooling to creativity.

American education has become lethargic in its efforts to revitalize school curriculum and foster creativity among its partakers. Liberal studies, an able vehicle for exploring and exploiting creative potential, has been devalued in the eyes of many. Vocational studies, models of education emphasizing knowledge as the end of education, and the mastery of easily measured skills are presently a consuming force in secondary and postsecondary education. We are in the midst of a creativity crisis. The current focus on technical training in higher education and the focus on mastery of discreet, measurable behaviors in elementary and secondary education leaves little time for teacher and students to pursue activities that are traditionally called liberal learning pursuits. This paper argues the existence of liberal learning and creativity parallels. It will also suggest that vocational and competency models of education have to a large degree replaced society's idea of what constitutes an educated person.

In the mid-1970s the public began to question the health of American public education. One state legislature after another passed laws enacting minimum competency testing for high school students. Proponents argued that the high school diploma was devalued to the meaning of a certificate of attendance and a long trend of declining SAT scores pointed to something gone awry in the schools. Invariably, states adopted testing policies that set minimum passing scores on achievement tests to be administered at different grade levels. Some states tied competency testing to high school graduation and, by 1978, 49 states had minimum competency testing or planned to implement a testing program within two years (Cohen & Haney, 1978; Haney & Madaus, 1978).

Competency-testing models are akin to what has been described as the industrial model of education. This is an input/output design where the "bottom line" is student performance on objective tests. The mastery of hierarchies of skills and knowledge is the focus of these curricula. Measurement of objective mastery is necessary in this model. Many vocational skills—and basic mathematics skills can be objectively tested—and mastery of these skills are important to employers. Unfortunately, many goals of traditional liberal learning cannot be objectively measured. Indeed, it is highly questionable whether the process of reading can be broken down into measurable objectives (Lyons, 1981). Critical thinking, skills of analysis, synthesis, and evaluation cannot be objectively measured and there will probably never be an objective test that satisfactorily approaches description of these abilities. The technical problem of testing and evaluating high-level intellectual activity, combined with an attitude of "If it can't be measured, it ain't worth teaching," has helped to lead curriculum designers to include only educational objectives that focus on knowledge or discreet measurable skills. This movement has in turn encouraged thinking that relegates intellectual process skills to the class of irrelevance.

The competence approach to education is dependent upon the concept of an "objective" body of knowledge. It is at its very core antithetical to the "subjective" approach of liberal learning—the questioning of how knowledge has been constructed by others—the essence of creative and critical thought. Competency models encourage teaching to the test, they reinforce the "right answer" mentality in students, and they reward quick thinking and quantity of answers rather than reflective consideration. Observing these characteristics in American elementary and secondary classrooms in a major study of schools, Silberman (1970) called American teachers "mindless." He found classroom instruction to focus on objectives of how, what, where, and who but hardly ever on why. Educators who focused on the overlearning of the basics of reading (particularly instruction in phonics) have found their students to be good word readers but poor comprehenders (Farr, 1977). Analysis of a recent National Assessment of Educational Progress report reveals that students are calculating and computing with numbers well but have hit an all-time low in applying computational skills to real problems (Friedman & Kilodiy, 1983). This confusion of means and ends led Silberman to conclude that educators need to focus on the aims of education rather than the intermediate products. Short-term measurement of acquired skills and knowledge is valuable only within the context of long-term goals. Have students learned too well the unintended lessons of schooling?

Competency testing, it is argued by proponents, provides accountability for education; it makes schools and students accountable for learning. Critics decry the competency-testing movement to be socially regressive—fulfilling a social sorting function for employers and reducing the function of teaching to preparing students to pass tests. Indeed, the impetus for competency testing is often attributed to business interests, in particular, the interests of labor-force employers. Opponents argue, correctly, that many complex or higher level skills always valued by American society and usually included in curriculum objectives cannot be tested by paper-and-pencil examinations. Accountability models that feature competency testing obscure other traditional curriculum objectives, and, in effect, the minimum competencies are elevated to the status of maximums.

Parallel to this movement of competency-testing accountability is the appearance of increasing interest in the vocational validity of secondary and postsecondary education. A retreating national economy throughout the 1970s undoubtedly played a large role in the questioning of the relevance of liberal arts curricula. College graduates with degrees earned in the liberal arts had great difficulty finding jobs as the economy trended upward amidst the infant technological revolution. College enrollments shifted from liberal arts to business administration and majors providing technical training for the largest growing sector of the economy (Kinney, 1979). In 1970 there was virtual parity in the number of liberal arts majors nationally; by 1979 the job-related fields held a two-to-one advantage (Litt, 1981). The social idealism and activism that characterized the college student of the 1960s and early 1970s gave way to the career-oriented students of the present. Without making value judgments of these two student types, it is clear that learning career skills necessary for employment are a much greater concern to college and secondary students than they were 10 years ago. A recent *Boston Globe* article (McCain, 1983) offered that "after a decade of disorganized retreat before the forces of career education, defenders of the liberal arts in the college curriculum have begun to regroup and fight back. . . ."

In a fashion, post-college employability has become equated with competence. The widely held, if inaccurate, perception that professional careers are successfully filled only by those with concentrated technical, management, or vocational-skills preparation has pushed the liberal arts into retreat and put the liberal arts student in the position of defending career and life choices.

One unfortunate symptom of the vocational attitudes that has developed is what may be called the ticket-punching syndrome. Although certainly not universal, large numbers of students view a college education as simply a means of getting the right holes punched in a ticket that admits them to a good job. It would be blaming the victim to attribute responsibility for this orientation to some personality of the student population. It is to a certain degree symptomatic of the times that we lose perspective of the goals of liberal education because of the need to see immediate and measurable results (punches in the ticket) which can be accumulated like tokens to "buy" the right employment. Liberal education is difficult to "sell" in a consuming society that is encouraged at every turn to seek immediate gratification for effort expended. Student preference for training, as opposed to education, simply reflects the marketplace and perhaps school experience. Jencks and Riesman (1968) commented, "the majority of those who enter college are plainly more concerned with accumulating credits and acquiring licenses than with learning any particular skill while enrolled" (p. 134). In other words, higher education in the eyes of many students is a matter of certification, not education.

Litt (1981) describes the "vocational university" as

a knowledge apparatus explicitly designed to create and apply ideas that are functional to dominant national policies. . . . By contrast, the internal core of the liberal arts curriculum is the mastery over political events as well as subject matter through cultivation of the rational and expressive faculties. Human concerns, not those of policy makers, are the core of liberal education. (p. 1)

Litt attacks government regulation and selectivity in the funding of research as a major cause of decline in liberal education offerings in large universities. He describes the wholesale move of the public university to an "applied, business-like direction in which marketable skills become the first order of course offerings and degree programs (p.10). He warns,

There are two key issues here: First, the success of the liberal arts in the fierce struggle for scarce resources, in which their move toward vocational status confronts the genuine, established articles in the schools of business, engineering, pharmacy, and so forth. Second, even some measure of success in a mutation to practicability runs directly into the second order problem—will the adaptation of the liberal arts to the world of job relevance cause the loss of sensibilities that have sustained the humanities throughout Western Civilization and the social sciences since the nineteenth century? (p. 10)

In a study of contemporary college curricula, a (1977) Carnegie Foundation study concluded that

faculty and student preferences now seem more toward specialization and atomization of the curriculum and away from integration and coherence. It is a pull toward a command of a narrow subject matter in great depth at the expense of the familiarity with the principles and methods of thought and inquiry that makes it possible for educated persons to deal with a variety of subjects on a fundamental level. (p.184)

Steven Muller, president of Johns Hopkins University, complained that

most undergraduates in effect write off their undergraduate years in terms of intrinsic value. They are not "real" years; they are only "pre" years. Their value is seen to be mostly in what follow them, not in what they themselves contain. Stated simply, they are not regarded as years of learning but of years of effort to qualify for something else; and learning and trying to qualify can be two entirely different things. (p.35)

These commentaries characterize the frustrations of those who see danger in the vocationalism of American higher education. However, vocationalism is not new to American higher education. As stated by Jencks and Riesman (Carnegie Foundation for the Advancement of Teaching, 1977), "The question always has been *how* an institution mixed the academic with the vocational, not whether it did so" (p.14).

Indeed, histories of American colleges suggests that curriculum has seldom existed apart from vocational interests, as the student from Harvard who said, "The degree of Harvard College is worth money to me in Chicago," pointed out. It would be error, however, to think the degree of movement in higher education toward work-related subjects and job preparation to be near typical of any period in history.

If we can, for the moment, make the vocationalism of higher education a presupposed reality, we will proceed to describe what aspects of traditional liberal learning are most critically absent in the present state of affairs and which are not critically and unfortunately in a trend of decline.

The evolution of college curriculum over the past 300 years makes impossible any short generalizations concerning the purposes of higher education; at any moment in history, diversity of existing institutional purposes defies the equation of education and purpose. Entire histories have been devoted to tracing curriculum evolution from Harvard College's mission (Carnegie Foundation for the Advancement of Teaching, 1977) "to advance learning and perpetuate it to posterity: dreading to leave an illiterate ministry to the churches ..." (p. 28), Yale College's advice that "every student shall consider the main end of his study to wit to know God in Jesus Christ and answerably to lead a Godly sober life" (Rudolph, 1977 p. 8) to the incredibly diverse missions of today's colleges. Defining the "liberal arts" is no easier task than defining the purpose of a college education for the liberal arts have changed shape along with the missions of colleges.

The liberal arts of today is quite dissimilar to its progenitor described as "inherited from the Middle Ages, modified by the Renaissance, and transmitted to the American Republic" (Jones, 1966, p. 7). Liberal arts, for the past half-century, has represented a way of thinking rather than a structure of the study of disciplines. It has emphasized the process of acquiring knowledge of the world and self through reflection upon the work of others and on contemporary problems. The liberal arts has valued the general more than the specific. It is concerned with modes of thinking rather than bodies of knowledge. In its best form, the liberal arts is epistemological, philosophical, and concerned with the ends of knowledge. Knowledge for its own sake is inherent in a contemporary philosophy of liberal arts—not a value for *a* body of knowledge, but rather a detachment from concern for knowledge as an objective end of learning. Liberal learning questions the status quo, the assumptions of and about knowledge, and critically examines how civilization disposes of its knowledge. These may be my wants of liberal education, but these wants have characterized most liberal arts agendas for the past 50 years, in theory if not in practice.

At the present time, in setting the agenda for higher education in the 1980s and 1990s it is imperative for reasons without need of statement that we remember Socrates' dictum: "The unexamined life is not worth living." Curriculum concerns of liberal education, as forwarded above, need to be articulated and generalized at a level practical enough that we can observe in the teaching/learning environment these vital concerns. These purposes of college curricula or mission are obscured by other values today. Not surprisingly, many college students do not know that these *are*, or *were*, important values of the college experience; they are thus victimized for not knowing how to think critically and reflectively when, in fact, secondary and postsecondary education has neglected these values and not taught students how to think. We cannot begin by trying to restate and reinstate a liberal learning (thinking) curriculum. We must begin by describing what typifies today's college experience vis-à-vis a liberal learning experience.

College liberal arts curricula, in the main, are normally similar to curricula of the past. The structure of college departments is still along "discipline" lines or according to subject fields (realms of knowledge). Traditional "divisions" of these departments are called the social sciences, humanities, and natural sciences. With the possible exception of the humanities, each division has become more specialized in a field of knowledge, more closely linked to its associated professions, and more likely to teach courses that prepare students for specialized vocations. It is no coincidence that the humanities, subject to the least change in orientation toward specialization, has suffered the greatest depopulation of students in recent years (Carnegie Foundation for the Advancement of Teaching, 1977). The professionalization of the college major has led to a new concept of "general education" (Jones, 1966) that is in actuality a restatement of liberal studies' values divorced from the upper level (major) courses in the "liberal arts" curriculum. General studies, or the nonmajor core requirements in most liberal arts colleges and professional schools within universities have become a symbol of pedagogy in and of themselves. Professional schools and upper-level course instructors expect that general studies (required English, mathematics, rhetoric, introductory courses to the disciplines) will ensure that upperclassmen can read, write, follow discourse, and be generally prepared to master a field of knowledge and skills (or subfield). In essence, the vocational interest of students and institutions has assigned the teaching

of critical and reflective thinking of a general and knowledge-indepen-
dent nature to a corner of the curriculum. Hubris dominates the de-
partmental structure, each set to its own purpose of disseminating
specialized knowledge and skills, unaware and uncaring of what other
departments do with "their" students. If true, in whole or part, these
statements underscore the need to reconsider the role of liberal learning in the college, for the fragmented curriculum has become the accepted norm, or invisible reality of the contemporary American college.

What is wrong with curricula that compartmentalize liberal learning
goals? Liberal studies become a subject to study rather than a means of
studying and a way of thinking. Liberal arts becomes tacked on to the
curriculum rather than being an integral part, or worse, liberal thinking
skills are assumed to be learned elsewhere.

Professional schools are no less capable of providing liberal learning
objectives for students; they are, however, at greater risk of absolving
themselves from responsibility for liberal learning and leaving that responsibility to colleagues in the "other" school (the liberal arts college).
However, there is the opportunity for schools detached from the liberal
arts college to provide integrated liberal learning experiences equal to,
or better than, the fragmented offerings that may exist in the liberal
arts. Again, the question is not if vocational objectives will be pursued
by colleges, but how.

If potential exists for the professional school to integrate liberal
learning objectives with and throughout its specialized or technically
oriented curriculum, more opportunity lies with the liberal arts college
to reintegrate its liberal learning objectives within its "major" courses
of study—not as a prerequisite, but as an integral theme of study—the
organizing structure or world view. But why and how should this be
done?

Let's begin with the assumption that vocationalism in secondary and
postsecondary education will not go away. Let's also assume that the
best direction for discussion is to talk about how we will live with vocationalism without abandoning the essence of the values of liberal
learning. A failure to integrate liberal learning can separate—and has
to a large degree separated—liberal studies and academic specialization
and will continue to fuel hypervocational attitudes, that is, the current
perception that the need for more technical and job-related knowledge
necessarily must limit time devoted to more irrelevant pursuits. It is also
necessary to "show relevancy" of liberal learning to constituents. Jager
(1981) reasoned that

> our culture has developed the means (often willy-nilly) and encouraged
> the attitudes (often inadvertently) to insure that students will feel uneasy

if they lack swift, clear answers to questions of this kind: What are you going to do with your education? What are you studying for? What is the effort *for*? . . . The pressure of this vague burden of professionalism upon the beginning college student is most regrettable: unfair to students as individuals, subversive to educational values, and thoroughly unfair as social policy. (p. 89)

Students are part of a culture that is becoming increasingly specialized, more expert, and more overcome by what Toffler described as future shock. The shortsighted fears of employers concerned with short-term employment needs and limited resources to do in-house training become mediators of perceptions about survival in life after college. Most recently, representatives of business, perhaps aware that their highly skilled technical people are growing into the age of management and decision making, have taken a new look at the value of general education and what that implies. In the words of Green (1981):

. . . genuine job security lies in having the flexibility for change and personal growth. Such flexibility is better provided by broad conceptual, analytical, and communication abilities than by specific skills or information. . . . important is the willingness of faculty and administrators to realize the limitations and, indeed the transient value of "professional" curricula in the development of abilities essential for both changing job markets and personal growth." (p. 73)

A casual reading of organizational development literature reveals the importance of "change" skills to the new generation of workers.

Ironically, college professors are finding a bonanza of consulting work (particularly those in the fields of English, psychology, and sociology) teaching communication skills, interpersonal relations, personal growth strategies, values clarification, and providing corporate counseling to executives, technical people, and middle management in private industry. Although humanities majors have difficulty finding jobs in the private sector, business leaders complained to educators at a meeting sponsored by the National Foundation for the Humanities and the Association of American Colleges that "many students, especially engineering, science, and business majors cannot communicate adequately in memos, reports or speeches" (Fowler, 1983, p. D19). In fact, at this meeting, AT&T Chairman Charles L. Brown reminded participants that a study conducted by his company investigated administrative skills including planning, organization and decision-making leadership, oral communication, intellectual ability including verbal and quantitative skills, and on-the-job motivation of 200 managers of scientific-technical or humanities background and found that humanities and social science majors achieved the best overall performance. They demonstrated strong interpersonal skills and were similar to business majors in administrative ability and motivation for advancement.... We found extremely pertinent evidence that humanities/social science majors were most suited for change, which is the leading feature of the high-speed, high-pressure, high tech world we now occupy. (p. D19)

At this meeting the chairman of General Foods quipped, "Business is fundamentally the relationship between human beings, but few business schools teach much of this—they leave it to Dale Carnegie and the Japanese" (p. D19).

The liberal arts are practical. Arthur Levine, president of Bradford College (Haverhill, MA) stated that the "Liberal Arts have always been practical. If you go back to the Middle Ages ... students studied rhetoric, logic and Latin because that was one social path to mobility ... a job with the church" (McCain, 1983, p. 7). Even Terrel Bill, Ronald Reagan's high-tech secretary of education, stated that "careerism" threatens college with becoming "glorified work-preparation institutes.... We ought to be examining whether we have distorted the priorities of our colleges and universities" (p. 7).

Are we as concerned with broadening our students intellect as we are with making graduates competent in the job-skills sense? Perhaps the groundwork for revitalizing liberal learning is the articulation of why general education is practical, valuable, and necessary to career and life success. Perhaps the most important step is integrating liberal arts into the major, raising its status from a prerequisite to "advanced knowledge." Failure to do so sends a clear message to students: We'll let you get the requirements out of the way in years one and two so that you can spend years three and four on the "real stuff."

In Toffler's (1971) future world, the technology will not require

millions of lightly lettered men [*sic*], ready to work in unison.... It requires not men who take orders in unblinking fashion, aware that the price of bread is mechanical submission to authority, but men who can make critical judgments, who can weave their way through novel environments, who are quick to spot new relationships in the rapidly changing reality." (p. 402)

Toffler cannot be called a proponent of the liberal arts, but what better to call the liberal learning experience than preparation as societal and self-critic. The creative individual of the future will be that critic.

Revitalizing liberal learning is a popular trend, but it not a bandwagon. It is happening in a small ballpark. Positive steps toward restating the values of liberal studies are found in new offerings of modes-of-thinking courses, integrated studies, topical approaches to critical thinking and values, reinstitution of "core" course requirements and increased faculty dialogue about the aims of education in a holistic sense. The immediate obstacle to function of this endeavor is the absence of a language to express the commonalities of diverse majors and schools and their relationship to liberal learning. The specialization of purpose and the distinctiveness of bodies of knowledge render past unifications of intellectual process and mastery of knowledge obsolete. Scientific method is a disputed entity of cross-disciplinary usage given the quantum leaps of knowledge and specialized modes of knowledge acquisition. Writing as a general intellectual process is spurned by the specialist who demands specific styles of writing. Teachers learn how to teach reading in social studies as opposed to teaching reading in science. The specialization of pedagogy has kept pace with the rest of society. (We even have the new field of andragogy or the teaching of adults as opposed to children's pedagogy.)

I propose an old idea as a potential, if partial, solution to the absence of a common language for unifying liberal learning process and the acquisition of specialized skills and knowledge. It is proposed as a beginning point for trial and discussion. It is a model of human intellect that embraces liberal learning values (or is embraced by liberal learning) and underlies creativity in all its forms. It is practical and consistent with vocational aspirations. This nonmagical entity is a list of process skills that are a part of the doing of all disciplines and a part of functional working and living.

Benjamin Bloom and his colleagues (Bloom, Englehart, Furst, Hill, & Krathwohl, 1956) defined educational objectives in three domains: cognitive, affective, and psychomotor. These objectives have appeared in curricula with vacillating popularity since. We will consider the cognitive domain here of immediate interest because its objectives are most easily related to the emphasis of college instruction. The affective and psychomotor domains, although of less immediate interest, are of no less importance to full consideration of the aims of education. Bloom's hierarchy of cognitive objectives (which imply skills) is presented as follows:

1. Knowledge
2. Comprehension
3. Application
4. Analysis
5. Synthesis
6. Evaluation

These objectives and their implied cognitive skills are common to all disciplines of study and in a more general sense to intellectual or thinking activity. The intellectual behaviors are arranged from simple to complex, each class of behavior building upon behaviors of a "lower" class. It is a simple list of thought processes that represent levels of thinking. The use of the term thinking behaviors should not be inferred to represent a behavioral view of learning although some represent it as such.

Knowledge objectives include knowing (remembering) terms, specific facts, procedures, concepts, and principles. Knowing is a low level of intellectual activity but critical to all higher levels of thinking. Even a complex theory can be recalled if memorized and this is a knowledge-level activity.

Comprehension implies understanding; comprehension is required to grasp the meaning of material, translate it into different forms, interpret information (explain or summarize), and predict or estimate outcomes.

Application means using what is learned in concrete ways, doing things with the knowledge, applying rules, methods, concepts, principles, laws, and theories to solve problems or change something.

Analysis, breaking the whole into parts, is a high-level task requiring application and comprehension. The concept includes identifying substructures of ideas and objects and the organizational patterns or principles involved. Analysis requires comprehension of the structure of things.

Synthesis refers to putting parts together to create new wholes. Learning outcomes in this class stress creative action with emphasis on new patterns or structures.

Evaluation, the highest level of cognitive activity, is concerned with judging the validity of ideas or concepts for some particular purpose. Judgments are based on definite criteria, internal or external. This is the highest level of cognitive activity and is dependent upon the other levels of thinking. It is making informed value judgments. I have previously called this skill critical thinking and the essence of liberal learning.

A small amount of elaboration and example make this structure of learning comprehensible to students of upper elementary grades and beyond. The propagation of this model has a number of advantages for students and educators. First, it makes the learning process (goals and expectations) explicit to students. It fosters discourse between students and teachers about classroom instruction and interactions; it helps students and teachers understand the true meaning of curriculum and encourages a congruity of student and teacher goals. Essay examination questions utilize directions such as "Analyze," "Synthesize," "Compare and contrast," "Identify," and the like. Many assumptions are made by students and teachers about what thinking processes are to be invoked to answer the question. Discussion of the process model of learning reduces ambiguity in teacher directions and expectations. I suspect it also facilitates learning.

Second, a model of cognitive processes provides a common language of discourse for educators from different disciplines to engage in discussion of the general aims of education—what should our graduates know and what should they be able to do. Course, department, and school missions can be made more meaningful to students and to *employers*.

Third, utilizing this taxonomy, teachers can more consciously balance learning objectives, better relate specialized knowledge to other fields and general (universally applicable) intellectual skills.

Fourth, this discourse is evidence of the relevance of liberal learning to the world of work, and students through this discourse can value the traditional liberal arts disciplines when outcomes are articulated through these terms, for these are the intellectual skills that make for creative managers, engineers, lawyers, and inventors.

Fifth, students can be encouraged to be synectic thinkers, cross-discipline synthesizers—they will profit from the "big picture" by the learned privilege of taking a step back from specialized method and knowledge. A common language of skills can make curriculum more coherent and more integrated.

Bloom's model is not "the" model but only one of many competing taxonomies. It was chosen for example here because of its simplicity and comprehensiveness. No such model should or will replace the uniqueness of intellectual processes required by different specialized fields, but there are commonalities of process (I believe that Bloom is an example of this) that need to be made explicit to the academic community and the world of work. We are not doing this effectively.

A language of process skills will make thinking, reading, and writing across the curriculum more viable concepts, and these are great potential unifiers of curriculum. It can lead to a better understanding by content specialists of what general educators (teachers of "core" communications and quantitative courses) are trying to provide students and a greater responsibility for the continuation of this process through "advanced" courses. Reading, writing, oral communication, and quantitative skills can be viewed less as skills that are mastered in one or two courses, but rather as skills that need to be developed through a lifetime of intellectual activity, in school, at work, and through leisure activities in pursuit of the good life.

Bloom's affective domain (elaborated by Krathwohl, Bloom & Masia, 1964, mentioned above) addresses the human processes of valuing and fulfillment. It is no less a part of intellectual development than the cognitive model and its values are no less dear to liberal learning. Appreciation of learning, beauty in art and literature, valuing humanity and seeking organization and symmetry in life are a few of the educational objectives that it addresses.

Implementing an intellectual development scheme using a thinking skills model should produce some very observable phenomena in classroom instruction. More student writing, in every classroom, regardless of subject, should be encouraged. More concern for the historical development of a discipline with consideration of ethical questions past, present, and future will provide a cultural context for study. The communication of ideas should be given the equal treatment of knowing. Interdisciplinary seminars and symposia can bring heightened awareness and appreciation of different insights into questions of concern to all. Most importantly, an understanding of what the liberal arts *can be* in terms of career and life development can be found in an integrated curriculum. Creative man is born of it.

The marriage of professional preparation and liberal learning goals needs to be a priority for educators. The ideas offered here for beginning a dialogue about the goals of a college education cannot stand alone and are not offered as a solution. It is hoped that discussion of these suggestions will encourage new and more institutionally tailored initiatives that will help us to redefine what it is that we want graduates to be, and what we want them to be able to do.

REFERENCES

Bloom, B.S., Engelhart, N.D., Furst, E.J., Hill, W.H., & Krathwohl, D.R. (1956). *Taxonomy of educational objectives, handbook, I. Cognitive domain.* New York: McKay.

Bronowksi, G.J. (1958). The creative process. *Scientific American, 199,* 59–65.

Carnegie Foundation for the Advancement of Teaching. (1977). *Missions of the college curriculum.* San Francisco, CA: Jossey-Bass.

Clifford, G.J. (1964). A culture-bound concept of creativity: A social historian's critique. *Educational Theory, 14,* 133–143.

Cohen, D. & Haney, W. (1978, December). *Minimums, competency testing, and social policy.* Cambridge, MA: National Consortium on Testing.

Dellas, M. & Gaier, E.I. (1970). Identification of creativity. *Psychological Bulletin, 15* (1), 55–73.

Farr, R. (1977, April). Is Johnny's/Mary's reading getting worse? *Educational Leadership. 34,* 521–527.

Fowler, E.M. (1983, May 4). Humanities majors in business. *New York Times.*

Friedman, S. & Kilodiy, G. (1983). A model program for developing verbal and quantitative reasoning skills. *Problem Solving, 5*(9), 1–2, 5.

Golann, S.E. (1963). Psychological study of creativity. *Psychological Bulletin, 69*, 548–565.

Green, C.S., (1981) Klug, H.G., Neider, L.A., Salem R.G. Careers, curricula, and the future of liberal learning: A program for action. In C.S. Green & R.G. Salem (Eds.), *New directions for teaching and learning: Liberal learning and careers* (pp. 67–80, 87–94). San Francisco, CA: Jossey-Bass.

Haney, W. & Madaus, G. (1978). Making sense of the competency testing movement. *Harvard Educational Review, 48*, 462–484.

Jager, R. (1981). Career and curriculum. In C.S. Green & R.G. Salem (Eds.), *New directions for teaching and learning: Liberal learning and careers*. San Francisco, CA: Jossey-Bass.

Jencks, C. & Riesman, D. (1968). *The academic revolution*. New York: Doubleday.

Jones, H.M. (1966). Uses of the past in general education. *Harvard Educational Review, 36*(1), 3–16.

Kinney, J. (1979). Lack of basic skills among community college students causes alarm. *Humanities Report, 1*(9), 9–14.

Krathwohl, D.R., B.S. Bloom & Masia, B. (1964). *Taxonomy of educational objectives. Handbook II: Affective domain*. New York: McKay.

Litt, E. (1981). Higher education and the American political economy. In C.S. Green & R.G. Salem (Eds.), *New directions for teaching and learning: Liberal learning and careers* (pp. 1–12). San Francisco, CA: Jossey-Bass.

Lyons, K.M. (1981). *A validity study of a domain-referenced minimum competency reading test for secondary level students and a proposed model for assessing the context dependence, reliability, content and construct validity of similar criterion-referenced reading measures*. Unpublished doctoral dissertation, Boston University, Boston.

McCain, N. (1983, November 23). The liberal arts fight. *Boston Globe*. pp. 1, 7.

Pearlman, C. (1983) A theoretical model for creativity. *Education, 103*(3), 294–305.

Rudolph, F. (1977). *Curriculum*. San Francisco, CA: Jossey-Bass.

Silberman, C.E. (1970) *Crisis in the classroom: The remaking of American education*. New York: Vintage Books.

Toffler, A. (1971). *Future shock*. New York: Random House.

White, R.W. (1959). Motivation reconsidered, the concept of competence. *Psychological Review, 66*, 297–333.

White, R.W. (1960). Competence and the psychosexual stages of development. In M.S. Jones, (Ed.), *Nebraska Symposium on Motivation*.

Young, R.E. (Ed.). (1981). *New directions for teaching and learning: Fostering critical thinking*. San Francisco, CA: Jossey-Bass.

SYMPOSIUM

PANEL 4

Comments

Laura Hourtienne

By way of opening, I should like to state that I believe that Professor Lyons has done an admirable job of describing the problems facing liberal learning as it attempts to adjust to the demands placed upon it by the practical world. However, I am not sure that he has sufficiently addressed the problem of creativity, or rather the crisis resulting from a dearth thereof in the world today.

Professor Miliora has given us a thought-provoking description of the conditions prerequisite for engaging in the creative process. But I think we find ourselves groping for a way to integrate these ideas and approaches into the liberal learning setting, or any other institutional setting for that matter. Nevertheless, a challenge is there for us, and I believe this challenge must be taken up.

Because of the diversity of the material presented and the great distance between the two papers, I shall address each separately.

I agree with Professor Lyons' general presentation of the problems and his concern with the need to maintain a balance between vocationalism and liberal learning. However, I feel that in attempting to establish the practical value of liberal learning in the marketplace, he has underemphasized the primary justification of liberal learning: the holistic aspect by which it aims at preparing the whole human being to lead a fulfilled life, addressing not only material needs but also spiritual ones. I am sorry that he places primary emphasis on Bloom's hierarchy of cognitive objectives, while merely alluding to, and thereby relegating to secondary importance, the affective domain, which includes, as he does state, the teaching of appreciation of learning, beauty in art and literature, valuing humanity, and seeking organization and symmetry in life.

Also, I share with Professor Lyons his concern about the trend away

163

from integration and see attempts to reintegrate, such as modes of thinking courses, integrated studies, topical approaches to critical thinking and values, and reinstitution of "core" course requirements, as positive. However, I think it is not enough to suggest that what we want to integrate are critical thinking skills across interdisciplinary lines. The goal of liberal learning in the past has been the integration of the individual, the development of the individual into a many faceted human being capable of valuing his own and others' humanity. Borrowing a quote from Litt used by Professor Lyons: "Human concerns, not those of policy makers are the core of liberal education."

This leads me to raise another question concerning the relationship of the liberal learning institution to the political-economic order of the day. In discussing the threat posed by vocationalism in higher education, Professor Lyons quotes from Litt. I consider this quote so important that I would like to repeat it again. Litt describes the "vocational university" as "a knowledge apparatus explicitly designed to create and apply ideas that are functional to dominant national policies. . . . By contrast, the internal core of the liberal arts curriculum is the mastery over political events as well as subject matter through cultivation of the rational and expressive faculties." The question that this quote prompts is of fundamental importance. Is it the purpose of the liberal learning institution merely to prepare students to serve, and thereby be subservient to the existing political-economic order, or is it to develop in them the qualities of mind and judgment which will enable them to have mastery over these events?

Professor Lyons has stated, and it is generally agreed, that we are faced today with a crisis in creativity. If we accept Professor Miliora's description of the qualities or preconditions necessary to develop or nurture the creative attitude, the reason for the existence of such a crisis is, I think, immediately apparent. Professor Lyons has referred to the absence of a language in which to express the commonalities of diverse majors and schools and their relationship to liberal learning. Professor Miliora's presentation brings home very forcefully the fact that between the language of creativity and the language of institutions there exists a language gap of monumental proportions. The vocabulary with which she describes the creative attitude is totally foreign to institutions, including those of liberal learning. Joy, trust, spontaneity, celebration, affirmation of life beyond life, inspiration, illumination, transcendence, curiosity as playfulness, listening to the impulse, the leap into the unknown are terms used to express spiritual experience, and many of them have their origin in mysticism. It would perhaps be too radical to propose that psychosynthesis be adopted as a central objective of the liberal arts curriculum. However, if those of us who are advocates of liberal learning continue to profess as one of the central goals of liberal learning the development of the whole individual, and we are sincere in our intent to foster creativity and are not merely paying lip service to it, then we have to listen very carefully to the message contained in Professor Miliora's presentation. A casual glance at the vocabulary I just mentioned makes glaringly apparent how foreign this realm of creativity is to the high-speed, high-pressure, high-tech world we now occupy.

For a moment, for our consideration, I would like to juxtapose the prerequisites to success in this high-speed, high-pressure, high-tech world and the prerequisites to the creative process as described by Professor Miliora.

On the one hand we have:
—success orientation
—strong ego drive
—a critical, judgmental attitude, also toward self
—stress upon efficiency, results
—control
—aggressiveness, frenetic pace, and much cacophony
—an exaggerated, almost obsessive preoccupation with security (job and other)
—future orientation (expectations are that one will forego in the present in order to advance in the future)

On the other hand we have:
—willingness to risk ridicule and failure
—some freedom from attachment to a self-image
—a nonjudgmental, accepting attitude toward self, an attitude of "letting be"
—curiosity as playfulness, a childlike wanting to explore what is not known, an attitude of "letting go"
—calm, quiet, relaxation
—willingness to take great risks and to welcome the unexpected and unknown
—ability to become lost in the present (the idea that life is realized and fulfilled in the present)

With such polar distances separating these two worlds, is there any way of reconciling them, or is this description of the creative attitude too "far out" to be practicable in, or applicable to, the world we occupy or the world of learning that we know?

I don't believe for a moment that there is any easy way to bring together or synthesize these diametrically opposed world views. But I think it is important that we recognize the realities contained in both, not just one; both deserve our attention equally. It is not enough to hear only the demands of the marketplace. There are other voices also demanding to be heard. Hundreds of thousands of people, young people and people of all ages across this country and Europe today, are turning to New Age organizations and Eastern gurus, are practicing many varieties of meditation, are practicing yoga and other body-discipline exercises and, in general, are searching for spiritual values because they do experience deeply the need to achieve a counterbalance to the materialistically dominated demands and dictates of the marketplace and the current political-economic order. They are searching for a balance between materialistic and spiritual values, the kind of balance that has always characterized liberal arts objectives.

The priorities of the culture in which we live do determine the type of creativity that is permitted to thrive and prosper. The crucial question is: Should we accept and conform our lives to the priorities set up for us by the marketplace—or do we continue to accept the challenge to educate young people in such a manner that they will be able to shape and critically reshape (transform) those priorities and choose for themselves the way in which they express their creativity, that they will be able to use their creativity in an independently responsible way to implement change in directions other than those dictated by the current power structure? If the answer is the latter, this involves more than developing the rational mind alone. It includes also developing the elements central to Professor Miliora's description of the creative attitude: the imagination and the intuitive powers that lead to higher consciousness.

Nineteenth-century thinkers in their idealism chose to confer upon the ancestor of modern man the appellative *homo sapiens*, man the knower, the wise. The twentieth century, through its love affair with technology, has transformed his contemporary descendant into *homo faber*, man the manufacturer, manipulator, fabricator, technologist, and technician. Liberal arts education in the past has always aspired to strive for wholeness and balance. I believe the real challenge to liberal arts education today is whether we are going to be satisfied with, and accept, this new nomenclature, accept as our reduced assignment the task of preparing young people for material success in the marketplace—which is not synonymous with life fulfillment, or whether we are going to continue to insist upon developing not only minds to serve but also imaginations and spirits to master.

SYMPOSIUM

PANEL 5

PROSPECTS FOR TEACHING CREATIVITY

New Directions in the Teaching of Creativity

Joseph M. McCarthy

This paper is part of a larger study which is intended to be a broad resource supporting any future effort the college may make to integrate the study and teaching of creativity into its curriculum and/or to establish a center or institute for studying creativity. This larger study will produce a guide to research and practice in the teaching of creativity and a file of program/curricular models, both intended to introduce users as quickly as possible to the state of the art in creativity training. As part of that larger effort, this paper develops an analysis of the successes and failures of experimental and other research into creativity training and suggests a new direction or axis for future research.

At the outset, it is useful to note the incredible volume of recent research literature on creativity. The term "creativity" first came into currency during the Renaissance and related the power of the artist to the creative power of God (Nahm, 1965). Like God, that power was seen as mysterious and unexplainable. In modern psychological and educational literature, the term/concept, initially neglected, has enjoyed a remarkable currency. During the 1930s and 1940s, only 186 books and articles on creativity were published (Guilford, 1950). In 1965, however, *Psychological Abstracts* listed 132 items on the subject (Getzels & Madaus, 1969). The first edition of the *Encyclopedia of Educational Research*, published in 1941, made no mention of creativity. In 1950, the second edition added the term to its catalogue of higher mental processes. By the third edition, in 1960, "creative thinking" was a subsection of the article on higher mental processes. The first full treatment came only in the 1969 edition. By the period 1979–1983, the ERIC system was logging over 700 articles and documents a year dealing with educational aspects of creativity. For the purposes of studying the teaching of creativity, only a fraction of this literature is directly pertinent. A great portion of it is devoted to study and speculation of the nature and definition of creativity, and much of it is concerned with teaching creatively rather than teaching creativity. When we factor out items in which the word appears as an attractive buzzword with scant regard for rigorous usage, this huge literature is rendered into a manageable quantity. Even then, a great many promising items prove to deal rather with intelligence or giftedness or with the personal characteristics of creative persons than with educational strategies that facilitate, liberate, or promote creative behavior.

Nevertheless, the sheer volume of potentially useful material is daunting, and the range of applications evidences an interest on the part of the educational community that is broad as well as intense. A large quantity of the recent educational literature on creativity concerns the teaching of the gifted and talented (Callahan and Renzulli, 1977; Huber, 1979; Keating, 1980; Linder, 1981; Lowenfels, 1979; Navarre, 1979; Renzulli & Callahan, 1975), but a great deal of it also concerns the teaching of special needs and disadvantaged children (Alvarez, 1983; Callahan, 1974; Jaben, 1983; Jegard, 1981; Landmann & Schroder, 1981). Every age group has been studied in relation to creative training, from preschool and elementary (Claguetweet, 1981; Kalmar & Kalmar, 1980; Khatena, 1971b; Khatena & Dickerson, 1973; Rodriguez, 1981, Schempp, 1983), through secondary (Carter, 1984; Clements, Dwinell, Torrance & Kidd, 1982; Dacey, 1971; Shepherd, 1982; Smith, 1980), to college and adult levels (Chambers, 1973; Jones, 1980; Khatena, 1970, 1971a; Whitman, 1983). The expected "creative" subject matters have received due attention: art (Jones, 1980; Smith, 1980; Torrance, 1980a); drama (Clements, et al., 1982); and writing (Alvarez, 1983; Callahan & Renzulli, 1977; Evans, 1983; Raimo, 1980; Rouse, 1983; Shepherd, 1982; Tway, 1980; Vitiello, 1983; Youngkin, 1982). Yet other subject areas have received their due meed of attention: business education (Fox, 1981; Golen, 1983); journalism (Moriarty, 1983); physical education (Carlson, 1979; Schempp, 1983); reading (Martin, 1982); science (Penick, 1983); and social studies (Brown & McFarlin, 1980; Claguetweet, 1981; Wragg, 1983). Teachers have been studied as well as students (Chambers, 1973; Glover, 1981–82), and sex, ethnicity, and socioeconomic factors as well as classroom circumstances (Haley, 1984; Moreno & Hogan, 1976; Rodriguez, 1981). In addition to schools, interest has been expressed in training programs in business and industry (Basadur, Graen, & Green, 1980; Dunette, 1963; Raudsepp, 1983; Stein, 1974). Nor is the literature on creativity training merely a phenomenon of the English-speaking countries (Hlavsa, Balonova, & Kolaj, 1980; Kalmar & Kalmar, 1980; Landmann & Schroder, 1981; Muradov, 1982; Vojtko & Pachinova, 1981).

In analyzing this research literature, it is useful to begin with the experimental research tradition. In the recent literature, only one review of the research has been strongly positive regarding the teachability of creativity (Torrance, 1972). This evaluated 142 experiments using empirical evidence and involving elementary and secondary school students. The studies were classified into nine categories based on method of facilitating creativity: Parnes' creative problem-solving procedures; other disciplined procedures; complex programs involving packages of materials; the creative arts; media and reading programs; curricular and administrative arrangement; teacher-classroom variables; motivation, reward, and competition; and facilitating testing conditions. The study claimed an overall success rate of 72%, with a range from over 90% for Parnes' procedures and other disciplined procedures to a low in the 50% range for curricular/administrative arrangements and teacher-classroom variables. There is, however, a problem, or series of problems, with the nature of the evidence. Very few students of creative training have utilized sufficiently thorough research methodology to be able legitimately to claim external validity.

The biggest single stumbling block is the continuing disagreement over the nature and definition of the concept of creativity. Professor Webb has explored some of the dimensions of this problem in his paper and is certainly correct in referring to the concept as "a slippery beast." In attempting to define creativity, researchers variously focus on creative products, the creative process, or the creative situation. If one studies creativity through its products, one must first define the nature of those products. The usual list of characteristics of creative products— that they are novel or original in the experience of an entire civilization, teleological, aesthetically pleasing, capable of dissemination, and tending to create new conditions of human existence—provides grounds for almost endless arguments and is, in any case, indicative of a definition much too exalted to be altogether useful in dealing with the learning achievements of schoolchildren. In the absence of complete resolution of these arguments and full study of the application of these characteristics to evaluating the products of children's activity, it is all too easy to fall back on a reductionist acceptance of self-reports, question-begging instruments testing "creativity," and other dubious procedures.

Should one prefer to see creativity as process, the range of possibilities announces the difficulty of the task. The creative process can be viewed and studied as autobiography, through analysis of such factors as associational fluency, originality, adaptive or spontaneous flexibility, and sensitivity to problems, through tests of convergent versus divergent thinking, by eliciting creative responses under controlled conditions, by testing hypotheses about details of the process, or by computerized problem solving and artificial intelligence. If one engages in the study of creative persons, selection of the subjects offers thorny problems. Performance on tests of creativity may not equal real-life creativity, prestige of subjects may contaminate the study, criteria emphasizing "self-actualization" are vague. Finally, the notion of the creative situation is analyzable only to the extent that an empirical basis can be discovered for specific agreement about types of circumstances that promote creativity (MacKinnon, 1968). Although all of the above taken together constitutes a singularly rich research agenda, it presents to the researcher on creative training some knotty methodological problems that are too often glossed over or ignored entirely, most often through unintentional reification of "creativity" or by excessive simplification in seeking an operational definition.

It is often forgotten that "creativity," for all the currency of the term, is only a hypothetical construct, an inference based on the observation of "creative" behavior. Enough hypothetical constructs linked one to another can provide a theory, which can be experimentally tested and verified or disproven. To reify a hypothetical construct so that it takes on in our assumptions the attributes of a real thing is to poison the wells of testing or discussions, and yet this is often done with "creativity." Beyond this, the attempt to define the term operationally for the sake of empirical investigation often does violence to the investigation and/or trivializes it. To define "creativity" by counting the number of correct answers on a test of divergent thinking is common in research studies of creativity training. When we ask ourselves whether creativity can be taught, therefore, we're often asking whether we can increase students' scores on tests of divergent thinking. Despite a large research literature on divergent thinking tests, their relation to real-life characteristics and skills that we would recognize as "creativity" is assumed rather than proven (Kogan & Pankove, 1974).

In addition to these basic conceptual problems, studies evaluating the effectiveness of creativity training often do not control adequately for the effects of motivation and response sets, to which tests of divergent thinking are vulnerable, fail to control for teacher effects or teacher modifications of procedure, fail to control for Hawthorne effects, fail to assign students or groups randomly, include in the program tasks too similar to the criterion tests, use individual scores rather than classroom means as the unit of statistical analysis, and use several univariate analyses rather than a single multivariate analysis (Mansfield, Busse, & Krepelka, 1978). Moreover, most inferential research of this type examines the significance of differences between experimental and control groups but does not assess how powerful the effect of treatment was on subjects (Rose & Lin, 1984).

These conceptual and methodological problems are pervasive enough and serious enough as to engender debate whether creativity can really be taught. Reviews of the literature have tended to be pessimistic. The first article on creativity to appear in the *Encyclopedia of Educational Research* began its treatment of the educational facilitation of creativity by observing that numerous strategies had been proposed, but usually without evidence of effectiveness (Getzels & Madaus, 1969). A lengthy study of the effectiveness of creativity training in the *Review of Educational Research* emphasized the methodological problems outlined above (Mansfield, et al., 1978). This study served as the basis for the section on training and education of the article on creativity in the most recent edition of the *Encyclopedia of Educational Research*, which concluded that, despite some effort to train divergent thinking abilities, most theories of creative process have had little effect on real-life situations in schools and that the task of the 'Eighties may be to apply these theories to education, especially of the gifted (Mansfield & Busse, 1982). The most recent review of the literature attempts to use the statistical technique of meta-analysis to examine how much impact treatments have on subjects across a wide range of inferential studies. Although it concludes that training does affect creativity, it laments the paucity of systematic research on program evaluation and does not do a great deal more than reinforce the positive findings of previous researchers with regard to the brainstorming approach as refined by Parnes (Rose & Lin, 1984).

For all this, a number of approaches have shown enough potential to warrant further experimentation. The first requisite would be a tightening of experimental methodology so as to deal with the serious criticisms that have been leveled at past studies (Isaksen, Stein, Hills, & Gryskiewicz, 1984). In this case, the most promising method on which to focus would be the Parnes program, which has been used with college students as well as with younger groups. The primary technique of this program is brainstorming, in which group participants are encouraged to share whatever ideas come to mind, no matter how unusual or impractical, without evaluation or criticism (Parnes & Noller, 1971, 1972a, 1972b, 1972c, 1973). Supplemental use of a variety of other techniques has made it difficult to assign effectiveness to specific techniques. The best designed evaluation studies dealt with uses of the program among both university and secondary school students, and show consistent and impressive results on measures of fluency, flexibility, originality, elaboration, and sensitivity (Reese & Parnes, 1970; Renner & Renner, 1971). Other studies, however, have suggested that individuals working alone produced more ideas than those brainstorming in groups and that the real value of group brainstorming is as a warmup for individual brainstorming (Dunette, 1963; Lindgren & Lindgren, 1965; Taylor, 1958). Nonetheless, the Parnes program has shown success, perhaps because of the age of the students, length of exposure to the technique, and high teacher involvement, and is arguably the most successful method of creativity training (Mansfield et al., 1978). The method is continually being utilized and improved upon at the Creative Education Foundation at the State University of New York College at Buffalo, which distributes books and teaching materials embodying the system. Parnes and his collaborators have developed a very useful guidebook which is currently in its second edition (Parnes, Noller, & Biondi, 1977).

Rigorous criticism of experimental research methodology does not mean that creativity cannot be taught, nor does it mean that experimental research cannot be valuable in illuminating the ingredients of creativity and the processes by which it may be fostered. It simply means that, as of the present moment and on the basis of available research, the verdict on creativity training most nearly approximates the traditional Scottish verdict of "not proven." There is excellent reason to think that creative behaviors are teachable, despite the significant definitional problems encountered in dealing with creativity, but experimental research may not be the most useful means of establishing the how and what of such a process. A good part of the problem is the tendency of educators in recent times to rely excessively upon psychology in its most experimental form as the most valid technique for study-educational reality. Education is, after all, a phenomenon susceptible of analysis through a variety of methods: philosophical, historical, sociological, anthropological, among others. Any of these methodologies has its strengths and limitations, and must be used in combination with others to provide a true, useful, and good synthetic picture of any educational institution, structure, or approach. Experimental psychology, by insisting upon a strict standard of laboratory repeatability, studies a situation that is by definition artificial, and often screens out as inimical to experimental conditions charismatic behaviors crucial to success in the classroom.

In studying creativity training, it is time to turn from the measurement of outcomes by instruments of supposedly high validity to the description of classroom processes by sophisticated observers intent upon the interpersonal and cultural aspects of fostering creative behavior, with validation on the basis of structural corroboration, referential adequacy and agreement among independent observers, research in the tradition of Philip Jackson's *Life in Classrooms*, Louis Smith and William Geoffrey's *The Complexities of an Urban Classroom* and Sarah Lawrence Lightfoot's *The Good High School* (Eisner, 1984). Studies such as these, using a method more typical of anthropology than experimental psychology, may well prove to be the most useful and illuminating way of discovering what it is in classroom interaction that best stimulates creative behavior. It is surprising, therefore, that so little interest in the topic has been displayed by educational anthropologists. The remarkable volume of studies on creativity includes almost no studies using anthropological method. The one study that uses this method, and does so with suppleness and discernment, is an essay by the late Jules Henry which clearly demonstrates the excellence of the approach (Henry, 1972). Yet this would seem to be the best way to bypass the wheel-spinning that has been characteristic of recent experimental research.

Those interested in creativity training primarily for action rather than further research will find available a large practitioner literature of uneven quality. A great deal of this is to be found in texts which attempt to distill from the research literature the most workable approach and describe some of the techniques elaborated by practitioners which seem to work but haven't necessarily been experimentally validated (Davis & Rimm, 1985; Foster, 1971; Gowan, Khatena, & Torrance, 1981; Guilford, 1968; Jones, 1972; Lytton, 1971; Marksberry, 1963; Parnes et al., 1977; Sanders & Sanders, 1984; Williams, 1972). The most recent of these, Davis and Rimm's 1985 *Education of the Gifted and Talented*, devotes two chapters to creativity. The first of these explores the characteristics of creative students (including a discussion of the relationship of creativity and intelligence), the creative process, and creative dramatics. The second begins with a discussion of the teachability of creativity and continues with a presentation of various techniques. The principal author's AUTA model (awareness, understanding, techniques and actualization) is treated first. Then the chapter proceeds to personal creative thinking techniques and standard creative thinking techniques (third step of the AUTA model). With regard to the first—personal creative thinking techniques—the authors present a series of examples, from artists and composers to cartoonists and columnists, from writers and filmmakers to professional comedians, and draw principles from them. With regard to standard creative thinking techniques, they present brief descriptions of a variety of methods, beginning, of course, with brainstorming (a disproportionately lengthy treatment) and continuing with attribute listing, attribute modifying, attribute transferring, morphological synthesis, idea checklists, synectics, direct analogy, personal analogy, and fantasy analogy. The chapter ends with a section on creativity-stimulating activities and exercises. Another intriguing text, *Teaching Creativity Through Metaphor: An Integrated Brain Approach* (Sanders & Sanders, 1984), provides discussion and approaches to teaching creativity based upon the tradition of left-brain/right-brain research as applied to understanding creativity (Bruner, 1979; Youngkin, 1982).

Another category of practitioners' literature is to be found in journal articles and items in the ERIC system which describe successful classroom practices. This literature, of course, tends to be highly subjective and especially vulnerable to enthusiasm. Yet even those who have been socialized into experimental research traditions can comprehend the particular usefulness of subjectivity in such a research area as creativity, and even if a great many self-reports are discounted or discarded, a great many remain to vitalize individual classroom practice. Some titles may be noted as indicative of the variety of this literature: "Creativity through the Microcomputer" (Bass, 1980); "Stimulating Creativity in a Large-enrollment History Class" (Brown & McFarlin, 1980); "Message for Business Educators: Injecting Creativity into the Classroom" (Fox, 1981); "Developing Creativity through the Reading Program" (Martin, 1982); "Yes, Creativity Can Be Taught—And Here Are Some Devices for Teaching It" (Moriarty, 1983); "Fifteen Ways to Cultivate Creativity in Your Classroom" (Timberlake, 1982). Perhaps even more indicative of variety is the fact that these articles appeared in such journals as *History Teacher, Journal of Business Education, Reading Teacher, Journalism Educator*, and *Childhood Education*. It should also be noted that not all such articles are about classroom practices, as witness "Creativity Training: Management Tool for High School Department Chairmen" (Burstiner, 1973) and "The Production of Metaphor in Poetry Therapy as a Means of Achieving Insight" (Goldstein, 1983). Whether pieces of this sort digest the fruits of experimental research for practitioners or report on individual or classroom activities that have subjectively been judged successful, they constitute a resource rich in suggestions for curriculum development and program building.

Beyond this, it is worth noting that "creativity" has recently become a trendy management buzzword and over 100 consultants and companies are offering creativity training workshops and aids for managers. Systematic research on the nature and effectiveness of such activity may well enrich the literature on creativity.

This paper has been concerned with the research aspects of new directions in the teaching of creativity. For too long, research on creativity teaching has been bogged down in an excessively narrow experimentalism which, despite its pretensions, is too often reductionist and lacking in rigor. This may be inevitable: The study of "creativity" may be sin-

gularly resistant to the demands of experimental research, too spontaneous for an artificial situation to yield external validity. If there are to
be new directions in research on creativity training, these must take
their origin in more supple, more real-life-oriented techniques of research, must pay much more attention to the characteristics of teachers
and their interaction with particular students in uncontrived situations.
Two new directions in particular seem to merit exploration. The first is
to put creativity teaching on the priority list of educational anthropologists and other nonexperimental researchers in both social sciences
and humanities. The second is to pay more attention to the people in
the trenches, teachers who must facilitate creative behavior and live with
the success or failure of their efforts, unvalidated though those may be.
The already voluminous literature on creativity would be remarkably
enriched by even a few high-quality studies of this sort.

REFERENCES AND BIBLIOGRAPHY

Alvarez, M.C. (1983). Sustained timed writing as an aid to fluency and creativity. *Teaching exceptional children, 15* (3), 160–162.

Amabile, T.M. (1983). *The social psychology of creativity.* New York: Springer-Verlag.

Barry, F., & Harrington, D.M. (1981). Creativity, intelligence and personality. *Annual Review of Psychology, 32*, 439–476.

Bartlett, M.M., & Davis, G.A. (1974). Do the Wallach and Kogan tests predict real creative behavior? *Perceptual and Motor Skills, 39*, 730.

Basadur, M., Graen, G.B., & Green, S.G. (1980). Training in creative problem-solving: Effects on ideation and problem finding and solving in an industrial research organization. *Organizational Behavior and Human Performance, 30* (1), 41–70.

Bass, G.M., Jr. (1980, June 23–25). *Creativity through the microcomputer.* Paper presented at the National Educational Computing Conference (ERIC Document Reproduction Service No. ED 190 128).

Brown, D., & McFarlin, H.A. (1980). Stimulating creativity in a large-enrollment history class. *History Teacher, 13* (2), 187–197.

Bruner, J. (1979). *On knowing: Essays for the left hand.* Cambridge, MA: Belknap.

Burstiner, I. (1973). Creativity training: Management tool for high school department chairmen. *Journal of Experimental Education, 41* (4), 17–19.

Busse, T.V., & Mansfield, R.S. (1980). Theories of the creative process: A review and a perspective. *Journal of Creative Behavior, 14* (2), 91–103.

Callahan, C.M. (1974). Development and evaluation of a creativity training program. *Exceptional Children, 41* (1), 44–45.

Callahan, C.M., & Renzulli, J.S. (1977). The effectiveness of a creativity training program in the language arts. *Gifted Child Quarterly, 21* (4), 538–545.

Carlson, J.B., (1979). Extending the boundaries of the imagination. *Journal of Physical Education and Recreation, 50* (4), 28–29.

Carter, L.K. (1984). The effects of multimodal creativity training on the creativity of twelfth graders. *Dissertation Abstracts International, 44* (7–A), 2091.

Chambers, J.A. (1973). College teachers: Their effect on the creativity of students. *Journal of Educational Psychology, 65.* 326–334.

Claguetweet, C. (1981). The effects of the implementation of creativity training in the elementary school social studies curriculum. *Journal of Creative Behavior, 15* (1), 70–71.

Clements, R.D., Dwinell, P.L., Torrance, E.P., & Kidd, J.T. (1982). Evaluation of some of the effects of a teen drama program on creativity. *Journal of Creative Behavior, 16* (4), 272–276.

Covington, M.V., Crutchfield, R.S., Davies, L., & Olton, R.M. (1974). *The productive thinking program: A course in learning to think.* Columbus, OH: Merrill.

Crockenberg, S.B. (1972). Creativity tests: A boon or a boondoggle for education? *Review of Educational Research, 42.* 29–45.

Cronbach, L.J. (1970). Intelligence? Creativity? A parsimonious reinterpretation of the Wallach-Kogan data. *American Educational Research Journal, 7*, 351–357.

Dacey, J.S. (1971). Programmed instruction in creativity and its effects on eighth grade students. *Dissertation Abstracts International, 32*, 2479A.

Davis, G.A. (1982). A model for teaching creative development. *Roeper Review, 5* (2), 27–28.

Davis, G.A., & Rimm, S.B. (1985). *Education of the gifted and talented.* Englewood Cliffs, NJ: Prentice-Hall.

Davis, G.A., & Scott, J.A. (1971). *Training creative thinking.* New York: Holt, Rinehart & Winston.

Demo, M.P. (1983). Creative activity in the classroom: The ERIC connection. *Children's Theatre Review, 31* (1), 27–30.

Dunette, M.D. (1963). The effect of group participation on brainstorming effectiveness for two industrial samples. *Journal of Applied Psychology, 47*, 30–37.

Eisner, E.W. (1984). Passionate portraits of schools. *Harvard Educational Review, 54* (2), 195–200.

Evans, P.O. (1983). A formula for writing poetry. *English Quarterly, 16* (2), 21–24.

Feldhusen, J.F., Speedie, S.M., & Treffinger, D.J. (1971). The Purdue creative thinking program: Research and evaluation. *NSPI Journal, 10* (3), 5–9.

Firestien, R.L., & Treffinger, D.J. (1983). Creative problem solving: Guidelines and resources for effective facilitation. *G/C/T, 26*, 2–10.

Foster, J. (1971). *Creativity and the teacher.* London: Macmillan.

Fox, H.W. (1981). Message for business educators: Injecting creativity into the classroom. *Journal of Business Education, 57* (2), 43–45.

Getzels, J., & Madaus, G. (1969). Creativity. *Encyclopedia of educational research.* (4th ed., pp. 267–275). New York: Macmillan.

Glover, J.A. (1980). A creativity-training workshop: Short-term, long-term, and transfer effects. *Journal of Genetic Psychology, 136* (1), 3–16.

Glover, J.A. (1981). Developing creative responding: Training and transfer effects. *Small Group Behavior, 12* (2), 167–181.

Glover, J.A. (1981/82). Implementing creativity training of students through teacher inservice training. *Educational Research Quarterly, 6* (4), 13–18.

Goldstein, M.I. (1983). The production of metaphor in poetry therapy as a means of achieving insight. *Arts in Psychotherapy, 10* (3), 167–173.

Golen, S. (1983). How to teach students to improve their creativity in a basic business communication class. *Journal of Business Communication, 20* (3), 46–57.

Gowan, J.C., Khatena, J., & Torrance, E.P. (1981). *Creativity: Its educational implications* (2d ed.). New York: Wiley.

Grossman, S.R. (1982). Training creativity and creative problem-solving. *Training and Development Journal, 36* (6), 62–68.

Guilford, J.P. (1950). Creativity. *American Psychologist, 5,* 444–454.

Guilford, J.P. (1968). *Intelligence, creativity and their educational implications.* San Diego, CA: Knapp.

Haley, G.L. (1984). Creative response styles: The effects of socio-economic status and problem-solving training. *Journal of Creative Behavior, 18* (1), 25–40.

Henry, J. (1972). Spontaneity, initiative and creativity in suburban classrooms. In J.I. Roberts & S.K. Akinsanya (Eds.), *Schooling in the cultural context: Anthropological studies of education* (pp. 183–194). New York: McKay.

Hlavsa, J., Balonova, E., & Kolaj, D. (1980). [Effectiveness of group creativity training]. *Ceskoslovenska Psychologie, 24,* (6), 503–508.

Huber, J. (1979). Self-instructional use of programmed creativity-training materials with gifted and regular students. *Journal of Educational Psychology, 71* (3), 303–309.

Isaksen, S.G., Stein, M.I., Hills, D.A., & Gryskiewicz, S.S. (1984). A proposed model for the formulation of creativity research. *Journal of Creative Behavior, 18* (1), 67–75.

Jaben, Twila H. (1983). The effects of creativity training on learning disabled students' creative written expression. *Journal of Learning Disabilities, 16* (5), 264–265.

Jarial, G.S. (1981). An experiment in the training of nonverbal creativity. *Journal of Creative Behavior, 15* (1), 72–77.

Jegard, S. (1981). Creativity training for mentally handicapped children and young adults. *Dissertation Abstracts International, 41* (9–B), 3601.

Jones, J.E. (1980). The elderly art student: Research and the participants speak. *Art Education, 33* (7), 16–20.

Jones, T.P. (1972).*Creative learning in perspective.* New York: Wiley.

Kalmar, M., & Kalmar, Z. (1980). [Creativity training experiment with residential nursery school children]. *Magyar Pszichologiai Szemle, 37* (1), 21–37.

Keating, D.P. (1980). Four faces of creativity: The continuing plight of the intellectually underserved. *Gifted Child Quarterly, 24,* 56–61.

Khatena, J. (1970). Training college adults to think creatively with words. *Psychological Reports, 27,* 279–281.

Khatena, J. (1971a). A second study training college adults to think creatively with words. *Psychological Reports, 28,* 385–386.

Khatena, J. (1971b). Teaching disadvantaged preschool children to think creatively with pictures. *Journal of Educational Psychology, 62,* 384–386.

Khatena, J., & Dickerson, E.C. (1973). Training sixth grade children to think creatively with words. *Psychological Reports, 32,* 336.

Kogan, N., & Pankove, E. (1974). Long-term predictive validity of divergent-thinking tests: Some negative evidence. *Journal of Educational Psychology, 66,* 802–810.

Kramer, D.E., & Bayern, C.D. (1984). The effects of behavioral strategies on creativity training. *Journal of Creative Behavior, 18* (1), 23–24.

Landmann, W., & Schroder, U. (1981). [Training of creativity with slow learners]. *Psychologie in Erziehung und Unterricht, 28* (5), 267–274.

Lewis, C. (1979). Creativity: An examination of some important issues. *G/C/T/, 9,* 22–23, 25.

Lima, L. de O. (1983). Archaic schooling, creative schooling. *Prospects, 13* (2), 145–160.

Linder, T.W. (1981). Organizing a course on creativity: Theory and practice. *Journal for the Education of the Gifted, 4* (3), 211–224.

Lindgren, H.C., & Lindgren, F. (1965). Brainstorming and orneriness as facilitators of creativity. *Psychological Reports, 16,* 577–583.

Lowenfels, M. (1979). Releasing creativity through image-making. *Gifted Child Quarterly, 23* (4), 801–806.

Lytton, H. (1971). *Creativity and education.* London: Routledge & Kegan Paul.

MacKinnon, D.W. (1968). Creativity: Psychological aspects. *International encyclopedia of the social sciences* (Vol. 3, pp. 434–442). *New York: Macmillan.*

Mansfield, R.S., & Busse, T.V., (1974). The effectiveness of creativity training programs. *Childhood Education, 51* (1), 53–56.

Mansfield, R.S., & Busse, T.V. (1981). *The psychology of creativity and discovery: Scientists and their work.* Chicago, IL: Nelson-Hall.

Mansfield, R.S., & Busse, T.V. (1982) Creativity. *Encyclopedia of educational research* (5th ed., Vol. 1, pp. 385–394). New York: Macmillan.

Mansfield, R.S., Busse, T.V., & Krepelka, E.J. (1978) The effectiveness of creativity training. *Review of Educational Research, 48* (4), 517–536.

Marksberry, M.L. (1963). *Foundations of creativity.* New York: Harper & Row.

Martin, C.E. (1982). Developing creativity through the reading program. *Reading Teacher, 35* (5), 568–572.

Mitchell, B.M., & Wilkens, R.F. (1979, Feb. 19–21). *The measurement of attitude change in creative problem solving programs.* Paper presented at the Annual Conference of the Association of Teacher Educators (ED 164 4771).

Moffat, J.A., & Shephard, W.J. (1983). Facilitation: A selected bibliography. *Journal of Creative Behavior, 17* (1), 65–70.

Moreno, J.M., & Hogan, J.D. (1976). The influence of race and social class on the training of creative thinking and problem-solving abilites. *Journal of Educational Research, 70,* 91–95.

Moriarty, S.E. (1983). Yes, creativity can be taught—And here are some devices for teaching it. *Journalism Educator, 38* (2), 13–16.

Muradov, S.N. (1982). Training creative specialists. *Soviet Education, 24* (3–5), 234–241.

Nahm, M. (1965). *Genius and creativity: An essay in the history of ideas.* New York: Harper.

Navarre, J. (1979). Incubation as fostering the creative process. *Gifted Child Quarterly, 23* (4), 792–800.

Noller, R.B. (1971). Some applications of general semantics in teaching creativity. *Journal of Creative Behavior, 5* (4), 256–266.

Olton, R.M., & Crutchfield, R.S. (1969). Developing the skills of productive thinking. In P. Mussen, J. Langer, & M. Covington (Eds.), *Trends and issues in developmental psychology.* New York: Holt, Rinehart & Winston.

Parnes, S.J. (1984). Learning creative behavior: Making the future happen. *The Futurist, 18* (4), 30–32.

Parnes, S.J., & Noller, R.B. (1971). The creative studies project: Raison d'etre and introduction. *Journal of Research and Development in Education, 4* (3), 62–66.

Parnes, S.J., & Noller, R.B. (1972a). Applied creativity: The creative studies project. I. The development. *Journal of Creative Behavior, 6* (1), 11–22.

Parnes, S.J., & Noller, R.B. (1972b). Applied creativity: The creative studies project. II. Results of the two-year program. *Journal of Creative Behavior, 6* (3), 164–186.

Parnes, S.J., & Noller, R.B. (1972c). Applied creativity: The creative studies project. III. The curriculum. *Journal of Creative Behavior, 6* (4), 275–294.

Parnes, S.J., & Noller, R.B. (1973). Applied creativity: The creative studies project. IV. Personality findings and conclusions. *Journal of Creative Behavior, 7* (1), 15–36.

Parnes, S.J., Noller, R.B., & Biondi, A.K. (1977). *Guide to creative action: Revised edition of creative behavior guidebook.* New York: Scribner.

Pearlman, C. (1983). A theoretical model for creativity. *Education, 103* (3), 294–305.

Penick, J.E. (1983). What research says: Encouraging creativity. *Science and Children, 20* (5), 32–33.

Perkins, D.R. (1981). *The mind's best work.* Cambridge, MA: Harvard University Press.

Powell, M. (1981/82). Nuts and bolts from the ivory tower. *Educational Research Quarterly, 6* (4), 46–51.

Raimo, A. (1980). Stimulating creative written communication through divergent thinking. *Journal of Creative Behavior, 14* (2), 125–132.

Raudsepp, E. (1983). Stimulate your creativity. *Hydrocarbon Processing, 62* (2), 71.

Reese, H.W., & Parnes, S.J. (1970). Programming creative behavior. *Child Development, 41,* 413–423.

Renner, V., & Renner, J.C. (1971). Effects of a creativity training program on stimulus preference. *Perceptual and Motor Skills, 33* (3), 872–874.

Renzulli, J.S., & Callahan, C.M. (1975). Developing creativity training activities. *Gifted Child Quarterly, 19* (1), 38–45.

Richardson, G.E., & Jordan, R. (1981). Strategies for creative emergence. *Health Education, 12* (1), 14–16.

Ridley, D.R., & Birney, R.C. (1979). Long-term effects of training procedures on originality tests. *Journal of Educational Research, 72* (3), 128–131.

Ripple, R.E., & Dacey, J.S. (1967). The facilitation of problem solving and verbal creativity by exposure to programmed instruction. *Psychology in the Schools, 4,* 240–245.

Rodriguez, E. (1981). Impact of creativity training on academic achievement and creative thinking skills concerning four ethnic-sex groups in the fourth grade. *Dissertation Abstracts International, 41* (8–A), 3334.

Rose, L.H., & Lin, H. (1984). A meta-analysis of long-term creativity training programs. *Journal of Creative Behavior, 18* (1), 11–22.

Rosen, R.D. (1982). Training your creative mind. *Psychology Today, 16* (11), 84.

Rostafinski, T.J. (1982). Brief creativity training: A controlled comparison of self-instructional and associational procedures. *Dissertation Abstracts International, 42* (11–B), 4562.

Rouse, J. (1983). On children writing poetry. *Language Arts, 60* (6), 711–716.

Sanders, D.A., & Sanders, J.A. (1984). *Teaching creativity through metaphor: An integrated brain approach.* New York: Longman.

Schempp, P.G. (1983). Influence of decision-making on attitudes, creativity, motor skills, and self-concept in elementary children. *Research Quarterly For Exercise and Sport, 54* (2), 183–189.

Shepherd, D. (1982, Nov. 12–13). *Progressive nurturing of creativity in high school writing classes.* Paper presented at the Annual Meeting of the Illinois Association of Teachers of English (ED 226 3471).

Shively, J.E., Feldhusen, J.F., & Treffinger, D.J. (1972). Developing creativity and related attitudes. *Journal of Experimental Education, 41*, 63–69.

Smith, N.R. (1980). Development and creativity in American art education: A critique. *High School Journal, 63* (8), 348–352.

Stein, M.I. (1974). *Stimulating creativity* (Vols. 1–2). New York: Academic Press.

Taylor, D.W. (1958). Does group participation when using brainstorming facilitate or inhibit creative thinking? *Administrative Science Quarterly, 3*, 23–47.

Taylor, I.A., & Getzels, J.W. (Eds.). (1975). *Perspectives in creativity.* Chicago, IL: Aldine.

Timberlake, P. (1982). Fifteen ways to cultivate creativity in your classroom. *Childhood Education, 59*, (1), 19–21.

Torrance, E.P. (1972). Can we teach children to think creatively? *Journal of Creative Behavior, 6*, 114–143.

Torrance, E.P. (1979). An instructional model for enhancing incubation. *Journal of Creative Behavior, 13* (1), 23–35.

Torrance, E.P. (1980a). Creative intelligence and 'an agenda for the 80's.' *Art Education, 33* (7), 8–14.

Torrance, E.P. (1980b). Creativity and futurism in education: Retooling. *Education, 100* (4), 298–311.

Torrance, E.P., & Torrance, P. (1973). *Is creativity teachable?* Bloomington, IN: Phi Delta Kappa Educational Foundation.

Treffinger, D.J. (1971). *Improving children's creative problem solving ability: Effects of distributions of training, teacher involvement, and teacher's divergent thinking ability on instruction.* West Lafayette, IN: Purdue University Press.

Treffinger, D.J., & Goawn, J.C. (1975). An updated representative list of methods and educational programs for stimulating creativity. In W.R. Barbe & J.S. Renzulli (Eds.), *Psychology and education of the gifted* (2d ed., pp. 371–386). New York: Halsted Press.

Treffinger, D.J. Isaksen, S.G., & Firestien, R.L. (1983). Theoretical perspectives on creative learning and its facilitation: An overview. *Journal of Creative Behavior, 17* (1), 9–17.

Treffinger, D.J., Speedie, S.M., & Brunner, W.D. (1974). Improving children's creative problem solving ability: The Purdue Creativity Project. *Journal of Creative Behavior, 8*, 20–30.

Trostle, S.L., & Yawkey, T.D. (1981). *Creative thinking and the education of young children: The fourth basic skill* (ED 204 0151).

Tway, E. (1980). How to find and encourage the nuggets in children's writing. *Language Arts, 57* (3), 299–304.

Vitiello, J. (1983). The development of poetic intuition in children: A study in the practice of nonviolence. *Language Arts, 60*, (6), 740–748.

Vojtko, A., & Pachinova, E. (1981). [Effect of training on the course of creative-thinking]. *Studia Psychologica, 23* (1), 93–94.

Wallach, M.A. (1970). Creativity. In P.H. Mussen (Ed.), *Carmichael's manual of child psychology* (3d ed.). New York: Wiley.

Warren, T.F., & Davis, G.A. (1969). Techniques for creative thinking: An empirical comparison of three methods. *Psychological Reports, 25* (1), 207–214.

Weaver, R.L. (1979). Kindling the creative spark (ED 168 0981).

Whitman, N. (1983). Problem-solving and creativity in college courses. *AAHE-ERIC/Higher Education Research Currents* 1 (ED 226 6501).

Williams, F. (1972). *A total creativity program for individualizing and humanizing the learning process.* Englewood Cliffs, NJ: Educational Technology Publications.

Wragg, P.H., & Allen, R.F. (1983). Developing creativity in social studies: Generating analogies. *Georgia Social Science Journal, 14* (1), 27–32.

Young, R.E. (Ed.). (1981). *New directions for teaching and learning: Fostering critical thinking.* San Francisco, CA: Jossey-Bass.

Youngkin, B. (1982). The mind: Creativity, the hemispheres of the brain, and teaching composition. *CEA Forum, 12* (4), 6–11.

SYMPOSIUM

PANEL 5

Beyond Creativity

John C. Berg

This symposium is concerned with two questions, related but different. The first is how to teach creativity; the second, which partly motivates the first, is the purpose of liberal arts education and of a liberal arts college. I shall have quite a bit to say about creativity later on; but I think it's important first for us to get a little perspective about our basic purpose as a liberal arts college.

There is a big difference between saying we want to teach creativity and saying that it is our basic purpose to do so. There is a simple operational definition of our basic purposes: they are required for graduation. If we decide that a particular skill, ability, or piece of knowledge is truly fundamental, that its possession is one of the defining marks of the College of Liberal Arts and Sciences (CLAS) graduate—then, if you don't succeed in acquiring that skill, ability, or piece of knowledge, you shouldn't graduate.

These requirements can vary a lot over place and time. At the University of Wisconsin, where I went to college, they included the ability to swim and—for men at least—to climb a 20-foot rope. A friend at Wellesley at about that time was required to take Bible. Every student in Texas, by state law, has a required semester in Texas government.

A few years ago we adopted a new curriculum here in CLAS, and I think it's a pretty good one. Our basic educational purposes, as operationally defined, now include some knowledge and ability in mathematics, writing, literature, logic, and communication, and, with some choices, in humanities, natural science, and social science. If you pass all these required courses, complete a major, accumulate 122 credits, and maintain a C average, you can graduate.

There is no requirement in creativity. It is true that one of the topics for this symposium is the development of creativity through the teaching of other subjects; but certainly you can *pass* these courses without being creative. Even term-paper extensions and permission to take make-up exams can usually be obtained by nothing more creative than mumbling a few words about a death in the family.

This is as it should be. We should not require creativity for graduation for two reasons. First, it would be counterproductive to do so. Despite all the talk about switching mechanisms in the brain and computer programs with creative abilities, creativity cannot be reduced to a method. It emerges best in its own way and at its own pace. Although we can encourage it, I am convinced that any attempt to force its development would fail. And, because the university couldn't afford to tell significant numbers of students that they weren't creative enough to graduate, the dreary result would be development of some substitute, a set of C-average behavioral objectives which we would *call* creativity, which students might even *believe* was creativity, but which would be very far from the real thing.

The second reason is that what we can and do require is more important—at least, as part of the liberal arts and sciences. I want to suggest, in particular, that every CLAS graduate should have developed two things: a significant amount of substantive knowledge, and an understanding of the existence and viability of multiple points of view.

I have heard that faculty at schools of management are alarmed at the high proportion of new MBA recipients who take jobs with consulting firms. The students do this for a simple and good reason: the consulting firms pay more. What these firms do is tell their clients how to make more profits, and they do it by subjecting the clients' books to mathematical analysis. It works; by making the right calculations, they can tell their clients which operations are not worth their cost. New MBA recipients are highly trained in quantitative analysis, and the consulting firms are glad to pay them for it.

Why the concern? Some business faculty are afraid that we may be developing a generation of corporate management which knows a lot about calculating profit and loss but doesn't know enough about how to produce anything. This is part of the general national problem of declining industries, poor quality goods, and uncompetitive rates of productivity. If you are making cars, and are not making money at it, it is easy for modern management science to tell you to shift some of your capital into real estate; this may even be the best thing for your company and for your career. But figuring out how to make better cars requires solid, substantive knowledge of automobiles. As more and more people learn how to invest money, and fewer and fewer how to make cars, the system defeats its own purpose; there is less and less to invest in.

This modern approach to business decisions is related to some of the more cybernetic concepts of creative thinking. Both involve an initial free association (or, for computers, universal scanning) and a subsequent testing stage to see if the associations thus formed are valid ones. Both have their uses, particularly in the short run. But neither can take the place of an approach based on substantive knowledge.

I don't think that this problem can be solved by educational reform. As I said before, students go into consulting because it pays more. Business schools put method above substance because there is a demand for it. Corporations favor MBA holders over engineers or chemists because it is more profitable to do so. We are at a stage in the development of capitalism where finance capital is more important than productive capital. From the point of view of the individual firm or the individual investor, it is more profitable to shift funds from firm to firm, from industry to industry, or from country to country than to settle down to improving the productivity of the firm, industry, or country you are already in. In a capitalist society, it is such individual decisions which determine what happens. Unfortunately, what's good for individual firms and investors can have some negative consequences for society as a whole, as our basic industries become inviable.

To solve this problem we would have to restructure our economy, so that private and public interests coincide. I'm not talking about how to do this, but about the role of liberal arts education—and especially the social sciences—in looking for such solutions. We need creative thinking, yes, but creative thinking grounded in substantive knowledge. We need economists who understand the structure and dynamics of the U.S. economy, so that they can think about how it might be changed, not just economic technicians who can calculate the most profitable investment. We need sociologists who have some understanding of the causes of crime, so that they can think about how to reduce it, not just experts in more effective police procedures. We need political scientists who understand how our political system works, and why it works that way, so that they can think about how to make it more responsive to the public's needs, not just specialists in how to win elections. And we need informed citizens who have some understanding of these things, of our basic cultural values, and of the nature of the physical world we live in, to support and take part in the making of creative decisions about the future of our country and the world.

Howard Gardner is a psychologist involved in "Project Zero" at Harvard University, an exploration into the psychology of artistic creativity. He recently published *Art, Mind, & Brain: A Cognitive Approach to Creativity* (1982, New York: Basic Books), an integrated collection of 33 essays which set forth his ideas and findings on this topic. One of Gardner's interests is the artistic creativity of young children. Everyone who works with young children, whether as researcher, teacher, or parent, observes the beauty and originality of the pictures they draw, the songs they sing, and the stories they tell. By the time they reach school age, however, children enter what Gardner calls a "literal stage," in which their art decreases in quantity and loses its imaginative quality. Their concern now is to copy the world around them, in both its physical appearance and its conventional symbolism. Adults commonly see this as a loss and blame the stultifying effect of conformist schools and society; but Gardner does not agree. He and his colleagues in "Project Zero" have concluded that this literal stage is a necessary part of the development of mature artists, providing the symbolic vocabulary and technical tools which make a more profound originality possible.

Our concern in this symposium has been with creative thinking, not artistic creation, but I think that there may be a parallel. You need not be educated in the liberal arts and sciences in order to think creatively. Creative thinkers can be found among young children, uneducated adults, and those with narrowly specialized training. But a liberal education provides you with a broader range. To use my own field as an example, creative political reform must be grounded in knowledge of how politics works. And creative solutions to today's political problems are likely to require knowledge of science and of cultural values as well. Such broad substantive knowledge is one of the essentials of education in the liberal arts and sciences.

A second essential is the understanding of different points of view. That phrase, "points of view," is deliberately vague, and meant to refer to many different levels of thought. It includes ideologies, theories, world views, paradigms, sciences, discourses, and philosophical systems. To say it in more technical language, a point of view is a particular appropriation of reality; and different, contradictory appropriations may be equally valid.

At least, that is how I would put it from my own point of view. Others, who prefer not to speak of an objective reality, would say simply that there are multiple realities.

By and large, the contemporary philosophy of knowledge finds it more useful to judge differing appropriations of reality by their relative usefulness, rather than to insist on a standard of absolute truth. This is because no theory is ever absolutely true. Any coherent world view is a simplification and, therefore, false. To discredit a system, it is not enough to find a counterexample; you have to find another system which works better, with the meaning of "better" depending on the purpose for which you want to use the system.

I think that this view of the nature of knowledge is widely accepted today; but it is generally ignored in professional education. Accountants, architects, automotive engineers, lawyers, medical doctors, and professional managers are taught the methods of their professions in a straightforward, unquestioning manner. Whether or not it is said explicitly, the assumption that this method is absolutely true is naturally encouraged by this. The understanding that competing truths exist is an important contribution of the liberal arts and sciences.

A few years ago, as part of the CLAS curriculum changes, we redesigned our introductory course in government. Previously, we had taught one semester of American government and one of comparative government. The course content naturally varied from year to year and from instructor to instructor; but the underlying structure of the course just as naturally implied that the basic purpose was to learn important facts about the political systems of a number of countries.

Our new course focuses on contrasting approaches to the study of politics, with emphasis on behavioralism, phenomenology, and Marxism. We chose to organize the course this way in good part in order to provide intellectual coherence; to allow us to present international relations, political theory, American and comparative government, and public policy as parts of a common enterprise. We are now able to cover the subfields of political science more inclusively, so that the course is a better introduction to the discipline.

However, there has been another major benefit of the change. Open-mindedness has become an issue in the course. I do not mean to say that we or our students had closed minds before 1982; but the structural emphasis on methods and points of view now encourages teachers and students alike to notice the merits of competing scientific systems, and to notice in particular that there is likely to be some merit to both sides of a dispute.

This sort of open-mindedness has many benefits. First, and most obvious, it makes for a more tolerant society. You don't have to know much about the nuclear arms race to see the dangers of the view that one side is absolutely right, and the other one, absolutely wrong. The history of religious conflict provides further examples.

Second, understanding of others' points of view is itself an important kind of substantive knowledge. Every so often one of our national pundits announces that the Soviet Union is on the brink of economic or political collapse because of some perceived crisis, such as consumer-goods shortages or the treatment of dissidents. In fact, the Soviet Union has proved remarkably stable. The mistake, I believe, comes from assuming that the average Soviet citizen thinks the same way that the average U.S. citizen does, rather than trying to understand the internal dynamics of Soviet culture and ideology. Such understanding would not necessarily lead to agreement; but it would improve our ability to predict the behavior of Soviet citizens and leaders alike.

Finally, openness to multiple points of view can contribute to creative thinking. Knowledge of a variety of theoretical frameworks can suggest new ways of thinking about problems, provide useful analogies, and make it easier to devise original theories when existing ones are inadequate.

I want to conclude with some examples of how these two things, broad substantive knowledge and openness to varying points of view, have contributed to creative thinking about practical social problems. But first I want to make one more point about what creativity consists of. The *Prospectus* for this symposium suggests a "marriage" between the liberal arts and Herbert Simon's curriculum in design, a curriculum which "uses computerized decision rules to search for what we might call creative solutions to business and engineering problems" (Tuerck, 1985, p. 5). Presumably the marriage would involve applying the same methods to the solution of other problems as well. I have already suggested some objections to this approach, but there is one more. The focus on creative problem solving is too narrow; there is much more to creative thinking than solving problems. Sometimes the most creative approach can be to reject a problem completely; to find a problem which no one had noticed before; or to cause a problem yourself, so that someone else will have to solve it. A good example of this is the action of Rosa Parks. When she refused to give up her seat on that bus in Montgomery, AL, she upset what had seemed to be a nonproblematic situation, incited a boycott, and *caused* a tremendous problem for the powers-that-were in Montgomery. They didn't have to be creative to come up with the solution—desegregated buses—they just needed to overcome their own stubbornness; and they would never have done that if Rosa Parks hadn't created a problem for them.

Two or three decades ago the electric-power industry looked at the problem of how to meet the growing demand for electricity which it anticipated. They came up with what seemed to be a creative answer, nuclear reactors. Today the countryside is littered with the ruins of unfinished reactors and with utility companies on the edge of bankruptcy, because the opponents of nuclear power turned out to be more creative than its supporters. Instead of looking for a better solution to the problem as defined—how to meet the rising demand for electricity—the antinuclear movement *rejected* the problem and put a new one in its place. If the growing demand required nuclear reactors, they reasoned, maybe the real problem was how to reduce demand. This turned out to be relatively easy, both because there was a lot of waste available for elimination, and because the decision to use less was a decentralized one, made independently by millions of consumers eager to save money, out of the hands of the unsympathetic utility companies and regulatory agencies.

The movement did a lot more, too, of course, from direct action to demonstrations to legislative lobbying to lawsuits, and all of these tactics contributed; but their victory (which is still only partial) came basically because the supply-and-demand picture changed so that it would no longer be profitable to operate the plants even if they were completed— the result of creative rejection of one problem for another one.

Now some of you may be thinking that I am playing with words here. Each of these examples can be seen as problem solving if you define the problem correctly to start with. That is, Rosa Parks's action was a good solution to the problem of how to start a civil rights movement in Montgomery, and energy conservation was a creative solution to the problem of making nuclear power economically inviable. But you can never be certain at first that you have defined the problem correctly; cybernetic creativity routines, therefore, are likely to spend a lot of their time trying to find creative solutions to problems which turn out to be the wrong ones. Attempts to define a method of creative thinking cannot help but limit it.

To recapitulate, I am arguing that the essential distinguishing features of a liberal education should be acquisition of substantive knowledge in a broad range of fields, for example, as embodied in our all-college requirements, and an ability to understand and evaluate multiple interpretations of reality, which should be developed through the way the various subjects are taught. Deeper knowledge of a specialized major subject, which we also require, does not distinguish the liberal arts and sciences from other kinds of education; but the subjects themselves are broader and more basic, and so more likely to contribute to open-mindedness and theoretical flexibility.

A good liberal education can inspire creativity, but I do not think that we can teach creativity in the sense that we can guarantee it to our graduates. And I think that the attempt to do so would be more likely to result in limiting it to a narrow technical procedure. Moreover, I do not believe that the liberal arts and sciences are any more likely to produce creative thinkers than any other sort of education. Engineers, nurses, accountants, and foresters can all be creative, but none is likely to be trained in the liberal arts. What we have to offer is not more creative ability, but more knowledge and understanding for that creative ability to work on. I do believe that this makes liberal arts graduates—at least, those educated in the way that I am suggesting—more suited to coping with the problems of our society, and consequently that we would all be better off if more students chose liberal arts colleges.

I would like to conclude with three examples which illustrate the importance of broad substantive knowledge, understanding of multiple points of view, and an open approach to creativity in dealing with social problems.

My first example deals with the contemporary health care system in the United States, and particularly with the impact on that system of the Medicare and Medicaid programs. What interests me about these programs is the degree to which they failed to achieve some of their major purposes and achieved quite different ones instead.

When Congress enacted Medicare in 1965, with Medicaid added as a last-minute political compromise, its supporters expected the program to help elderly people get better health care, to make that care cheaper, and to be the first step toward the creation of a comprehensive national health system. The American Medical Association and the insurance industry shared these expectations and fought the program tooth and nail because of them; the opposition was so strong that it took 12 years of debate and the Democratic landslide in the 1964 election to overcome it.

The first objective was achieved; elderly people get much better health care today than they did in 1964. Because of the addition of Medicaid, so do the poor. But the elderly also pay more for health care than they did in 1964, a lot more. In fact, the two programs have driven up health-care costs so much that we all pay more, and they have made the costs of a national health insurance program so high that its possibility has receded into the distant future.

Some of the cost increase is due to improvements in care; a little is probably due to the unionization of health care workers, although theirs is still one of the most poorly paid occupations; but a lot of it is due to the payment structure of the Medicare and Medicaid programs. In both cases doctors, hospitals, and other health-care providers are paid on a fee-for-service basis, with the payment coming from the federal or state government. This means that providers have an economic incentive to provide more services and to charge more for each service provided, while consumers have little or no incentive to either contest the provider's recommendation or to shop around for the lowest prices, because they are not paying directly for what they receive. The only force for cost control is government regulation, cumbersome and ineffective.

This explanation is oversimplified; for example, Medicare patients do share some of the costs of the health care they receive. Moreover, there are ways to deal with the problem, although they are too complicated to discuss here. But my point remains valid. The architects of Medicare had very clear ideas about what it would accomplish, and it turned out to do something quite different. This is what I want to try to explain.

The mistake was certainly not due to overly hasty action; as I said, the Medicare program was debated for at least 12 years before final adoption, and its designers, led by Wilbur Cohen of what was then the Department of Health, Education, and Welfare, were among the most knowledgeable social welfare planners in the world. It is true that Medicaid was added to the bill at the last minute, and that Wilbur Mills, the chairman of the House Ways and Means Committee, later said that he proposed the addition in order to "build a fence around the Medicare program," so that it wouldn't grow into a national health insurance system. But Cohen accepted the compromise almost immediately, and did not seem to anticipate any trouble from it. In any event, the inflationary features of Medicaid are present in Medicare as well.

What was lacking, I think, was sufficiently broad knowledge about economics and politics. The planners of Medicare assumed that doctors' and hospitals' fees would continue to be about what they had been, despite the new method of payment they were proposing. They assumed that the political climate of support for the welfare state which had existed for the previous 32 years would continue, so that if any problems arose they would be able to issue regulations to correct them. And they assumed that, because the American Medical Association (AMA) had waged an all-out campaign against Medicare up to the last minute, the program's adoption would spell the end of the AMA's dominating power.

All of these assumptions proved wrong. The increase in third-party payments allowed medical fees to rise rapidly; and the AMA, once it finally acknowledged its defeat, shifted quickly from implacable opposition to intimate involvement with regulatory decision making, in a new political climate which enabled the AMA to render government cost-control efforts ineffective. In the face of these incorrect political and economic assumptions, expertise in demographics and social security proved insufficient.

I am speaking from hindsight, of course, and it would be misleading to pretend that all of the problems should have been foreseen. Moreover, even if they had been foreseen, Medicare and Medicaid might still have seemed acceptable compromises; we are certainly a lot better off with them than we would have been without them. But if the unforeseen effects of these programs had been known back in 1965, when strong political support for them existed, their backers might have chosen to fight for some of the corrective measures, such as prospective budgeting, which are being developed so timidly today.

That was an example of how things might have been better if the principles I am advocating had been more fully realized—in this case, the principle of broad, substantive knowledge. Now I want to discuss a success story, the creation of the independent state of Zimbabwe, in which my second principle—understanding multiple points of view—played an important part.

There are a lot of problems in Zimbabwe today, but I call this a success story because things turned out so much better than most people had expected them to a few years earlier. At that time, the white settler minority, led by Ian Smith and the Rhodesia Front, had declared unilateral independence from Great Britain in order to maintain its absolute rule, and appeared to be intractable in this course. The black majority was badly divided between the Zimbabwe African National Union led by Robert Mugabe, and the Zimbabwe African People's Union led by Joshua Nkomo—ZANU and ZAPU—two leaders, two parties, even two separate guerrilla armies, based in different neighboring countries and divided by ideology, ethnicity, and international alignments. On top of that, even if the independence movement managed to overcome its division enough to win it seemed likely that the settlers, who held the country' rich agricultural and industrial base in their hands, would sabotage it before giving it up. In this context, the calling of a London peace conference, by a British government which had shown itself unwilling to act against Smith in the past, seemed hopeless indeed.

What happened was far from perfect. A great many problems remain today, notably the worsening divisions between Mugabe and Nkomo. But the success was striking. Rhodesia became Zimbabwe, ruled by the black majority but without the massive flight by, and sabotage from, the white settlers which had been feared. Smith, along with his black ally Abel Muzorewa, agreed to yield power and to accept a constitution based on majority vote. Mugabe and Nkomo, at that time tenuously united in the Patriotic Front (PF), agreed to accept provisions in the constitution which they found morally repugnant—in particular, the earmarking of "for whites only" seats in the Zimbabwean parliament, in numbers far beyond the white proportion of the national population—in order to make the white settlers feel more secure in the face of the change.

The key to the settlement, I think, was the ability of the leaders of the Patriotic Front to understand the point of view of the Rhodesian whites, and the ability of Lord Carrington, the British negotiator, to understand the differing points of view of all sides. The essential problem was that black people and white people believed themselves morally entitled to ownership of the same land. What was a racist insult from one point of view—that is, the insistence on a constitution which made one white vote worth five or six black ones—was at the same time, from another point of view, seen by the settlers as a necessary protection for the land which they firmly believed their grandparents had wrested from the wilderness.

Part of the achievement of the Patriotic Front leaders was that, without sharing this view, they were able to understand it enough to realize that they had to give in to it or go on with the civil war for many more years; and that they could give in to it without jeopardizing the attainment in practice of genuine majority rule. Part of the failure of Ian Smith, on the other hand, was that he did not understand his opponents—the PF leaders and the black people of the country—but apparently had deluded himself into the belief that his ally Muzorewa could win a significant number of seats in a free election. In this, Smith was simply falling victim to his own propaganda, because he had been presenting Muzorewa to the world as a *bona fide* African leader; he proved not to have the flexibility of mind to see beyond his own point of view.

The end result was the necessary component of all successful negotiations, a settlement which seemed better than the *status quo* to any party which had the capacity to block it. This result was a triumph for Mugabe and ZANU on the one hand, and for Lord Carrington, the British negotiator, on the other, in each case because of their willingness and ability to understand—although not necessarily agree with—not only the interests, but the ideological world views of the opposing parties. For me, the role of ZANU is particularly striking because other revolutionary movements so often have failed to develop such understanding and so have isolated themselves from large parts of their own people; but that is a topic for another day.

Carrington and the British were able to retire into the background after independence, having removed a thorn from their side and restored an important member to the Commonwealth. For Mugabe and ZANU, the problems were just beginning. They now face the task of transforming a compromise among opposing interests into a unifying national ideology and of resolving the conflicts of interest enough to provide a material base for such a unifying ideology. We have made this tough problem a case study in our introductory politics and government course, so any of you who are government majors may have some familiarity with it. We show a film which includes an interview with some black farmers, and another with a family of white settlers, both of whom speak very movingly and intensely about their devotion to the land, what it means to them, and what they have done with it and on it over the years. Of course, it turns out that they are talking about the same piece of land, which they both regard as historically and morally theirs. That is the sort of problem the leaders of Zimbabwe will have to resolve in order to create a stable nation-state. Even more difficult will be to resolve the deepening conflicts between the two independence movements. Again, reaching a solution is going to require a willingness to understand differing points of view.

I want to give you one more example, to illustrate the point I made earlier that creativity shouldn't be defined as the ability to find solutions to problems, but should be broadened to include the rejection of problems and the creation of new problems as well. In honor of the tremendous efforts David Tuerck has put into organizing this symposium and making it a success, I'd like to draw this example from his discipline, economics. In doing so, I do not have to go very far afield, because economics and government have grown closer together over the years. Federal government action is now thought by almost everyone to have the most significant impact on our economic health, and presidential candidates are increasingly judged by their impact or potential impact on the economy. For this reason we now urge all government majors to take at least one year of economics—a suggestion not always received by the students with the enthusiasm it deserves.

When we look more closely at the interaction between government and the economy, one of the things we notice is that government economic policy does not work very well, and that it works increasingly poorly as time goes by. John F. Kennedy's slogan in the 1960 campaign was "Let's get this country moving again." That year the unemployment rate was 5.5%. As of this writing, a rate of 7.0% (June, 1984) is being heralded as the sign of a galloping recovery. Conservatives in 1960 worried that the inflation rate, a GNP deflator of 1.7%, might sap the nation's vitality. As of this writing, bringing the rate down to 3.2% (for the second quarter of 1984) is one of the success stories of the Reagan administration. The President's Democratic opponents don't dream of saying that this is still too high, but only that the high federal deficit threatens to drive it back up again. Economic policy has consisted of trading unemployment for inflation, then trading back again for more of each.

I think a major reason for this is that the problem has been defined as follows: How should government regulate the business cycle? There are various answers to this: Use fiscal policy; use monetary policy; let it run its course unchecked. The trouble is that there is something wrong with each answer. Unfortunately, the business cycle performs important functions in a capitalist system. Whether you call it shaking out or devalorization of capital, a depression or recession every so often gets rid of inefficient and unproductive capital which has been keeping profitability down and makes it possible for there to be a new spurt of growth. A successful attempt to moderate the cycle interferes with this. Inefficient companies keep operating, obsolete equipment is not replaced, and the period of growth is shorter and weaker than it would need to be to achieve an unemployment rate as low as there had been before. On the other hand, an unmoderated depression causes so much suffering that it is neither politically possible nor humanly desirable.

What we need to do is to reject the problem of how to moderate or regulate the business cycle and define a new problem: How we, as a nation, can get control of our tremendous national wealth and productive capacity and use it to provide all of us with a good life in a free and peaceful world. I suspect that, not for the first time in our history, this will happen only through problem creation—the refusal of workers, the poor, women, minority racial and ethnic groups, and others to accept solutions which leave them out, thereby moving us from the problem of regulating the business cycle to the larger problem of holding our society together.

I am not suggesting that liberal arts colleges themselves should undertake the task of problem creation. To do so would require a monolithic institutional commitment to a particular point of view which would be contrary to the educational philosophy I am advocating here. I am arguing a different point: that an education in the liberal arts and sciences ought to produce women and men who are open-minded and flexible, and at the same time well informed, in their approach to life; and that this sort of education is more likely to produce creative thinkers, and particularly those able to think creatively about improving society, than any more narrowly defined curriculum in "creativity" or "design."

There is one more point to be made. I have argued that the defining features of the liberal arts and sciences are two: broad substantive knowledge and openness to multiple points of view. But the responsibility for achieving these goals rests mainly on the college as a whole, not on the individual teacher. To seek to exclude teachers who have expertise in a narrow field, or who approach their subjects in a narrow-minded, even a dogmatic, way, would be nothing but another kind of closed-mindedness. My personal approach to teaching is to encourage more than one way of looking at things; but on a college-wide level, students can acquire this ability just as well from being exposed to teachers who argue passionately for strongly held points of view, particularly if these points of view are not all the same. The true spirit of a college of liberal arts and sciences is not to propagate solutions, not even such valuable solutions as creativity or open-mindedness, but to foster well-informed and open-minded debates about the human condition.

REFERENCES

Gardner, H. (1982). *Art, mind, & brain: A cognitive approach to creativity*. New York: Basic Books.

Marmor, T.R. (1982). Congress adopts medicare: The politics of legislative certainty". In J.E. Anderson (Ed.), *Cases in public policy-making*, (2d ed., pp. 85–99). New York: Holt, Rinehart, and Winston.

Tuerck, D.G. (1985). *Prospectus: Suffolk University conferences on creativity in honor of the college's 50th anniversary*. Unpublished manuscript, Suffolk University, Boston.

SYMPOSIUM

PANEL 5

Comments

Alexandra D. Todd

"True intellectual creativity is antithetical to university life" is often-repeated folk wisdom in American intellectual circles. Given the fragmentation of disciplines, the pressures on students of grades and examinations, the pressures on faculty of promotion and tenure, not to mention the finite increments of time awarded classroom subject matter, it is no wonder that this proclamation resounds in the halls of academe. I am happy, however, to see this platitude laid to rest here at Suffolk as evidenced by the wide variety of creative thought and suggestion raised over the past several weeks in this symposium.

This series of talks was introduced by Robert Webb and Kenneth Greenberg examining that elusive "product," creativity. Webb posited creativity within the individual, reaching out to understand how to socially grasp, teach, and understand the phenomenon. Greenberg, in a reversal of Webb's approach, focused on the contextual, social influences on the individual, claiming creativity as group product rooted in culture, time, and place. Throughout this symposium the papers have woven back and forth between the "processes" necessary for creativity to arise and questions of what the end "product" of creativity might look like.

Today's authors, John Berg and Joseph McCarthy, shift the factors away from intrinsic product and concentrate on extrinsic process, adding a new twist. The questions they raise provide a paradigm shift of sorts. Berg denies that a liberal arts education should require creativity of the student and McCarthy questions its possibility, even if thought reasonable. Neither, of course, denies the existence or desirability of creativity; they simply raise a new set of questions around its feasibility.

John Berg concludes his paper with the statement that "the true spirit

196

of a college of liberal arts and sciences is not to propagate solutions, not even such valuable solutions as creativity or open-mindedness, but to foster well-informed and open-minded debates about the human condition." In like manner, in his paper, he offers creative insight that itself veers away from a solution and concentrates on process, not product. Rather than dwelling on the ever-elusive questions, "What is creativity?" or "Once we figure it out, how do we teach it?" he takes a step back to look at the purposes of a liberal arts education. Within these purposes lies not a solution but a direction. A solid education should produce open-minded, well-informed students and only then can any of them hope to fulfill Berg's ideal of creativity—creativity being the ability to improve society. And here we have another twist. Berg introduces into our conception of creativity that always enriching issue—ethics. The idea that creativity has a moral component, the undertaking of making a better society, brings up that age-old argument (also embedded in Greenberg's paper) between the "art for arts sake" (creativity for creativity's sake) and art (creativity) embedded in political/social arrangements. Berg's commitment to improving the human condition, a condition ever in need of improvement, allows us to think of creativity, or an aspect of it, in a more graspable, tangible way. Thus, a liberal arts college should concentrate on what it does best—producing open-minded, as well as well-informed people—and creativity for the social and individual good becomes a possible result, if not requirement.

This is a direction that could inform the work of McCarthy, for he, in his intellectual speculations, keeps looking for that tantalizing pot of gold at the end of the rainbow. He wants answers to the big questions—the hows, whats, and whys. At first glance, answers appear to be elusive: "These conceptual and methodological problems are pervasive enough and serious enough as to engender debate whether creativity can really be taught." But McCarthy tentatively disagrees with this conclusion, suggesting the need for broader conceptual and methodological frameworks in the taming of what Webb has called that "slippery beast," creativity. McCarthy's points are intriguing. But while the big questions are raised and we are given a new way to think about the answers, there is not enough detail to judge what is really possible here. He sets his sights high. While suggesting that there is no such a thing as a creative product, he sets about searching for it. Berg's work moves the expectation level down a few notches, changes the questions around here and there, and comes up with more realizable possibilities.

Both positions are valuable. Stemming from Berg's work, we can follow a creative process we all need as teacher, student, and scholar—a process that lends itself to making the most of our skills, leading, in turn, to a better and more enlightened world. But we also need a touch of McCarthy's idealism—to seek beyond what we think we can do, asking the unanswerable, raising impossible questions, if only to knock them down and start over. It is both of these approaches that make a liberal arts education both an art and liberal.

COLLOQUIUM

PANEL 1

CREATIVITY AND TECHNOLOGY

Computers, Knowledge, and the Human Mind

Zenon W. Pylyshyn

INTRODUCTION

Anyone who reads newspapers and magazines these days has heard the term "Artificial Intelligence." It inspires awe in the business community and concern or puzzlement in most other places. Discussions of the limits of machine intelligence, though they still occur, have largely been replaced by concern over the social and economic significance of this new technology.

I'm one of those who is awed and impressed by the potential of this field and have devoted some part of my energy to persuading people that it is a positive force. I have done so largely on the grounds of its economic benefits and its potential for making the fruits of computer technology more generally available to the public—for example, to help the overworked physician; to search for oil and minerals and help manage our valuable resources; to explore, mine, and experiment in dangerous environments; to allow the noncomputing public access to vast libraries of important information and even advice and, in the process, give real meaning to the freedom of information act; and last, but not least, to entertain people—for if we do not blow ourselves off this planet, entertainment in its most general sense, including *education*, will surely be the major industry of the future.

These are fruits of the new technology that many of you may be familiar with, at least in a general way. You may also be aware of the many pitfalls that stand between us and their realization, including the military misuse of such work. What I would like to do today is concentrate on another aspect of the new technology—and, to some extent, of technology in general—which has received much less press. I want to concentrate on the *intellectual* significance of the recent developments in computer science, and particularly in artificial intelligence.

I might begin by asking a question that may be in the minds of many of you here today: Why should those of you who do not plan to be computer specialists or who are not the least bit interested in technological wizardry want to know about artificial intelligence? This and many other institutions of higher learning are dedicated to the development of wiser and more sensitive human beings who may, as a result of their education and other experiences, be in a better position to lead a fuller and more meaningful life. I am very much in favor of liberal education. I believe, like many of you, that the broadening of one's sensibilities and the exercise of one's creative potential are top priorities in education. Nonetheless, I also believe that liberally educated people cannot afford to be completely ignorant of technology, or even worse, to be smug about the playful indulgence of the modern technocrats.

There are several reasons why I hold this view. Probably the most obvious is that those who are growing up to be in a position of influence—to be opinion leaders in one way or another—should have some valid understanding of the major forces that are shaping our world. There can be no doubt that computers—and artificial intelligence in particular—will be among those forces in the coming decades. Unlike many other works of science, there is something about the direct relevance of computers to one's intellectual transactions with the world that make it particularly disturbing and disquieting. There is also something about the complexity and opacity of this form of technology that makes it particularly susceptible to misunderstanding and to prejudice. It is the duty of the intellectual to attempt to get a perspective on the nature of this beast before passing sentence on it, as I have frequently seen done.

The second, and more subtle reason that I believe that understanding the nature of computing and artificial intelligence is relevant to a liberal education, is that the ideas of computing, information, and artificial intelligence bring with it changes in one's world view, and in particular to one's view of human nature. Because this may not strike some of you as obvious, I would like to take a moment to reflect on the role of technology in shaping a world view, because this role has not always been adequately recognized.

The process of understanding and of articulating one's tenuous grasp on an evolving picture of nature is not unlike the process of creating a work of art, such as a sculpture. In both cases there are three major elements: the imagination and curiosity of the creator, the nature of the tools available, and the resistance offered by the materials. A sharp knife on soft wood yields a very different result from a massive chisel on granite rock, quite independent of the sculptor's initial intention. Similarly, a brilliant man tackling the world's mysteries with only his eyes, ears, and the concepts with which his native tongue provides him, will have different experiences, and will carve them up differently than will a person with the tools of a technological culture—even though the world may be essentially the same in both cases.

Technology, by which I mean to include not only the design of artifacts, but everything that involves a codified system of methods or *technique*, proves both instrumental tools to help us make observations and calculations, and conceptual tools that help us to see things in new ways. Such conceptual tools may be thought of as imagination prosthetics because they typically extend the range of the conceivable. Conceptual tools dominate periods of intellectual progress. Speaking of the importance of one such set of concepts—that provided by pure mathematics—physicist Freeman Dyson (1964) says,

> One factor that has remained constant through all the twists and turns of the history of physical science is the decisive importance of mathematical imagination ... For a physicist, mathematics is not just a tool by means of which phenomena may be calculated; it is the main source of concepts and principles by means of which new theories can be created. (p. 99)

Similarly, speaking of the development of new philosophical views, Susanne Langer (1962) put it this way:

> In every age, philosophical thinking exploits some dominant concepts and makes its greatest headway in solving problems conceived in terms of them. The seventeeth- and eighteenth-century philosophers construed knowledge ... in terms of sense data and their association. Descartes' self examination gave classical psychology *the mind and its contents* as a starting point. ... Hobbes provided the genetic method of building up complex ideas from simple ones. ... Pavlov built intellect out of conditioned reflexes and Loeb built life out of tropisms. (p. 54)

I believe that history will record that, around the mid-twentieth century, many classical problems of philosophy and psychology were transformed by a new notion of process: that of a *symbolic*, or *computational* process. Although the foundations for this idea were laid nearly a half-century ago by mathematicians like Alan Turing, Alonzo Church, Kurt Gödel, Steven Kleene, Emil Post, A. A. Markov, and others, it was not until the late 1950s that the availability of digital computers made it possible to begin the transformation that we see today in both artificial intelligence and the closely related field of study called cognitive science (a term used widely in recent years to designate the scientific study of the processes that underly knowing, reasoning, imaging, planning, remembering, perceiving, and the like—the exact boundaries being under constant review).

Although the computer is a logical continuation of the path of technological development that has been going on ever since *homo sapiens* began to make tools, in some ways it is also a radical departure from this path. In this talk I would like to explore the parallel between earlier technological trends and the development of computers. At the same time I will also examine what is *special* about computing. This discussion will lead me to consider what computing has in common with human thought that recommends it as a vehicle both for the understanding and for the exercise of intelligence. In doing this I shall consider three characteristics of this new technology: its capacity to increase the quantity and quality of complexity, its capacity to exhibit very nearly unbounded plasticity of behavior, and its capacity to determine actions on the basis of knowledge of the external world and certain goals related to this knowledge.

COMPUTERS AND THE QUALITY OF COMPLEXITY

The industrial revolution made technology supreme by giving us mass production based on the two fundamental ideas of *division of labor* and *standardization (and, hence, interchangeability) of components*. These two are closely related. The products of technology are decomposable into component parts—parts that are independently specifiable in terms of the *function* that they perform, and which can be used in *any* sample of the manufactured product. Because of this, it is possible to have such components designed and manufactured by specialists and then independently assembled at some later date. This idea is important in part because it leads to high productivity. Yet perhaps even more important than the increase in productivity is the fact that the dual principles of division of labor and interchangeability of components make possible a certain kind of *accumulation of complexity* which had never been seen before the twentieth century. Before the widespread adoption of these principles, the overall complexity of a project was limited to what could be conceived in the mind of the master designer (even the great pyramids and the wonderful cathedrals of Europe are no exception). Nowadays, no single person has more than a highly sketchy understanding of the major products of technology.

The two elements, which together may be referred to as the *modularity* of technology, have had an effect on every phase of modern life. Indeed it might be argued that Guttenberg's invention of movable type is an instance of the discovery of just this sort of modularity. In recent times a more self-consciously systematic and structured version of modularity has been developed to help organize large complex projects. Much of the dramatic successes of modern technology can be attributed to the exploitation of this idea. For example, there is very little in the way of new scientific principles or discoveries that went into the contemporary space program. The dramatic achievements in such things as landing a person on the moon is due entirely to the development of means for organizing complexity—for carrying the principles of modularity and division of labor to its extreme.

One of the fundamental characteristics of computer system design is that it makes the idea of the modular and hierarchical organization of complexity into a fundamental prescriptive principle and capitalizes on it to create enormously complex systems—yet systems that are still understandable and even repairable if they should fail to work properly. One way in which computing makes possible an extreme degree of modularity is worth examining because it sheds some light on the nature of the phenomenon of organization of complexity.

The one example I want to sketch relates to the idea of levels or layers of organization. Computer systems are typically designed by first implementing a set of general purpose facilities in hardware, then another independently designed set of facilities which might take the form of an interpreter for a programming language. Such facilities are specifically designed to suppress certain logistical details from the person who is concerned with the design of a system for some particular application. So-called high-level programming languages, such as Basic, Fortran, LISP, and so on, make it possible for a system designer to concentrate on the concerns of the particular task at hand. Such an individual almost never knows in detail how the computer electronically carries out the sequence of commands that he specifies in his design. Similarly, a designer can also use the computer language layer to create a new set of tools, such as a data base management system, which another designer can subsequently use to design still another complex system with no knowledge of how the facilities he is using are realized at the lower level. This deliberate *suppression of detail* is crucial to the orderly growth of complexity, because it allows different designers to each concentrate on a natural class of tasks that share common design principles.

This layering principle is fundamental to computer design and is carried to an extreme in such applications as the setting of standards for certain large-scale cooperative ventures, such as intercomputer communications.[1] The point of this layering is to provide a way to mediate between the diversity of specific machines and forms of information transmission on the one hand, and the need for identical standards on the other. This layering is just the idea of interchangeability of components and division of labor raised to a high art, in response to the enormous complexity of modern technological artifacts. It is the fact that technical objects can be organized in terms of this kind of conceptual layering that makes it possible for people to have sufficient understanding of such devices to operate them, repair them, and indeed even to design them.

This hierarchical style of design is both extremely natural for computing—for reasons having to do with the ease with which computers allow functions to be *composed* from subfunctions—and at the same time is the reason why computer systems can grow to such enormous complexity. This, in turn, is one of the factors that has contributed to the recent successes in artificial intelligence. Researchers now have the tools (i.e., some of the layers) with which to build systems whose complexity is sufficient to begin to produce behavior that we consider intelligent.

Those who remember the good old days of the early 1960s (how recent is the early history of artificial intelligence!) will recognize that programs such as the General Problem Solver were a very small fraction of the size of such current AI expert systems as Xcon or Mycin or Internist. This is critical because one of the lessons that has been learned in the past several dozen years is that intelligence arises from the interaction of a very large number of basic parts. In contrast with physics, cognition appears to have few general and powerful laws. Whatever else is required for the exercise of intelligence, it appears that one thing that is required is a large number of transactions on a large knowledge base. To a first approximation, to be intelligent is to know a lot and to be able to access the knowledge when it is appropriate. The commercial expert system Xcon has a representation of some 2,500 elementary facts, and Internist is said to have nearly a hundred times as much. And both of them are admittedly in the class of *idiot savants* that can perform intelligently only over a narrow range of problems. Clearly, in AI, we are dealing with large numbers. Without some general scheme for keep-

---

[1] For example, the International Standards Organization has devised certain standards and codes to be used for communications among machines (the so-called Open Systems Interconnect standards). These standards consist of a set of seven strictly independent layers—each of which can be realized in whatever way is appropriate for any particular computer or communication link, while enabling compatibility at some particular level.

ing control of such quantities, the designers of such systems would soon lose their way.

Before I come to my main point, which concerns the role of knowledge in the functioning of artificial intelligence systems, I want to sketch one additional property of computing that distinguishes it from the operations of other complex artifacts. I do this by going back a half-century or so to the origins of some of the ideas that form the theoretical foundations of computer science.

PLASTICITY OF COMPUTER FUNCTION

Alan Turing was a mathematician interested in exploring the limits of mechanization of mathematics. In the process he had to define the notion of "mechanism" as a fully specifiable, symbol-manipulating device, abstracted from any physical properties. He devised an extremely simple and ingenious design for such a device, which is now referred to as the "Turing Machine." What he discovered was that such an extremely simple device has the remarkable property of being *universal*. This means that one can design a particular Turing machine in such a way that by varying the symbols it reads on its input tape it can be made to behave like *any possible symbol-manipulating machine*. In other words, a universal Turing machine can simulate every conceivable symbol-processing mechanism without changing its basic structure. Because every computer you buy nowadays is a variant of a Turing machine, this result is also true of all our computers—they can be made to carry out *any* formally or mechanistically specifiable function. This is another way of saying what most people know about computers, that they are programmable to carry out almost[2] any function we know how to describe in the right way.

This extreme plasticity of behavior is one of the reasons why computers have from the very beginning been viewed as artifacts that might be capable of exhibiting intelligence. Those who were not familiar with this basic idea have frequently misunderstood the capacity of machines. For example, the Gestalt psychologist Wolfgang Kohler (1947) viewed machines as too rigid to serve as models of biological or mental activity. The latter, he claimed, are governed by what he called "dynamic factors"—an example of which are self distributing field effects, such as the effects which cause magnetic fields to be redistributed when we introduce new pieces of metal. He contrasted such dynamic factors with

---

[2] The qualification arises here because Turing was also able to prove that there exist uncomputable functions, thereby demonstrating a formal limit of mechanization. The relevance of such a limitation to cognitive science is not clear at the present time.

what he called "topographical factors" which are structurally rigid. He says,

> To the degree to which topographical conditions are rigidly given, and not to be changed by dynamic factors, their existence means the exclusion of certain forms of function, and the restriction of the processes to the possibilities compatible with those conditions. . . . This extreme relation between dynamic factors and imposed topographical conditions is almost entirely realized in typical machines . . . we do not construct machines in which dynamic factors are the main determinants of the form of operation. (p. 65)

That *computers* violate this claim is one of their most important and unique characteristics. Their topographic structure is completely rigid, yet they are capable of *maximal* plasticity or variability of function. It is this very property that led Turing (1964) to speculate that computers would be capable in principle of exhibiting intelligent behavior. The combination of extreme plasticity of function, together with an organization that gives rise to the orderly growth of complexity (due to the layering and distribution of labor principles mentioned earlier) make computers a powerful new form of technology. I will come back to the reason for this plasticity of function later. But first I want to introduce what, in my view, is the aspect of computers that establishes them as the most radical departure from the lineal descendants of early *homo sapiens* tools. Roughly speaking, it is the fact that computers, like people, can be made to *act on the content of information they are given*. Because this is not a familiar idea, I shall devote the remainder of my talk to discussing this claim and its ramifications.

COMPUTING AS KNOWLEDGE-BASED

It is commonplace nowadays to accept computers as a major new medium for the storage, transmission, and transformation of information. It is becoming clear to the public now, as it was not when I first began to teach computer science a number of years ago, that computers are not just lightening-fast calculators, but *information handlers*. Nonetheless, it is not generally appreciated how the information-handling capacity of a computer is different (except for its speed and efficiency) from the information-handling capacity of such devices as books, files, tape recorders, telephones, libraries, television sets, and so on, all of which in some sense store, transmit, process, and transform information. But that it *is* different should be abundantly clear. Computers, unlike books or even television sets, *do* things because of the particular information they contain. Moreover, the nature of the behavior that they exhibit appears to be directly attributable to the *content* of the information they have— or what the information is *about*. This is not true of any of the other information-handling systems we can think of—with the obvious exception of people or other higher organisms.

This observation is fundamental and bears some elaboration. Those who work with computers know that they can be coherently and consistently described as behaving in certain ways *because they know or have representations of certain things*. For example, a programmer might say that the computer predicted a rise in corporate spending at a certain time because it "has an econometric model" and was told the current values of certain parameters, or that it printed a check for so many dollars because it knows what the individual's salary is and what deductions have to be made according to the contract and the income tax law. The programmer might also correctly describe a computer as making a certain chess move by saying that it did so "in order to avoid having its knight captured by the opponent's queen." A more complex computer system, say one which diagnoses infectious diseases (e.g., the MYCIN system—see Shortliffe, 1976), might be described as *inferring* that a patient has a certain infection and *recommending* a particular treatment based on its *knowledge* of symptoms and of the actions of certain drugs. Indeed, the successor to MYCIN (a system called Teriesias) will even *explain* to the physician how it came to its decision by citing certain things it *believes* and certain inferential processes that it carried out.

Are these sorts of descriptions just convenient anthropomorphisms— like saying, for example, that the thermostat believes the room is too cold so it turns on the furnace? It's beginning to look very much like the answer has to be *no*. For one thing, the case of such artifacts as thermostats is easily excluded on the basis of a version of Occam's Razor (known to biologists as de Morgan's canon); *viz*, don't attribute philogenetically higher capacities when lower ones will suffice. In the case of devices such as thermostats, nothing whatever is lost in describing its functioning in physical terms. All its regularities are adequately captured in an electro-mechanical description, with no need to refer to goals, beliefs, knowledge, and so on. In such cases there is no genuine "level" of organization or of functioning beyond the electromechanical. But this is simply *not* the case for higher organisms, and it turns out not to be the case for the kinds of artifacts being designed in artificial intelligence. Such machines exhibit systematic patterns of behavior that could not adequately be captured by describing their physical structure. They must be described as being governed by internal symbolic representations: In other words, their behavior is dependent on the *knowledge* that is encoded in them. Because whenever I say this, people look at me

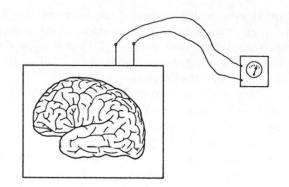

Figure 1. Systematic patterns of behavior recorded from an unknown black box. The problem is to explain the observed regularity. (Pylyshyn (1985), p. 68.)

with suspicion, I had better take a few moments to at least hint at why this is so.

REPRESENTATION-GOVERNED PROCESSES

The regular pattern of behavior exhibited by some systems can only be understood if we assume that aspects of their internal states are representations—that they are physical instantiations or tokens of symbols that stand for something, or that they function as codes for something. This is really a very simple and unproblematic point, though it sometimes strikes some people as a puzzling claim. Here is a simple example to illustrate this point (needless to say, it is not an example of an intelligent system—only of this simple idea of the need to refer to what states represent in giving an explanation of a system's functioning).

Suppose I showed you a black box into which I had inserted an electrode or some other response recorder (as illustrated in Figure 1). We need not be concerned with what is in the box. As we observe the box go about its usual function, we discover that the ensuing record exhibits certain regularities. For example, we observe that either individual short pulses or pairs of such short pulses frequently occur in the record, and that when there are both pairs and single pulses (as sometimes happens), the pair appears to regularly precede the single pulse. After observing this pattern for some time, we discover that there are occasional exceptions to this order—but only when the whole pattern is preceded by a pair of long and short pulse sequences. Being scientists, we are most interested in giving an explanation of this regularity. What causes this particular pattern to occur, as opposed to some other pattern? What kind of explanation for the pattern will be appropriate?

The answer, I maintain, depends upon what sort of device the black box is—and, in particular, on what its *capacity* is beyond the particular behavior we have just been observing (i.e., not on what it is doing, or what it typically does, but on what it *could* be doing in certain counterfactual situations). In this particular example, chosen deliberately to make a pedagogical point, I can confidently tell you that we would not find the explanation of its behavior in its internal structure or in any properties intrinsic to the box or its contents.

Now that might strike some people as an odd claim. How can the behavior of a system not be explainable in terms of its internal construction or its inherent properties? What else could possibly explain the regularities it exhibits? In the end, of course, it is the existence of certain properties in the box that govern the totality of its behavioral repertoire, or its capacity. But as long as we have only sampled some limited scope of this repertoire, (say, what it "typically" or "normally" does) we may not be in any position to infer what its intrinsically constrained capacity is, hence the observed regularity may tell us nothing about the internal structure or inherent properties of the device.

To make this point concrete, I can now reveal to you that the real reason the black box exhibits this regularity is simply that it processes or transmits English words encoded in International Morse Code. Thus the regularity we have discovered is not a direct result of the structure of the box but is attributable entirely to a spelling rule of English (*viz.*, *i* before *e* except after *c*). And the reason that providing a detailed description of the component structure and the operation of the box would not explain this regularity is that the structure is capable of exhibiting a much greater range of behaviors—*the observed constraint on its behavior is not due to its intrinsic capability but to what its states represent*. Because, as I have already pointed out, computers are extremely labile in the range of behavior that they can potentially exhibit. Hence, most of their behavioral regularities are not due to their structural properties, but to the representations that they embody.

Here are a few other, not so trivial, examples. I will make the point

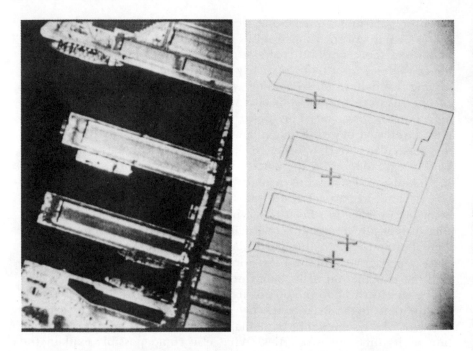

Figure 2. Aerial photograph of ships. [Ballard & Brown (1982), p. 3]

in this case by asking what is needed in order to design a system which exhibits a certain pattern of behavior, rather than what do we need to know in order to explain the regularities in its behavior? In fact, explaining and designing are much more closely connected activities than most people are willing to admit—which is one reason I maintain that the role of technology in shaping our understanding of the world has been underrated.

The examples I want to sketch are miniature problems that occur in systems falling into the category of artificial intelligence: The first one is from a system that analyzes aerial photographs. Suppose that it is looking for ships in aerial photos such as the ones shown in Figure 2. How can it do this? There are two different ways it might attempt to solve this task, and these two ways illustrate a prime difference between AI technology and other engineering technologies. The first way might be to search for image properties that are frequently (or even invariably) associated with ships—for example, patterns of a certain size and shape and appearing at certain coordinates or wavelengths. I will call such reliable indicators "signatures" of what we are looking for. When signatures are available—as they are for a few important features such as ground moisture—then this is certainly a useful approach.

However, signatures of man-made entities are rare because such entities are more often characterized by their function than by their shape or other physical characteristics. After all, a ship can be of many different sizes and can appear as quite different patterns on an image, depending on the season, the lighting condition, the surrounding geography, and so on. But human photointerpreters do very well at the task of locating them. How do they do it? The answer appears to be that they analyze the images by making use of what they know about ships, harbors, water bodies, rivers, the shipping industry, and anything else that might possibly turn out to be relevant.

In the sample image shown here, for example, some of the ships are barely visible. Yet they *can* be detected if you know what to look for and where; if, for example, you keep in mind that ships tend to be located on water near docks, that some rectangular protrusions of the shoreline may be docks, that contours that separate water from shoreline have characteristic shapes that provide evidence as to which is water and which, shore (e.g., at the mouth of rivers), that one can usually rely on such very general facts as that a contour does not change from being a water-land boundary at one place to a land-water boundary at another place as we follow it around. There are dozens and dozens of such obvious commonsense facts that go into the photointerpreter's skill, as well as some not-so-obvious things he may look for. Thus, although an expert photointerpreter may describe what he does as "just looking," we know that such "looking" covers a large amount of knowledge-based reasoning—reasoning that the interpreter may be unaware of doing. A system that did photointerpretation as well as an expert—and, over a range of situations, as broadly as the expert—is unlikely to be able to get away with searching for a "signature." It would invariably have to resort to inferences based on knowledge that is represented in a form that allows it to reason.

Here is another example which shows that carrying out a certain task requires that we appeal to knowledge. Suppose we wish to design a system that understands English sentences. Clearly, in order to understand an English sentence, the system will have to uncover what is called its "thematic structure": it will have to determine "who did what to whom." This requires that a number of things about the sentence be determined, one of which is simply to decide what all the pronouns or other anaphoras refer to. But how are we to determine what the italicized pronoun refers to in sentences such as the following?

- The city councilors refused the demonstrators a permit because *they* feared violence.

• The city councilors refused the demonstrators a permit because *they* were communists.

As in the code-box example, there is no *general* fixed structure or mechanism for doing the right thing in all cases, in this case for assigning references. There is no way of wiring a machine once and for all so it gets all such examples right. Why not? Because it is patent that what the pronoun refers to depends on knowledge of such things as what city councilors are like, what the attitude of people in authority is to communists in certain countries, perhaps on recollections of recent history or the day's news, and so on, without limit. Only factors like this would explain why the pronouns are typically assigned different referents in the two sentences and why the reference assignment can be easily changed by altering the context, and hence rendering some particular piece of knowledge relevant to the assignment. For example, I recently inadvertently provided an example of the effect of context myself when I used these sentences in a talk I gave in Florence, Italy. I had forgotten that the city council of Florence was in fact drawn primarily from the communist party. Because of this, my audience had assigned the same referent to the pronoun in both sentences and the point of the example had been largely lost!

It is important to realize that all this talk about how certain regular features of behavior can only be understood in terms of the use of knowledge and the making of inferences and decisions based on goals is *not just a matter of expedience or convenience*. The fact is that there are certain systems in nature whose behavior is explainable only if we take into account the organization that they have at a certain level: namely, the level at which they can be described as having representations of knowledge and goals. No matter how accurately and completely you described their physical or neurological structure, you would still not understand why they displayed certain patterns of behavior—unless you also took into account this level of organization.

By the way, the existence of this level of organization is closely related to my earlier point about the behavioral plasticity of certain systems. One important reason why we have to postulate representations is in order to account for the rather radical plasticity in human behavior. Psychologists who conduct laboratory studies on human behavior must take extraordinary precautions in the way they instruct subjects and in what they might inadvertently lead subjects to believe about the experiment. The reason is that behavioral regularities are extremely sensitive to subjects' beliefs, which in turn are influenceable by the content of any information or clues that the experimenter might provide. Whatever regularities in behavior we might observe under some set of conditions can be altered in a systematic and logically coherent way (to a first approximation) by merely providing the subject with certain information—by telling or showing the subject something, or providing clues which together with other beliefs warrant some plausible inference (see Brewer, 1972, for excellent examples of this in human conditioning experiments). This responsiveness of behavior to the content of *information-bearing events*, by the way, is one of the main reasons for the downfall of behaviorism.

The radical alterability of behavior patterns has led some people to conclude either that a rigorous predictive science of psychology is not possible, in which case one should resign oneself to predicting statistical properties of behavior (i.e., what people will do *most* of the time) or they have concluded that we have been on the wrong track when we have been trying to model mental activity in certain mechanistic terms. Kohler (1947), whom I cited earlier, was one of the people who took the second option, because he felt that "mechanical" models were too constrained in their behaviors by their structure, or what he called "topographical factors." But, as I noted earlier, Kohler was simply mistaken in this view, as Turing was able to prove. What I did not mention in my earlier discussion, is that in order to prove the universality of the simple Turing machine, Turing had to introduce the idea of symbols or of reference, and hence of representation. In order to simulate another machine, the universal machine has to have some representation of the machine to be simulated (e.g., it has to be given the instructions that the second machine would have carried out). Thus what was missing from Kohler's analysis was the notion that a machine could have another level of organization—one in which it is described as having and using *symbols*, and hence *representations*.

Finally, I want to conclude by saying something about the notion of *cognizing*, which I have been using loosely all through this talk.

IS *COGNIZING* A NATURAL CLASS OF PHENOMENON?

The qualitative growth in complexity and speed-of-information handling that computers have made possible has been more generally recognized than has their character as knowledge processors or, as Dan Dennett has called them, "semantic engines," which enables them to act on the *content of knowledge*. At the turn of the century, philosopher-psychologist Franz Brentano argued that the mark of the mental (and consequently the mark of the uniquely human) was the possession of what he called "intentionality"—by which he referred to the fact that mental states are "about" something—they have what we would call "representational content." The problem of understanding intentionality remains one of the tougher problems in philosophy of mind. Yet many of us believe that whatever the eventual satisfactory analysis of this notion, it will include features of what computers do, as well as what the human mind does. Indeed, computers are the only nonliving systems we know that appear to support a level of organization which corresponds to having and using representations, and hence that corresponds closely to what Brentano called intentionality. They do this despite the fact that at the moment nobody wants to say that such machines are *conscious*—hence it appears that intentionality may be independent of consciousness.

There is an important point here, if this analysis is correct. Revolutionary changes in our view of the world frequently have had the character of discovering new groupings of phenomena—groupings that philosophers call *natural kinds.* The discovery that violent and natural motion were not different kinds of phenomena, subject to different principles, as Aristotle had taught, was one of the first steps in the development of the new physics. It went hand in hand with the reclassification of the motion of heavenly bodies into the same category as the motion of middle-sized objects like stones and cannonballs. The modern concept of "physical object," as anything that has mass and location—whether or not it is visible, or even detectable in principle, and whether or not it is in motion or at rest—seems totally natural for us today. Yet, this was not always the case. Indeed, Galileo was ridiculed for his assumption that things he could see only through a special instrument (the rudimentary telescope) were of the *same natural kind* as things that could be seen with the naked eye. And perhaps we can understand why. Classing such things in the same natural category was to make an enormous conceptual leap: the leap of seeing a new fundamental grouping of things.

What people who work in the fields of artificial intelligence and cognitive science believe is that certain aspects of human capacity must also be regrouped or reconceptualized. Man has been variously understood as a creature of special creation, as a social entity and, in the late nineteenth century, as a biological object. What some of us now believe is that there is another natural category to which cognitive or rational action should be assigned. That category is one which also includes certain sorts of machines as members in good standing: machines whose behavior is governed by what they represent—by what they know. These are knowledge-driven systems, or what George Miller picturesquely refers to as *informavores*, or systems that are nourished and guided by information. If this regrouping or reconceptualization is correct, it means that certain forms of human behavior should be explained in precisely the same way that we explain certain forms of computer behavior. Thus, contrary to a widely held view, the computer is not a metaphor for mind, anymore than mathematical structures are metaphors for the physical world, as Freeman Dyson insisted in my earlier quotations, or geometry was a metaphor for space to Galileo. Rather, computing is a literal description of aspects of cognitive processes, stated in terms of a more manageable member of the same natural kind (*viz.*, the natural kind *cognizer*). This, then, is the new heresy: man the *informavore*, not only a cousin of the ape, but of the computer.

If all this turns out to be true, and the new natural kind becomes assimilated to the general view, as did the Galilean categories over the Aristotelian ones, we shall be witnessing a revolution in our image of man, perhaps greater even than the Darwinean or the Freudian. We shall also be witnessing a revolutionary change in the nature of our environment as we extend ourselves electronically. For the extension will be unlike that brought about by electronic communication media, which, as my countryman Marshall McCluhan pointed out, simply extended our senses. This new extension will literally place replicas of some of our most cherished functions—like thinking, deciding, recommending, evaluating, and pursuing goals—out there in our environment, along with other people and animals. As autonomous, active gatherers and exploiters of knowledge, they will represent a new and still incomprehensible form of externalized intellectual activity. Although in a sense they will still be tools, they will also be active participants in our intellectual activities, and we shall have to learn to live with them on those terms.

REFERENCES

Ballard, D.H. & Brown, C.M. (1982). *Computer vision.* Englewood Cliffs, NJ: Prentice-Hall.

Brewer, W.F. (1974). There is no convincing evidence for operant or classical conditioning in adult humans. In W.B. Weiner & D.S. Palermo (Eds.), *Cognition and the symbolic processes.* Hillsdale, NJ: Erlbaum.

Dyson, F.J. (1969). Mathematics in the physical sciences. In National Research Council Committee on Support of Research in the Mathematical Sciences (Ed.), *The mathematical sciences.* Cambridge, MA: MIT Press.

Kohler, W. (1947). *Gestalt psychology: An introduction to new concepts in modern psychology.* New York: Liveright.

Langer, S. (1962). *Philosophical sketches.* Baltimore: Johns Hopkins Press.

Pylyshyn, Z.W. (1985). *Computation and cognition: Toward a foundation for cognitive science* (2d ed.). Cambridge, MA: MIT Press/A Bradford Book.

Shortliffe, E.H. (1976). *Computer-based medical consultations: MYCIN.* New York: Elsevier.

Turing, A.M. (1964). Computing machinery and intelligence. In A.R. Anderson (Ed.), *Minds and machines.* Englewood Cliffs, NJ: Prentice-Hall. (Original work published 1950)

COLLOQUIUM

PANEL 1

Comments

Maria Teresa Miliora

It is my purpose not only to offer comments on what are for me the salient points in Professor Pylyshyn's paper, but also to relate the ideas on creativity which I expressed in my paper, "The Creative Attitude," delivered at our symposium on creativity last fall to those of Professor Pylyshyn's on artificial intelligence presented here. In order to establish a conceptual framework within which my comments may be appreciated, I will state my belief that the rational intellect is only one of several modes of human cognition. Further, I contend that within our society and our educational institutions there is probably an overemphasis on developing the rational intellect to the near exclusion of the other functions—in particular the imagination and the intuitive faculty.

I imagine there are those of us who, upon hearing Professor Pylyshyn's presentation, are uncomfortable with the idea of further computer technology, fearing that creativity will suffer, that technological development will exacerbate the alienation among people, and that human interactions and processes will be further dislocated. Others of us are probably impressed and excited with the capability of computer wizardry that he describes. I find myself at the midpoint of these polar positions.

From my perspective, Professor Pylyshyn has given us a lucid description of machine intelligence, explained why it is called intelligent, and presented a persuasive argument that this is a positive force and that the continued development of this new technology is inevitable.

I agree that liberally educated people cannot afford to be ignorant of technology. All of us, regardless of discipline, need to be equipped in order to be involved in making decisions that will determine the directions that this new technology will take and how this force will be used in the future. We must assume it will affect our lives; how it will do so is within our control.

Professor Pylyshyn states that ideas regarding artificial intelligence can bring with them "changes in one's world view, and in particular to one's view of human nature." He suggests that those who use only their perceptions will have different experiences from those who have technological tools because technology enables us to extend the range of the conceivable, to see the world in new ways. He calls these conceptual tools "imagination prosthetics." I agree that technological tools can extend the range of human experience. However, when we speak of technology having the capability of moving human experience to new directions, there is, for me, an implication that we have reached the limits of human experience—that is, the limits of human perception, imagination, and the intuitive level of cognition. I do not believe we have reached those limits; indeed I believe we have barely scratched the surface of our potential for cognition that extends beyond the realm of the analytic, rational intellect. I hope that we do not develop artificial intelligence because we believe that we have fully developed ourselves in these other realms.

Professor Pylyshyn presents a convincing argument that computers are more than tools. According to him, the special nature of computers derives from their "capacity [1] to increase the quality and quantity of complexity, [2] to exhibit very nearly unbounded plasticity of behavior and [3] to determine actions on the basis of knowledge of the external world and certain goals related to this knowledge." In discussing the first of these characteristics, the quality of complexity, he states that computers have the capacity to "allow functions to be composed from subfunctions" and that "intelligence arises from the interaction of a very large number of basic parts." It should be noted that the mental activity reproducible by these artifacts which Professor Pylyshyn describes as intelligent is entirely in the realm of the analytic mode of cognition.

He explains that the third characteristic is perhaps the most dramatic—that computers "like people can be made to act on the content of the information they are given," that their behavior is attributable to what the information is about. He describes them "as being governed by internal symbolic representations [and that] their behavior is dependent on the knowledge that is encoded in them." He connects the necessity for postulating the utilization of representations or symbols in computer systems to the utilization of representations by humans in order to account for the plasticity of both human and computer behavior, that is, to account for the fact that the behavior of both are influenceable and responsive to information-bearing events. It appears to me that representations have to be postulated because of another assumption, as well, that this plasticity of behavior is qualitatively and quantitatively the same for both humans and computer systems. I, for one, have yet to find two humans who will react exactly the same, if we consider both internal and external processes, when exposed to the same event. If it is concluded that computers behave or can behave as individualistically as humans, I would argue that that conclusion derives from the fallacious assumption that individual, internal human processes can be objectively known, described and communicated.

I find Professor Pylyshyn's conclusion about intentionality disturbing. He states that "computers are the only nonliving systems we know that appear to support a level of organization which corresponds to having and using representations." Thus, according to Professor Pylyshyn, computers satisfy Brentano's definition of intentionality. He goes on to say that because "at the moment nobody wants to say that such machines are conscious—it appears that intentionality may be independent of consciousness." I do not agree with this conclusion and would argue that human intentionality is governed by both unconscious and conscious processes, the extent of each in humans is highly individualistic. Further, I believe that a major goal of human development should be to bring ever greater consciousness to intentionality and that to do otherwise or to presume that it cannot be done is to diminish human nature.

Professor Pylyshyn asks the question, Is cognizing a natural class of phenomenon? He describes fundamental groupings of phenomena as "natural kinds." He states that "cognitive or rational action" is such a natural category and that in this category belongs the human cognitive process and the artificial intelligence system. He states that "if this regrouping is correct, it means that certain forms of human behavior should be explained in precisely the same way that we explain certain forms of computer behavior." To the extent that Professor Pylyshyn's remarks about human behavior are limited to the rational, intellectual level of human behavior alone, I do not disagree with his conclusion. There is for me, however, some ambiguity of intention when I consider his statements, "the computer is not a metaphor for mind" and "man the *informavore*, not only a cousin of the ape, but of the computer." I wonder whether some, upon hearing these remarks, might not make a quantum leap and interpret these as meaning that humans are like computers in all aspects of their respective cognitive processes.

I do not believe that development of human creativity and development of artificial intelligence are mutually exclusive endeavors. Indeed, because each is a manifestation of a different level of human experience, one focusing on sensory, imaginal, and intuitive functions and the other on the analytic, rational intellectual functions, the development of both will further human development and enable a fuller expression of human potential. What I fear, however, is the continued polarization of what for me are simply two aspects of human experience, what some call right-brain and left-brain processes, represented by artists and humanists on one hand and scientists and technocrats on the other. Further, I believe that if there is polarization, it is the creative, the intuitive, process that will suffer because historically we have tended to favor rational intellectual pursuits rather than the former. I believe that development and integration of both within our individual human experience should be the goal of education, and I challenge our liberal education institutions to that end.

COLLOQUIUM

PANEL 1

Comments

Daniel C. Dennett

First, I want to offer my congratulations to Suffolk University on its 50th anniversary. I look forward to the next 50 years—indeed, the next 100 years.

I agree so wholeheartedly with almost everything Zenon Pylyshyn has said that I will not play the usual philosopher's role of arguing and nitpicking and trying to refute what he said. Perforce, agreeing with Professor Pylyshyn means that I must disagree somewhat with what Professor Miliora has just said. I will leave to Pylyshyn the task of responding to the bulk of her remarks, as he wishes. But I'm going to single out one point with which I want to express my disagreement, and that is her suggestion that there is an important division between, on the one hand, the analytic or rational and, on the other hand, the creative, imaginative, or intuitive.

One of the things I think we have learned in artificial intelligence is that any deep notion of rationality or of analytic power involves deep notions of creativity and imagination and intuition—that if you have a vision of analytic power or of rationality which is sheer brute mechanical computation with no leaps of imagination, then you have an impoverished view of what the analytic is—of what the rational is. And some of the most exciting work in artificial intelligence is precisely the work that shows how any rational agent—whether it is a robot or a theorem prover or a medical diagnosis system—has to have, in effect, creative powers of imagination. I can't hope to defend my view at length here; I would simply suggest that it is no longer obvious that there is a sharp break where Professor Miliora wants to make one—between the intuitive and the imaginative and creative, on the one hand, and the analytic and the rational, on the other.

Professor Pylyshyn says that computers can be, as he puts it, prosthetics of the imagination—a theme with which I am in complete agreement. What we are facing is growth in our ability to think, a growth
enhanced by the tools—both the hardware tools and the conceptual
tools—provided by the computer and the computer revolution. Some
of these changes are not just changes in the world views of the academics and the researchers who are working on these projects but are trick-
ling down into popular culture in a way that you are all familiar with,
and which perhaps alarm some of you. In the popular culture we have
smart cars, smart cash registers in supermarkets, and smart elevators. I
was fascinated to see this morning, as I was taking my shower, that there
is even smart shampoo these days. I noticed that on the bottle of shampoo it said that my shampoo "responded to the special cleansing needs"
of my hair. And I thought, how clever of this shampoo! Apparently it
has some rules in it for what the optimum treatment of the hair is and
it sends out its little molecular testers that see just exactly what the
deficiencies are in my hair and then does some calculations and some
computations and then provides just the right treatment! (Perhaps I'm
being a little gullible about that shampoo.)

We have no doubt gone overboard in attributing intelligence to this
fluid in a jar. And, of course, some people would say we've gone overboard in attributing intelligence to the thermostat or the elevator or the
computer—no matter how fancy the computer is. Professor Pylyshyn's
closing remarks had to do with the proposition that we have a new
natural kind. We have to move some boundaries. We now have the category of the informavore or the cognizer, which includes, not just us
and a few of our closest mammalian relatives, but also some artifacts
that we have made. This is a shocking idea to many people. I want to
say that I think he is absolutely right that we've got a new category. But
I don't quite agree with him about the placement of the boundary so I
am going to pick a fight with him about that.

What about our thermostats now? Pylyshyn suggests that it's merely
a bit of convenient anthropomorphizing to say that the thermostat is
one of these knowledge users, that it has any real intentionality, that
it has any real representation in it. And he suggests that it is easy
enough to see what the difference is between a thermostat and, say, a
fancier AI system. The AI system, he says, cannot really be understood
in its operation without attributing to it a level at which it is processing information and at which it has a representation of knowledge,
say, about the world that it consults in the course of its operation.
You have to go up to this knowledge level, to what Allen Newell calls
the knowledge level and to what I call the intentional stance level, in
order to explain the system's behavior. This, he says, is different from

the thermostat, whose behavior you can understand without ever ascending to that level.

I think that's true in a certain sense. You can indeed understand any particular commercial thermostat. You can understand its behavior and the regularities in its behavior without ever ascending to the intentional stance level. But, if you only understand the thermostat at that level, you've left out something important. After all, if you're willing to devote the rest of your life to it, you can understand any artificial intelligence system of whatever complexity at the design level or at the electronic or physical level. And, if you do, you will, nevertheless, be missing something very important about the design (and rationale of the design) of that artifact. Science has up to now dealt primarily with a certain class of questions. It has dealt excellently with the *what* questions, the *where* and *when* questions, and even with the *how* questions, but it hasn't had much to say about the *why* questions. One question that we might want to answer about the thermostat is not just "How does it work?" or "Where does it get its inputs?" or "Where does it send its outputs?" but "Why is it there and what is its function?" A thermostat, in effect, has a *raison d'être*—it has a reason for being. It occupies a certain niche in the world. And if it didn't have certain powers, it wouldn't be there.

I'm going to give you a list of *why* questions which, I want to claim, reveal that they have something important in common when you set out to answer them. One of them is, "Why did the diagnostician decide that the patient had an infection of the blood of a certain sort?" That's a why question. Independent of whether the diagnostician is a human specialist or an artificial intelligence specialist, that question has an answer in terms of the information that was consulted and the reasons and the reasoning that went on. "Why did the chess player move his rook to rook-4?" is a similar sort of question with a similar sort of answer in terms of strategies, reasons, knowledge about the position on the board, and so forth. But now I want to consider a somewhat different question: "Why do some moths have those startling eye spots on their wings so that when they open their wings up they look like much larger creatures with big glaring eyes?" Finally: "Why do houses have thermostats?" In each case, there is an answer to be given in terms of reasons, in terms of these items being parts of larger systems, the design and operation and activity of which are responsive—either swiftly or slowly—to reasons that are there.

A thermostat can be understood very simply as replacing a not very intelligent person whom you might hire to play a role for you. And you might say to that person, "Here is my command to you: This is what I'm going to pay you for. I want you to stand here and turn on the furnace whenever it feels too cold and to turn off the furnace whenever it feels just right." And if the person is not very good at sensing the temperature, you might hand him a thermometer and say, "I want you to watch that thermometer, and whenever the mercury gets down below this mark, I want you to turn the furnace on and whenever it goes back up above this mark, I want you to turn the furnace off." And if the person didn't have a very good memory, you could write those directions down on a piece of paper and give the piece of paper to the person, and the person could stand there all day long looking at the thermometer and looking at the directions and checking to make sure he or she was following orders.

That gives you the essence of the thermostat. If you think, though, of the niche that that person is occupying, you realize that there is a switch to the furnace and two sources of input. There's the source that tells you the temperature and there's the source that tells you what the desired temperature is, a command: Keep it at 68, keep it at 72, keep it at 65. And, my point is this: Whether you have a person or a thermostat in that niche, it has to have two ways of sensing the world, one to sense the actual temperature and one to sense the desired temperature. It has to have an output—its switch—and it has to have what is known in computer science as conditional branching so that it can "decide" what it's going to do next, depending on what it senses about the way the world is.

If you think about a thermostat in those terms, you realize there are many different devices you could put on the wall utilizing different principles of physics, different design principles. Some of them might spell things out in very different ways. After all, in the case of our human thermostat, we have a written instruction and a thermometer that is being visually inspected to determine the temperature. All these systems have something in common. And what they have in common is that they are all information-processing systems. What makes the thermostat special is simply that it is about as simple a system as you can have that has these properties. So, contrary to Professor Pylyshyn, I would say that the thermostat belongs in the natural kind with the human being and the smart computers. It's just like the paramecium—a very simple case. And it's none the worse for that; in fact, it's simplicity makes it a very nice example to draw out the very principle of information and information utilization that Professor Pylyshyn wants to stress.

Now, go back to the moth. Why does the moth have the eye spots on its wings? Well, certainly not because the moth—any more than the shampoo—is clever enough to figure out the rationale and has painted the spots on its wings in order to deceive the predators. Nevertheless, that is the rationale for those spots. It's not in the moth's tiny head. And

Darwin has shown us that it's not necessarily in God's head, either. The process of evolution by natural selection has itself been responsive and sensitive to the information in the environment over a much longer time scale than, say, a human designer would be or could be responsive to the same things.

An information-sensitive system, such as the process of natural selection, is not necessarily an information-*representing* system. When you want to speed up the responsiveness to reasons and when you want to increase the plasticity and versatility of a system's responsiveness to information, you have to build into the system a system of representation. Our thermostat can represent only two things—desired temperature and actual temperature. And then it just compares the two representations and turns on the furnace if they are different. If you want to have a more elaborate system of representation, you have to build in something like a language which can systematically represent many different possible world situations and then permit the system that has those representations in it to make its decisions based on its appreciation of those representations of the way the world is. The thermostat is about as simple a case as there can be.

Artificial systems of the sort that Professor Pylyshyn was describing are not even halfway, in their complexity, to the complexity of what we have between our ears. We couldn't understand them—these artificial intelligence systems—if they didn't have a level-by-level modular breakdown so that we can understand individual levels independently of the astronomically complex details of the lower levels. It's this idea—that we can divide the problem of intelligence (and creativity and rationality and intuition) into manageable subproblems at different levels and analyze them—that has given us the power (not yet the actuality, but the potential) to understand the workings of our own minds by understanding the workings of other simpler members of this new class of informavores.

In closing, I would say that there's only a difference of degree between us and the thermostat, just as there is only a difference of degree between us and the paramecium. And, as for the question of conciousness, I would go out on a limb that even Professor Pylyshyn did not go out on and say that we're on the verge of explaining conciousness itself as an elaboration on the information process and capacities of these cognizers and informavores. But that's a story we're not yet quite ready to tell.

COLLOQUIUM

PANEL 1

Comments

Stuart Goldkind

I find myself in the somewhat awkward position of agreeing (for the most part) with Professor Pylyshyn's remarks. This, of course, makes my role as commentator more difficult. I apologize to Professor Pylyshyn in advance for my method of extricating myself from this position, because it is possible that someone could construe my commentary as a criticism of his statements. That is not so, however. The situation as I see it is this: Professor Pylyshyn, in his discussion, has blurred over several issues whose resolution would not tell against his position no matter how they might be resolved. It is quite clear from Professor Pylyshyn's other writings that he is perfectly cognizant of these issues, and it seems most likely that he did not wish to become involved in the many complications which a technical discussion of these problems would raise. Nonetheless, I feel that some of the problems are quite important, and I will try, in the short time alloted to me, to give a thumbnail sketch of some of the difficulties surrounding one of these issues (without in any way attempting to resolve them).

REPRESENTATIONS: *FOR* VERSUS *OF*

There is a distinction which I believe deserves a more prominent place in current discussions of cognitive science. This is the distinction between a representation being a representation *of* something versus being a representation of something *for some entity*. This is a distinction closely related to an important question for cognitive science. Put roughly, the question is: How do representations represent? or, Where does the content of representations come from; how is it to be accounted for? Professor Dennett, one of our other commentators, has written an interesting book (if I have the title right, it is *Content and Consciousness*) which takes this question very seriously. Unfortunately, in the short time allowed here I can do no more than recommend the book to your attention.

Professor Pylyshyn states that AI systems can act on the basis of the content of information they have. There is much truth to this and, as Professor Pylyshyn points out, its importance cannot be overemphasized. However, it is also a statement whose ultimate import is far from clear. To illustrate: Consider a map of London. This map represents various facts about London, yet one could not correctly say that a book containing this map *believes or knows* anything about London (not even the facts represented by the map). There is a certain minimal sense to *"having a representation"* such that it would be correct to say that a book has a representation (or more than one) of the fact (for example) that Sherlock Holmes was given to periods of lassitude followed by periods of frenzied activity (depending on whether or not a case was under investigation). In this minimal sense, there is nothing wrong with saying that computer systems have representations. There is, however, another richer sense in which this attribution is more problematic. This is the sense in which we would not want to say that the book has this representation, or the representation that Sherlock Holmes is tall, or any other. We would not want to speak in this way because the book has such representations only in virtue of the fact that it might have them *for someone else*. That is, the set of symbols representing the fact of Holme's tallness, does not in any way, shape, or form, represent this fact *for* the book.

Similarly, it is not enough that information be present in a computer system in order to say (in the richer sense) that the machine has a representation of that information. Or, put another way, it is not enough to say that the machine *believes, or knows*, the information. What more is required in order to justify the application of the richer statement (which, by the way, would put the representing in a class along with allegory, analogy, literary symbolism, metaphor, and others) is an extremely difficult question. It is clear that something must be said about the functional role which the representation plays in the behavior of the entity which is said to *"have"* the representation. But the connections between representations and behavior are complex and not easily analyzed. (We have only to remember the difficulties with dispositional accounts of belief—does King Knute's gesture and command to the sea to recede signify that he believes that he can control the tides, or does it show that he believes that he can most effectively dispel the myth that he has this power by precisely that action?) The exact explication of the functional role a representation must play in order to qualify as a belief (or a representation *for an entity*) is one of the greatest challenges faced by cognitive scientists.

COLLOQUIUM

PANEL 1

Reply

Zenon W. Pylyshyn

Well, there isn't really anything to rebut. People are generally being nice to me, quite unlike the way they are at philosophy meetings. I have a few comments to make, however, and I'll make them in reverse order of the speakers because of the recency effect on memory.

First, a quick remark about Dr. Goldkind's point about knowledge: "Whose knowledge is it and who are these representations for? Where does the content come from?" These are some of the most difficult philosophical problems in the philosophy of mind and in cognitive science. Cognitive scientists usually don't worry about these questions too much because it doesn't affect their day-to-day work. But it does affect how one is to interpret the nature of artificial systems—whether they are to be taken to be strongly equivalent to human cognition or whether they are taken to be mere mimicry. Which of these we opt for depends on how we answer the question, "*Whose* knowledge makes the system work the way it does?" Is it the designer's knowledge, or does the machine possess the knowledge? The distinction is between the sort of knowledge we find in a book and the knowledge we have in our minds. The knowledge in a book just sits there. It is the knowledge that an author puts into it and the knowledge that a reader gets when he reads it, but it's no more knowledge *for* the book than it is splotches of ink.

There is reason, however, to think that the situation is very different in the case of a computer (though not in the case of the thermostat— we'll come back to that in a minute). In the case of the computer, the knowledge doesn't just sit there. It actually enters into the process of determining actions. How the content of knowledge can determine actions is a problem that has no philosophically satisfactory solution at the moment—either for computers or for people. Yet we have to say things like: "The computer recommends Neomycin because it believes the patient has a streptococcus infection." In doing this we've given an explanation. For example, we've given an explanation for why a machine printed something out, and part of the explanation requires use of such words as streptococcus. But the streptococcus has not caused the machine to behave in any way. There is no causal relationship between a streptococcus virus or germ and the behavior.

In natural science, we're not used to dealing with that sort of thing. When you say X happened because of Y, then it's because Y has entered into a causal relationship, and there is actually a physical law—a natural law—that says that if you have Y then you will get X. In cognitive science, there is no causal law that connects some things that are mentioned in the explanation with the action. That's because the things that are mentioned in the explanation are semantic contents. The relationship of words or symbols to things like viruses is an informational or referential relationship, and referential relationships can't cause things. So why do we need them in that story? Well, there is no good general answer to that, although there have been several attempts to develop different kinds of semantical theories to explain how it's possible for a system of codes to have semantic content. The problem is not unrelated to the problem of how words get to have meanings. How does my referring to Chicago connect with Chicago? There are attempts to deal with that, but it's a very difficult problem.

A comment about Dan Dennett and, at the same time, Professor Miliora. The power of the analytical mode—I think Dan is exactly right—has been vastly underestimated. There are analytical, rational processes going on whose implications go well beyond what we might have expected. To make a rational system work, we need to hypothesize processes of which we as humans have absolutely no awareness. Otherwise, there would be no way to explain how it's possible for us to do the simplest thing like assign the referent to a pronoun.

When you read a sentence which has a pronoun in it, you know what the pronoun refers to, but your awareness of how you come to know it is just blank. You're not aware of any process going on. Cognitive scientists, however, have very good reason to believe that there is a rational, complex, articulated, computational process going on. It may seem to you that you arrive at some cognitive state by pure intuition, but that's just to say that you're not aware of what's going on. Saying it's intuition is not to give an explanation of how it happened. I don't agree with Dan, by the way, that the problem of conciousness is going to be explained by computational methods. I don't think it's going to be explained in any way for a long time because I don't think that it's a puzzle. I think that it's a mystery, and the distinction between the two is that, in the case of a puzzle, if somebody had a correct solution to it, everyone would say, "Wow, isn't that a nice solution." If somebody had a solution to the problem of what conciousness is, no one would recognize it because we don't know well enough what the problem is. So, at the moment, it resides in the domain of a mystery.

Now the thermostat issue: I'm simply not going to rise to that bait. Dan and I have had this argument a number of times. I think that thermostats are qualitatively different from representation-governed systems, and hence are not members of the category of cognizers. I don't think that we can force them into that category by explaining them in terms of some rationale for why they behave the way they do. Such a teleological story may explain why certain systems occur in certain ecological niches, but it does not imply that such systems possess a "knowledge level" of organization. I think that there is no knowledge level of organization in degenerate cases like thermostats.

Suppose you take a human, put him in a place where the thermostat is and give him a switch and a set of instructions to do exactly what the thermostat does. The human would be cognizing. The thermostat doing the exact same thing, wouldn't be. The reason is that we can't infer the underlying process from a fragment of behavior: the human could do other things, too, and the thermostat couldn't. Furthermore, the other things that a human could do could be changed very systematically by just informing the person, for example, that you're not going to pay him for doing that after all. And suddenly he's going to stop behaving that way. Information will change the behavorial regularity of the human in that position. It won't change the behavioral regularity of the thermostat. Dan is attempting to lead me on with a slippery-slope argument that I will not pursue.

To Professor Miliora, I already said something about consciousness. Primarily, I said that I'm not going to say any more about it because I don't understand what it is to impute consciousness to another organism. I know what it is for me to be conscious, but I don't know what it is for someone else to be conscious, at least I don't know what it is in the right way. I don't know what it is in a way such that if I had an explanation of it, you or I would be satisfied with it.

There is a point that Professor Miliora raised concerning rational or analytic cognition, as opposed to other forms of cognition, that I think is worth a remark. First of all, I'm not recommending that we train people only in this rational or analytical mode of operation. I think one needs to encourage people to deal with the world without deliberately thinking things out. We need to encourage them to use the kind of processes that go on without their conscious awareness, and we need to encourage them to trust intuition or to discipline intuition, and so on. This almost always happens when we become expert at some task.

There are many examples of processes that we count as intuitive because they happen in a flash. Yet, in most cases, we have very good reason to believe that what was going on is just the sort of thing that's going on when you are thinking to yourself, except that it happens very quickly. The simplest illustration is the phenomonon called "subitizing." I flash a number of spots on the screen—three, four, or five spots. You have the very strong impression that you know how many there are and you haven't had to count them. That is what "subitizing" refers to. But, if you examine the process very carefully, it turns out that what's going on is very rapid counting—something on the order of 30–40 milliseconds per item. It goes so fast that you are not aware of it, so that you might say that you knew intuitively how many dots there were. But more careful analysis reveals that what was going on was a rational process.

It's been a discovery—an empirical discovery of no small consequence—that you make better progress if you don't put things that you are aware of in a category distinct from those processes of which you are not aware. It turns out that you are able to develop a systematic theory of cognition by blurring the distinction between things of which you are, and are not, aware.

I will agree with Professor Miliora that there is not only one kind of thing going on in what we informally call cognition. I believe cognition in the technical sense overlaps to a large extent with the informal sense of cognition. But it does not overlap entirely. There are a lot of things that we would like to count as cognition or reasoning that are not going to end up in the natural scientific category that I called "cognizing." For example, a great deal of effort in psychology has been spent trying to understand learning as a cognitive process in which one builds up new concepts by a process of logical analysis or computation. I think there is very good reason to think now that learning does not take place this way. A good deal of learning is just not going to fall into this category of explanation. The answer to the question how I learned that something is a dog or a chair or a member of some such natural category will probably not be that I worked it out by a process of reason and problem solving.

A child can learn certain concepts by ostention. Suppose the first time the child encounters a dog, you point to it and say "dog." Even if the child does not learn that label immediately, the naming event initiates a process about which we know very little, except that it is neither a process of association nor of problem solving. The child does not simply entertain a hypothesis such as that you may be referring to things that are approximately two feet long and have four legs, fur, and so on. That is not what's going on. Rather, there seems to be a biological predisposition for a certain kind of category, "doglike," and what we have done is trigger that biological predisposition. It is not an uncontroversial view, I should say, but it's a view that, in the case of concept attainment and in the case of language learning, is gathering more and more credibility. I cite this example because it's a process that many people might have assumed fell into the category of cognizing, but it probably won't turn out to work that way.

A lot of other phenomena—such as the developmental stages and other phenomena studied by Piaget—will probably also turn out not to be a case of building representations the way some cognitivists believe but, rather, will turn out to be the result of the maturation of certain kinds of mechanisms. Other things—the effects of moods, the effects of emotions on our dispositions to behave or to believe certain things— will probably also not be accounted for by the same kind of principles that go into explaining how it is that a person understands a particular sentence or solves problems. So we have no right a priori to say what's going to fall into this natural category of cognition. It might be that a lot of the things Professor Miliora is interested in, which we informally think of as aspects of reasoning and thinking, are just not going to be a part of this science, and we have no right insist in advance that they be put there. It's a matter of empirical discovery exactly where the boundaries of this science are.

It was one of the achievements of physics that it discovered the boundaries of physical laws. What sort of phenomena can be accounted for by the laws of physics? It turns out that the motion of planets can be accounted for that way, as can the motion of subatomic particles. But the movement of worms has to have different principles. The movement of living things, and even semiliving things like viruses, have to have a completely different set of principles for explaining their trajectories. Similarly there are likely to be lots of areas of human mentation which are not going to be part of cognitive science.

COLLOQUIUM

KEYNOTE SPEECH

A Liberal Education Meet for These Times

Mark H. Curtis

I feel honored to have been asked to address this colloquium. Its theme is a challenging one—Creativity and the Implementation of Change: Liberal Learning in the Practical World. Liberal learning now, as in both the recent and remote past, is laden with promise for the practical world. Yet undergraduate education is in disarray and it is going to take vision, creative leadership, and dedication to the high calling of college teaching to restore coherence to the undergraduate programs of our colleges and universities—to forge from the diverse and fragmented curricula a revitalized liberal education meet for these times.

The substances of my remarks comes from the report on baccalaureate education which the Association of American Colleges released last week at its 71st Annual Meeting in Washington. This report, which you may have read in the *Chronicle of Higher Education*, contains the findings and recommendations of a Select Committee established by the Association at its Boston meeting in 1982. Entitled *Integrity in the College Curriculum*, it is founded on a premise that we tend, these days, either to ignore or take for granted. This premise is that undergraduate education is *still* a matter of utmost importance and has purposes that give it far-reaching significance not only for college students but for our whole society.

I believe the continuing significance of undergraduate education can be summarized in these propositions:

1. That going to college still means to most people attending an institution of higher education to pursue studies leading to a baccalaureate degree.

2. That baccalaureate education still has a distinctive intrinsic value for students which justifies it for its own sake.
3. That baccalaureate education, as a terminal program of formal education for many persons and as the foundation for professional and advanced studies for others, still has a civic purpose that is vital to the health of American democratic society.

To return to the first proposition: Statistics on college enrollment clearly demonstrate what going to college means to most people. In 1980, the largest single contingent of students in all institutions of higher education was the group of 5.6 million undergraduates who were attending four-year colleges and universities to pursue courses of study creditable towards a bachelor's degree. They comprised over 46% of the total enrollment of 12,234,644. In addition, a substantial number, though not a majority, of the nearly 3.8 million undergraduates attending two-year colleges were also engaged in studies that could be used for transfer to four-year institutions offering baccalaureate programs.

Statistics on the degrees awarded in 1980 are even more conclusive. Seventy percent of the degrees granted by four-year colleges and universities were bachelor's degrees. Even if associate degrees are included in the base, they still constitute more than 53% of the total.

But statistics of this sort indicate only that baccalaureate education is an important matter to a lot of people but do not say anything about why they believe it to be important. What place does baccalaureate education have in the sequence of experiences that make up formal education?

The state that has befallen higher education is not, despite the opinion of many, the "consequence of unplanned and unchecked democratization" which holds that every American has the right to be wrapped in sheepskin. Nor is the cause of its decline a kind of marketplace philosophy of higher education, where the students are the consumers and the faculty are the purveyors of learning. Such a development, which someone has called a Green Stamp approach to education, is not so much the cause as the symptom of academic troubles. If either or both of these factors were the source of our problems, we could restore integrity to our educational programs by simple measures such as stiffening the admission requirements or tinkering with the offerings for general education and tightening up the limits on the number of courses permitted for a major.

Unfortunately, the disarray in undergraduate education has deeper roots. If you have had a chance to read the report that was issued last week, you found there a historical analysis that traced the source of the problem to the collapse of any coherent educational philosophy under

the impact of several developments which occurred in the late nineteenth century and whose consequences have been unfolding ever since.
The chief ones were the rise of research universities with their graduate
programs to train professional research scholars, the growing popularity
of the land grant colleges with their emphasis on agriculture and the
mechanical arts, and the elective principle, which became an Occam's
razor to cut through the rigidities of the old curriculum, only to permit
later the proliferation of narrow, specialized courses. Distribution and
concentration requirements arrested for a time, but could not halt, the
final dissolution of the curriculum. In the last thirty years, changes, such
as the unprecedented rise in enrollments, the rapid introduction of new
fields of study, especially in technical and professional areas, and the
increasing hegemony of graduate and postbaccalaureate professional
schools, have each vitiated the intrinsic meaning and purpose of baccalaureate education. The Committee concluded:

> [The undergraduate] course of study has been battered by history and by
> every group that shares an interest in it. Successive generations of stu-
> dents carry differing expectations to the academic enterprise, and they
> leave their mark. Today's student populations are less well-prepared, more
> vocationally oriented, and apparently more materialistic than their im-
> mediate predecessors. . . .The credential is for most students more impor-
> tant than the course. Therefore, it is critically important for academic
> institutions to pay more attention than they have to the course for which
> they are prepared to deliver the credential. (Association of American Col-
> leges, 1985, pp. 5–6)

Having made such a diagnosis of the state of undergraduate education, the Committee's prescription calls for reform of college education
and college teaching in root and branch. As they looked to ways to
achieve reform, they called on the faculty to resume its ancient responsibility for the curriculum as a whole and to take the profession of
teaching seriously. All of them being, or having been, faculty, they sym-
pathized with, but still spoke forthrightly to, their colleagues.

Let me briefly cite what they had to say about teaching.

> There is considerable discontent among the professors themselves with
> the quality of teaching generally; most of them welcome words of serious-
> ness about teaching and are willing to acknowledge that something im-
> portant was missing in their graduate school education. For while all of
> them were prepared to be professional economists or physicists or what-
> ever, none was prepared for the profession of undergraduate teaching,
> for the ethical standards and levels of performance appropriate to the

responsibility of being not only the professor of a subject but a college teacher. (Association of American Colleges, 1985, p. 11)

They call on faculty, senior tenured faculty as well as junior faculty, to become serious about teaching. They must:

1. Teach undergraduates regularly and for a significant portion of the academic year.
2. Develop courses that show commitment not only to the interests of their departments but to the educational ideals and mission of their institutions.
3. Teach in such a way that they illuminate the general purposes of the curriculum and relate their special field to the whole realm of learning.
4. Give time ungrudgingly to the counseling and personal aspirations of students.

In making these strong recommendations, the Select Committee, most of whose members are distinguished scholars as well as teachers and administrators, did not denigrate or belittle the importance of research. Indeed they recognized and asserted that "the finest teachers are often the best researchers" (p. 11). What they deplore is the pervasive spirit in American academic circles "that says that [research] is the only worthy or legitimate task for faculty members" (p. 11). They criticize not the inclusion of research among the responsibilities of faculty but the imbalance of a system that pits research against teaching and makes it an ultimate that overrides concern for teaching. They realized that to correct this long-standing problem, the faculty, who are the indispensable agents for achieving significant academic reform, need the leadership and commitment of presidents, provosts, and deans representing the corporate authority of colleges and universities.

With respect to reform of the curriculum itself, their recommendations require determination and concerted intellectual effort by all. They demand inventiveness and creative imagination sufficient to break down ingrained faculty habits and to break through the incrustation of institutional bureaucratic practices. As the Committee puts the matter:

The elements of our minimum course of study do not add up to an invitation to establish prescribed survey courses in literature and science, nor do they suggest solving the curricular problems of higher education by simply strengthening distribution requirements and adding multi-disciplinary general education courses. We believe that either one of these old

solutions is more likely to perpetuate than remedy the conditions that
brought our committee into existence. Both of them are comfortably appealing, for they do not challenge the ways in which power and responsibility have been used in the past. (p. 24)

What they proposed was a "minimum required program of study for
all students, consisting of the intellectual, aesthetic, and philosophical
experiences that should enter into the lives of men and women" (p. 15).
Their report continues:

> We do not believe that the road to a coherent undergraduate education
> can be constructed from a set of required subjects or academic disciplines.
> We do believe that there are methods and processes, modes of access to
> understanding and judgment, that should inform all study. While learning
> cannot, of course, take place devoid of subject matter, how that subject
> matter is experienced is what concerns us here. We are in search of an
> education that will enable the American people to live responsibly and
> joyfully, fulfilling their promise as individual humans and their obliga-
> tions as democratic citizens. (p. 15)

A close study of their nine fundamental characteristics of a minimum
curriculum will quickly demonstrate the depth of their conviction. When
they, for instance, speak of "inquiry, abstract logical thinking, critical
analysis" (p. 15), they are dealing with fundamentals that should be
learned in the study of any subject. They are directing attention to the
need to develop facility in performing the basic intellectual activities,
weighing evidence, developing inferences on the basis of observation,
determining why we put faith in what we know. To take another example: "Understanding numerical data" (p. 17) is not the outcome of
mastering the content of a single course, but results from using numerical analysis and reasoning in various courses through the curriculum.
Such understanding can awaken students to ways in which numerical
data lead to levels of knowledge inaccessible by any other means, and
at the same time arm them to recognize misuse of numerical data and
how misrepresentation based on such errors can be refuted. Likewise,
literacy in writing, reading, speaking, and listening (p. 16) is something
that should be developed across the curriculum. They develop critical
understanding and empower persons to use clarity, directness, simplicity, and cogency in expressing their hard-won knowledge and judgments
to others. In a practical world, where written memoranda and clear
verbal statements are important in getting business done, nothing is
more essential than literacy. As a final example from their list of nine,
I shall cite science, (p. 19) which is widely neglected by today's undergraduates unless they major in the natural sciences. The Committee

emphasized that the study of science which they advocate will make it possible to realize that science is a way of knowing—a means by which acts of human intelligence explain the universe in which we live. It will develop an appreciation for how theories are formed, what evidence validates them, and how one can discriminate between conclusions that rise from mere assertions and those that are developed from the use of scientific reasoning. As the chairman of the board of the Massachusetts Institute of Technology puts it, the kind of study they recommend will make it possible for educated persons to distinguish the meretricious from the meritorious in the fields of science and technology.

The rest of their list consists of historical consciousness, values that prepare men and women to make real choices and have the courage to live with the consequences of their decisions, appreciation of both the fine and performing arts, international and multicultural experiences, and study in depth.

It is important to note that all the elements of their minimum required curriculum are not subject matters but characteristics of mind and intellect. As such, they can be significant features of studies in technical and professional fields as well as in the traditional academic programs. The Committee recognized that more than 60% of the baccalaureate degrees awarded these days are earned by students pursuing programs in engineering, business, allied health science, education, and other professional fields studied at the undergraduate level. They took seriously the advice they received from leaders in undergraduate professional education, who advised that professional competence encompassed more than technical learning and included skills, abilities, and habits of thinking commonly believed to be acquired through the liberal arts. They argued that professionals, when they exercised their technical skills on real-world problems, were dealing with multidisciplinary situations and needed to understand the contextual matrix of the problems that brought their technical expertise into play. Furthermore, they believed that a baccalaureate degree in their fields should signify that their graduates had attained the same attributes of intellect and character that graduates in the liberal arts fields were expected to have. As a consequence, they recommended that a finding by the 11 institutions that cooperated with the Select Committee, namely, that the very distinction between the liberal and the vocational that runs through two millenia of educational theory is no longer a universal, should be taken into account. Their report, states: "Education in a professional or vocational field may, if based on the skills and attitudes of our minimum curriculum, and presented in a liberal spirit, also provide a strong and enriching form of study in depth" (p. 30).

In making its plea for integrity in the college curriculum, the Committee addressed its argument to the American academic community, particularly to the faculties of American colleges and universities, for they are the key and indispensable agents of fundamental reform in the undergraduate curriculum. At the same time they recognized that faculties cannot fulfill their responsibilities without the leadership and support of other key authorities in the academic community. Faculties will not be able to restore vigor to curriculum committees, to reform the value system which permeates the academic profession and which places greater importance on research than on teaching, and to counterbalance the entrenched interests of departments leading to overspecialization, if the whole academic community on each campus does not provide corporate support for their efforts. Presidents and deans have an essential role in preparing the conditions conducive to academic change, providing real incentives which will animate the faculty as a whole and resume responsibility for the curriculum as a whole.

Unless I seriously misread the signs of the times, the Select Committee on the Meaning and Purpose of Baccalaureate Degrees has truly voiced an uneasiness among colleagues in the academic community and sounded a warning that the public at large exhibits a growing concern that college education is falling short of all it could be. In either case, all of us who have any responsibility for the quality of higher education are challenged to bring fresh thinking to policies and principles we have long taken for granted. To revive liberal education and make it meet for these times, we must realize that tinkering with the curriculum is no longer fruitful. The questions that tinkering tries to avoid will rise up to embarrass us.

What kinds of questions do I have in mind? Let me illustrate. Can we any longer take for granted that it is possible to define educated persons merely in terms of the subjects they are supposed to have covered? Haven't the turf fights between ardent defenders of one field or another led us to a stalemate? Even if some of us still have a heart for that kind of battle, hasn't every blast from the knowledge explosion of the last generation further fragmented the curriculum and repeatedly demonstrated the futility of trying to cover in four years all that our ingenious scholars and reseachers have revealed about the physical universe and the cultures in which we live? If all that is known cannot be acquired in four years, we need to change our question. We must now ask what should students learn that will enable them—indeed empower them— to cope with the new knowledge, to judge whether it is valid, and to understand its meaning for themselves and for the world around them.

In one sense, we need again to consider what we mean by the liberal arts. Are they nothing more than items in a canonical list of revered subjects or are they intellectual capacities that enable educated persons to understand and come to terms with reality in all its variety and complexity? Fresh inquiry into questions such as these may open up the possibility that we shall discover that the dichotomy between the liberal and the practical is not real. We may find that the two are inextricably related. Yet, examination of how and why they depend upon one another could well lead to insights into what should be taught in college and how it should be offered.

One consequence of posing such basic questions about the nature of the liberal arts could well be a new openness in considering what aids to thinking and knowing, besides speech, writing, reading, and mathematics, must be added to their number. What new intellectual technology may now be desirable, if not essential, for the enhancement of learning or the strengthening of our modes of knowing?

The ultimate question, of course, is: What does it mean to be free persons today and tomorrow? Much emotion and ink has been spilled about the value of the liberal arts for their own sake. Is this not verging on academic idolatry? The liberal arts, noble as they are, are not sacred icons separate from the human beings that possess them. They are human capacities and as such they are in the fullest sense of the word, practical. If we are to realize our full potentialities, if we are to grow and adapt to the constant changes that are our lot, if we are to perform our offices, both public and private, as responsible moral persons, and if we are to keep faith with one another, we need to cultivate the human capacities—the intellectual arts—that free us to do all these things. Therefore, we cannot afford to disregard new opportunities to enhance our freedom on the ground that we would be adulterating the pure liberal arts with something useful and mundane. What we must acquire is the assurance that the cultivation of new liberal arts will indeed enhance our humanity as much as the old ones have helped us preserve it through ages of change and challenge.

REFERENCES

Association of American Colleges. (1985). *Integrity in the college curriculum: A report to the academic community*. Washington, DC: Association of American Colleges.

COLLOQUIUM

PANEL 2

CREATIVITY AND SCHOOLING

Critical Pedagogy and the Role of the Resisting Intellectual

Henry A. Giroux

There is a strange paradox that haunts the discourse regarding the crisis facing public education in the United States.[1] On the one hand, this crisis is characterized as a failure of the schools to prepare students adequately for the ever-changing demands of a sophisticated technological economy; or it is described by less vocal critics as the growing failure of schools to prepare students to think critically and creatively with regard to developing the sophisticated literacy skills necessary to make informed and effective choices about the worlds of work, politics, culture, personal relationships, and the economy. Underlying both sets of criticisms is the notion that schools have failed to take the issues of excellence and creativity seriously and in doing so have undermined the economic and academic possibilities that could be conferred upon both students and the larger society.

On the other hand, educational reformers have responded to the

[1] The discourse of crisis in public education has been dealt with in a series of reports and books, including the following: The National Commission on Excellence (1983); Task Force on Education for Economic Growth (1983); The College Entrance Examination Board (1983); Twentieth Century Fund Task Force on Federal Elementary and Secondary Education Policy (1983); Carnegie Corporation of New York (1983); Goodland (1984); Boyer (1983); and Sizer (1984). For a critical analysis of these reports and the ideologies behind them, see Aronowitz and Giroux (1985).

crises in public education primarily by offering solutions that either ignore the role of teachers in preparing learners to be active and critical citizens or by suggesting reforms that ignore the intelligence, judgment, and experience that teachers might bring to bear on such issues. In this case, the call for excellence and improved student creativity has been accompanied by policy suggestions that further erode the power teachers have over the conditions of their work while simultaneoulsy proposing that administrators and teachers look outside of their schools for improvements and needed reforms. The result is that many of the educational reforms appear to reduce teachers to the status of low-level employees or civil servants whose main function seems to be to implement reforms decided on by experts in the upper levels of state and educational bureaucracies. Furthermore, such reforms embrace technological solutions that undermine the historical and cultural specificity of school life and further weaken the possibilities for school administrators and teachers to work with local parents and groups in improving schools from the vantage point of concrete educational needs and interests. Underlying the paradox of work in the discourse of school reform is a dual failure. First, there is the growing public failure to recognize the central role that teachers must play in any visible attempt to revitalize the public schools. Secondly, there is the failure to recognize that the ideological and political interests underlying the dominant thrusts in school reform are at odds with the traditional role of organizing public education around the need to educate students for the maintenance and defense of the traditions and principles necessary for a democratic society.

I want to argue that part of the growing crisis in public education centers around the declining competence of students and others to effectively interrogate and communicate ideational content. In other words, what is in jeopardy is not merely the ability of students to be creative, but the very capacity for conceptual thought itself. Moreover, because democratic social, cultural, and political forms depend on a self-motivated and autonomous public, the precondition for which is critical thinking, the crisis at hand may be the very existence of democracy itself.

My main point will be that the crisis in creativity and critical learning has in large part to do with the developing trend toward the disempowerment of teachers at all levels of education. This involves not only a growing loss of power among teachers around the basic conditions of their work, but also a changing perception of their role as reflective practitioners. In effect, I will argue that teacher work is being increasingly situated within a technical and social division of labor that either reduces teachers to the dictates of experts removed from the context of the classroom or serves to widen the political gap between those who control the schools and those who actually deal with curricula and students on a day-to-day basis. In the first instance, teachers are relegated to instrumental tasks that require little or no space for oppositional discourse and social practices. Pedagogy, in this case, is reduced to the implementation of taxonomies that subordinate knowledge to forms of methodological reification, while theories of teaching are increasingly technicized and standardized in the interest of efficiency and the management and control of discrete forms of knowledge.[2]

Teachers are not simply being proletarianized; the changing nature of their roles and function signifies the disappearance of a form of intellectual labor central to the nature of critical pedagogy itself. Moreover, the tendency to reduce teachers either to high-level clerks implementing the orders of others within the school bureaucracy or to the status of specialized technicians is part of a much larger problem within Western societies, a problem marked by the increasing division of intellectual and social labor and the increasing trend towards the oppressive management and administration of everyday life. The current tendency to reformulate the status and nature of teacher work is evident in a number of historical and sociological tendencies that need to be mentioned briefly before I argue for an alternative view of how teacher work should be viewed, and what the implications might be for a critical theory of schooling.

TOWARD A PROLETARIANIZATION OF TEACHER WORK

Historically, the relationship between the role of educators and the larger society has been mediated by the image of the school teacher as a dedicated public servant reproducing the dominant culture in the interest of the common good, and the university community as a body of social scientists who, in their capacity as experts, "were to educate the masses and provide direction for moral and social progress" (Popkewitz, 1984, p. 108). With the advent of the twentieth century, the administration and organization of public schools were increasingly brought under the influence of the instrumental ideologies of corporate business interests; moreover, the growing professionalization of academics and their respective disciplines resulted in a redefinition of the theoretical nature of the social sciences. Increasingly, university social scientists shifted from the terrain of social reform to the role of expert as policy advisor. Within this context, the relationship between knowledge and power took on a new dimension as the development of social

---

[2] An example of this trend in the teaching of reading through a mastery learning approach can be found in Shannon (1984).

science became closely linked to supporting the ideological and social practices of a business society. In charting the rise and success of the academic social sciences, Silva and Slaughter (1981) ably document how the emerging professional associations of the developing social sciences between 1865 and 1910 in the United States lent their skills and knowledge to the economic and social problems faced by the rising corporate liberal interests. In commenting on the rise of the American Economic Association, they provide an insight into the general political direction in which the professional associations and the social sciences in general were moving:

> As economists were more routinely called to expert service and initiated in the politics of power, they refined their notion of constituency. Although using the rhetoric of objective science and the public welfare, their clientele was the Progressive wing of corporate capital and other professionals. . . . Claiming to be impartial and scientific arbiters of social questions, they used the ideology of expertise in the interests of social control and developed pragmatic, technical mechanisms to consolidate and finance colonial fiscal policy, federal industrial relations commissions, and the income tax. Thus, social science experts became advocates for the existing order, hegemonic intellectuals serving the emerging national corporate elite. (chap. 5, p. 2)

As the theoretical tenets of the natural sciences began to provide the model for dominant academic discourse and inquiry in the social sciences, the move toward the reduction of critical thought and reason to its merely technical dimensions marked the ascendency for its models of inquiry and pedagogy. Within this positivistically oriented discourse, research techniques became increasingly freed from value judgments, useful knowledge was measured next to its managerial capabilities, and science become synonomous with the search for transhistorical laws and the requirement that theory explain rather than constitute or determine the object under analysis.[3]

It is important to stress that the primacy of technical and economic rationality did more than devalue the importance of moral and religious reason in everyday life; it also strengthened relations of dependency and powerlessness for ever-widening groups of people through the social practices of an industrial ideology and psychology that reached far into the culture industry and other spheres of public life (see Marcuse, 1964; Ewen, 1975). Underlying this technical rationality and its accompanying rationalization of reason and nature was a call for the separa-

---

[3] For a general critique of positivism, see Horkheimer (1974); see also Habermas (1973), especially Chapter 7. For a specific critique of the legacy of positivist thought and its influence on educational theory and practice see Giroux (1984).

tion of conception from execution, the standardization of knowledge in the interest of managing and controlling it, and the devaluation of critical intellectual work for the primacy of practical considerations. The history of this emerging technocratic rationality in both the schools and in public life has been repeated many times, and it need not be reinvented here, but its effects have taken on a special significance in the 1980s and can be seen in a number of areas (see Spring, 1972; Tyack, 1974; Adorno & Horkheimer, 1972).

One area in which the dominance of technocratic rationality is manifest is in the training of prospective teachers. As Kliebard (1973), Zeichner (1983), and Giroux (1984) have pointed out, teacher education programs in the United States have long been dominated by their behavioristic orientation towards issues of mastery and methodological refinement as the basis for developing teacher competence. The normative and political implications of this approach are made clear by Zeichner (1983).

> Underlying this orientation to teacher education is a metaphor of "production," a view of teaching as an "applied science" and a view of the teacher as primarily an "executor" of the laws and principles of effective teaching. Prospective teachers may or may not proceed through the curriculum at their own pace and may participate in varied or standardized learning activities, but that which they are to master is limited in scope (e.g., to a body of professional content knowledge and teaching skills) and is fully determined in advance by others often on the basis of research on teacher effectiveness. The prospective teacher is viewed primarily as a passive recipient of this professional knowledge and plays little part in determining the substance and direction of his or her preparation program. (p. 4)

Within this model of education, teachers are viewed less as creative and imaginative thinkers who can transcend the ideology of methods and means in order to critically evaluate the purpose of educational discourse and practice than as obedient civil servants dutifully carrying out the dictates of others. All too often, teacher-education programs lose sight of the need to educate students to be teacher-scholars by developing educational courses that focus on the immediacy of school problems and substitute the discourse of management and efficiency for a critical analysis of the underlying conditions that structure school life. Instead of helping students to think about who they are and what they should do in classrooms, what their responsibility might be in interrogating the means and ends of specific school policy, students are often trained to share techniques on how to control student discipline, teach a given subject effectively, organize a day's activities as efficiently and orderly as possible. The emphasis is on finding out what works! The form of technical rationality that underlies this type of educational training is not confined to undergraduate programs; its logic exercises a strong influence on graduate programs as well, programs that are often intended to promote what is often euphemistically called "educational leadership." For instance, it was noted in a recent study of doctoral programs in education that "research in education is preoccupied with techniques, rather than with the inquiry into the nature and course of events-with 'how to' rather than 'what,' with form rather than substance.... Too often students in education ... have difficulty even finding serious questions worth addressing" (Winkler, 1984, p. 11).

If prospective teachers are often trained to be specialized technicians, future school administrators are trained in the image of the social science expert. Richard Bates (1980) and William Foster (1980), for instance, have pointed out that much of the training for school administrators, principals, and superintendents is narrowly technical, concerned primarily with producing a marriage between organization theory and the principles of "sound" business management. Inherent in such training is the notion that complex language systems, management controls, and systems of accountability are beyond the grasp of either teachers or the average layperson. The technocratic consciousness embodied in this view is not only at odds with the notion of decentralized control and the principles of participatory democracy, but also presents an ahistorical and depoliticized view of school governance and policy. Schools are not seen as sites of struggle over different orders of representation, or as sites that embody particular configurations of power that shape and structure activities of classroom life. On the contrary, schools become reduced to the sterile logic of flow charts, a growing separation between teachers and administrators, and an increasing tendency toward bureaucratization. The overriding message here is that the logic of technocratic rationality serves to remove teachers from participating in a critical way in the production and evaluation of school curricula. For example, the form that school knowledge takes and the pedagogy used to legitimate it become subordinated to the principles of efficiency, hierarchy, and control. One consequence is that decisions and questions over what counts as knowledge, what is worth teaching, how one judges the purpose and nature of instruction, how one views the role of school in society, and what the latter implies for understanding how specific social and cultural interests shape all levels of school life is removed from the collective influence of teachers themselves. The relationship between the bureaucratization of schools and the specific structuring of knowledge is illuminated in the following:

The major demands placed upon the structure of knowledge by bureau-cratized schools are: that the knowledge be divided into components or relatively discrete components; that the units of knowledge be ordered in sequence; that the knowledge be communicable from one person to an-other using conventional media of communication; that success in acqui-sition of part, if not most of the knowledge is recordable in quantifiable form; that the knowledge be objectified in the sense of having an existence independent of its human origins; that the knowledge is stratified into various levels of status or prestige; that knowledge based upon concrete experience be treated as low status, but that knowledge expressed in ab-stract and generalized principles be regarded as having high status. (Wake, 1979, p. 16)

The increasing tendency to reduce teacher autonomy in the devel-opment and planning of curricula is also evident in the production of prepackaged curriculum materials that contribute to a form of deskill-ing among teachers. For instance, Apple (1982) has pointed to elemen-tary school science curricula packages whose underlying rationality oriented teachers to simply carrying out predetermined content and instructional procedures. Similarly, the principles at work in this ration-ality are also found in many school textbooks and what I call manage-ment pedagogies. In many school textbooks knowledge is broken down into discrete parts, standardized for easier management and consump-tion, and published with the intent of being marketed for large, general, student audiences (see Apple, 1984). Futhermore, there is a growing adoption by schools of forms of pedagogy that routinize and standardize classroom instruction. This is evident in the proliferation of instruc-tional-based curricula and management schemes, competency-based learning systems, and similar approaches such as mastery learning. These are basically management pedagogies because the central question re-garding learning is reduced to the problem of management, that is, "how to allocate resources [teachers, students, and materials] to produce the maximum number of certified . . . students within a designated time" (Shannon, 1984, p. 488).

The principles underlying management pedagogies are at odds with the notion that teachers should be actively involved in producing cur-ricula materials suited to the cultural and social contexts in which they teach. Questions regarding cultural specificity, teacher judgment, and how student experiences and histories relate to the learning process itself are ignored. One could go even further and say that the issues embodied in such questions represent a mode of teacher autonomy and control that is a positive hinderance to those school administrators that believe that excellence is a quality to be displayed primarily in higher reading, math, and college board scores. This becomes more obvious in light of the major assumption underlying management pedagogy: that the behavior of teachers needs to be controlled and made consistent and predictable across different schools and student populations. The payoff for schools' systems is not merely the touting of more manageable forms of pedagogy; this type of school policy also makes for good public relations in that school administrators can provide technical solutions to the complex social, political, and economic problems that plague their schools while simultaneously invoking the the tenets of accountability as an indicator of success. In other words, if the problem can be measured, it can be solved. The following statement by some Chicago school administrators enamored of management pedagogy points to the ideology behind the growing proletarianization and deskilling of teacher work.

> Providing materials that were centrally developed and successfully field tested would: 1) reduce greatly the time needed to prepare and organize materials; 2) require little inservice time; 3) be economical for schools in Chicago and elsewhere to implement; 4) standardize the definition, sequencing, and quality of instruction necessary for mastery of each objective; 5) reduce greatly the time needed for developing lesson plans; and 6) be easy for substitutes to use. (Katims & Jones, 1981, p. 7)

Underlying this approach to educational reform is a mode of technocratic rationality that restricts curricula and student diversity and simultaneously refuses to address seriously the issue of how to deal pedagogically with less privileged learners. In the first instance, the narrowing of curricula choices to a back-to-basics format, and the introduction of lock-step, time-on-task pedagogies operates from the pedagogically erroneous assumption that all students can learn from the same materials, pedagogies, and modes of evaluation. The notion that students come from different histories, embody different experiences, linguistic practices, cultures, and talents is ignored. Similarly, the current drive among school reformers to deny a high school diploma to students who don't pass a comprehensive graduating exam, or to deny entrance to undergraduate and graduate schools to students who don't measure up to the call for higher scores on any one of a number of tests represents a technological solution to a highly charged political and social problem. The central issue that needs to be interrogated is how public schools and institutions of higher education might be systematically failing certain groups of students, or how they might re-evaluate the nature and structure of their own approaches to teaching and learning so as to take seriously their obligations to educate *all* students to be productive citizens. K. Patricia Cross (1984) sums the problem up well in her comment:

> Clearly, we cannot afford to 'improve' educational institutions at the expense of society. But it is distressing to see how many well-meaning but short-sighted legislators and educators are taking advantage of the current mandates for excellence by supporting proposals that can have the effect of eliminating from local high schools and colleges the very students who need them most. Some years ago, a wag said of Admiral Hyman Rickover's elitist recommendations for education, 'Save the best; shoot the rest.' Selection is the easy route to quality—but it is a swinging-pendulum solution that fails to address the underlying problems of curriculum, instruction, and teacher training. (p. 171)

RETHINKING THE ROLE OF THE TEACHER AS INTELLECTUAL

What I have tried to do in the previous section is point to the various ideological and material forces at work in the United States that currently undermine the role and conditions of work necessary for teachers to assume the posture of thoughtful, critical, educational leaders. In what follows, I want to argue that one way to rethink and restructure the nature of teacher work is to view teachers as intellectuals. The category of intellectual is helpful in a number of ways. First, it provides a theoretical basis for examining teacher work as a form of intellectual labor; secondly, it clarifies the ideological and material conditions necessary for intellectual work; thirdly, it helps to illuminate the various modes of intelligibility, ideologies, and interests that are produced and legitimated by teacher work.

By viewing teachers as intellectuals, we can illuminate and recover the rather general notion that all human activity involves some form of thinking. That is, no activity, regardless of how routinized it might become, can be abstracted from the functioning of the mind in some capacity. This is a crucial issue because, by arguing that the use of the mind is a general part of all human activity, we dignify the human capacity for integrating thinking and practice, and in doing so highlight the core of what it means to view teachers as reflective practitioners. Within this discourse, teachers can be seen not merely as "performers professionally equipped to realize effectively any goals that may be set for them. Rather, [they should] be viewed as free men and women with a special dedication to the values of the intellect and the enhancement of the critical powers of the young" (Scheffler, 1968, p. 11).

Furthermore, viewing teachers as intellectuals provides a strong critique of those ideologies that legitimate social practices that separate conceptualization, planning, and designing from the processes of implementation and execution. It is important to stress that teachers must take active responsibility for raising serious questions about what they teach, how they are to teach it, and what the larger goals are for which they are striving. This means that they must take a responsible role in shaping the purposes and conditions of schooling. Such a task is impossible within a division of labor where teachers have little influence over the ideological and economic conditions of their work. There is also a growing political and ideological tendency as expressed in the current debates on educational reform to remove teachers and students from their histories and cultural experiences in the name of pedagogical approaches that will make schooling more instrumental. What this generally means is that teachers and students alike are "situated" within curricula approaches and instructional management schemes that reduce their roles to either implementing or receiving the goals and objectives of publishers, outside experts, and others far removed from the specificities of daily classroom life. This issue becomes all the more important when seen as part of the growing objectification of human life in general. The concept of teacher as intellectual provides the theoretical posture to fight against this type of ideological and pedagogical imposition.

Moreover, the concept of intellectual provides the theoretical groundwork for interrogating the specific ideological and economic conditions under which intellectuals as a social group need to work in order to function as critical, thinking, creative human beings. This last point takes on a normative and political dimension and seems especially relevant for teachers. For, if we believe that the role of teaching cannot be reduced to merely training in the practical skills but involves, instead, the education of a class of intellectuals vital to the development of a democratic society, then the category of intellectual becomes a way of linking the purpose of teacher education, public schooling, and in-service training to the very principles necessary for the development of a democratic order and society.

Neither teacher-training institutions nor the public schools have seriously viewed themselves historically as important sites for educating teachers as intellectuals. In part, this has been due to the pervasiveness of a growing technocratic rationality that separates theory from practice and contributes to the development of modes of pedagogy that ignore teacher creativity and insight; it is also due to the predominance of theories and forms of school leadership and organization that give teachers little control over the nature of their work. The latter not only shape the structure and experiences of what teachers do in schools, but also the way in which they are prepared in teacher-training institutions. What is generally the overriding concern in most teacher education programs is the emphasis on having prospective educators master pedagogical techniques that generally eschew questions of purpose and the discourse of critique and possibility.

I have argued that by viewing teachers as intellectuals we can begin to rethink and reform those historical traditions and conditions that have prevented schools and teachers from assuming their full potential as active, reflective scholars and practitioners. But I want to both qualify this point and extend it further. I believe that it is imperative not only to view teachers as intellectuals, but also to contextualize in political and normative terms the concrete social functions that teachers perform. In this way, we can be more specific about the different relationships that teachers have to both their work and to the society in which such work takes place. I want to develop this position in a more detailed way below.

Any attempt to reformulate the role of teachers as intellectuals has to also include the broader issue of how to view educational theory in general. It is imperative to view educational theory as a form of social theory. I say imperative, because if seen as a form of social theory, the discourse of educational theory can be understood and interrogated as representing forms of knowledge and social practice that legitimate and reproduce particular forms of social life. Educational theory in this case is not viewed as merely the application of objective scientific principles to the concrete study of schooling and learning. Instead, it is seen as an eminently political discourse that emerges from and characterizes an expression of struggle over what forms of authority, orders of representation, forms of moral regulation, and versions of the past and future should be legitimated, passed on, and debated within specific pedagogical sites. All forms of educational theory and discourse represent a form of ideology that has an intimate relation to questions of power. This is evident in the way such discourses arise out of, and structure the distinctions between, high- and low-status knowledge, legitimate cultural forms that reproduce specific class, racial, and patriarchal interests, and help to sustain specific organizational patterns and classroom social relations.

Educational theory should also be seen as having a deep commitment to developing schools as sites that prepare students to participate in, and struggle to develop, democratic public spheres. This means that the value of educational theory and practice should be linked to providing the conditions for teachers and students to understand schools as public spheres dedicated to forms of self and social empowerment. It also means defining teacher work against the imperative to develop knowledge and skills that provide students with the tools they will need to be leaders rather than simply managers or skilled civil servants. Similarly, it means fighting against those ideological and material practices that reproduce privileges for the few and social and economic inequality for the many.

By politicizing the notion of schooling and revealing the ideological nature of educational theory and practice, it becomes possible to be more specific in defining the meaning of the category of the intellectual and to interrogate the political and pedagogical function of the intellectual as a social category. There are two related but separate points by which to venture a definition of the intellectual. The more general definition is rooted in a quality of mind that is characterized as having a creative, critical, and contemplative relationship to the world of ideas. Richard Hofstadter (1963) epitomizes this position in his distinction between the meaning of intellect and the meaning of intelligence. Intelligence, for him, is

> an excellence of mind that is employed within a fairly narrow, immediate predictable range; it is a manipulative, adjustive, infailingly practical quality. . . . Intellect, on the other hand is the critical, creative, and contemplative side of mind. Whereas intelligence seeks to grasp, manipulate, reorder, adjust, intellect examines, ponders, wonders, theorizes, criticizes, imagines. (p. 25)

Paul Piccone (1981/1982) provides a similar distinction but places it within a larger social context.

> . . . unless one fudges the definition of intellectuals in terms of purely formal and statistical educational criteria, it is fairly clear that what modern society produces, is an army of alienated, privatized, and uncultured experts who are knowledgeable only within very narrowly defined areas. This technical intelligentsia, rather than intellectuals in the traditional sense of thinkers concerned with the totality, is growing by leaps and bounds to run the increasingly complex bureaucratic and industrial apparatus. Its rationality, however, is only instrumental in character, and thus suitable mainly to perform partial tasks rather than tackling substantial questions of social organization and political direction. (p. 116)

Herb Kohl (1983) is more specific and provides a definition of the intellectual that relates it directly to teachers. He writes:

> An intellectual is someone who knows about his or her field, has a wide breadth of knowledge about other aspects of the world, who uses experi-

ence to develop theory and questions theory on the basis of further experience. An intellectual is also someone who has the courage to question authority and who refuses to act counter to his or her own experience and judgment. (p. 29)

In my view all of these positions make distinctions that are important but fall into the problem of suggesting that intellectual inquiry is either the repository of specific groups of people or that the quality of intellectual inquiry is only operative within specific social functions. This is not meant to suggest that the question of what qualities of mind constitute intellectual inquiry is not an important one. These positions are informative in that they suggest that intellectual inquiry is characterized by someone who has a breadth of knowledge about the world, who views ideas in more than instrumental terms, and who harbors a spirit of inquiry that is critical and oppositional, one that is true to its own impulses and judgments. But a distinction has to be made in this case between those characteristics of intellectual inquiry as they exist in various degrees and proportions among different individuals *and* the social function of intellectual work itself. In his attempt to turn the issue of the nature and role of the intellectual into a political question, Antonio Gramsci (1971) provides a more helpful theoretical elaboration on this issue. For Gramsci, all men and women are intellectuals, but not all of them function in society as intellectuals. Gramsci is worth quoting at length on this issue.

When one distinguishes between intellectuals and non-intellectuals, one is referring in reality only to the immediate social function of the professional category of the intellectuals, that is, one has in mind the direction in which their specific professional activity is weighted, towards intellectual elaboration or towards muscular-nervous effort. This means that, although one can speak of intellectuals, one cannot speak of non-intellectuals, because non-intellectuals do not exist. But even the relationship between efforts of intellectual-cerebral elaboration and muscular-nervous effort is not always the same, so that there are varying degrees of specific intellectual activity. There is no human activity from which every form of intellectual participation can be excluded: homo faber cannot be separated from homo sapiens. Each man [*sic*], finally, outside his professional activity, carries on some form of intellectual activity, that is, he is a "philosopher," an artist, a man of taste, he participates in a particular conception of the world, has a conscious line of moral conduct, and therefore contributes to sustain a conception of the world or to modify it, that is, to bring into being new modes of thought. (p. 9)

For Gramsci (1971), all people are intellectuals in that they think, mediate, and adhere to a specific view of the world. The point here, as mentioned previously, is that varying degrees of critical and common-sense thought is endemic to what it means to be human. The signifi-cance of this insight is that it gives pedagogical activity an inherently political quality. For instance, Gramsci's view of political activity was deeply rooted in the task of raising the quality of thought of the working class. At the same time, by arguing that all people do not function in their social capacity as intellectuals, Gramsci provides the theoretical groundwork for analyzing the political role of those intellectuals who had to be considered in terms of the organizational and directive func-tions they performed in a given society.

In the broadest scene, Gramsci (1971) attempts to locate the political and social function of intellectuals through his analyses of the role of conservative and radical organic intellectuals. For Gramsci, conservative organic intellectuals provide the dominant class with forms of moral and intellectual leadership. As agents of the status quo, such intellec-tuals identify with the dominant relations of power and become the propagaters of its ideologies and values. This group represents a stra-tum of intellectuals that gives ruling classes a homogeneity and aware-ness of their economic, political, and social functions. In the advanced industrial countries, organic intellectuals can be found in all strata of society and include specialists in industrial organizations, professors in universities, journalists in the culture industry, and various levels of executives in middle management positions.

To Gramsci, radical intellectuals also attempt to provide the moral and intellectual leadership of a specific class, in this case, the working class. More specifically, radical organic intellectuals provide the peda-gogical and political skills that are necessary to raise political awareness in the working class in order to help the members of that class to de-velop leadership skills and to engage in collective struggle.

Gramsci's categories are helpful in that they illuminate the political nature of intellectual work within specific social functions. Moreover, Gramsci's analysis helps to shatter the myth that the nature of intellec-tual work is determined by one's class location. On the contrary, there is no immediate correspondence between class location and conscious-ness; but there is a correspondence between the social function of one intellectual's work and the particular relationship it has to modifying, challenging, or reproducing the dominant society. In other words, it is the *political nature* of intellectual work that is the issue at hand. In my mind, this is a major theoretical advance over the ongoing debate among Marxists and others as to whether intellectuals constitute a specific class or culture.[4] Furthermore, by politicizing the nature of intellectual work,

[4] For an overview of this debate, see Boggs (1979).

Gramsci strongly challenges dominant theoretical traditions that have decontextulized the role that intellectuals play in education and the larger society. In other words, he criticizes those theorists who decontextualize the intellectual by suggesting that he or she exist independently of issues of class, culture, power, and politics. Inherent in such a view is the notion that the intellectual is obligated to engage in a value-free discourse, one that necessitates that he or she refuse to make a commitment to specific views of the world, refuse to take sides on different issues, or refuse to link knowledge with the fundamental principles of emancipation. Such a view reinforces the idea that intellectuals are free floating and detached in the sense that they perform a type of labor that is objective and apolitical.

Similarly, Gramsci's (1971) notion that intellectuals represent a social category and not a class raises interesting questions as to how educators might be viewed at different levels of schooling in terms of their politics, the nature of their discourse, and the pedagogical functions they perform. But Gramsci's terms need to be expanded in order to grasp the changing nature and social function of intellectuals in their capacities as educators. The categories around which I want to analyze the social function of educators as intellectuals are: (a) resisting intellectuals, (b) critical intellectuals, (c) accommodating intellectuals, and (d) hegemonic intellectuals. It is imperative to note that these are somewhat exaggerated, ideal-typical categories whose purpose is to bring into bold relief the cluster of integrated elements that point to the interests and tendencies which they legitimate. Needless to say, there are teachers who move in and out and between these categories and defy being placed in any one of them; moreover, it is conceivable that teachers under different circumstances may opt out of one tendency and move into another category. Finally, these categories are irreducible to any one specific political doctrine. They point to forms of ideology and social practice that could be taken up by any number of diverse political positions or world views.

RESISTING INTELLECTUALS

Resisting intellectuals is a category that suggests that teachers as intellectuals can emerge from and work with any number of groups, other than and including the working class, that advance emancipatory traditions and cultures within and outside of alternative public spheres (see Gramsci, 1971; Freire, 1984). Utilizing the language of critique, resisting intellectuals employ the discourse of self-criticism so as to make the foundations for a critical pedagogy explicit while simultaneously illuminating the relevance of the latter for both students and the larger society. Central to the category of resisting intellectuals is the task of making the pedagogical more political and the political more pedagogical. In the first instance, this means inserting education directly into the political sphere by arguing that schooling represents both a struggle for meaning *and* a struggle over power relations. Thus schooling becomes a central terrain where power and politics operate out of a dialectical relationship between individuals and groups who function within specific historical conditions and structural constraints as well as within cultural forms and ideologies that are the basis for contradictions and struggles. Within this view of schooling, critical reflection and action become part of a fundamental social project to help students develop a deep and abiding faith in the struggle to overcome injustices and to humanize themselves. Knowledge and power are inextricably linked in this case to the presupposition that to choose life, so as to make it possible, is to understand the preconditions necessary to struggle for it.

In the second instance, making the political more pedagogical means utilizing forms of pedagogy: treat students as critical agents, problematize knowledge, utilize dialogue, and make knowledge meaningful so as to make it critical in order to make it emancipatory. In part, this suggests that resisting intellectuals take seriously the need to give students an active voice in their learning experiences; it means developing a critical vernacular that is attentive to problems experienced at the level of everyday life, particularly as these are related to pedagogical experiences connected to classroom practice. As such, the starting point pedagogically for such intellectuals is not with the isolated student but with collective actors in their various cultural, class, racial, historical, and gendered settings, along with the particularity of their diverse problems, hopes, and dreams. It is at this point that the language of critique unites with the language of possibility. That is, resisting intellectuals must take seriously the need to come to grips with those ideological and material aspects of the dominant society that attempt to separate the issues of power and knowledge, which means working to create the ideological and material conditions in both schools and the larger society that give students the opportunity to become agents of civic courage, that is, citizens who have the knowledge and courage to take seriously the need to make despair, unconvincing and hope, practical. In short, the language of critique unites with the language of possibility when it points to the conditions necessary for new forms of culture, alternative social practices, new modes of communication, and a practical vision for the future.

CRITICAL INTELLECTUALS

Critical intellectuals are ideologically oppositional but do not see them-selves as connected either to a specific social formation or as perform-ing a general social function that is expressively political in nature. Their protests constitute a critical function, which they see as part of their professional status or obligation as intellectuals. In most cases, the pos-ture of critical intellectuals is self-consciously apolitical, and their rela-tionship to the rest of society is best defined as free floating.[5] As individuals they are critical of inequality and injustice, but they refuse to move beyond their isolated posture to the terrain of collective soli-darity and struggle. Often this retreat from politics is justified on the basis of arguments that posit the impossibility of politics for reasons as ideologically diverse as the claim that we live in a totally administered society, or that history is in the hands of a technology out of control, or the simple refusal to believe that human agency has any effect on his-tory.

ACCOMMODATING INTELLECTUALS

Accommodating intellectuals generally stand firm within an ideological posture and set of material practices that supports the dominant society and its ruling groups. Such intellectuals are generally not aware of this process in that they do not define themselves as self-conscious agents of the status quo, even though their politics further the interests of the dominant classes. This category of intellectuals also define themselves in terms that suggest that they are free floating, removed from the va-garies of class conflicts and partisan politics. But in spite of such ratio-nalizations, they function primarily to produce and mediate uncritically ideas and social practices that serve to reproduce the status quo. These are the intellectuals who decry politics while simultaneously refusing to take risks. Another more subtle variation is the intellectual who disdains politics by proclaiming professionalism as a value system, one which often entails the spurious concept of scientific objectivity.

HEGEMONIC INTELLECTUALS

Hegemonic intellectuals do more than surrender to forms of academic and political incorporation, or hide behind spurious claims to objectiv-ism; they self-consciously define themselves through the forms of moral and intellectual leadership they provide for dominant groups and

[5] The concept of the free-floating intellectual as used here is similar to that expressed by Mannheim (1936).

classes. This stratum of intellectuals provides various factions of the dominant classes with a homogeneity and awareness of their economic, political, and ethical functions. The interests that define the conditions as well as the nature of their work are tied to the preservation of the existing order. Such intellectuals are to be found on the consulting lists of major foundations, on the faculties of major universities as managers of the culture industry, and, in spirit at least, in teaching positions at various levels of schooling.

For fear of these categories appearing to be too rigid, it is important to stress more specifically that the teachers who occupy them cannot be viewed merely from the perspective of the ideological interests they represent. For instance, as Erik Olin Wright (1978) has pointed out, the positions that teachers hold must also be analyzed in terms of the objective antagonisms they experience as intellectuals who occupy contradictory class locations. That is, like workers, they have to sell their labor power and have no control over the educational apparatus as a whole. On the other hand, unlike workers, they do have some control over the nature of their labor process, that is, what to teach, how to teach, what kind of research to do, and so on. Needless to say, the relative autonomy that teachers have at different levels of schooling differs, with those in higher education having the most autonomy. Moreover, regardless of the ideological interests such teachers represent there is always the possibility for real tensions and antagonisms between the lack of control they have over the goals and purposes of schooling and the relative autonomy they enjoy. For example, in a time of economic crisis, teachers have been laid off, given increased course loads, denied tenure, and forced to implement administratively dictated pedagogies. It is within these tensions and objective contradictions that the possibilities exist for shifting alliances and movement among teachers from one category to the next.

THE DISCOURSE AND ROLE OF EDUCATORS AS RESISTING INTELLECTUALS

In order to fight for schools as democratic spheres, it is imperative to understand the contradictory roles that resisting intellectuals occupy within the various levels of schooling. In the most immediate sense, the notion of resisting intellectual makes visible the paradoxical position that radical educators face in the public schools and in the universities. On the one hand, such intellectuals earn a living within institutions that play a fundamental role in producing the dominant culture. On the other hand, they define their political terrain by offering to students forms of alternative discourse and critical social practices whose interests are often at odds with the overall hegemonic role of the schools and the society it supports. The paradox is not easy to resolve and often represents a struggle against being incorporated by the university or school system through its efforts to reward those educators willing to either remove critical scholarship from their teaching or to remove it from any relation to concrete political movements. At the university level, there is enormous pressure, for example, for radical educators to peddle their academic wares merely as viable commodities for academic journals and conferences. Under the banner of accountability, teachers at all levels of schooling are sometimes subtly and, sometimes not so subtly, pressured to respond to the issues, modes of research, discourse, and social practices deemed legitimate by the dominant culture. Erik Olin Wright (1978) is worth quoting on this issue:

> [Radical] theorists within ... universities are under tremendous pressures to ask questions structured by bourgeois problems, bourgeois ideological and political practices. Such pressures are often extremely direct, taking the form of tenure criteria, blacklisting, harassment, etc. But often the pressures are quite subtle, played out through the intellectual debates within professional conferences and journals. To publish in the proper journals one has to ask questions which those journals see as relevant, and such relevance is dictated not by the centrality of the questions to [radical social theory and practice], but to the dilemmas and problems within bourgeois social science. (p. 16)

Rather than surrender to this form of academic and political incorporation, it is important for educators to make clear the theoretical elements that give meaning to the role of the resisting intellectual as well as to the type of critical educational theory in which such a role is grounded. One starting point would be to define the role of the resisting intellectual around what I have referred to earlier as the discourse of critique and the discourse of possibility.

By employing these discourses, resisting intellectuals can make clear the way in which power functions in schools in both a negative and positive way. Power is viewed in this instance as both a negative and positive force; its character is dialectical and its mode of operation is always more than simply repressive. In other words, domination is never so complete that power is experienced exclusively as a negative force. On the contrary, it means that power is the basis of all forms of behavior in which people resist, struggle, and fight for their image of a better world. What is essential is to understand how power is manifested in schools within the contradictory forms that it takes. One important pedagogical task that emerges from this perspective is to interrogate how knowledge, language, and power come together within the formal and hidden curricula of schools so as to actively silence people.

For instance, rather than viewing knowledge as objective, as merely something to transmit to students, teachers can demonstrate how it is constructed through a selected process of emphasis and exclusion. Such an interrogation could be analyzed around questions such as the following:

—What counts as school knowledge?
—How is such knowledge selected and organized?
—What are the underlying interests that structure the form and content of school knowledge?
—How is what counts as school knowledge transmitted?
—How is access to such knowledge determined?
—What cultural values and formations are legitimated by dominant forms of school knowledge?
—What cultural formations are disorganized and delegitmated by dominant forms of school knowledge?

There is also the central issue of making clear the role that language and power have at all levels of schooling. Language must be viewed as more than a tool for merely displaying thought; nor can it be reduced to issues that are technical and developmental in nature. In this case, resisting intellectuals can provide critical analyses of language as linguistic practices which embody forms of power and authority. If language itself is seen as a locus of meaning, it becomes possible to raise questions about the authority patterns that legitimate and utilize language in order to allocate resources and power to some groups while denying them to others. Central to this position is the notion that language practices can only be understood in terms of their articulation with the power relations that structure the wider society. In other words, language as both the subject and object of power represents, in part, an embattled epistemological terrain on which different social groups struggle over how reality is to be signified, reproduced, and resisted. Foucault (Giroux, 1983) captures this issue in the following comment:

Education may well be ... the instrument whereby every individual, in a society like our own, can gain access to any kind of discourse. But we all know that in its distribution, in what it permits and what it prevents, it follows the well-trodden battle lines of social conflict. Every education system is a political means of maintaining or of modifying the appropriation of discourse.... What is an educational system after all, if not the ritualization of the word; if not a qualification of some fixing roles for speakers; if not the distribution and an appropriation of discourse, with all its learning and its powers.[6]

The point here is that institutionally legitimated language practices introduce teachers and students to specific questions, specific ways of life, and are constitutive of specific social relations. By establishing a relationship between language and power, it is possible for teachers to interrogate specific language practices around the questions they raise, the incapacitating silences they harbor, and how the latter bear down on students in the form of impositions that disorganize and delegitimate certain experiences and ideas. Such a view of language points to more than the need for teachers and students alike to deconstruct its hidden codes and meanings; it is also imperative for them to develop alternative rhetorical structures and discursive practices, which both challenge and affirm forms of thinking, speaking, and acting that support a critical pedagogy.

The relationship between power, on the one hand, and knowledge and language, on the other, needs to be supplemented with an understanding of how power works on the structure of the personality and the body so as to promote certain forms of learning. More specifically, the latter points to how educators can address the issue of how learning takes place outside the realm of mediated consciousness and rationality. For instance, how is it possible to understand learning as a function of habit, as part of the fabric of ongoing social practices that become part of what might be called sedimented histories? Put another way, how is it possible for teachers to understand how learning is mediated and produced though the unconscious so as to promote among themselves and students, for instance, forms of behavior that represent an active refusal to listen, to hear, or to engage in activities that might threaten one's world view, or, in some cases, even to affirm one's own possibilities? Of course, this issue raises serious questions about how schools, through various rituals, social practices, and rules, become implicated in forms of domination that bear down on the body and psyche, that "penetrate" the body in order to locate it in a grid of technologies and practices that serve to anchor in it specific ideologies and values conducive to the larger society.

The other side of this view of learning, one that engages the discourse of possibility, is that if needs can be constructed they can be unmade and reconstructed in the interests of emancipatory concerns. For example, for teachers to simply explain the ideology of sexism in order to teach students about how it oppresses women and denigrates men may be meaningless if students have internalized such an ideology as part of

[6] Foucault, cited in Giroux (1983) p. 207.

the habits and structure of their psyche and personality. As a constellation of needs, sexism becomes a material force that has to be reflected upon, and reconstructed through, new social practices and experiences lived concretely within non-sexist classroom relations. At stake here is the notion that if creativity and talent are largely a function of social conditions, it is important to unravel how ideology as both a set of ideas and a material practice in both the overt curriculum and in those aggressively engendered silences that make up the hidden curriculum either block or promote forms of critical teaching and learning.

All of these aspects of schooling suggest the need for teachers to be more critically attentive to the ideologies embedded in the hidden curriculum and how they work to shape different aspects of school life. American educational theory has always posited a slavish attachment to that which could be seen and observed in classroom life; this emphasis on the literal has been a formidable obstacle in preventing teachers and others from looking beyond the immediacy of classroom events to that which is unspoken and unseen so as to probe deeper into the meanings, values, and ideologies at work in all aspects of school life (see Giroux, 1983).

Another central task for resisting intellectuals is to investigate the relation of popular and subordinate cultures to the dominant modes of schooling. This means investigating school cultures as a set of activities which are lived and developed within asymmetrical relations of power. Culture in this case is seen as a form of production whose processes are intimately connected with the structuring of different social formations, particularly those that are related to gender, age, race, and class. Culture is not merely a warehouse of knowledge forms, social practices, and values to be accumulated, stored, and transmitted to students. Such a view of culture refuses to engage institutionalized and dominant culture as a selected and privileged discourse that can function to legitimate specific interests and groups.

Culture must be fully implicated and understood as part of the terrain of politics and power. In this view, culture can be analyzed as a form of production through which human beings attempt to mediate everyday life through their use of language and other material resources. Most importantly, culture is viewed in this sense as a sphere of struggle and contradictions, and it must be seen in a real sense as unfinished, as part of an ongoing struggle for individuals and groups to define and affirm their histories and place in the world; In a nonreductionist sense, culture is a form of praxis that has a dialectical quality that is manifested in cultural forms and practices that can serve either dominating or emancipatory interests. As a form of domination, it serves to actively silence subordinate cultures. As an emancipatory form, it is a concrete expression of the ways in which people affirm, resist, desire, and struggle to re-present themselves as human agents establishing their rightful place in the world.

As part of a critical theory of education, this suggests that resisting intellectuals argue for a notion of cultural power that takes as its starting point the social and historical particularities of the students with whom they work. This means working with the experiences that students, adults, and other learners bring to schools and other educational sites. It means making these experiences in their public and private forms the object of confirmation and debate. It also means legitimating such experiences in order to investigate how they become constitutive of social reality. By affirming the cultural capital that gives meaning to students' lives, resisting intellectuals can help to establish the pedagogical conditions in which such students display an active voice and presence. Such an approach also points to the pedagogical conditions necessary to critically engage the languages, dreams, values, and encounters of those students whose histories are often actively silenced. In this instance, cultural power refers to the need to work *with and on* such experiences. It also means engaging other cultural experiences and forms of knowledge as part of the need to critically appropriate them so as to help students gain the skills, values, and sense of responsibility they need to be creative, critical, and ethical citizens.

Finally, it is imperative for resisting intellectuals to form alliances among themselves, to engage in a critical dialogue with other teachers in the schools, and to work with oppositional groups willing to fight for a qualitatively better life for all. In the first instance, teachers and academics who function as resisting intellectuals can collectively organize in order to engage in projects designed to understand the critical role that educators play at all levels of schooling in producing and legitimating existing social relations. This might take the form of establishing social projects in which teachers critically interrogate existing school curricula, the hidden curricula, policy formation at the local and state levels, the form and content of school texts, and the working conditions that characterize specific schools. Not only would such projects provide a theoretical and political service by critically engaging the nature of school life, they would also give teachers the opportunity to begin to communicate with each other about their common concerns.

Furthermore, such alliances provide the possibility for university and public school people to redefine the traditional theory-practice relationship. This means abolishing the pernicious institutionalized social division of labor between those who do theory at the university level and those who merely apply it at the elementary, middle, and secondary school levels. One step in this direction is for resisting intellectuals from these different spheres to forge alliances around common social and political projects in which they share their theoretical concerns and practical talents. At stake here is the recognition that these different educational sites give rise to various forms of theoretical production, and that such sites cannot be seen as separate places for the development of theory and the implementation of practice.

Such projects also have value because they open the possibility for resisting intellectuals to develop and work with movements outside of the limiting contours of academic disciplines, symposia, and reward systems that have become the traditional referents for intellectual activity. One benefit of working outside of the university and school system is that resisting intellectuals can organize their work around concrete issues and problems that point to different forms of accountability. Such relations provide the opportunity for teachers to broaden and examine the political nature of their work, to reflect on the theories they employ, and to constantly interrogate the questions they ask and the methods they use, particularly as these relate to emancipatory concerns. In effect, I am arguing that teachers as resisting intellectuals need to become a movement marked by an active involvement in democratic public spheres in which the primacy of the political is asserted anew. Resisting intellectuals can join with any number of social groups engaged in forms of emancipatory struggle. For example, by linking up with ecology, feminist, peace, and neighborhood groups, resisting intellectuals can bring their skills and talents to bear on vital forms of engagement at the local level, for example, locally based efforts against toxic-waste dumping, nuclear power, consumer fraud, racial and sexual discrimination, and so on. Within this context, the political becomes pedagogical. In other words, intellectuals learn from and with others engaged in similar political struggles.

Such alliances are absolutely necessary if teachers, particularly within the public schools, are to be able to bring outside force to bear on fighting for ideological and material conditions within the schools that will allow them to function as intellectuals, a point I raised earlier in this essay. Teachers need to operate within conditions that will allow them to reflect, read, share their work with others, produce curriculum materials, and publish their achievements for others outside of their local schools. At the present time, teachers labor in the public schools under organizational constraints and ideological conditions that leave them little room for collective work and critical pursuits. Their teaching hours are too long, they are generally isolated in cellular structures and have few opportunities to teach with others, and they have little say over the selection, organization, and distribution of teaching materials. Moreover, they operate under class loads and within an industrial time table that is oppressive. Their salaries in the United States are a matter of scandal that is only now being fully recognized by the American public. The issue, of course, is that intellectual work needs to be supported by practical conditions buttressed by concomitant democratic ideologies. By fighting for conditions that support joint teaching, collective writing and research, and democratic planning, teachers will make inroads into opening up new spaces for creative and reflective discourse and action. The importance of such a discourse cannot be overstressed. For, within such a discourse, teachers can develop an emancipatory pedagogy that relates language and power, takes popular experience seriously as part of the learning process, combats mystification, and helps students to reorder the raw experiences of their lives through the perspectives opened up by history, philosophy, sociology, and other related disciplines. Through such a discourse, resisting intellectuals can invent a language of possibility, one that proposes extensive philosophic and programmatic changes in education, on the one hand, while giving new meaning to the pedagogical and political necessity of creating the conditions for emancipatory forms of self and social empowerment among both teachers and students on the other.

REFERENCES

Adorno, T., & Horkheimer, M. (1972). *The dialectic of enlightenment.* New York: Herder and Herder.

Apple, M. (1982). *Education and power.* Boston: Routledge & Kegan Paul.

Apple, M. (1984). The political economy of text publishing. *Educational Theory, 43* (4), 307–319.

Aronowitz, S., & Giroux, H. (1985). *Education under siege.* South Hadley, MA: Bergin and Garvey.

Bates, R. (1980). Bureaucracy, professionalism and knowledge: Structures of authority and structures of control. *Educational Research and Perspectives, 7*(2), 66–76.

Boggs, C. (1979). Marxism and the role of intellectuals. *New Political Science, 1* (2/3), 7–23.

Boyer, E. L. (1983). *High school: A report on American secondary education.* New York: Harper & Row.

Carnegie Corporation of New York (1983). *Education and economic progress: Toward a national education policy.* New York: Author.

College Entrance Examination Board (1983). *Academic preparation for college.* New York: Author.

Cross, K.P. (1984). The rising tide of school reform reports. *Phi Delta Kappan, 66* (3), 171.

Ewen, S. (1975). *Captains of consciousness.* New York: McGraw-Hill.

Foster, W. S. (1980). The changing administrator: Developing managerial praxis. *Educational Theory, 30* (1), 11–23.

Friere, P. (1984). *The politics of education.* South Hadly, MA: Bergin and Garvey.

Giroux, H.A. (1983). *Theory and resistance in education.* South Hadley, MA: Bergin and Garvey.

Giroux, H.A. (1984). *Ideology, culture and the process of schooling.* Philadelphia, PA: Temple University Press.

Goodland, J. (1984). *A place called school: Promise for the future.* New York: McGraw-Hill.

Gramsci, A. (1971). In Q. Hoare & G. Smith (Eds. and Trans.), *Selections from the prison notebooks.* New York: International Publishers.

Habermas, J. (1973). *Theory and practice.* Boston: Beacon Press.

Hofstadter, R. (1963). *Anti-intellectualism in American life.* New York: Random House.

Horkheimer, M. (1974). *Critique of instrumental reason.* New York: Seabury Press.

Kliebard, H. (1973). The question of teacher education. In D. McCarty (Ed.), *New perspectives on teacher education.* San Francisco, CA: Jossey-Bass.

Katims, M., & Jones, B. F. (1981, April). *Chicago mastery learning reading: Mastery learning instruction and assessment in inner city schools.* Paper presented at the annual meeting of the International Reading Association, New Orleans, LA.

Kohl, H. (1983). Examining closely what we do. *Learning, 12*(1), 29.

Mannheim, K. (1936). *Ideology and utopia.* New York: Harvest Book.

Marcuse, H. (1964). *One dimensional man.* Boston: Beacon Press.

National Commission on Excellence (1983). *A nation at risk: The imperative for educational reform.* Washington, DC: Author.

Piccone, P. (1981/1982). Symposium on the role of the intellectual in the 1980s. *Telos, 50,* 116.

Popkewitz, T.S. (1984). *Paradigm and ideology in educational research.* Philadelphia, PA and London: Falmer Press.

Scheffler, I. (1968). University scholarship and the education of teachers. *Teachers College Record, 70*(1), 11.

Shannon, P. (1984). Mastery learning in reading and the control of teachers and students. *Language Arts, 61*(5), 484–493.

Sizer, T. (1984). *Horace's compromise: The dilemma of the high school.* Boston: Houghton Mifflin.

Silva, E.T., & Slaughter, S. (1981). *Prometheus/bound: Knowledge, power, and the transformation of American social science, 1865–1920.* Unpublished manuscript, University of Toronto.

Spring, J. (1972). *Education and the rise of the corporate state.* Boston: Beacon Press.

Task Force on Education for Economic Growth (1983). *Action for excellence: A comprehensive plan to improve our nation's schools.* Denver, CO: Education Commission of the States.

Twentieth Century Fund Task Force on Federal Elementary and Secondary Education Policy (1983). *Making the grade.* New York: Twentieth Century Fund.

Tyack, D. (1974). *The one best system.* Cambridge, MA: Harvard University Press.

Wake, A. (1979, July). *School knowledge and the structure of bureaucracy.* Paper presented at the conference of the Sociological Association of Australia and New Zealand, Canberra, Australia.

Winkler, K.J. (1984). Research focus of education doctorate is too ill-defined, officials say. *The Chronicle of Higher Education, 29*(11), 11.

Wright, E.O. (1978). Intellectuals and the working class. *The Insurgent Sociologist, 8*(1), 5–18.

Zeichner, K.M. (1983). Alternative paradigms on teacher education. *Journal of Teacher Education, 34*(3), 3–9.

COLLOQUIUM

PANEL 2

Comments

Kevin Ryan

There is much to agree with in Professor Giroux's paper, particularly in his identification of the problems confronting the schools, teachers, and teacher-education institutions. Specifically, teachers have lost power in recent years; there is a dangerous tendency to make teachers mere clerks and technicians; teacher education is a deeply flawed activity in our society; much of the research that is being done in education is trivial; schools in our society are becoming increasingly bureaucratized; and, finally, teachers should be intellectuals. Although there is much, then, with which I agree, reading the paper was an exercise in mental convergence and divergence. I found myself sometimes agreeing with the problem, but not the cause or the solution, and sometimes agreeing with the solution, but not convinced about the stated problem. And, happily, there were times when I found myself in agreement with both problems and solutions.

Take for instance, the bureaucratization of schooling. In the last half-century the fundamental nature of education has been changed through the move to increase the size of schools and consolidate school districts. In 1932 in this nation there were approximately 128,000 districts. Fifty years later, in 1982, the number of teachers and students had more than doubled, but the number of school districts had shrunk to 16,000. The face-to-face relationships among teachers, administrators, and school board members have been replaced by personal directives, labor management procedures and a cult of efficiency mentality.

On another issue, I think Professor Giroux and I would differ on why teachers have less power today, with my own judgment being that, in the last 15 years, teachers have made a series of poor political choices that have had little to do with education and gone a long way toward eroding the public's normally positive attitude toward them. In effect, teachers signed aboard the trade union movement after the boat had left the dock.

But these are small matters. One abiding problem I have with Professor Giroux's work, which is reflected in this paper, too, is a certain inaccessibility. He uses specialized language about issues that need public discussion. His language is the language of a small group whom one suspects of writing for one another. I believe his views would receive a much wider hearing if he would translate them into the language of children and teachers and schools, that is, into standard English.

A second, more troubling issue for me is his tendency to move from "what ought to be" to "what is not" and use that to justify his point. For instance, teachers ought to be intellectuals. They ought to have a quality of mind characterized by a creative, critical, and contemplative relationship to the world of ideas.

However, they are not. Giroux suggests that they function as clerks and technicians as a direct effect of conscious decisions of some undefined, powerful forces in the nation. I think this is too easy. It also underestimates the rarity of the intellectual. For an individual to become an intellectual is a rare and wonderful social event. I don't think intellectuals can be mass produced. I don't think there are enough to go around. And, even if we as a society were blessed with many more, I am not sure they should be massed in elementary and secondary schools. We need them in corporate boardrooms, military headquarters, religious hierarchies, television networks, and lots of other places. We need them in think tanks and in isolated garrets, writing the poems and essays that will shape the future mindscape.

In effect, to request that teachers be intellectuals is to make a request that we, as a society, can never deliver on. The result is to dampen our hope by seeking goals we can never achieve. Although making this a condition of school reform may be good for the soul, it strikes me like coaching a baseball team to go to the plate and swing for a home run every time. School reform is long and hard work. It is won with hard-earned singles rather than home runs. It is similar to demanding that all teachers be saints, people of extraordinary virtue and purity of heart. Indeed, this goal seems more achievable than that two-and-a-half million elementary and secondary school teachers become intellectuals.

In my own life, I have had some very good teachers, but I don't think I encountered an intellectual until university. I have had three children in schools in three states and don't think they have yet encountered an intellectual. And, I believe they have had very good education from their teachers.

There is a note throughout this paper that the modern modes of production and the economic interests surrounding them have taken something away from the teacher, have diminished his or her autonomy, and reduced the teacher to an intellectual serf. This seems a very ahistorical view, from my point of view as a former history teacher. The teachers in New England's public schools of a century ago were not autonomous intellectuals, functioning as self-directed professionals. In Massachusetts in 1874, male teachers received a monthly salary of $24.51 and women were paid $8.07, well below the scale for semiskilled workers. There was a regular outing from segments of the public about this intellectual qualities of teachers. Teaching was considered a work for young unmarried women or misfit men, people who could be easily controlled by the community in every aspect of their work and private lives. If anything, the history of the teacher in this country has been one of slow and uneven, but rather consistent, expansion of their personal and intellectual freedoms.

The schooling of teachers has been a similar story of struggle, from postelementary normal schools to the current inadequate, but nevertheless improved, situation. Although our current university-based teacher education may be unsuccessful in preparing the teacher-intellectual, it is a major improvement from the technique-dominated normal schools.

And let us turn to technique for a moment. Professor Giroux has made something of a whipping boy of technique and of training in technical skill. He says,

> Instead of helping students to think about who they are and what ... their responsibility might be in interrogating the means and ends of specific school policy, students are often trained to share techniques on how to control student discipline, teach a given subject effectively, organize a day's activities as efficiently and orderly as possible. The emphasis is on finding out what works!

Well, of course it is. That is what a professional school is for, whether we are talking about medical schools or architecture schools or military academies. However, to prepare people in the technical skills of their profession does not mean that technique is cut off from its larger purposes. It does not mean that teachers are robots making robots. Although I personally have decried the over technication of teacher education, I fault Professor Giroux for undervaluing the contribution that skill makes to teaching and overvaluing an oppositional approach by the teacher.

And let us turn to this last point.

What I find most distressing in Professor Giroux's paper is the one-sided view of the person who should emerge from our elementary and high schools. His student suggests to me a person who has a firm grasp of all the injustices in life, but none of the true causes of those injustices; a person who is automatically in opposition to those in power without understanding the need for power in human affairs; a person who has a knee-jerk reaction to the status quo without understanding the cultural achievements it represents. The student becomes a social critic without an appreciation of culture or the complexity of the human condition. Instead of learning, first, to know our cultural inheritance and, second, to take pride in it and finally to see his or her role as extending the benefits of our culture to more people, the picture that emerges to me in Professor Giroux's work is that of a student who protests too much. Although a critical mind is the hallmark of any educated person, it is not the only mark. Education requires a more balanced approach than is being advocated here.

Reading Professor Giroux's paper brought to mind an observation by John Gardner, that militant moderate who has performed so many services to our country. Gardner considered how 23d century scholars would view the decline of 20th century institutions. These scholars would, he observed, trace this decline to a clash between "uncritical lovers" and "unloving critics." On the one hand, those who loved our institutions ignored their faults and protected them from criticism. On the other hand, those who criticized our institutions denied them the nurturing needed to survive. "Between the two, the institutions perished."

COLLOQUIUM

PANEL 2

Comments

Michael R. Ronayne

As a natural scientist, I feel more comfortable with quantitative theory than with social theory. As a member of a local area school committee, I do, however, have a few comments to make about the practical aspects of Henry's paper.

Henry Giroux and I sat together at lunch today and had a little preview of this afternoon's session. At the end of lunch, Henry and I agreed that I should become more hopeful of what can be and he should become more practical about what can be. I agree that school teachers in this country have been totally undervalued, poorly educated, scandalously paid, and generally abused by society. I find them to be a nervous lot, under more stress than many other people, and extremely sensitive. When I try to understand why, all I have to do is look at the multiple stresses and pressures we put on them. School teachers are supposed to provide day care and moral and ethical instruction, as well as instruction in the various fields of learning. The role of the church and the family seems to have dissolved, with the result that people make unbelievable demands on local school systems.

People tell my school committee that we should take care of their children from age 2 on, 5 days a week, from 7 o'clock in the morning to 4 in the afternoon. A recent state of Massachusetts education bill called for mandatory early childhood education. One gets the idea that the state should step in and take care of the children from arrival in the delivery room, on through nursery school, and beyond. One of the biggest problems facing schools these days arises from the demands that parents place on them to do things they really shouldn't be doing.

We don't seem to value teaching in this country. We certainly don't pay for it. At the college level, we provide no training in teaching. Ph.D.

candidates, who graduate on the strength of their theses, are foisted on the college population with no more training or experience than they received as unsupervised teaching assistants. At the elementary and secondary levels, we ask our teachers to teach just about everything. I understand the problem that Henry raises over teacher-proof science modules, but I am relieved that my daughter is being taught science by someone who at least has a teacher-proof module.

Why are our expectations about the performance of our teachers so low? The answer lies with the teacher-training institutions in this country, including the one with which I am affiliated. We simply do not produce intellectuals in these programs. The blame lies with the state certification agencies. I said something to this effect just the other day in a letter to the Boston *Globe*. The Education Department here asked me if I could have waited until the state certification team had finished their review of our program before I said this. The state certification team is coming here next week, and we hope that they do take all this in the way it's intended. Or perhaps we hope they don't take all this in the way it's intended.

John Brademis has been a leader in Congress and is now president of New York University, where he expects to raise a billion dollars by the end of the century. In a recent issue of *Daedalus*, he tells of how he couldn't get the superintendent of schools in Indiana to give him a teaching job. He had graduated magna cum laude from Harvard and had just finished his Ph.D. at Oxford, but he was not allowed to teach. He didn't have the methods courses. That's a travesty—a crime. Just think what would have happened to public school education in Indiana if John Brademis had stayed there.

Recent articles in the press have described the protests that have been coming from private institutions of higher learning in Massachusetts over the Commonwealth's certification rules. People from Mt. Holyoke, Wheaton, Suffolk, and other institutions have pointed out the difficulties that are associated with teaching in the Commonwealth. A sharp physics major from Mt. Holyoke simply can't teach in Massachusetts because she's not certifiable. There ought to be better ways of encouraging young people—intellectuals in their disciplines—to enter teaching in Massachusetts. We ought to pay them, but we also ought to find some inventive way to certify them.

There are rising intellectuals to be found among the undergraduates in our institutions of higher learning. If I were looking for one and trying to direct him to become a quality teacher, I would recommend a bachelor's degree in a quality undergraduate program and perhaps a master's degree in education. Perhaps that kind of paradigm would define a resisting intellectual.

Henry appears to suggest that the resisting intellectual should make changes outside the system. I wouldn't think so. It is endemic to the current system that we train teachers to be practitioners rather than intellectuals. Teachers trained in this tradition have a vested interest in the status quo. They have a powerful union.

I hope that some of them are resisting intellectuals. I think that I have seen some who are. The way to attract more such teachers is to convince parents and the school committees that we need resisting intellectuals to teach critical and creative thinking. Then we might see the school system hiring and tenuring people who will work within the system to make changes of the kind that both Henry and I would like to see.

COLLOQUIUM

PANEL 2

Comments

Ronda Goodale

I am very pleased to be here and have the opportunity to comment on Henry Giroux's paper. His paper is both exciting and timely. It comes at a time when the teaching profession is moving in a very critical direction, toward a more technical frame of reference and more accountability for schools and teachers.

If you go into any classroom, particularly in the urban centers of Massachusetts, you will find increasingly stringent curriculum requirements written for every single course. Concern over the rising number of dropouts and other perceived school-system failures has led school systems to implement measures of progress that increase accountability and that can be measured quickly. The attainment or non-attainment of specific curriculum requirements are easier to measure and test. Test scores can be looked up readily; a rise in test scores (one piece of data) is too often used as a major basis for determining success or failures of a school system. For example, although SAT scores have risen for minorities, dropout rates for minorities, particularly Hispanics, continue to rise at an alarming rate at both the high school and college level.

These statistics indicate that we have to look for solutions that go beyond enhancing specific skill acquisition including test-taking skills. Self-esteem as well as problem-solving abilities are also essential components in student academic success.

We need teachers who can teach the basics but who can also seriously address critical thinking abilities. We need teachers who can accept student skills as they are when they enter school and build upon these skills. Teachers need to model critical thinking behavior in their own classrooms. Most teachers, however, when asked to identify primary inservice needs respond with: How can I teach reading more effectively?

275

How can I manage behavior? Of course, these are important pedagodcical questions, but there are other salient issues that we need to wrestle with in education: cultural understanding, problem solving skills, and attitudes.

I think, therefore, we must accept and address teachers' concerns as they arise, but must also infuse all courses teachers take with these other ingredients. For example, if a teacher asks for something to help teach reading, we should respond with a course that not only teaches the mechanics of reading but also explores why we teach reading and the power of reading. Our teacher-education courses should not only serve the pragmatic needs of the teacher, but also be a model for developing critical thinking and evaluative skills in the classroom.

Paolo Frere emphasizes that one can not just discuss reading; you also need to focus on what the student understands. As we try to correct the past failures in our school system, we must be careful not to build a new system that is so rigid that it ignores or understates the need for thinking and understanding. The current trend in educational philosophy, centered in the testable, puts more abstract concepts and social and emotional goals in jeopardy. We need more accountability but not at the expense of analytical and intuitive abilities.

Dr. Giroux's paper, therefore, is well timed in view of education bills that have passed or are being considered throughout the United States. With stress on accountability and competency teaching, it is even now more critical to attend to the interactive models suggested by Dr. Giroux.

We are well aware that most of the potent education that goes on in schools consists of social and emotional elements that make up the classroom's hidden agenda. Students gain their concept of education from the interactions, the teacher modeling, peers, and so forth. These may not be the concepts we intended to teach, but they are the "curriculum" the students are learning. We must therefore be more sensitive to the unstated curriculum. In fact, it is this curriculum that may be impacting upon school success much more powerfully than our articulated curriculum.

Therefore, I strongly agree with Dr. Giroux that we need to examine carefully our educational goals. What is it we really want students to get out of education? How can we hold teachers accountable for goals, when many of the most important are not clearly defined? Teachers usually do not have the opportunity to even participate in formulating these goals that they must teach. Too often, teachers themselves, when asked to plan a curriculum, request a consultant from a university. We need to bolster teacher self-esteem and afford them more opportunities in actively participating in establishing goals and using their own critical thinking abilities.

We have an important obligation to teach students to read, even when challenged by poor attendance records, students who move from one school to another, and students in special education programs.

Considering the large number of nonreaders and the importance and power in learning to read, we need to have a mandated, consistent curriculum in reading. However, this is only the beginning; unless our schools continue to address social, emotional, and cultural concerns, as well as critical thinking, we will continue to fail.

COLLOQUIUM

PANEL 2

Reply

Henry A. Giroux

You've been terribly patient. I know it's been awfully long. I'll be brief. I'll start with some of the simpler questions and then try to answer some of the others. First, I don't believe that teachers who are resisting intellectuals or teachers who take a stance that necessitates some sort of critical risk should work exclusively outside the system. They should work *in and outside* the system. It seems to me that there are a number of roles teachers, as intellectuals, can play.

Second, I don't believe in conspiracy theories. I do believe that certain powers come together in specific ways to impose certain conditions on the way people live. And I don't think we can run away from that. But, at the same time, I do believe that the question of power is an important one. We do have to ask how certain economic and political conditions come into play in given societies so as to place limits upon teachers, how these conditions often place teachers in a position where they can't do the work we would like to see them do. In other words, how do we come to grips with both the specific and the larger context in which teachers work?

When I talked about teachers as intellectuals, I was in no way merely suggesting that teachers are "smart." I was simply utilizing a category through which we could begin to unravel more specifically a critique of the roles that teachers are often asked to perform. By utilizing the concept of intellectual, I hope to begin to use a language that allows us to rethink the very nature of the work that teachers do, the social functions they perform, and the conditions under which they work. To be an intellectual means that you need time to think. You need time to work with your colleagues. You need time to publish. It means you need time to become cognizant of the very principles upon which you act.

I don't believe that technical competency is unimportant. Of course it's important. I would never argue that it's not important. But I think that we have to be able to reflect upon the principles inherent in the methods that we use. Social practices and techniques are not neutral. You feed a kid M & M's to get him to learn. That has certain political and philosophical implications, just as it has certain interest embodied in it. Or you love him or her to death—that has another set of implications and interests. We've got to be able to identify those interests. So, on one level, we've got to be purposive, reflective, and theoretical, but at the same time we've got to be practical. There really is a combination of elements to consider. It's not a matter of opposing one with the other. I think that's a bad opposition. It's certainly not one that I would support. Again, if that was what I seemed to imply, it is not what I meant.

Lastly, there is the question of culture. I must firmly agree with one of my favorite colleagues. Culture is not common. I don't believe that there is a common culture. I believe there are dominant and subordinate cultures. There's popular culture. There is mass culture. But in every case, the culture and the practices it suggests are related to questions of power.

I want to raise a question about culture. How do you make pedagogy or schooling meaningful so as to make it critical? How do you make it critical so as to make it emancipatory? The point is that knowledge doesn't speak for itself. A theory of culture is really a theory of learning. Students come to classes and they bring histories to those classes. Schools often teach specific forms of culture. In some cases, those forms silently disconfirm the history that kids bring to school by excluding their histories, their dreams, their languages. We've got to become cognizant of that and how it works. I don't think that teachers actively sit back and impose a culture on kids that in some way disconfirms and prevents them from learning. I think it's often done through a whole series of commonsense methods and commonsense assumptions.

I was in a school somewhere—maybe it was in Detroit—somewhere like Detroit. The school was 95% black. There was a huge poster on the wall. It depicted a typical, white, middle-class family. Underneath the poster, the caption read: "Be proud of your school and family." That's culture as a weapon. That's culture that doesn't speak to difference. It speaks to silent relations of power that disconfirm before the process of learning can even begin. And that's something we have to be aware of. That's not to say the dominant culture doesn't have a number of wonderful things that should be critically appropriated. Of course it does. It's not all of one piece. But the way in which power and culture come together has got to be analyzed critically. Culture is not a warehouse. It's not all of one piece. It's more than that.

COLLOQUIUM

PANEL 3

CREATIVITY AND LITERATURE

The Text and the Self: The Study of Literature as a Creative Activity

Lillian Feder

There is no single method of teaching literature effectively, but one requisite, it seems to me, is that instructors be aware that they are not only "educating feeling," as Susanne Langer (1962/1964, p.83) expresses it, but developing capacities for creative thought, which is intrinsic to an aesthetic response to a work of art. For this reason, I will not delineate a particular method of teaching literature but rather attempt to analyze the creative experience of a literary work, an understanding of which is essential to any effective approach to teaching. Suggestions regarding methods of teaching will emerge from my discussion, but these should be regarded not as directions but rather as outgrowths of my belief that imaginative literature is an important stimulus to intellectual and emotional development.

The study of literature involves two kinds of creativity: the first, revealed in the texts that are read, which are usually chosen because they are the products of a special quality of genius that alters fundamental ways of apprehending reality; and the second, that of the students, which can be described as a more general human capacity to develop individual modes of assimilating and expressing internalizations of experience. It is this second type of creativity that I will be emphasizing in my discussion, but a major question that my subject suggests, and to which I will return later, is how the two act on each other, that is, how studying the literary work of creative genius affects the capacity to experience reality creatively. First, it seems necessary to consider the nature of the self involved in this process, for as Henri Bergson has taught us, the human self is our fundamental act of creation.[1]

THE SELF

What is this self to which everyone alludes yet which seems to defy a generally accepted definition? At present, it is a highly controversial issue. One of the most prominent contemporary psychoanalytic move-ments bases its theory and practice on the psychology of the self. Con-currently, a great deal of effort is being expended by deconstructionist philosophers and literary critics to prove its nonexistence. Meanwhile, studies of selfhood in the work of literary figures—Montaigne, Defoe, Pope, Stendhal, Yeats, to name but a few—continue to appear. Imagi-native writers, moreover, often refer to the need to express the self, the individual voice, in the work. Further confusing the issue are the fre-quent lamentations over narcissism in contemporary society, which er-roneously equate it with a desire for self-fulfillment.

The complexity of the self makes it extremely difficult to define. Al-though many impressive books have appeared recently (e.g., Mahler, 1975; Kahn, 1983; Nozick, 1981; Harth, 1982; Burridge, 1979) which treat selfhood from a psychological, philosophical, anthropological, or bio-logical point of view, no one of them offers what I consider a brief, precise formulation of the actual experience of selfhood that can serve as a point of reference in considering the common human capacity for creativity. Heinz Kohut (1977), whose works on the current psychoan-alytic approach to the psychology of the self are widely known, explains his failure to define the self on the basis that, "like all reality," it is "not knowable in its essence" (pp. 310–311). In fact, no essence need be sought. The self is not an essence but a complex way of transforming biological, psychological, and social activity into an individual concep-tion. Furthermore, if feelings of selfhood are as diverse as are individual human beings, they also have common bases and properties: the very processes that enter into self-creation.

My own definition of the self or self-creation (terms I use interchange-

[1] Most modern conceptions of personal identity as an act of self-creation derive from Henri Bergson's view (1907/1944) that each moment of life is "a kind of creation," that "we are creating ourselves continually." Bergson defines existence for a "conscious being" as follows: "to exist is to change, to change is to mature, to mature is to go on creating oneself endlessly" (pp. 9–10). The validity and usefulness of adaptations of this approach are demonstrated in Gilbert Rose (1980).

ably) has been influenced by recent approaches (especially Rose [1980] and Harth [1982]) that treat it as an ongoing process, but it differs from them in several respects, especially in its emphasis on both unconscious and conscious elements and on the interaction between psychic and external determinants. As I view it, the experience and concept of the self are continual creations of the individual mind, involving multiple processes, chiefly internalization, integration, and expression. These are all functions of the ego, the mediation among the manifold processes of the self—unconscious, conscious, impulsive, rational—which produces human possibilities and limits in relation to time, nature and society, cause and effect (Feder, 1980).[2] In self-creation, which is necessarily each person's way of adapting his or her biological, cognitive, and psychological characteristics to external nature and society, the processes of internalization, integration, and expression, however varied their functioning, develop conceptions of reality, which include the self's own nature. Thus, selfhood is both reflexive and outwardly directed.

Internalization is an individual conversion of familial and social values and regulations, which includes adherence to, and ambivalence or antagonism toward, these norms. Through perception, assimilation, idealization, distortion, denial, and repression, human beings form conceptions of their roles in their immediate and extended environments. Integration, perhaps the most complex of all the operations involved in selfhood, is both the principle and act of organizing as a unit varying unconscious and conscious experience: bodily attributes and functions; physical and psychological needs, deprivations, pleasures, and pains; unconscious drives, memories, dreams, fantasies; and preconscious and conscious thought processes. Essentially, integration is a consciousness that functioning is itself definition and direction of these diverse elements. As a vehicle of the self, expression consists of the various means by which individuals test and respond to their society's and their own conceptions of reality. Words, other sounds, gestures, acts, plans, hopes, participation in or withdrawal from society, all express a self-image reacting to the world outside.

Obviously, such brief descriptions can do no more than suggest the physiological and psychological complexity of internalization, integration, and expression, each of which comprises the multiple intellectual and psychic processes to which I have referred. But, in defining the self in relation to the study of literature, it seems sufficient to have identified their functions and to indicate that they account for both consistency and change in the self. Internalization, integration, and expression

---

[2] The brief description of the ego here is quoted in part from my earlier discussion of this concept in *Madness in Literature*, pp. 17, 135, which was based on definitions of Freud (Federn, 1953) and Kris (1952/1964).

function as combined genetic and culturally acquired constituents of each individual developing consistent modes of shaping ever-changing physiological, psychological, and social experience as an image of the self.

As Risieri Frondizi (1953/1971) points out, "The self is not something already made but something that is always in the making." Discussing the self as a function, Frondizi views it as "memory projected toward the future, memory hurled ahead. The future conditions the nature of our self not only as it merges with the present but while it is still more distantly future." A concept of the future, he goes on to say, not only concerns the self "as a system of ideas and intentions; it also enters into the formation of the self through our emotions" (pp. 145–146). The future is intrinsic to both the experience and the concept of self-creation. "The I's self-synthesis," says Robert Nozick (1981) in *Philosophical Explanations*, "includes a self-conception which projects itself into the future" (p. 105). An image of the future is part of the continuous development of the self; its revaluations of its earlier stages as deviations from its present goals or preparations for them, its conceptions of the present as an enactment of plans, desires, fears, and losses that in varying degrees will help to create the self and its world in time to come. Self-projection into the future is a way of assigning meaning and purpose to individual existence and its products in society and history.

The cognitive and psychic activities involved in self-creation are as distinct as the human beings who claim or recognize identities, yet people do communicate to each other, explicitly and symbolically, their individual means of integrating varied and sometimes contradictory experience of themselves, others, and external nature and society. In so doing, they reveal obliquely how common psychological processes create the enormous diversity of human personality and experience. Such disclosure is a basic ingredient of communication, encompassing likeness and difference, the endless reduplication, variety, and change in the formation of what we call human nature.

Of course, forms of self-revelation are determined by social roles and customs. Even when people describe their preferences, their personalities, the events of their lives, and their feelings, they simultaneously reveal and disguise their motivations and concerns, often from themselves. But distortion may itself serve as a form of disclosure, for the listener, responding with an awareness, albeit largely unconscious, of his own perceptions, responses, and most important, of his own continuous accommodations of psychic to social demands, assimilates the other's unique adaptations of common psychic processes. The awareness that these adaptations are different from his own enlarges his perception of the world outside himself; they are evidence of its separate existence even as it is recreated by individual internalization, integration, and expression.

THE FICTIVE CHARACTER AND THE SELF

Knowledge of other selves, however, is not restricted to association with actual persons, which, no matter how rich and varied one's life may be, must necessarily be limited. Even the self which exists in the most mundane environment can be enriched by its experience of the characters and personae of literature, for these are imaginative constructs of self-creation, which enlarge and intensify readers' awareness of both themselves and external reality. But the means by which fictive characters or selves stimulate such apprehension, while portraying the psychic experience entailed, differ greatly from those of actual selfhood. Although these literary constructs reflect a mind and a social and cultural history creating them, they should not be taught as elements of an author's fictionalized biography. The conversion of autobiographical material should be considered only as it operates within the limits of the world created on the printed page.

The fictive self, however related to the actual experience and concept of selfhood, differs from it in other important respects. The fictive self is not to be confused with a fictional character, since a character, unlike a living human being, can function without developing as an individual self. Many of the great archetypal characters—for example, Achilles, Clytemnestra, Orestes, Oedipus—in their earliest appearances in literature are not portrayals of individualized human beings. Yet their myths symbolically enact unconscious processes that are channeled in self-creation. Although their individual development is precluded by the nature of mythical narrative, their involvement in the elemental problems of human adaptation to communal life makes them prototypes of the fictive self.

The most obvious, and at the same time the most complex, characteristic of the self in any literary work is its limits, which can also be its means of extending the reader's boundaries of emotional and cognitive experience. In this respect, its genesis and mode of operation are the opposite of those of actual selfhood. Out of infinite biological and psychological processes and environmental influences, human beings select perceptions, sensations, memories, and responses to define their existence, excluding from their very consciousness those that threaten the survival and continuity of their sense of self. But the fictive self, whose limits are established by words on a page, can release and extend the reader's perceptions, memories, and feelings by aesthetic means, which provide their own controls. The very economies that formal requirements impose on the constructions of fictive characters' pasts and their memories, on the delineation of their social and personal environments, and on the representation of their conflicts, resolutions, and visions of the future grant coherence and form to individual life. Thus, through simultaneous identification with and distance from the fictive self, the reader can learn consciously to experience processes of self-creation in a communal and historical context.

The fictive self can emerge slowly, approximating the actual dynamics of selfhood and continue to create itself until death or the end of the poem, novel, or play; or it can confront the reader on first acquaintance with its claim of more than half a lifetime's struggle for definition and integration, which continue throughout the work. It can be depicted in explicit detail or in symbolic action. In any case, the fictive self of character, persona, or speaker is often the focal communicant between writer and reader, a creation that refutes the contention that writing is "the negative where all identity is lost" on the part of the author or, indeed, the characters. Whereas it is absurd to regard fictive characters and events as merely an expression of an "author's person, his life, his tastes, his passions,"[3] it is equally absurd to consider language as functioning on its own through an automaton erroneously named the author. The fictive self is no more an "essence"[4] than is the living self but, unlike actual selfhood, it is a construct, an aesthetic arrangement of the psychic, historical, and social elements which together produce the concept of individual existence.

The fictive self is produced by common techniques of literary creation; thus narration, description, symbolization, action, interior monologue, and dialogue can be analyzed as aesthetic adaptations of psychic means of internalizing, integrating, and giving expression to experience. These techniques create fictive selves through some or all of the following: representations of characters' feelings regarding their own mental and physical attributes; depictions of memories, dreams, and verbal thinking; overt references to, or enactments of, internalization of the physical, personal, social, and political environment; development of relationships among characters; and portrayals of their active involvement in the events of their time. The unconscious and conscious processes of fictive selfhood, whether depicted symbolically or overtly, are always more discrete than they are in actual life. Drives, motivations,

---

[3] Barthes (1977). Barthes sets up straw literary historians and critics "to be found in ordinary culture" who have an "image" of works of literature as entirely derived from, and explained by, the biographies of their creators (pp. 142–143).

[4] Barthes (1977) oversimplifies the history of criticism by positing a sweeping decline from Aristotle's just conception of character as "subsidiary" to action to a "later" tendency to view characters as "psychological essences" (pp. 104–105).

and actions, however complex, are always limited by language itself as well as by other formal and thematic considerations. Paradoxically, the techniques of aesthetic creation, with their inherent limits, stimulate mediation between a prototypical or naturalistic self composed of words on pages and the self of the reader.

As any recognition of the infinite variations in the processes of actual selfhood demands an apprehension of external reality, so the variety of possible responses to the self in the text points up its referential function. In fact, the fictive self at its most effective is a chief agent in uniting psychic with aesthetic creation, the individual writer and reader with literary, cultural, and social history.

THE ALTERNATE WORLD OF THE LITERARY TEXT

Of course, not only the fictive self or the protagonist but the whole created world of a literary work—its setting, plot, atmosphere, and narrative and thematic structure—can deepen and illuminate human experience. The basic psychological importance of this aesthetic effect as potentially creative is validated by D.W. Winnicott's work (1971) on the "intermediate area of *experiencing,* to which inner reality and external life both contribute" (p. 2), but which is different from both. Beginning with the infant's earliest engagement with a "transitional object" (p. 13), Winnicott goes on to demonstrate that the "intermediate area" of psychic functioning develops as "a resting place for the individual engaged in the perpetual human task of keeping inner and outer reality separate yet interrelated." This "intermediate area" involves "the substance of *illusion,* that which is allowed to the infant and which in adult life is inherent in art and religion" (pp. 2–3). Winnicott considers the "interplay between originality and the acceptance of tradition as the basis for inventiveness" one of many examples "of the interplay between separateness and union" (p. 99). The "potential space between subject and object" is "that of cultural experience which is a derivative of play. . . . It can be looked upon as sacred to the individual in that it is here that the individual experiences creative living" (pp. 102–103).

Winnicott's description of the "intermediate area" as a psychological function that can employ illusion constructively is illuminated by Susanne Langer's (1953) discussion of illusion as the basis of aesthetic experience. The "illusion of experience, or 'virtual life'" of a poem, she says, "is established with the opening line" and maintained throughout (pp. 213–214).

> The virtual world in which poetic events develop is always peculiar to the work; it is the particular illusion of life those events create, as the virtual

space of a picture is the particular space of the forms in it. To be imaginatively coherent the "world" of a poem must be made out of events that
are in the imaginative mode—the mode of naive experience, in which
action and feeling, sensory value and moral value, causal connection and
symbolic connection, are still undivorced. (p. 217)

Langer 1952/1964 would identify Winnicott's "intermediate area" as
the realm of the imagination, which she regards as "the source of all
insight and true beliefs, . . . probably the common source of dream, reason, religion, and all true general observation" (p. 81).

Drawing on Winnicott's work and aware of Langer's, Gilbert Rose
(1980) introduces the concept of the "transitional process," which is
extremely useful in defining the nature of creative imagination. According to Rose, a "dynamic equilibrium" between the individual self and
external reality is experienced continually throughout life. The "adaptation of everyday life and the originality of creative imagination both
represent a continuing 'transitional' interplay between self and reality."
Adaptation necessarily involves "a greater accommodation to reality"
than creative imagination, which refashions it. But the processes are not
discrete since "creative imagination must also accommodate to reality,"
whereas adaptation is creative in integrating the elements of reality that
each individual selects. Together these processes create the self's physiological and psychological responses to the outside world (pp. 111–
113).

Rose (1980) emphasizes the psychological ambiguity inherent in the
aesthetic structure of works of art and in individual responses to them.
He summarizes his extensive discussion of the source, nature, and effect
of aesthetic form as follows:

> [Aesthetic] structure has to do with the dialectic between separation and
> fusion, control and ambiguity, tension and release, thought and feeling
> or action, change and constancy, present and past.
>
> The relevance of aesthetic experience derives from its biological roots
> in the individual's need for constant orientation in a relatively fluid con-
> temporary reality.
>
> And we can see all this as part of an overall, ongoing *transitional process.*
> The aesthetic experience reflects and sharpens this transitional process,
> which informs all experience. (p. 211)

Rose (1980) makes basic contributions to an understanding of the importance of aesthetic experience in the development of individuality
and autonomy. Concerned as he is with human adaptation to external
resources and demands, his emphasis is necessarily on the individual
psychology of the artist and his intended audience. However, in consid-

ering the creative value of aesthetic experience and in particular of literary study, one must also consider the fact that a work of art is both an individual and a social product.

A poem, novel, or play has a multiple history—individual, social, political, and literary—fused and transformed by its author into an alternate world, different from the actual one that he and his audience inhabit yet inevitably connected with it. Study of a literary work should reveal that the society it conveys, however indirectly, is neither mirror image nor vehicle of escape but a conception of life rooted in, yet often antagonistic to, historical reality. Octavio Paz (1974) has described this relationship as a "contradiction between history and poetry" which exists in "all societies" and is particularly "manifest" in "the modern age." This "contradiction" or "discord," he says, results from the ways in which poetry "transfigures" time: "From its earliest days modern poetry has been a reaction against the modern era, tugging first in one direction then another as the manifestations of the modern have changed" (pp. V–VI).

Actually the contradictory relationship between literature, history, and society is inherent in aesthetic creation and in the creative response it elicits. From its origins in myth and throughout its continuous history, literature has given form to unconscious drives and feelings projected on a social framework. The "illusion of experience" that a literary text creates releases such drives and feelings in the context of domestic, social, and political reality. Thus, many significant works of imaginative literature simultaneously incorporate and challenge a society's prevailing assumptions. They do so not by propaganda or argument but by creating an aesthetic structure of the "intermediate area of experience" that also participates in the formation of cultural history. It enters into the consciousness and definition of both the society in which it originated and others, contemporary or later, whose language and culture may be different, as an alternate view of reality which discloses ignored or repressed contradictions inevitable in the very act of adapting biological and psychological processes to communal life.

In a literary work, the leading protagonist, the fictive self, or the persona has a major role in engaging the reader in creative participation in this cultural experience, for it is he or she who, in portraying the ambivalence inherent in individual adaptation to communal life, illuminates the ways in which social institutions channel but never quite resolve this ambivalence. In so doing, the character or persona confronts the reader with the elemental and continuous challenges of human life: mortality and its inevitable limitations as well as its extraordinary possibilities of transcendence in love, religion, magic, science, and art.

The study of literature, whether it is the earliest extant poetry of Western civilization or contemporary fiction, is not a passive reception of the contents and background of a work. In reading the *Iliad*, for example, students must be taught how the mythical, nonrealistic elements of the epic portray more deeply than any historical account both the individual's and society's accommodation to war, death, and the yearning for immortality. Perhaps the most creative aspect of this process lies in their apprehension of how partial and threatening this accommodation has always been and still remains.

Homer's portrayal of Achilles' choice of a short glorious life over a long inglorious one, with its tragic consequences, induces the reader to experience with more clarity and intensity than he could generally risk in actual life the intricate connections between personal feelings and values and political and social issues. The heroic code by which a warrior ironically achieves immortality through death in battle incorporates the values of a tribal society, which grow out of its economic, social, and political institutions. But such values also incorporate the deepest human fears and desires: the threat of death and its conquest. Achilles' acceptance and questioning of this code engage the reader intellectually and emotionally in the tragic cost of any choice that involves mortality as well as in the ambivalence inevitable in what seems the firmest of decisions. The mythical elements—the choice itself, the involvement of deities in the Trojan War and in the individual contests of the heroes, the role of *moira*, or fate, that pervades the entire poem—enact such fears and desires in relation to societal demands, which in actual life encourage denial as a psychological defense against ambivalence.

If students are taught to experience myth in literature as conveying the earliest formal expression of psychic narrative converted to political, religious, and cultural vehicles, they will respond to its remnants of dream and fantasy as these relate to their own lives in society. This experience allows them to question their psychic defenses and the stock responses to personal conflict and societal demands they have adopted without conscious awareness.

I have said earlier in this paper that the very limits imposed by aesthetic requirements can release latent cognitive and emotional capacities in the reader. In studying the *Iliad*, for example, one participates imaginatively in Achilles' extremes of wrath, pain, and love as he reacts against what he considers a violation of justice which calls into question a code of conduct which has defined his being. His withdrawal from battle results in sorrow and death; the fulfillment of his wish that the Greeks suffer from his absence brings him no satisfaction, only the anguish of losing his beloved friend Patroclus. Yet Achilles emerges with tragic insight into the code he accepted, as he portrays the price of the choice he made to live and die heroically. The extremity of Achilles' wrath and grief, which involve gods, heroes, and natural forces, removes the epic narrative from actual experience. Furthermore, the poem's organization, its highly stylized language and meter, its heroic portrayal of character and motivation distance it not only from ordinary life but from the realm of dreams and imagining to which it is surely related. Even the dreams to which the epic refers, for example, Achilles' dream of Patroclus (XXIII, 62–101) or the dream to which Achilles' pursuit of Hector is compared in a simile (XXII, 199–201), are structured in relation to the narrative. The *Iliad* indeed reflects and stimulates what Winnicott names the "intermediate area," uniting individual imagination, thought, and feeling with historical and contemporary reality. This area or process is "a resting place," as Winnicott calls it, only in the sense that the reader is not physically involved in the conflict he experiences vicariously, but his aesthetic distance does not preclude engagement. In fact, it intensifies his emotional and intellectual participation. He can undergo the experience of questioning internalized social values, the disintegration of long-established assumptions, without practical consequences. Thus, he is freed, at least to some extent, from his customary denial and repression of ambivalence toward untested loyalties.

Aesthetic response implies shared experience, not only with a character or a persona but with all those who have participated in a literary work's cultural history—readers, scholars, critics, and those who have used and alluded to it in later works of art. Thus, the reader's empathy with Achilles in his isolation is a shared aloneness, in which the cost of individual integrity is invested with communal value. Furthermore, evocation of buried or unacknowledged feelings is directed by the structure of the epic toward the hero's and the reader's ultimate enlightenment. As a result, memories and associations that might be painful in actual experience are channeled into aesthetic satisfaction.

This is intensified by the language and stylistic elements of the *Iliad* which, even in translation, can convey traditional associations along with particular emotional significance. As everyone knows by now, the *Iliad*'s pervasive formulae, characteristic of oral epic, were not invented by Homer but adapted from earlier poetry. The epic formula, as Cedric Whitman (1958/1965) describes it, is "an artificially devised unit of semantic, grammatical, and metrical functions. As such, it has clearly transcended the discursive function of speech and has become a vividly presentational medium, in short, an art form." The formula is "imagistic," says Whitman, "and appeals directly to the senses." It "is functional ... not merely in the sense that it assists in creating verse, but also because it is a sort of poetic atom, a fragment of technically transformed speech whose structure is already that of art, not logic." One of Whitman's major contributions in this discussion is his demonstration of how Homer uses this traditional language in an original and creative manner, how the poet's "immense range" and adaptations of formulae "with reference to association and design" exploit "the genius of the style itself." "When formulae are combined and recombined as they are in Homer's battle scenes," he goes on to say, "it is like the falling of glass chips in a kaleidoscope. Patterns constantly are formed, always with consistency of color, and always with pieces of the same shape, yet always different and always luminous with surprise" (pp. 110–124).

This traditional form, with its rhythmic and associative recurrences and variations, exemplifies Winnicott's concept of the "interplay between originality and the acceptance of tradition as [a] basis for inventiveness" for both author and reader. Among the many recurrent formulae describing the death of a warrior in battle, two that are sometimes paired are: "He fell with a thud and his armor clashed upon him." The contrast of the sound of a lifeless body hitting the earth with that of active combat portrays the tragic irony of the heroic contest through auditory associations shocking in their juxtaposition. The condensation of the formulae is like that of a dream, the implications of which are left to the reader. These two formulae do not always occur together. Sometimes one is joined to a different formula, suggesting the individuality of death within the general slaughter. The line, "He fell down, head-foremost, and his armor clashed upon him" stimulates visual associations in contrast with auditory ones. Another variation is the description of Patroclus wounded by Hector: "He fell with a thud, and the Achaean host greatly lamented" (XVI, 822). The absence of the sound of clashing armor, by now all too familiar in this context, is itself important, for it should remind the reader that Patroclus is wearing the borrowed armor of Achilles, in which he has dared to disobey his friend's command only to drive the Trojans from the ships. His fall is typical, but the usual formula is not suitable here for his armor with its ambiguous connotations of borrowed glory and daring. The description of the lamentation of the Achaeans prefigures the extended mourning of Achilles, which is to dominate the remainder of the poem.

The emotional impact of the formulae extends beyond associations with the Trojan War and its consequences to the larger issues of which the war is a part. Heroes and even Zeus himself exemplify the human disposition to reckless impulse caused by blindness of judgment, expressed in the Greek noun ἀτη *(atē)* and the verb ἀάω *(aaō)*. Early in the *Iliad* (I, 407–412), Achilles asks his mother Thetis to persuade Zeus to help the Trojans so that Agamemnon may become aware of his *atē* in denying Achilles the honor due him. His wish comes true when, on two occasions, Agamemnon admits his recklessness and offers to make amends (IX, 114ff.; XIX, 86ff.). On the second of these, having declared that it was *atē* sent by the gods to infatuate him that brought so much suffering to the Greeks, he goes on to speak of Ἄτη *(Atē)*, the eldest daughter of Zeus, the personified essence of recklessness and blindness of judgment. Twice he uses the formula: Ἄτη, ἥ πάγτας ἀᾶται *(Atē,* who deludes or misleads all, XIX, 91, 129), the language revealing the very process by which inner experience is eternalized in myth. Encompassing human and divine limitation, the formula also applies to Achilles, who has been warned against *Ate* in vain (IX, 504–514), the great Zeus, who was deceived by her (XIX, 95–133), and finally the reader who faces his own propensities to self-delusion projected on a goddess who enacts them in a transitive verb. The very structure of the formula stimulates the imagination to perceive the tendency to project human limits on a malevolent deity and to apprehend the psychological and aesthetic processes involved in such projection.

Studying the *Iliad* unites the reader to the early and continuous emotional history of Western civilization and helps to develop a concept of the individual's role within it. As students perceive that the very recognition of human limitations is simultaneously the price and the reward of the struggle against them, they convert ambivalence into a mode of creative response. As the myths, formulae, and action of the epic are involved in the "transitional process," or the "interplay between self and reality," students integrate these formal elements into their particular adaptations to existing circumstances. Feelings and ideas stimulated by this alternate view of reality and directed by its aesthetic structure demand new forms of cognitive assimilation and linguistic expression. The creative connections between language, thought, and feeling are thus reawakened.

Although I have concentrated on the *Iliad* as an example, I do not mean to imply that it is only or chiefly study of the ancient classics that can stimulate a creative response. I chose the *Iliad* in an effort to demonstrate, however briefly, that the very nonrealistic and formal qualities which may make it seem inaccessible to a modern audience can actually constitute its deepest appeal. From the onset, these elements determine the nature of the epic's "virtual" realm where creative act and response converge. But later literature, even realistic fiction, can also involve the reader in an alternate world, however close this may seem to present reality.

In a contemporary novel, V.S. Naipaul's *A House for Mr. Biswas* (1961/ 1978), which is utterly different from ancient epic in its setting, characters, language, and structure, the unprepossessing protagonist engages in a contest as moving and, in its way, as heroic as Achilles' to assert his contradictory view of reality in an unreceptive society. Mr.

Biswas' impractical, often comic, efforts to own his own home, in the face of poverty, his own ignorance, and the skepticism of his family, enact his struggle for autonomy. The house, into which he and his family move near the end of the novel and where he dies not long after, reflects the flaws and limitations of its owner and the petty corruption of his society, but it remains standing.

Equally important and intimately related to this visible sign of the self-respect he wrests out of inevitable defeat is the meaning of reading and writing for this poor, ill-educated Indian living in Trinidad. With less than 6 years of elementary schooling, without guidance or encouragement, Mr. Biswas (as he is called from infancy to death) turns to reading and later to writing as vehicles of self-creation. In his youth, discovering the inspirational works of Samuel Smiles, an English writer of the second half of the nineteenth century, he identifies himself with Smiles's portraits of humble, self-taught young men who rose to great success. Later, he finds consolation and self-definition in philosophy and fiction.

Driven by his only partly articulated unwillingness to accommodate himself to the routine jobs to which his class and role in society have assigned him, and by his need to express the imaginative, often bizarre, interpretations of events he formulates mentally, he becomes a journalist. At first his assignments allow him to express his "fantasy," his "facetiousness," "something of his own" (p. 323). But his job offers no more security than do any of the other economic or social conditions of his life. When a "new regime" takes over his newspaper, rules he regards as ridiculous are enforced, and Mr. Biswas is assigned to cover funerals, courts, and cricket matches. In retaliation, he asserts himself in the only ways he can—by "mentally [composing] many sonorous letters of resignation, varying from the abusive to the dignified to the humorous and even to the charitable," and fantasying that he will "start my own magazine" (pp. 373–375).

Reality seems to offer no avenue for self-expression. Even when he is reassigned to the writing of features, editorial restrictions do not permit him to reveal his feelings openly. Responding to a letter from his former editor, he pours out his bitterness. On rereading the letter and realizing "how much he has revealed of himself" (p. 384), he tears it up. The self his words have portrayed is too uncompromising to survive in the world to which he must somehow adapt, yet, even as he destroys this evidence of its existence, he is aware that he has created it.

A House for Mr. Biswas should be studied in relation to Naipaul's (1962/1981) journalistic writings on Trinidad and his (1984) "Prologue to an Autobiography," an account of his father's life, on which the novel is based. Even more important than students' awareness of the background provided by these works, is their comprehension of the connections and differences between the factual material and the imaginative portrayal of self-creation. It is the "intermediate area" where Mr. Biswas' self emerges in the most unpromising conditions, in defiance of a society that would deny its claims, that produces a creative response to the actual world, which his house and his words profoundly enrich.

REFERENCES

Barthes, R. (1977), *Image-music-text* (S. Heath, Trans.). New York: Hill & Wang.

Bergson, H. (1944). *Creative evolution* (A. Mitchell, Trans.). New York: Random House. (Original work published 1907)

Burridge, K. (1979). *Some one, no one: An essay on individuality*. Princeton, NJ: Princeton University Press.

Feder, L. (1980). *Madness in literature*. Princeton, NJ: Princeton University Press.

Federn, P. (1953). *Ego psychology and the psychoses* (Edoardo Weiss, Ed.). London: Imago.

Frondizi, R. (1971). *The nature of the self: A functional interpretation*. Carbondale: Southern Illinois University Press. (Original work published 1953)

Harth, E. (1982). *Windows on the mind: Reflections on the physical basis of consciousness*. New York: William Morrow.

Kahn, M.M.R. (1983). *Hidden selves: Between theory and practice in psychoanalysis*. London: Chatto & Windus.

Kohut, H. (1977). *The restoration of the self*. New York: International Universities Press.

Kris, E. (1964). *Psychoanalytic explorations in art*. New York: Schocken Books. (Original work published 1952)

Langer, S. (1953). *Feeling and form: A theory of art*. New York: Charles Scribners & Sons.

Langer, S. (1964). *Philosophical sketches*. New York: Mentor Books. (Original work published 1962)

Mahler, M. (1975). *The psychological birth of the human infant: Symbiosis and individuation* (F. Pine & A. Bergman, Trans.). New York: Basic Books.

Naipaul, V.S. (1978). *A House for Mr. Biswas*. New York: Penguin Books. (Original work published 1961)

Naipaul, V.S. (1981). Trinidad. *The middle passage: Impressions of five societies—British, French and Dutch—in the West Indies and South America*. New York: Vintage Books. (Original work published 1962)

Naipaul, V.S. (1984). *Finding the center: Two narratives*. New York: Knopf.

Nozick, R. (1981). *Philosophical explanations*. Cambridge, MA: Harvard University Press.

Paz, O. (1974). *Children of the mire: Modern poetry from romanticism to the avant-garde*. Cambridge, MA: Harvard University Press.

Rose, G. (1980). *The power of form: A psychoanalytic approach to aesthetic form*. New York: International Universities Press.

Whitman, C. (1965). *Homer and the heroic tradition.* New York: Norton. (Original work published 1958)

Winnicott, D.W. (1971). *Playing and reality.* London: Tavistock.

COLLOQUIUM

PANEL 3

Comments

Leslie Epstein

I had always assumed the last word on creativity, particularly its effect upon the reader or viewer, was the first: Aristotle's. The Athenian will be purged or cleansed of precisely those feelings of pity and terror that the dramatist, through the spectacle of the fall of a great man, has first aroused. Or, as the sceptical Heraclitus put it, a man hopes to make himself clean by bathing in mud. The mud, in the ancient formulation, those feelings, was clearly material belonging to the unconscious—as is made most clear by the Oedipus story, which both Aristotle and later Freud took as the paradigm of their respective and related theories.

The chief virtue of Professor Feder's paper, and of her theory of self-creation through aesthetic experience, is that it deals with areas of the psyche generally more accessible to conscious manipulation and control: in her terms, internalization, integration, expression. That is, the work of self-creation is, essentially, an ego function. And what she is most concerned with, it seems to me (though this was true of Freud as well), is enlarging the boundaries of the ego—which means, in artistic terms, using fantasy, play, illusion, imagination, and all the tricks of the trade in the service of a wider, enhanced, and finally stronger definition of reality.

The hidden agenda here is this: Our readers, our students, can be taught to live a little more of life—meaning, more complexity of life, more ambivalence of feeling, more sheer danger—through first experiencing it with our defenses entranced, even lulled, in works of art, and (again I think it is her great strength here) with our wits sharpened, our very capacity for thought and judgment invigorated.

Lest I merely repeat lamely what she has said well, let me give an example: Don Quixote (rather, one scene from *Don Quixote*). This is an appropriate example for many reasons as you'll instinctively feel, not least from its working its way through, struggling through, to becoming the first novel.

Everything Professor Feder argues depends upon what one reads. The reason Quixote goes mad, (and perhaps what made Cervantes mad behind him) is that, in Langer's language, the world of chivalric romances is one in which "action and feeling, sensory value and moral value, causal connection and symbolic connection" are not unified but divorced, whereas Quixote chooses—and this is the great joke of the book—to act as if they were whole. The result is that Quixote the man as well as *Don Quixote* the novel (and so the entire genre of the novel) becomes split, devoured by pastiche and parody and pastoral; and the great task for Cervantes is how man and book can be created, that is, made whole, with their sense of reality enhanced.

Think of Professor Feder's persuasive suggestion of how the enlargement of reality within the self occurs primarily through the apprehension and appreciation of the other, of the other's recreation of the world, which only then takes on a separate existence. That will bring us to the quite beautiful scene near the end. (Think how important it is that this work, unlike so many others, especially these days, *has* an end. When was the last time you read a novel that was as fully satisfying at its conclusion as at its start? Where all the premises set up in the first half were resolved in the second? It is the mark of our disunified world, of our unimaginative mode—the chivalric mode, if you will—that no work is really finished: Ending implies finitude, limits, mortality, which is, as Professor Feder suggests, that aspect of reality hardest for our defenses to bear.) So we come, after these thousands of pages, to the scene in which the Don will at last win his beloved Dulcinea Del Toboso, for it is established beyond doubt that she will be disenchanted, and free to love the Don, once Sancho Panza submits to 3,300 lashes.

Bargaining takes place. It is agreed that Sancho will administer the blows himself, and that the servant will—though Quixote wonders whether this will affect their efficacy—be paid a certain sum for each.

The scene is deep night. A clump of beech trees. A whip, "powerful and flexible," has been made from a donkey's halter. The Squire sets about his self-flagellation, while the Don waits outside the grove. After six strokes, Sancho bargains for a higher rate, and the Don happily agrees to double the sum for each blow. Then Sancho, as we are told, "let the lashes rain down: Rascal that he was, however, he stopped laying them on his shoulders and let them fall on the trees instead, uttering such moans every now and then that it seemed as if each blow was tearing his heart out."

Soon the trees shake, the bark flies in all directions, birds take to the

air, an agonized wail rends the night, and just here a strange and wonderful thing occurs: The Don rushes forward, seizes the cruel lash, and
forbids his servant to continue. "Fate, my dear Sancho," he says, "will
not have you lose your life to please me, for you need it to support your
wife and children. Let Dulcinea wait for a better occasion." And he takes
off his cloak and puts it around Sancho's broad shoulders.

It is here that the wonderful event occurs: through grace, through a
miracle—but we know it is through imagination—Quixote's sanity, his
grip upon an enhanced reality if you will, is restored: "The mercy that
I speak of," says Don Quixote, "is that which God is showing me at this
moment—in spite of my sins. My mind now is clear, unencumbered by
those misty shadows of ignorance that were cast over it"—cast over it
by his "bitter and continual reading" of the "hateful books of chivalry."
He continues, speaking upon his deathbed: "I am no longer Don Quixote De La Mancha but Alonso Quijano, whose mode of life won for
him the name of good." But we have been reading, too. What of our
minds? No less than the Don, we have passed through those hateful
books—and not always in parodied form. And we too, in our lives, as
in the novel, stand at midnight outside of a dark and mysterious grove.
As the Don's heart launched out toward the reality of another, as he felt
that suffering more in his imagination than Sancho bore it in reality, so
too do our hearts launch outward toward his mystery, his being, his
separateness. He soon fades, faints, disappears. But we are left more
courageous, more compassionate, more clear-headed, in short, made
whole, made more imaginative, for having read his adventure and the
other adventures in other books that Quixote calls—and surely Professor Feder would agree—the very "light of the soul."

COLLOQUIUM

PANEL 3

Comments

Gerald Richman

Yesterday when I met Professor Feder for the first time, she said that she had a bone to pick with me in response to a first draft of these comments that I had sent to her. She suggested that I reread the paper. Last night I did just that, but I am afraid that Professor Feder will still have a bone to pick with me.

Professor Feder presents an interesting and sophisticated version of an old idea in terms of modern theories of the psychology of the self. The old idea is that literature is didactic. It teaches us something. In the modern version, instead of moral truths, literature helps the reader in the continual process of creating the self. Implicit in this, I think, is the argument that this is a positive creation of the self. We learn from the characters of the poem, novel, or play by simultaneously identifying with them and distancing ourselves from them. This gives us an "illusion of reality" which "releases our unconscious drives and feelings" (an idea very close to what Professor Epstein said about Aristotle's definition of catharsis), thus helping the reader to create the self.

As a teacher of literature I find this argument appealing. But, as much as I want to be convinced by Professor Feder's plausible model or even by Aristotle, I remain skeptical, because neither Professor Feder nor Aristotle provides the evidence to demonstrate that readers actually do what she says they do—that reading literature actually helps readers create the self. When Professor Feder writes about Achilles and the *Iliad*, she is very convincing, but when she writes about the reader's response to the poem, I am nagged by the question, "Says who?"

Take, for instance, Professor Feder's opening remarks and her excellent discussion of Achilles,

Homer's portrayal of Achilles' choice of a short, glorious life over a long, inglorious one, with its tragic consequences, induces the reader to experience with more clarity and intensity than he could generally risk in actual life, the intricate connections between personal feelings and values and political and social issues.

Now let me modify Professor Feder's statement to read:

Homer's portrayal of Achilles' choice of a short glorious life over a long, inglorious one, with its tragic consequences, induces the reader to *observe* [I change experience to observe] with more clarity and intensity than he could generally risk in actual life, the intricate connections between personal feelings and values and political and social issues.

I made only one change: I dropped the verb *experience*, which Professor Feder used, and substituted the word *observe*. The difference between observe, or something that readers do from the outside, and experience, which the readers do from the inside (by internalizing the event or whatever is going on), is important. In the sense that Professor Feder uses it, the word *experience* indicates an important step in the creation of the self—a more or less profound change in the reader's psyche. Observations, however, can be made and quickly forgotten without significantly contributing to the creation of the self.

Professor Feder clearly demonstrates that works of literature can bring readers to the water, but she does not demonstrate that literature can make them drink. Reading can force us to observe, but it can't force us to experience and so help create the self. If literature, even rightly taught, can force readers to experience, in Professor Feder's meaning of the word, Achilles or Mr. Biswas or Lady Macbeth or Huck Finn or Don Quixote, readers would have created far better selves than they have. Having read Goethe's *Faust*, say, would have rendered it impossible for there to be educated Nazi concentration-camp commandants. But history tells us that the reading of Goethe did not help the Nazis create themselves, at least in any positive sense.

I want to emphasize again, that what Professor Feder says about Achilles and Mr. Biswas is excellent, and I agree one hundred percent. But when she switches from literature to the reader's response, I need to see more evidence before I can give her argument one hundred percent agreement. Her argument, it seems to me, as much as I want to believe it, is wishful thinking. I am not sure what evidence would convince me on this point. Perhaps, as an English teacher and not a social scientist, I would need to see written responses by a range of readers—

not just a few exceptional readers—that showed that they had not only observed the tragedy of Achilles, but had experienced it. For me, more evidence is necessary to support Professor Feder's argument.

COLLOQUIUM

PANEL 3

Comments

Sarah Smith

The modern reader's relationship to the text, about which Professor Feder has been so eloquent, seems to have developed about 1720. Before that, as far as we can tell from the scattered references to the process of reading, printed text seems to have been used essentially as an aid to memory. The writer-reader relationship was based on that between the speaker and the listener; text was an artifact of that relationship, and often no more than a pale reflection of it.

A crucial step in the transformation of this relationship seems to have been the printing of sermons. Starting in the 1640s and 1650s, and reaching its peak between 1690 and 1730, the printed sermon soon developed another goal from the spoken one. The reader, during the reading of a printed sermon, was to be influenced or "converted." A direct relationship developed between the writer, as writer, and the reader, as reader. We see the introduction into literature of direct address to the reader: "Gentle Reader," "Dear Reader." The writer speaks about the writing process. There begins to be a literature about the reading process, both in private letters and journals and within literary writing. By the 1720s we can say that this relationship has spawned the beginnings of what can be read as a secular literature, among the English essayists and particularly in Defoe, as well as creating interesting, though short-lived, hybrids such as Defoe's "sermon-novel" *Religious Courtship*. (To an extent, of course, all of Defoe's career fits into this middle passage.) By the 1740s, with writers such as Richardson, Fielding, Collins, or Gray, the idea that the writer should directly influence the reader begins to lead a robust secular life, and by 1800 it has led to the development in English literature of, to cite a few phenomena, the novel, the Sentimental movement, and the beginnings of Romantic literature.

One of the interesting sidelights of this conversion literature is that its development depended, to a degree, on pure technology. Printing techniques made great advances during this period. New type fonts were developed, better and faster presses, improved ways of making paper. Books became cheaper. At the same time, similar improvements were occurring in many other areas of English life, so that more people became prosperous. (It is interesting, in this context, that Defoe seems to have invented for the ordinary reader the concept of a middle class, mentioning the "middle state of life" in the first part of *Robinson Crusoe.*) The middle class could afford books, it read books, and it supported the first professional writers.

This is not the only case in which a new kind of creativity may be said to, in part, depend on, or rise out of, the development of new technology. Film is another well-known example, one following a strikingly similar chronological line. In 1893 (more or less) the film camera is developed for scientific purposes. In 1895 the first datable film show is given; it already includes entertainment films. Less than twenty years later, the first masterpieces have been produced within the new medium, by the new technology. New technological possibilities give rise to new creative possibilities and, as Professor Feder's work implies, to a new sense of audience: the movie audience, the visually educated heirs of the cinematic technology.

The equivalent new technology in 1985 is the computer. To list some of its more recent successes is to give an idea of its pace: fast processing, CMOS RAM chips, VLSI chips, improvements in operating systems, hard disks, bit-rastered displaying, image digitizing, real-time graphics generation, compatibility standards, and laserdisk technology, combined with the remarkable spread of computers throughout society.

We forget how quickly they have spread. The IBM PC was introduced into Boston in November 1982, only 2 years and 3 months ago. At that time, a two-drive system with 64K of memory and word-processing software cost about $5,000. Now, a true compatible with four or five major programs, 128K and, on a sale day, a printer, can be bought for as little as $1,395. The technology not only exists: It has spread, and is spreading still.

I want to veer a little away from Professor Feder's immediate subject and talk today about the effect of this technological change on us as creative people—creative makers of literature, of educational environments such as Professor Giroux has discussed, of computational environments such as Professor Pylyshyn has so eloquently described. And, taking advantage of my place as last programmed speaker of this conference, I would like to prophesy about the role of creativity to come in this new computer age. Specifically, I would like to discuss a new form

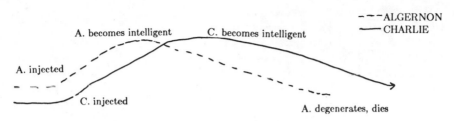

Figure 1. Linear narrative ("Flowers for Algernon").

of art and entertainment, one that hardly exists yet, in order to inspire this audience to help bring it to pass.

To do this I must speak briefly about the distinction between linear and modular narrative. Most books are read linearly: Starting at page 1, you go forward to the end. Books do not have to be a linear narrative, of course; some books, such as dictionaries, are never read this way, and even some literature, for instance Rilke's lyric poetry and *Finnegans Wake*, should be read in a different way. However, for most narratives of any reasonable length, we can say that the author expects the audience to read the pages in order, first pages to last.

Concepts like linearity and duration are basic to literary criticism. (See Figure 1.) We chart concepts such as the rising and falling action of a narrative, and say that a narrative has a beginning, a middle, and an end. Any author of perception takes advantage of this perceived linearity of form, so that many strong stories are inherently linear.

Let us take a very simple example, the science fiction story "Flowers for Algernon." There are two characters, a mentally retarded man, Charlie, and a laboratory mouse. The mouse, Algernon, is injected with a substance that's supposed to make it more intelligent; then the hero is injected with the same substance. The mouse gets more intelligent; then Charlie gets more intelligent. The mouse gets very, *very* stupid and dies, and Charlie ... The story is a rising and falling line: very simple, very powerful.

But not all stories need be constructed like that. Let's consider a different technology, a random-access narrative. Computers contain a certain amount of memory, and because of the way that memory is reached ("accessed"), it is just as easy for the computer to get to any part of that memory as it is to any other: the ability to get anywhere from anywhere is called "random access." Computer memories tend to be large, so that a great amount of information can be stored on them: more information than in the ordinary book. For these reasons, some persons in the computer field have for a long time been working on the idea of a "computerized book," something that would be easy to carry

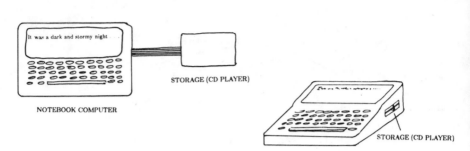

Figure 2. A simple hardware setup for modular narrative. The computer may include a storage device such as a CD player, or be slaved to one.

around and would have a great amount of easily reachable information inside it.

Let's construct, in our minds, what this computer might look like. We'll be very conservative, using only currently available, commercially tested technology. We'll confine this discussion to text-based systems, although graphics systems are already available, because graphics pose issues of storage and display that aren't fully resolved.

Take a small computer, like the Model 100 from Radio Shack. This is called a "notebook" computer or "lap portable," is very inexpensive, and weighs just over four pounds. [See Figure 2.] (There are many other lap computers; this model is used as an example only.) Taking this as a model, we might make a few modifications to it, such as a larger screen, and add to it for storage a compact laser disk player. One laser disk contains about 600 MB of storage: not kilobytes but megabytes, six hundred thousand thousand bytes of memory. To translate this into more familiar terms, a byte may be equivalent to a printed character, so that 600 MB could represent 600 million characters, or about 60 million longish words, or 250 novels the length of *Shōgun*.

600 MB of memory is room for either a very long story, or a different kind of story.

We've already seen examples of what this different kind of story—this non-linear narrative—might be. Computer games like "Adventure," starting with an initial situation, allow the reader to choose one of several possible outcomes. Instead of being linear, the narrative comes in modules; though the code is always the same, the ability to choose allows them to be read in multiple orderings.

We need to be content with a kind of creative ambiguity in defining "module"; it is a term, like Christian Metz's "episode," that varies according to the creative bent of the individual. A module is the atomic particle of a narrative: the element that, while not indivisible, is conveniently thought of as a unity. See Figure 3. In programming terms, it is

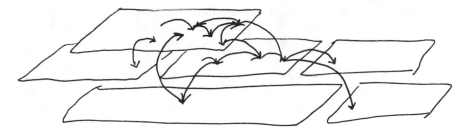

Figure 3. Modular narrative. Arrows represent possible paths from one module or group of modules to another.

a piece of programming code that contains no conditions requiring user input. (But, this is simplistic, because games programming is always looking at the user's resolution of previous conditions.)

Modules might be equivalent to an episode in conventional narrative or might be bounded by a change of direction, state, or protagonist. Related modules are linked into a kind of narrative constraint grid, one or more of which form the whole narrative structure.

It is relatively a short distance from "Adventure" or "D&D" to a form of computer-based narrative that has the goal, like literature, of confronting its audience with the "elemental and continuous challenges of human life." The distance is one of intention, not of form. To write well with these narrative constraints requires only that some persons of genius take them seriously.

Geniuses—immortal writers of the future—are you here now?

It would be imprudent of me to predict too closely what may be written in this form. Let me only suggest, imperfectly and incompletely, what may be some of its narrative questions and concerns:

—Classic narrative gives experience, generally though not universally, of single individuals at once. Computer-based narratives will be able to fully flesh out several. It is likely that computer-based narratives will more easily suit themselves to the portrayal of a group, to a story that shows progress less strongly than connection.

—To most linear narratives, the patterning of action toward an ending is vital. Modular narratives will show strong patterns of connected events, of course, but they are more likely to be interested in the patterns and moments of choice. More than one of these choices can be assumed to be valid, or at least interestingly false.

—The problems of modular narrative are likely to center around closure: knowing when to stop, knowing when the narrative has reached fullness. "The sense of an ending" will be by no means so clear to modular narrative as to linear. Perhaps, in fact, there will be new relationships between author and reader, in which a narrative is read in order to create a great reading, or a narrative is extended by a reader who can also program.

—Their greatest difference from linear narrative, especially from realistic narrative, will be in their double nature, as both world-system and, within the computer, lines of programming code. Programming and its special talents, such as heuristics strategy and optimization, is likely to provide a powerful metaphor for such art; and its great themes are thus likely to be negotiation, comprehension, exploration, and the necessity of choice.

Need such narratives be trivial? They cannot be. They involve ethics and morality, inescapably; in these created worlds, "better" and "worse" choices will bring with them notions of "better" or "worse."

Nor will they be intellectually timid. They deal with the making and unmaking of alliances, the nature of characters that makes decisions live or fail, the strength and structure of a world. The strategies of empire-makers are reflected in the most trivial of computer games; how much more so, in serious art!

It is an enormous new art that lies before us: "enormous" in physical scope because it requires so much and such careful writing; enormous still more because of the demands it puts on us. The nonlinear narrative will draw together science and art, the highest human aspirations, and the new powers of the computer—and with it, make writer and reader cocreators more literally, and no less enduringly.

Thank you, Professor Feder, and congratulations to you all at Suffolk University as you enter upon your new half-century.

COLLOQUIUM

PANEL 3

Reply

Lillian Feder

Because Professor Epstein and I agree to a large extent, I will not comment on his remarks except to say that I found his discussion, especially of Don Quixote, very beautiful. I'll turn to Professor Richman's remarks, because obviously we disagree. Then I will make a few comments on Professor Smith's remarks, though I am not really competent to discuss computers, since I still write with a pen that requires real ink.

Let me start with Professor Richman's first statement, that my theory was a new development of an old theme. That's wrong. I know what he's talking about. He's talking about an ancient theory which is stated in many places. Perhaps most explicitly in Horace's *Ars Poetica*, and that's the one most quoted. The statement is, *"Aut prodesse volunt aut delectare poetae,"* that is, "poets wish either to benefit or to delight." And then he goes on in the next sentence to say that they may wish to do both. This ancient idea is applicable in some respects to didactic literature, and ancient literature is largely didactic—which is not to criticize it. But this idea implies a certain moral judgment, whereas I am discussing a psychological process. I'm not talking about the work teaching you. The teacher does help the student to understand a literary work and the student sometimes helps the teacher to apprehend new facets of a work. But that's different from the reading process, which is an enlarging of one's being.

The second issue he raises—about the Nazis knowing Goethe—is a very complex one. Literature deals with that issue. Critics have interpreted Kurtz in Conrad's *Heart of Darkness* as an example of this problem. In general, what has been pointed out is that Kurtz was a very learned man who knew music and literature. He was a philosopher and an idealist. And, of course, Kurtz became a tyrant of the most vicious and ugly kind. This is one example of how literature deals with this very problem. But this complex issue is not the subject of our meeting. When I talk about the role of literature in the process of self-creation, I never would imply that it makes you a good person who would never turn into a Nazi. I can't discuss that because it's not anything that I would be so foolish as to suggest. The development of the self is an ongoing process that continues from the moment we are able psychologically to begin this process to the moment of death. I hope, personally, that as I am dying I will be trying to understand what death is, because that is my last chance to enlarge my being. And, incidently, deathbed stories very often have that character, whether they are true or not. And the role of literature is one aspect of self-creation. It is not the whole thing.

Another comment I want to make on Professor Richman's paper is that he used the word force—that literature forces you to create yourself—that really people don't experience; they simply observe. Now, the word force is incorrect. Any literary work that tries to force you to do anything is not going to have any effect on you. Literature can be a rhetorical art in the best sense of the word—not in its reductive sense. It can be an art of persuasion. It draws you into its charmed circle. It makes you, in a very famous phrase, "suspend your disbelief," because the experience of myth and all kinds of elements that are not naturalistic can make you better understand the natural world, your world, your being, the world of your being. Now, it's a slow, complex, difficult, delicate process. And I don't believe that any student, even a bad student, simply observes as he or she is reading. You respond to some extent emotionally, even if you dislike the work. You may read a book and say, "It's boring." Well, that's an experience. That's not simply an observation. As you go through the narrative structure or the thematic structure or just the experience of the rhythm of the language, you are responding to them physiologically, imaginatively, consciously, unconsciously. That is what I'm talking about in terms of enlarging experience.

I found Professor Smith's remarks very interesting and engaging, and I can only say that talking with Professor Pylyshyn last evening helped me to get a little bit of background into what Professor Smith was saying. I admire her aspirations and dreams of the future creative possibilities of the computer. I'm not competent to say whether I agree or not. But, good luck. I do want to say one thing, though. You mustn't assume that narrative has always been linear in literature and needs the computer to change it. Nonlinear narrative, nonlinear thinking, nonlinear elements have existed before in literature. Nonlinear literature is a modern mode and may very well influence computer narrative and vice-versa. I do, I must say, along with you people, certainly want to learn more about this new possibility. But it must never replace the feel of a book, the turning of a page, the owning of a book, just the whole experience of being alone and yet communally involved as you sit and read.

COLLOQUIUM

PANEL 4

Final Remarks

David G. Tuerck

About a year ago, in preparing for the creativity conferences of which this is the concluding session, the college circulated among potential contributors a conference *Prospectus* that raised a number of questions about the creative process and its relationship to liberal learning. The *Prospectus* offered for consideration the proposition that the undergraduate liberal arts college should organize its curriculum around an understanding of the creative process and, in so doing, dedicate itself to the enhancement of students' creative skills.

In the ensuing months, we have had a chance to evaluate this proposition from the perspective of the college faculty and now of the three distinguished speakers with whom I have the privilege of sharing this panel. The result is a collection of papers that reflect the disparateness of their authors' academic specializations as well as the challenge that the very notion of creativity poses for anyone who attempts to define or teach it.

Although a more prudent observer might resist the temptation to categorize these papers, I will nevertheless make a stab at it, as a starting point for this afternoon's discussion. The categories, as I see them are:

—Papers that attempt to reveal the cognitive foundations of the creative process;

—Papers that offer practical suggestions for teaching creative skills, as
through "psychosynthesis," "idea combining," or "rhetorical invention," within the framework of the existing educational system;
—Papers that support the idea of teaching creative skills but find the
existing educational system flawed in some way that, without correction, poses a barrier to such teaching; and
—Papers that question the desirability of attempting to teach creativity
as part of the liberal arts curriculum.

The papers offered during this colloquium, like those offered during
the faculty symposium, roughly divide themselves, I believe, between
these categories. Here and elsewhere, Professor Pylyshyn offers what
might be the starting point in any reassessment of the liberal arts curriculum: the notion that thinking or "cognizing"—whether of the
human or machine variety—requires the thinking mechanism to
incorporate representations of human beliefs and intentions into its
substrate.

Professor Feder also mentions the importance of " 'ideas and intentions' "—particularly, as they enter into the formation of the self. The
development of a fictive or "intermediate" self through the study of
literature permits—perhaps, we should say, forces—the reader to overcome the limitations of his or her own internalized social values.

In Professor Giroux's paper, I see two very different themes. One
offers still another perspective on what I am characterizing here as the
cognitive foundations of the creative process. This is the idea of a student's coming to the classroom endowed with certain "cultural capital,"
an understanding of which is necessary for the liberation of his or her
creative powers. I see Professor Giroux's cultural capital as meaning the
same thing as Professor Feder's internalized social values. The difference might be in how they would, as teachers, treat this particular form
of capital. I see Professor Feder as challenging it and Professor Giroux
as affirming it, although perhaps both would do some of each.

The second theme of Professor Giroux's paper puts the student, on
entering the classroom, at a fork in the road. The student can take one
of two paths. He can swear henceforth to suppress all creative thought
and quietly enter the ranks of bureaucratic capitalism; or he can sally
forth to do battle against what Professor Giroux apparently takes to be
the salient features of the capitalist system—toxic waste, consumer fraud,
and the like.

You will guess from this characterization of his paper that I will be
aiming my first (and probably only) question today at Professor Giroux.
I hope, Henry, that you will not think less of me for this. My problem
is not so much with the ideological content of your paper as it is with

your citing the American Economic Association as a force for the perversion of American education. I have been a member of the American Economic Association for 20 years now, Henry, and I know that anyone who considers it a force for anything—good or bad—has fallen into serious error.

Let me be a typical economist and pose a hypothetical question. You urge us as teachers to be sensitive to our students' cultural capital, and I agree that we should be. But suppose that this capital consists in part of the perception, ingrained and possibly correct, that the capitalist system, with all of its flaws, serves their interests well. What, then, are we, as purveyors of liberal learning, to do? If your answer is that we should challenge the material basis of this perception and strive to expand the value system from which it originates to include spiritual and aesthetic values, then I am completely with you. But if you mean, instead, that we should challenge the ideological basis of this perception, then I am forced to ask how you would equip the student to evaluate competing models of economic organization. How would you have him choose, say, between the prevailing brand of capitalism and some form of central planning? How would you have him evaluate a proposal to alleviate any of the examples of market failure to which your paper points? My concern is that by politicizing knowledge and the giving of knowledge you leave the student unequipped to subject any such issue to nonideological or, therefore, scientific consideration. Indeed, if all knowledge is merely the reification of someone's hidden agenda, then, I submit, there is no knowledge—only social struggle.

Before you respond—and, trust me, I really do mean to let you respond—I will share a rather practical concern. This is the concern that we in the liberal arts colleges have been losing our students to the professional schools by making just the mistake you correctly condemn: ignoring that part of students' cultural capital that includes their material values. Indeed, we confuse and alienate students by extolling materialism as a theory of social behavior and then condemning it as a life goal. The result is the strange process in which students turn to the professional schools for creative skills that lie naturally in the domain of the liberal arts colleges. When we find corporations trying to teach postgraduate employees such things as writing and ethics, then I think we can stop worrying that our teachers have sold out to the corporate establishment. More likely, perhaps, they have ignored the emerging reality that capitalism is here to stay and that what they had better do is get on with the business of educating tastes and cognitive skills within that framework.

Now, that, as everyone already knows, was more a statement of my personal views than a question. But one issue on which I would appreciate the opinion of all the speakers is that of the appropriate response by the liberal arts college to what may well be a genuine *laissez-faire* trend in the United States and Canada. The cultural capital of our students does affect their receptiveness to our efforts to imbue them with liberal values (in the nineteenth-century sense of the phrase) and with an ability to understand literature and the arts. Shouldn't we be asking such things as how the development of the fictive self is likely to improve a person's ability to function in the corporate environment into which he or she is probably headed, rather than, say, how we can turn the educational establishment into an instrument of social mobilization?

COLLOQUIUM

PANEL 4

Final Remarks

Henry A. Giroux

I find it hard to understand how anyone can argue that any form of knowledge represents a form of intelligibility that isn't grounded in some sort of interest. Knowledge is not neutral. All knowledge is ideological in that it is rooted in some particular relationship, in some form of constellation, around specific values and attitudes. To argue for objective knowledge is to argue that in some way we don't make selections, we don't make choices, that we don't abstract from a particular world view.

I don't want to talk about the value of truth or the value or the disvalue of capitalism as a specific ideological system or political system. People who read my work know how I feel about that. There are contradictions in this country. There are problems of sexism and racism. There is authoritarianism, as in other social systems. My concern is only the way in which we can empower students, both socially and collectively, to recognize all forms of authoritarianism, right and left, and to recognize how knowledge becomes linked to power. Students must be able to identify with the interests that underlie knowledge and with what those interests speak to in the terms of the kinds of social relationships that they legitimate—whether those social relationships speak to domination or not, whether those relationships empower people or not.

That raises another question, which is, "What is the particular relationship between schools and the social order, particularly the corporate order?" I want to argue, in the sense of Dewey, C. W. Mills, and others, that the discourse of freedom is much too important to reduce to the kind of instrumentality that is often associated with the interests that businesses and other corporations tend to place or want to embody in public education. To talk about educating people for jobs alone, to talk about utilizing and implanting in schools the kind of technical rationality by which education becomes measured in terms of individual achievement in economic success, may be important, but it is not the model for the discourse of freedom. I don't believe we should turn schools into "company stores."

The discourse of freedom is in other places. It is based on conceptions of democracy, of self, and of social empowerment, ideology, and power. It seems to me that the narrow model of economic rationality which we see so prevalent in this society, with its emphasis on efficiency and on all the concerns that I have mentioned earlier, in some way represents an enormous threat to what I would call critical pedagogy: understanding the nature of one's own world view; appropriating knowledge that in fact could be critically interrogated and utilized; having a sense of one's own history; understanding the relationship between the schools and the larger order; being able to confirm one's history and at the same time being able to critically move beyond it or at least interrogate it. These categories represent, not simply the language of critique, but also the language of possibility. They, it seems to me, provide the basis for a pedagogy that goes beyond the instrumental.

COLLOQUIUM

PANEL 4

Final Remarks

Lillian Feder

I want to begin by correcting something that David Tuerck said about my discussion of the fictive self. I don't like the use of the word *force*—that was a word used by one of my discussants. My point about the fictive self in relation to the development of, or the creation of, the self is that there is no force involved. It's a process of assimilating, growing with, and enlarging. Somehow there was a confusion, because I objected to the word *force* before, and for some reason David thought it was a word that I had used.

Now, to come to the issue that I think David Tuerck raised, which is the relation of teaching or classroom work to the particular social and political environment in which we live. Speaking for myself, I don't feel that it is my job—and I think Professor Giroux said the same thing—to persuade students to any political or social philosophy. I think that is their business. We live in a democracy, and it is the business of each individual to formulate for him or herself a political and social position and a cultural position. But I do think that the study of literature, as I said in my lecture this morning, always involves a response to society. Octavio Paz said that a poem is the product of both a poet and a society. No work of art is without some expression of the world from which it emerged. But it also has a literary history and a future history—it has a history of all who have responded to it. I have also said that much great literature—not all, but much—presents an alternate view, sometimes an antagonistic view, of the larger society and of history. This is not because literature is written by subversives but because literature deals with the individual attempt to adapt biological and psychological forces to a communal world. That is always a compromise, and compromises always leave unresolved areas: "civilization and its discontents."

319

Literature is both deeply attached to society and, at the same time, always questioning it. But literature doesn't question by propaganda or by political parties; it doesn't do so by platforms. It does so by revealing how human beings internalize the assumptions of their time and at the same time, whether consciously or unconsciously, question the assumptions of their time. I mentioned the *Iliad,* which is based on the heroic code, according to which an early death means dying for what one believes and therefore living forever, so that men will say that one fought heroically. At the same time, death at an early age means giving up what is most precious, which is life. Now, the heroic code is a social conception that grows out of society, a society in which war is a very important political, social, and economic factor. What the great work of art does is to present the assumption in all its complications, to question it, and most of all to show the cost in human terms and the recognition of that cost, all of which is rarely possible in daily lives and which no political party could ever do. So, literature is deeply attached to social, political, and cultural factors, but it is a unique form of expression, and should be taught as literature and not merely as a vehicle. I am sure most speakers would agree.

COLLOQUIUM

PANEL 4

Final Remarks

Zenon W. Pylyshyn

I would like to comment on something Professor Giroux said. He said that knowledge is not neutral. I find that so obvious that I don't want to argue about it. The selection and the presentation of knowledge is clearly imbued not only with the values of society, but also political values, that is, values of dominant groups. The question is, "What are we as educators supposed to do about this?"

The traditional view, one that I and others have taken, is to value critical thinking—to instill in students a disciplined critical sense rather than a desire to accept whatever they are told. What students need is a sense of intellectual responsibility. I tell my students that they may believe anything that they want but to be prepared to present reasons for believing what they do and to be responsible for it. Teaching critical thinking and teaching intellectual responsibility is how we approach it. It sounded to me as if Professor Giroux was opting for a more radical approach, but I would be very wary about doing anything more than teaching critical thinking and intellectual responsibility.

I would like to add to Professor Feder's claim that great literature questions the assumptions of our times. I think that great *anything*, including great technology, questions the assumptions of our times. We had a discussion last night about whether it's possible to be creative in that sense in a domain such as business. I don't see any reason why one can't. One can question, innovate, and create in any domain.

I would also like to make a point about the particular technology that I talked about because I think that it calls into question rather fundamental assumptions about one's self-image, which was the theme of Professor Feder's talk this morning. One of the things that we are discovering is that we as human beings share certain things in common with other parts of the universe. Bruce Mazlish talked about the fourth discontinuity in our view of ourselves. The first was the discovery, with the Copernican revolution, that we are not physically at the center of the universe. The second was the discovery, with the Darwinian revolution, that there is a continuity between us and the rest of the animal world. The third was the discovery, with the Freudian revolution, that we are not entirely rational beings, but are in fact governed by a great deal of unconscious activity (maybe not completely understandable activity). Now we have the discovery that many of our capacities—in fact, very cherished intellectual capacities—may also be capacities that we share with machines.

I don't see that this should be a problem, but it does take a while to adjust to. It is not as if we are going to turn out to be "mere" computers. We are not going to be IBM or DEC machines. It will simply turn out that a lot of things we do are cases of inferences or of the use of heuristics to further certain goals based on certain beliefs, and that these are functions we share with certain artifacts.

Throughout history, there has been a very important continuity between humans and their tools. As the tools become more important to us, as our lives become more dependent on them, a continuity develops whereby they become extensions of ourselves. What's happening now is that computing and artificial intelligence are becoming an extension of ourselves. It's a somewhat different kind of extension than with more passive tools and, perhaps because of that, it is more troublesome. But TV is an extension of our eyes, and jet airplanes are an extension of our ability to walk, and both have made qualitative differences to our lives. Similarly, the computer, equipped with encoded knowledge and the ability to draw inferences, is an extension of our cognitive ability. This doesn't demean us in any way. In fact, it shows us that some of the things that we do are not very mysterious. They are things that we can let our tools do. (It does not bother us to think about the automobile this way, although the advent of the automobile did bother a great many people, initially.) I think that it is a discontinuity that we are going to have to live with, and it's one of the ways in which technology and the products of technology shake up our view of ourselves and our relation with the rest of the universe.

Author Index

Subject Index